Raga Mala

Raga Mala

The Autobiography of

Ravi Shankar

Edited and Introduced by George Harrison

Additional Narrative by Oliver Craske

Welcome Rain Publishers

RAGA MALA: THE AUTOBIOGRAPHY OF RAVI SHANKAR
FIRST WELCOME RAIN EDITION 1999
ALL RIGHTS RESERVED
PRINTED IN ITALY

FIRST PUBLISHED IN GREAT BRITAIN IN 1997
IN A LIMITED, SIGNED AND NUMBERED EDITION BY
GENESIS PUBLICATIONS LTD.
2 JENNER ROAD, GUILDFORD, SURREY, GU1 3PL, ENGLAND
MANAGING EDITOR: OLIVER CRASKE
DESIGN AND ART DIRECTION BY FIONA ANDREANELLI,
DAN EINZIG AND DAVID COSTA AT WHEREFORE ART?

DIRECT ANY ENQUIRIES TO
WELCOME RAIN PUBLISHERS LLC
532 LAGUARDIA PLACE, BOX 473
NEW YORK, NY 10012

ISBN: 1-56649-104-5

FIRST EDITION: SEPTEMBER 1999

1 3 5 7 9 10 8 6 4 2

CONTENTS

FOREWORD

When I first met Ravi, I saw in him a quality that I'd always aspired to. I've never practised, never come anywhere near to what he does. In fact there isn't anyone I've ever heard of, in the West at least, who has got such brilliant musicianship.

Ravi became the bridge between my Western and my Eastern sides. In many ways I've felt just like a patch board: I like to plug one person into another, one type of idea into something else. Ravi was special to me, because without him I wouldn't have been able to get into the Indian experiences so easily. By having him as a friend, I could experience the best of India, and I was able to find it straight away. I said in an interview recently that without Ravi I would have ended up a boring old fart. Some people may still say I'm a boring old fart, but at least my life was enhanced and given much more depth through the ancient Indian culture, and Ravi was my contact with it.

Right from the start another thing I liked about Ravi was that, although on the one side he was a great classical musician, at the same time he was fun. He knew what was going on in the world, what books or films or plays were out. He'd always involve everybody who was around him. Even if we were travelling along in a car, he would make up a tune and get everybody to sing it, or teach us an old song or different time signatures and how to count them. With Ravi there's always something of interest going on, and a lot of happiness and laughing. Indian music has its very serious side, and then it also has a light side and a kind of comedy too. He shows that in his gestures, from what he learnt as a dancer, and his very interesting facial expressions. He's always been like a guru and a father figure,

but at the same time I think mainly of him just as a friend, because we joke around most of the time. Sometimes *I'm* like *his* dad. He can be so childlike.

In spite of always being curious about what's going on in the world, and having been subject to a lot of material problems too, he's still like a sannyasi in some respects. He's always retained a certain detachment from the situation. He doesn't make a big fuss. Give him some music and that will do.

Ravi laid down the groundwork for other Indian musicians who were later able to perform all around the world because of him. The world is now permeated with the acceptance of Indian music. But for him to go and study for seven years, eighteen hours a day, and become a master of an instrument which was obscure in most of the world, and for which nobody was particularly craving outside India, and then spend the rest of his life trying to hip everybody to it – what a thing to do!

Music is his life. He's spent so many years in this life practising and playing. He is the music and the music is him. Having toured for over fifty years, it's hard to stop. It drives him on, so he'll just keep on going, I'm sure.

Back in 1994 we were thinking of ways to mark Ravi's 75th birthday. I asked Brian if he wanted to publish a book and he said 'yes'. Ravi liked the idea too, and then we started to prepare for it – and it's actually taken over two years. It's always good to have Ravi, his music or his books, in my life.

Once when I was driving Ravi into London I put a cassette on, and it crossed my mind: 'He probably thinks this is really strange music.' When he asked, 'Who's that?', I replied, 'Oh, it's Cab Calloway, you won't know him.' And he said, 'Oh yes, I saw him at the Cotton Club around 1933!' So I already knew a lot about Ravi's story: his father being a barrister, about how he grew up in Paris with his brother Uday, and his trips to America. But I didn't know a lot of the details which now emerge in the full story in the book. It is such an amazing story – he has had an incredible life, and it still is!

Hari Om Tat Sat.

GEORGE HARRISON

PREFACE (TUNING UP)

By nature I don't think of the past; I think always of the future. Yet in my seventy-fifth year, the occasion for which this book was originally intended, there appeared to be some commotion being made about what I had achieved. This seems strange to me – although it makes me elated and grateful. I feel I have not been able to do more than a fraction of all the creative, musical and visual things that keep bubbling and brewing up in my mind.

And sitting here in Encinitas, California, in this lovely house with such beauty all around, I do feel that I would like to stay on this planet longer in order to accomplish as much as possible. One of my big motivations is my daughter, Anoushka, who has all the lakshana (signs) of being a yogya patri – literally a 'suitable pot'. I want to train her and give her as much as I can, so that she can carry on and travel much further along the never-ending path of our great music.

People ask me always what I want to be remembered by, and I would like it to be not for my mistakes, but for the things that I was able to achieve – those that have touched the hearts of the people in my own country and beyond. God has been kind to me, and I have been very lucky indeed to have gained recognition and appreciation almost all over the world. It has been my good fortune that there have never been any problems with communicating the greatness of our music. In places where the people had never even heard of it, nevertheless it has been an instant success, and still there are warm receptions today everywhere I go.

Unfortunately, one faces a lot of discordant things in life. Previous negatives I have fought against and not been much affected by, but in these later years it has been much harder, mainly owing to health problems. Yet, being an Aries, even when I fall down I always bounce back on my feet quickly. A little frustration does creep in when I am not actively doing any new creative work, but things are looking better now, as I have recently been nurturing some new projects which seem to be coming into blossom.

I have found great relief and comfort over the last few years since I married Sukanya. Not only are we completely in love with each other, but she has also relieved me of all mundane and worldly worries, especially by cleaning up the materialistic mess I had created over many years. She can be a hard taskmistress on occasions, but is so tender and loving at the same time. Though it was late in my life that she became my wife, I am again thankful to God for bringing her to me.

To write a book on one's own life is not an easy job, especially having gone through, as I have, a myriad of characters and a jungle of events and incidents happening in different parts of the world. I have never been an organised person; even when I have tried writing a diary regularly, I have never managed to continue it for more than seven or eight days! Now, writing from memory, I have been reliant on some records, letters, newspaper cuttings, photograph albums and a few very dear people, such as my most senior students and elderly relatives and friends, whose help has been invaluable. Nevertheless there are bound to be inaccuracies in some places, for which I apologise – though I cannot help it. The book is also directed at a very diverse audience, and in many places I have attempted to be explicit in describing our Indian traditions. Naturally these details are intended mainly for non-Indian readers.

The whole project took over two years to complete, much longer than was expected. Even a professional writer takes months (or years) of undisturbed attention to finish a book, and here I have been entrusted with squeezing in such a challenging task between my travels, concerts, recording and editing sessions, practising and teaching, while at times jet lag, tiredness or sickness have further burdened me. It has been a hard job, I tell you! But a rewarding one, too.

Then comes the question of being totally frank and writing everything: the TRUTH. That seems to be the name of the game today – and a big factor is that these titillating, lucid and sensational books sell well, too! Yet who doesn't have a skeleton (or a few) in their cupboard? Don't you? I believe in the middle path – though I have not always stayed on it myself – and have tried to say as much as is needed while avoiding anything hurtful to some people or in bad taste. There is a saying in Hindustani: 'Samajhdaron ke liye ishara hi kafi hai,' meaning, 'A hint is enough for an intelligent person to understand.'

And what is the truth, anyway? It is like beauty – in the eye of the beholder. The great Akira Kurosawa has shown this so wonderfully in his film *Rashomon*. Perspective plays a crucial role: I have tried to be as truthful as possible in stating the past and the present in relation to everyone and everything mentioned, including myself, but what I have told you here is the story of my life as I see it now.

There is no doubt that I have contradicted myself at many times and in many places over the course of my life. It will even have happened in this book, I am sure, because of how I have written it – in various places (California, Delhi, London, Glasgow, Henley and on several trains and planes), at various times (between 1994 and 1997) and in various ways (sometimes writing with a pen, sometimes dictating onto a tape, sometimes annotating drafts). We all contradict ourselves, and inevitably so. You can all too easily write an autobiography in which you praise one person to the heavens – your lover, your cook, or whoever – and omit to mention another person who was years ago the object of all your plaudits. In another ten or twenty years you may have a different partner, a different chef, a different perspective. Nothing is permanent in this life, and I can say this with the true confidence of one who frequently goes through changes of heart! Some of my views expressed here would have been different fifty years ago or twenty-five years ago – or sometimes last week! I make no apology for this because it is unavoidable, but it is always worth bearing in mind.

The title of this book is *Raga Mala* – 'Garland of Ragas'. Raga mala is a style of playing in which the performer refers to many different ragas while always returning to the main one. In a similar way, while writing the book I have time and again found that one recollection has sparked off another, which I might pursue before coming back to where I was. So perhaps you will find that reading this book is a little like listening to our raga mala style.

You will also notice that each of the chapters is named after a raga I have created. They are arranged in a sequence which follows the time theory associated with our North Indian classical music system, beginning with an early-morning raga, *Gangeshwari* (doubly appropriate since the river Ganga is the lifeblood of Benares, where my life began), through afternoon, evening and night ragas to *Parameshwari*, a raga of the very late night or early dawn. The epilogue is named after a dhun, a number in a lighter, folk style with which I usually end a concert.

I would like to thank all those who have helped me to bring this book into existence, mainly George, Sukanya, Brian and Oliver. I can never be thankful enough to God for leading me intact through such various paths of roses and thorns over seventy-seven years. Loving him, and being greedy for his love, I pray for his grace and blessings for my remaining years.

AUGUST 1997

ONE: GANGESHWARI

The whole world where I was born in Benares was like an India as it existed two thousand years ago. Apart from a few automobiles, cycles and other little emblems of modernity that were around me, everything was really old: the way of life, the city's temples and ghats. Ghats (literally 'sloping places') are the tiered steps on the banks of the river, and Benares is famous for its ghats, because it is there that you witness complete life itself, from childbirth to death. Everything happens there: there are plays going on, songs being enacted by dancers telling the story of Krishna and Radha, or the devotional kirtans sung in Bengali and bhajans sung in Hindi. Benares is so cosmopolitan; people come from all over India to this city of pilgimage. It has such power because these people's faith merges there; they come to Benares to die and to be cremated according to old Hindu rites, because they believe this will bring immediate nirvana and thus release them from the cycle of reincarnation.

Kashi is the oldest name for Benares. But it is another old name for the city, Varanasi, that has come into use again. The British couldn't pronounce many of the place names in India so they distorted them, and for a couple of centuries Varanasi was known as Benares.

My greatest joy and excitement as a child was to visit the ghats with my mother, my brothers and my brothers' friends. There was so much activity, so much natural entertainment, so many different types of music. In Benares, sound is everywhere. To hear the shahnai being played in the temples and palaces... All the maharajahs had their mansion or palace on the bank of the river, and many of them had their own shahnai-player. These musicians had five or six duties per day – early morning, mid morning, afternoon, early evening, evening and night. Constantly one heard the beautiful ragas of that particular hour, and altogether it created a music of its own. They blended so beautifully, into a harmony, really. That particular sound of the ghats in Benares was unique. It is still there, but no longer the same: now it is more of a cacophony and has become commercialised, mixed in with Hindi film music with its elements of pop, rock and rap.

Growing up in this supremely spiritual environment was an auspicious beginning for a young Indian destined to achieve the greatest heights in his nation's classical music. But the path of Ravi Shankar's evolution towards his accomplishments would not be a conventional one. His early years were to contain a blend of the sacred and the material, of deprivation and excess, of dedication and triviality, of East and West – an unconventional background for a distinguished Hindustani musician. Yet this diversity of ingredients fused in him to emerge ultimately in a truly global artistic concoction.

To begin at the beginning, Ravi Shankar was born on 7th April, 1920, at his family's rented house in the city of Benares, in a lane known as Tilebhandeshwar Galli. Thousands of years old, Benares is the most sacred place on earth for a Hindu, a city of two thousand temples situated along the banks of the great Mother Ganges, and reputedly the abode of Shiva.

Ravi's father, Shyam Shankar Chowdhury, was a Brahmin (a member of the priestly caste, the highest in the Hindu caste system) from Jessore in East Bengal (now Bangladesh). A highly educated and cultured Bengali, he achieved distinction as a statesman, lawyer, philosopher, writer and amateur musician. From about 1905 he had served as Diwan (chief minister) to the Maharajah of Jhalawar, a small native state in what is now Rajasthan. During this period Shyam had become estranged from Ravi's mother, Hemangini, and without divorcing he had remarried. (This was not an unlawful practice in India then, although it was rare and generally frowned upon. The Hindu marriage code prohibiting bigamy was only introduced after independence.) Shortly before Ravi's birth, he left to practise law in Calcutta and London. When Ravi was only a few months old, Shyam's eldest son Uday also left for London to study fine art at the Royal College of Art.

Hemangini was from the small village of Nasrathpur, about seventy miles from Benares. Her father, Abhoy Charan Chakrabarti, had been a prosperous zamindar (landlord) – as had Shyam's father – and in her youth she had lived in a beautiful stone mansion in the nearby town of Ghazipur. But those riches had disappeared as a result of the profligacy of the men in her family and, after Shyam had left, Hemangini brought up her children in Benares while surviving on a pension awarded to her by the Maharajah of Jhalawar. Ravi, or Robindra as he was named at birth, was her last child, nearly ten years separating him from the youngest of the four other brothers who survived infancy.

My full name as pronounced in Bengali is 'Robindro Shaunkor Chowdhury'. The name 'Ravi', meaning 'the sun', comes from Sanskrit, the origin of almoſt all modern Indian languages. The pronunciation has changed greatly from Sanskrit to Bengali, and thus 'Ravindra' and 'Ravi' in Sanskrit became 'Robindro' and 'Robi' in Bengali. So in Bengali I was originally called Robindro (although, ſtrangely enough, in the English ſtyle it was written 'Robindra'); it was only later, when I was about twenty or twenty-one, that I changed my name to Ravi, the equivalent used in the major part of India.

My nickname from childhood was 'Robu'. That's what a few of my family and friends call me. Similarly my brother Rajendra was known as Raju, and Debendra was Debu. I also called Raju 'Mejda' (meaning 'middle brother'), and Debu, 'Sejda' ('third brother').

Our original family name had been Chattopadhyaya. (The British could not pronounce that word either, so when they arrived they turned it into

The author revisiting the house where he was born, on Tilebhandeshwar Galli, Benares.

Chatterjee, which is why one now comes across so many Chatterjees, as well as Banerjees and Mukherjees – originally Bandopadhyaya and Mukhopadhyaya.[1]) Later the Muslim rulers of the day gave my ancestors land and made them zamindars. Along with that they were awarded the title 'Chowdhury', which from then onwards replaced Chattopadhyaya as our last name. For a few generations we were actually known as Hara Chowdhury, because we used to worship at a Shiva temple (Hara is another name for Shiva). While in Udaipur, where my brother Uday was born in 1900 (and from where his name was taken), my father had dropped the 'Chowdhury' and thereafter just used 'Shankar' – which we have all maintained since.

My mother actually had seven sons but, believe it or not, no daughters. She so much wanted to have a daughter – and I missed having a sister. Uday was the eldest son (and therefore known to us brothers as 'Dada'), the next child was stillborn, and then came Rajendra (born in 1905), Debendra (1908), and Bhupendra (1911).

Next was an unusual child, nicknamed Puchunia, who died at only ten months, although everybody thought he was two years old. He was big and healthy, and from the age of five or six months he used to do strange things that no one could believe. He started walking and talking very early, and was highly intelligent; there are baffling stories about the things he could do. The Maharajah used to visit sometimes because he was fond of this baby boy. Puchunia liked the Maharajah to smoke his cigar, and would even mime smoking a cigar and blowing out the smoke!

Bhupendra, whom I called Chhotda, was the tallest of us, about five foot eight inches. He was very handsome, with curly black hair, and used to write poetry and songs, which my brothers would tease him about. He wasn't interested in playing football or any other sports, though he was quite robust; sometimes they would say he was a sissy, and he would stay at home and then cry like a girl. I used to be the closest to him. We were like friends. Sometimes we would sit on the rooftop together: he would play the harmonium and we would both sing.

In 1917 or 1918, while my father was in Jhalawar, he had married an English lady named Miss Morrell. That was where the gulf between my parents had widened; they had been living separately, and then my mother was given a mansion there in Jhalawar. Miss Morrell died around 1925 or 1926, at a time when my father was in Calcutta practising law; they had no children. He then returned to the West to spend the rest of his life, splitting his time between London, Geneva and New York.

After he left Jhalawar for Calcutta in 1920, my mother came to Benares and lived there with me and my three brothers (Dada having already left home). Along with all of our belongings, she brought from Jhalawar two or three trunks that were full of presents she had received over ten or twelve

---

1. Over many years I have popularised a pun: 'Why is an allergy a Bengali disease? – Because it rhymes with Chatterjee, Mukherjee and Banerjee!' (Though a refugee is not always a Bengali...)

years. She was a great consort of the Maharani (the Queen) and, as was the custom in those days with royalty, on a festival day or on the birthday of anyone in the royal family, they would give presents – gold or diamond rings for the nose, a diamond earring, a gold bracelet, locket or chain, as well as expensive saris made of gold brocades.

It was fixed that we would get a pension sent to us from Jhalawar every month. Two hundred rupees was the amount set, which was very substantial in those days – but those were also the princely days when there were such thieves and robbers on the staff of the aristocrats, and some of these took five or ten rupees each. Within a year or two, by the time it reached us the pension had dwindled to sixty rupees, even though it was still officially two hundred in their books. Sixty rupees was nothing, really (about two American dollars at today's rate), for a mother to pay for her children and their education in college and school, house rent and household expenses, and myself the youngest of the four!

My father never sent anything to us, presumably because he believed that we were provided for. I don't know whether my mother was too proud to let him know that these people were not sending us the full amount. I think my brothers did try to contact him about it. To me it was a mystery, this side of my father; because whatever he was doing, he was always earning money – maybe not fabulous amounts, but he had an income through his legal-advice work or his teaching. He would help a few students in Calcutta with their studies by sending them each one pound (and in those days one pound was quite a sum), and he would also send money to my aunts (his sisters), some of whom had become widows. With all these people he was very generous, but as far as we were concerned he never sent any help. It seemed very strange at the time, although I did come to understand it better much later on.

I saw my mother suffering. With that small amount of money she would manage the house, pay for our education and never let us be hungry – but we lived in a very frugal manner. She was a great cook. Whatever she cooked was like nectar to us; even if she made plain spinach, it would be so tasty with the rice. My brothers would bring some of their friends round and they would all say, 'Oh, Auntie, we want to eat! We hear you cook so well.' My mother would never refuse, no matter whether she was prepared for it. They would ask for more and more, and we would all eat, too. But when they had left, there would be no food remaining and she would take some jaggery (a coarse brown sugar lump) and a pot full of water from the tap. I saw her do that so many times and I really felt for her. I was close to my mother. I saw all her pain and her loneliness, but even then she didn't show her bitterness; she was full of love.

When we were getting poorer she would open one of the trunks and take out a golden bangle or earring, or an expensive sari, and in the evening when the streets were emptier she would cover herself with a shawl, so people wouldn't recognise her, and take me with her to a shop in the main road at the end of the lane. This was a shop that sold all the different oils. The shop owner was also our landlord and very rich, and he accorded her a lot of respect, calling her 'Mother'. (It is an Indian tradition that elder ladies are called 'Mother' by a younger person, just as women of a similar age are called 'Sister', and much younger ones, 'Daughter'.) She would pawn one of the articles and get maybe twenty or twenty-five rupees. For those few years this was how she brought us up.

She also bought a Singer sewing machine, and to earn some extra money she would sew ladies' blouses for a person who would come and take them away. Her cousin Brija Bihari came to live with us in order to help her in this. My mother really struggled so much.

By now we were living in a different house, in the same street where I was born but on the other side. Opposite us there was a very rich Bengali family of landlords who lived like maharajahs. They had a mansion and tennis courts, plenty of land with flowers, trees, fruits and vegetables, and a motor car, which was quite something at that time. They held special functions that brought many famous musicians to the house. It was a joint family – two brothers, their children and their grandchildren. Amongst the grandchildren there was a boy called Bulu, who went to the same school as I did, and we became good friends. I used to go to their house and play, and my brother Mejda also used to visit for games of tennis.

Mejda was a sportsman, a champion at badminton for some time in Benares, and he used to play cricket also. He was a member of a social-cultural club called Sangeet Samiti, where he used to play musical instruments: cornet, harmonium, dilruba, esraj and even a small sitar, which was kept in the corner of a room in our house. There were a few instruments of his at our home, and they were the most important playthings I had. Whenever my brothers were away and my mother was busy in the kitchen, I would strum the sitar as best I could. The harmonium was easier, because all I had to do was press the keys as on a piano keyboard and operate the squeeze-box with the left hand. Whatever few songs I knew – and I was learning some songs by Rabindranath Tagore (we call them Rabindra Sangeet) from Bechu-da, a friend of Mejda – I would play and sing as well as I could train myself to.

In the afternoons I was passing my time playing with my friend Bulu in his large house opposite, and this was where I saw riches for the first time. The ladies upstairs there – the mothers, sisters and cousins – used to adore me. They fed me with such delicacies as puri, halua and a variety of sweets and fruits, all served on marble plates, with juices in marble goblets, on marble tables! You can just envisage what a big impact this had on me, as my own family were going through that very tight period financially at this time.

These were my early years, seeing everything all around, poverty and riches, and soaking in the sights, sounds and spiritual aromas of Benares.

Reading was my childhood passion from the moment I learnt to recognise the alphabets, principally in Bengali and then in English. At about the age of five I started reading in Bengali, mostly children's books, and I picked it up so quickly that within a year or so I was reading anything I could lay my hands upon. Around the house there were plenty of books belonging to my brothers: detective books, romances and other stories. I acquired a taste for Tagore and Dwijendra Lal Roy – who wrote wonderful songs as well as books, stories and plays – and the works of my favourite author, Sarat Chandra Chatterjee. Then, again and again, I became drawn to mythological books. The great epics *Mahabharata* and *Ramayana* soon became my favourites, just as my daughter has now become hooked on them as well.

Whatever I read stimulated my imagination, and because I was a loner it became my passion to stand in front of the mirror and act out all the stories: I was the hero, the heroine, the lover or the villain. There was hardly anyone to play with since my brothers were at school or college, so I entertained myself until I joined the school and made some friends there.

I studied at the Bengalitola High School for a couple of years only, between 1927 and 1929. I remember one curious thing that happened around the age of eight. A class friend of mine, who was very naughty, kept telling me for many days that his family was having a house built and electricity was being fitted, which very few houses had. Eventually he said, 'Come with me and I'll show you something fantastic there which will give you a nice feeling. You won't believe it! We have sweets and fruits, and you can have them.'

So one day after classes he took me to the unfinished house, which was not far from school. Like any new house being built, there were things scattered around. He took me to a wall and made me touch a raw electric wire – and I was electrocuted! What a traumatic experience! You can picture me

Bengalitola High School, where Ravi studied between the ages of seven and nine.

17

there: furious, shouting and crying at the same time, and wanting to hit him. It was so cruel of him, and so stupid of me – even now I think of it and cannot understand my foolishness. I never saw him again after that – I didn't want to!

(This reminds me of another 'electric' experience! In January 1995 my wife Sukanya and I were staying in Calcutta at a friend's house, where I was electrocuted while taking a shower. It seems there was a leakage from the water-heating geyser onto the wall, and when I touched the wall my whole system was jolted into a million vibratos and tremolos at the same time! With water and electricity involved together, it was a miracle – one of the many miracles in my life – that I survived.)

Another school friend told me one day that the Lord Shiva, one of our holy trinity (Brahma, Vishnu and Shiva), and his wife Parvati (the Mother Goddess) had come as human beings to a house. Naturally I was very curious, so we bunked a class and around one o'clock we went to a rich man's house. There were a lot of people sitting in a room singing bhajans, and I saw a gentleman with a beard like Shiva's, and coiled, matted hair. Around his neck he was wearing a garland of rudraksha, which is made from reddish-coloured dried fruit stones and is supposed to radiate spiritual powers. (It is worn by most devotees of Shiva). The lady was so beautiful, of fair colour, wearing an off-white silk sari with a red border; she too had matted hair, and had a round red tika on her forehead. They were so radiant, especially the lady, that I felt they really were Shiva and Parvati.

Many years later I discovered that she was the very famous lady yogi Mata Anandamayi (meaning 'mother full of bliss'). She had ashrams everywhere, with hundreds of thousands of disciples, but she was not affected by her success; she continued to be the same fantastic soul. After a few years of marriage, her husband became her disciple and remained so as long as he lived. I met her again in the early Sixties, and when I told her about the incident from my childhood days, she laughed! I became a devotee of hers until she died in the early Eighties. She was one of the greatest souls that I have ever encountered: a true ever-loving mother! I loved her so much, and was lucky to have received her love and blessings.

When my family had been in Jhalawar, there had been many chances to hear music. Jhalawar had no musicians of its own, but famous musicians and dancers often visited to perform at the court, so my mother heard some of them, especially the lady musicians and singers – famous names like Gohar Jan, Malka Jan, Zohra Bai and Kajjan Bai. After their regular progamme in the Maharajah's court, these female musicians would attend a zenana (ladies') court in the presence of the Maharani, who was accompanied by her close relatives, her friends and the wives of senior officials. Male musicians also performed sometimes, but on those occasions the ladies had to sit in the dark behind a curtain made from chik, very fine straw matting through which they could see but which veiled them from the men's gaze.

To this day there exists a tradition throughout India whereby the women from all generations sing together accompanied by the dholak (a drum). The ladies sang so beautifully for the different festivities, such as the birth of a child, a marriage, the harvest festival, the colour festival (Holi) or the light festival (Diwali). My mother had considerable musical talent, and was blessed with a soft but very melodious voice; she also knew a variety of folk music and semi-classical music such as thumri, kajri and dadra.

In Benares, I loved to lie on our flat third-floor roof in the evenings with my head on my mother's lap. She would pat me, and I would listen to her singing in her beautiful voice, looking up at the clear night sky (free from pollution in those days). I used to admire the sky much more without the moon; the light from the stars was so powerful that they would shed their own light. She would tell me the names of all the stars, and mythological stories about our gods and goddesses. Sometimes, because she had no one else to talk to, she would speak of her Jhalawar days, and how my brothers used to live like princes: they had been to the best schools and even had a little tiger cub to play with. She described the mansion with its large retinue of servants, maidservants and gardeners, and the sentries who would give a military salute to her and my brothers each time they passed. To me, all those stories sounded like a fairy tale, and made me feel slightly jealous.

Hemangini Shankar, Ravi's mother.

She also related stories about her childhood, in particular the eccentricities of her grandfather, who was hot-tempered and big-hearted at the same time, with an insatiable appetite for enjoying life and spending money on keeping the best wrestlers, horses and – as you might expect – concubines. He had been a very rich landlord. Indeed it was he who had had the mansion in Ghazipur built, and he also owned cottages and houses in Nasrathpur. He used a fast two-horse cart to travel between the two places, although he had more fun staying in Ghazipur which was really in its prime then. The mansion had been a fantastic house built entirely from stone and beautifully decorated with traditional-style filigree work, but after his death everything was allowed to fall into a state of disrepair. His sons started the family trend for living more in Nasrathpur, so that in my childhood whenever we went away from Benares, as we did every summer (during my brothers' school or college holidays), it was to Nasrathpur, not Ghazipur. I did go to the mansion, and stayed there for one or two nights, but by the time of my first visit there were only a few rooms worth living in.

Those couple of months I spent each year in Nasrathpur were unforgettable. Mostly we stayed at the large house of Chhoto Dadamoshai's, my mother's uncle. His single-storey home was arranged around a central square courtyard with a veranda. There was a huge garden – some parts of it with so many trees that it seemed like a forest – filled with about twenty different types of luscious tropical fruit: sitaphal (custard apples), jamuns (large blue berries with stones), mangoes, lychees, guavas, jack fruit. There would be about a dozen of my young aunts, uncles and cousins at the house, aged between four and fourteen, and together we would roam around the garden all day long, playing hide-and-seek, climbing trees and gorging ourselves on the fantastic fruits. In the sweltering weather, with temperatures of up to 114 degrees Fahrenheit, we were so grateful for the deep well in the garden. The water in it used to be ice cold, even in the severest summer. We would all sit down in a row and wait our turn as the servants collected water in a balti (bucket) from the well and then poured it on us one by one. We would shriek with pleasure!

Those of us from the cities were made to take an afternoon nap indoors in a dark room cooled by ingenious methods. In the centre of the ceiling was a special pankha (fan), which was operated by means of a cord pulled by a young servant who sat beside the wall. The windows and doors were blocked up with khus khus tatti, blocks of scented straw kept moist by being sprayed with water at intervals. The hot breeze from outside would blow through the straw as cool air. The effect was like air-conditioning with an added fragrance. It was so delightfully cool. How inventive were the people of olden days, surviving without the electricity upon which we are so reliant today!

I must also tell you about the great feasts we had in Nasrathpur (food always being a favourite topic of mine). All my elder mamas (maternal uncles) were hunters and every morning they would go off with their guns, returning with killings in abundance: ducks, pheasants and partridges, sometimes wild deer and once even a wild boar! They would also catch shrimps, crabs and other fish from their own large ponds and from distant lakes. My mother's aunt was in charge of the cooking. She was a tall, strong, attractive lady and a magnificent cook. We called her 'Boudi', the name we use for a sister-in-law, instead of 'Grandma', because she was so young for a grandmother. With the assistance of my mother and all the young aunts she would prepare dozens of delicious dishes – chicken, mutton, the hunters' catches of fish and meat, vegetables from the garden, salads, hot and sour condiments and chutneys, special breads and rice. All the cooking was done in pure ghee or mustard oil. Home-made rich creamy yoghurts were made from the milk of the cows and buffaloes which were kept at the house, and we ended each meal with malai, rabdi, kheer or other sweets. They were amazing feasts. Mind you, this all happened twice a day! We would have lunch at about two in the afternoon and then, after we overactive youngsters had collapsed, exhausted, at the end of our day's fooling around in the garden, we would be forced to wake up again for dinner at about ten or eleven in the evening. On top of all this were the hearty breakfasts and tasty snacks with our late-afternoon tea. I can still recall the aromas of all the exotic spices, and the food cooked with such expertise and invested with such love.

At home in Benares, every full moon we would perform Satya Narayan Puja, a special celebration worshipping Lord Vishnu. I used to love the food made as offerings for those occasions too: the chopped fruits and sweets, and especially sinni, a special sweet made out of milk, flour, chopped bananas, raisins, cashews, pistachios and other nuts. It tasted so good, especially as we never had much variety of food. My brothers had known it all during their earlier period in Jhalawar, but to me all of these simple things meant so much.

I felt so near to my mother at that period of my childhood. That was a beautiful time. She knew plenty of Bengali songs from theatrical plays. In those days there were only silent films, so the popular songs came mostly from famous musical stage plays. Each night at the time of Dassehra one of these stage plays would be put on. (Dassehra, also known as Durga Puja, is the annual festival held around September or October to celebrate Rama's defeat of Ravana, as told in the *Ramayana*. For four or five days of its duration we would visit the Durga temple very early in the morning, along with my brothers and a huge crowd of other worshippers.) There were several theatrical clubs, including Mejda's club Sangeet Samiti and some from Calcutta, which each rehearsed for three or four months to prepare a play. These were the main attractions at the Dassehra festival, and my mother knew many songs from them.

I would go along to some of these plays, and found them exciting, although I usually fell asleep after some time – as all children do! On one occasion, when I must have been seven or eight, a bizarre incident occurred during a performance by Sangeet Samiti of a play called *Bilwa Mangal*, variously attributed to several great fifteenth- and sixteenth-century saints. This was a story about a wealthy and likeable man who had a beautiful wife but became infatuated by a courtesan. She liked him, but she always told him, 'You have such a beautiful wife in your house. How can you leave her to come to me?' He lost his mind completely, and used to visit her again and again, to hear her sing and be with her.

Late one night it was raining and her front door was closed. He was shouting, desperate for her to let him in, but she refused. Then he saw a rope hanging from the veranda, and climbed up it to her room. Shocked to see him, she asked, 'How did you get in the house?' When he told her, she was perplexed since there was no rope hanging outside. They both went to look – and saw it was a snake! So she told him off: 'Why are you doing this? Just for this body of mine? You are so mad that you didn't know the difference between a rope and a snake! This love you say you have for me: if you could give one fourth of it to God you could have a darshan (glimpse) of him, and be liberated.' These words gave him a jolt, and he turned back and went home. Thereafter he became one of the greatest saints, and wrote beautiful bhajans.

That evening I could not sleep during the play! I was watching it with such intensity. In the intermission one of Mejda's friends was teasing me: 'How do you like that girl who is the heroine?' To me she really looked so beautiful, with wonderful make-up and costume. I was in love with that character! He asked me if I wanted to meet her. I thought it was not a proper thing to do, and I was shy – but still very excited. He took me backstage, to where all the actors were relaxing.

However, in those days it was men who took the female parts in these plays. Backstage, the actor had taken off his wig, blouse and artificial boobs. Sitting there, with the sari folded for comfort, he was quite dark-skinned, and he was smoking, of all things, bidi, a cheap cigarette made from dry leaves rolled with tobacco inside – mostly smoked by poor or working-class people. I couldn't understand it, since I had been told that 'he' was a 'she'. Mejda's friend was now in hysterics, repeating again and again, 'Robu is in love with you!' The actor looked like a hijra (eunuch) with a dark hairy chest and legs! Everyone else was laughing, but I started crying and wanted to go home, so I didn't see the whole play after all. What a shocking let-down!

We had a few cinema houses in Benares, and still fresh in my memory is my first experience of the cinema, when I was two and a half or three. I went with my brother Bhupendra and one or two of his friends to see a jungle film from Hollywood. I don't imagine it could really have been a 3-D film, but there was a scene where a tiger seemed to jump directly out from the screen – scaring the life out of me. I shrieked, and they had to carry me home in a high fever!

Little by little I would see some of the silent Bengali films which were made in Calcutta. In those days, Calcutta made pictures of real quality, such as *Kapal Kundala*, written by one of our foremost writers of the last century, Bankim Chandra Chatterjee. He also wrote the song 'Vande Mataram', which is one of our greatest national songs. The only other film I clearly remember was *Durgesh Nandini*, written by the same author, but I certainly saw a few others, including some from Bombay. I also vaguely recall some Hollywood movies featuring Douglas Fairbanks Senior and Elmo Lincoln. They were only silent films, but I adored the cinema. My passion for films started from right then.

When we left Benares for the West in 1930, we had to halt in Bombay for two days, and that was where I saw my first sound movie. This was part talking and part sound effects. My first fully-fledged talkie I saw later, in Paris.

We had a lot of respect for British culture, but of course we did not like their colonialism. So I was brought up with contradictory feelings about British people in general: love and hate. The period of about twenty-five years before the British departed, as nationalist feeling ran high and the Congress was becoming powerful, was a bad time because the British were really brutal and oppressive. The 'tommies' who were sent to India as policemen or administrators were the same type of people, I think, who were sent to run the penal camps in Australia: they were educated enough to run offices but not highly educated, and they were very hard people. They were chosen because the British were governing a country, and they couldn't send intellectuals and conciliators to do that. I can understand that, but unfortunately we thought all British people were like them. They would beat people up, and we were scared of them.

My political knowledge was very little – limited to that one region and period – yet being in Benares I used to

Ravi aged about seven, with his maternal uncle Kunjo Bihari Banerjee, known as Kunjo Mama. The photographer had told him not to blink while the photograph was being taken – hence the trance-like expression.

hear about Gandhi and the Congress of Non-Cooperation, or a freedom fighter shooting an English magistrate or collector. There was much apprehension and excitement. The underground movement came mostly from Bengal, Punjab and Maharashtra; and once in a while a radical activist would pass through Benares, creating an atmosphere of fear. Without any reason we felt scared whenever we saw a policeman, as if we ourselves had done something wrong.

Chatterjee's song 'Vande Mataram', meaning 'Hail to the Mother', was a powerful song in praise of Mother India, and it became a party song of the revolutionaries against the British. The book from which the song was drawn, called *Ananda Math*, was banned. 'Vande Mataram' induced acute paranoia in the British government. Everywhere there were local Indian police officers and detectives who were very obedient to the British, and they would arrest anyone who uttered even the first line. I was brought up hearing these things and sympathising but not being involved; and later on, when I read *Ananda Math* myself, it was like reading a dirty book and hiding it so that I would not be caught and sent to prison!

#78

y father first visited us when I was almost eight. This was the first time I had seen him in my life. He stayed in a very posh hotel in Benares, quite far from where we lived: the Hotel de Paris, which was in the cantonment area, a very clean locality where the few British and Indian high officials resided. My father was with two ladies: Madam Henny from Holland, who was his latest girlfriend, and Miss Jones, the younger cousin of the late Miss Morrell.

I was so awestruck. He arrived in a best Savile Row suit, very smart and handsome. The ladies never came to our house, but he came on his own early one morning to take me to the hotel where he was staying. I went and had breakfast with them, and was so scared.

Madam Henny was a little portly, very rich, nice-looking and smelt wonderful. Miss Jones was small and mousy, but extremely English. Madam Henny was trying to speak correct English, but I could tell she was speaking in a strong accent. It was my first experience of sitting at a table and having English breakfast. We ate fried egg and toast. I saw them using forks and cutting without a knife, and I didn't know what to do, because until then I had always used my hands. I was told by the ladies how to use the cutlery, but I was miserable and angry, almost in tears. I couldn't manage with the knife and fork, and didn't know what to do with the fried eggs – especially the yolk, which fell on my clothes. So then they instructed me on how to use the serviette, and my father was giving more directions from the other corner. I don't know how I got through that breakfast!

I met him for maybe three or four days that time. One day he bought me a huge balloon, which was very new to me, and then took me to the ghat; and as we were going down the steps, he met a friend – the person who had been our guardian when we first came to Benares. They started talking, so I amused myself by playing with the balloon. Fifteen minutes went by, then half an hour, and I was getting bored. All of a sudden there was a BANG as the balloon burst. My father looked at me and then carried on talking. Another fifteen minutes went by and I was getting even more bored, wanting to walk around and see more. At last the friend went away and I was ready to go back home, but my father took me by the shoulders and shook me. I was told later by my brothers that he would never beat anyone; when he was angry he just shook them by the shoulders and shouted. That was his only punishment. I don't even remember what he said – it was probably related to the balloon, or perhaps I was not standing properly –

(opposite and below) Ravi's father, Pandit Shyam Shankar. The inscription below reads: 'My dear son Robi, with blessings, your father, Shyam Shankar, 18th October 1934'.

but to me it was so hurtful. I had never felt any love from him; he had never taken me in his arms or touched me with affection. I cried, although I tried not to. I really didn't have much feeling for him then. He took me home and returned to his hotel.

I remember during this first meeting with him the good smell of cologne. He also gave me a beautiful bottle of red ink, which didn't smell at all like ink; it smelt of rose. I have always been very sensitive to smells, and that was strange and exciting. From then on I would sometimes open the pot and smell it, but never would I write with it.

He did one good thing that time: he bought us a medium-size Chevrolet van. Sejda had just passed his second year at college, but my father said, 'What is the use of studying? You should try something adventurous.' So we ran a bus service between Ghazipur and Mhow. It was successful, and we started earning good money. Later on a driver was engaged and then Bhupendra also joined, so the two brothers were doing this together.

But within eight or ten months there was an epidemic of plague in the area. Bhupendra fell ill with it, and died within three days. We were in Benares, where I was going to school, and his dead body was brought back on that same bus. This was my first encounter with death, and I was heartbroken. How I missed him! You can imagine how my mother felt, having lost her eighteen-year-old boy. We lost interest in the bus and sold it off.

My father was an unusual man. It was not until much later that I learnt all about him, so in my childhood I almost hated him, my sympathy naturally being with my mother. Being separated from my father while he was with other women caused her suffering, and seeing this was painful to me, though she would never say anything bad about him. But later on, after I learnt the facts, my feelings towards him gradually changed.

Theirs was an arranged marriage. His father, Barada Shankar Chowdhury, a zamindar from the village of Kalia, had organised it through a matchmaker. He received news of a zamindar's daughter in a remote village, and read her horoscope, as is the custom. My father had declined marriage many times, but for some reason he agreed this time, and they married. There was an age difference of about nine years: my mother was about eleven (not an uncommon age for a bride then) and he must have been twenty.

He was such an intellectual giant and my mother was so simple, a village girl. She knew no English, and she could hardly write or read any Bengali; her handwriting was like that of a child. He couldn't talk with her on any subject. He tried to teach her English and Bengali, and maybe he gave up too soon, but it was just one of those very sad things, really. He was always travelling here and there, and he found other people to whom he could relate. Whenever he visited her, he got her pregnant, and that's perhaps the only thing they had between them. I can understand how they never had a close relationship.

There was plenty of money coming in to his family, and he would have had a huge amount of land and property, but he said he didn't want it and just gave it away to his relatives. He never saved any money, nor sent us any, of course. Very worldly in many ways, he was at the same time so detached, to a strange extreme. I think my brothers (or at least Dada and I) inherited that tendency – the feeling of having everything but having nothing.

My father was a great Sanskrit scholar, took his MA at Calcutta University, became a Barrister-at-Law at the Middle Temple in London and a Privy Council member too. He studied yoga in a cave with a great yogi for almost two years, Vedic chants in Benares (and possibly in Maharashtra too) and French in Geneva. In 1931 he was awarded a Doctorate of Political Science from the University of Geneva for a thesis entitled *The Nature and Evolution of the Political Relations between the Indian States and the British Imperial Government*, supposedly the first Indian to gain his doctorate in French. Afterwards he obtained a legal position with the League of Nations in Geneva, and went on to teach Indian philosophy in New York, at the invitation of the Roerich Museum and later Columbia University.

He also specialised in voice culture, the technique designed to improve the voice-throw system. He followed the Western style, even though India had its own version – it was commonly used when people sang in large courtyards or palaces in the days before microphones. Nowadays, unfortunately, all our singers depend on the microphone, and some of them have almost a crooner's voice. I heard him once on a special occasion in a chapel in Geneva. He recited some Vedic chants, mostly from the *Sama Veda* – and I couldn't believe it was my father! I didn't know that side of him at all. As he chanted, it was reverberating all around In such a powerful, clear, melodious and rich voice. He used to give demonstrations of this when he gave lectures, reciting some Sanskrit shlokas (verses) from the Vedas in the original style.

He also wrote several books, although to my knowledge only two were published, both in London: the first, in 1914, was *Buddha and his Sayings*, a guide to the life, doctrines and dictums of Buddha; the second, *Wit and Wisdom of India*, in 1924, was a collection of humorous short stories from different parts of India. I do not know where the manuscripts are now. There were many other unpublished manuscripts, including one I remember seeing with a big 'L' on the cover: *Light, Life, Law and Love*. It was a discussion of the Indian way of life, mostly concerning the ideas of Manu Samhita.

The title pages from Shyam Shankar's two published books.

WIT AND WISDOM OF INDIA

A COLLECTION OF HUMOROUS FOLK-TALES
OF THE COURT AND COUNTRY-SIDE
CURRENT IN INDIA

BY

PANDIT SHYAMA SHANKAR, M.A. (London)

*Research Scholar of University College, London, Member of the Middle Temple
and Member of the Jhálwár State Council*

Author of
" BUDDHA AND HIS SAYINGS "

With an Introduction by
FRANCIS HENRY SKRINE, F.R.H.S.
Indian Civil Service (Retired)

ILLUSTRATED

LONDON
GEORGE ROUTLEDGE & SONS, LTD.
BROADWAY HOUSE : 68-74 CARTER LANE, E.C.
1924

BUDDHA AND HIS SAYINGS

WITH COMMENTS ON RE-INCARNATION
KARMA, NIRVANA, ETC.

BY

PANDIT SHYAMA SHANKAR

LONDON
FRANCIS GRIFFITHS
1914

Another one was called *The Religion and Philosophy of Universal Brotherhood*. These never appeared in print even though he was in a position to have them published through the Roerich Foundation in New York. All this shows further that he was not ambitious for money or fame.

From his somewhat lonely and Spartan childhood in Benares, Ravi was now to be whisked away at the age of ten to the glamour and tumult of Paris highlife, guided by his eldest brother, Dada: the legendary Uday Shankar, bringer of Indian dance and music to the West. Of this cultural pioneer, James Joyce wrote: 'He moves on the stage like a semi-divine being. Believe me, there are still some beautiful things left in this world.'

I have always felt deep love and enormous respect for Dada. I consider him one of my gurus, because in my early years that I spent with his troupe he was more like a father to me. He taught me some very important things, such as loving and respecting our art, culture and heritage – he was the first one to direct my attention towards that – and so much about stagecraft, showmanship, manners and discipline on the stage, all its rules, regulations and decorum. That really helped me. And yes, his insatiable passion for women and sex influenced me greatly in my life, too!

He had started off as a painter in London, but in May 1923 Anna Pavlova saw him choreographing and performing some dance in an Indian ballet in Covent Garden, apparently entitled *The Great Moghul's Chamber of Dreams*, which my father had written and produced. This was actually the first Indian ballet produced in Britain. My father was very musical and creative, even though he was not a professional, and since 1915 had produced a number of variety shows in London. He would also make suggestions to Dada about the choreography. Dada's mentor was Sir William Rothenstein, the head of the fine art section at the Royal College of Art, who was invited by my father to that Covent Garden performance. It was Sir William who brought along Pavlova. Dada had already received the Silver Medal of Merit at the Royal College of Art, and Sir William had great hopes for his future as a fine artist. But this evening was to change Dada's whole life and career.

Pavlova had previously been to India, and was charmed by what she saw there. She was very eager to do something with Indian dances and costumes, but felt she couldn't do it herself. When she saw my brother, she immediately sensed that here was a person who could help her. She proposed that he assist her with two ballets, *Hindu Wedding* and *Radha-Krishna*, which she wanted to produce as part of her *Oriental Impressions* presentation. Sir William was not happy about it; he was extremely fond of his student, and knew that Dada would have a brilliant future as a painter, but he could not prevent it. Dada, of course, was thrilled about such a brilliant opportunity. He spent nine months touring Canada, the USA, Mexico and South America with her troupe, choreographing the two ballets and dancing as Krishna, with Pavlova as Radha.

Dada did not really have that much background in dance. Having been in places like Benares or Nasrathpur, he had seen the performances of the communities of cobblers and washermen, and folk dances at different celebrations and times of the year. In Udaipur and Jhalawar he had seen the semi-folk dances Nautch, Ghangor and Ghumar, and he came across the festival dances known as Garba, Ras and Dandia while in Bombay. He also saw some other styles in Jhalawar, to where famous dancers came from different parts of India. He even saw the celebrated Goki-Bai, who used to dance on a platform mounted on the tusks of an elephant, with the sarangi and tabla musicians sitting on the haoda (seat) on the elephant's back! He imbibed all these dances and held them in his mind.

While studying fine art and going through books on the iconography of India, he was fascinated by the photographs and descriptions of the old caves in Ellora, Ajanta, Mahaballipuram and Bagh, with their stone sculptures and paintings of gods and goddesses in dance poses and wearing period costumes. Being a fantastic painter, he could visualise the dance movements merely from the poses in those still images.

THE ORIENTAL IMPRESSIONS (Three Miniatures)

(a) Dances of Japan.   1. Dojoji
                         2. Kappore
                         3. Takeau Bayashi

Arranged by Mr. Koshiro Matsumoto Fujima and Miss Fumi, Professors of Dancing at Tokyo.
The Overture and Orchestral Arrangement from original Japanese theme by Henry Geehl.

Scenery Designed and Painted by M. O. Allegri.

Mlles. Stuart, Friede, Coles, Glynde, Bartlett, Rogers, Nichols, Crofton.
M. Algeranoff.

(b) A Hindu Wedding.

The Bride	...	Mlle. Nakita
The Bridegroom	...	M. Vajinski
The Priests	...	MM. Domdslavski and Winter
Friends of the Bride	Mlles. Griffiths, Bartlett, Rogers, Elkington, Spencer, Ward	
Friends of the Bridegroom	MM. Oliveroff, Micolaitchik, Sabi, Labzelles	
Nautch Girls	Mlles. Stuart, Coles, Friede, Glynde, Lake, Faber, Faucheux, Gervis	

(c) Krishna and Rhada

Krishna	M. F. Uday Shankar
Rhada	Anna Pavlova
The Goppies	Mlles. Stuart, Coles, Friede, Glynde, Lake, Faber, Faucheux, Gervis

The Music for the two Hindu Scenes composed by Mlle. Comolata Banerji.
Dances arranged by M. F. Uday Shankar.

A detail from the programme for Anna Pavlova's Oriental Impressions sequence, which she presented in her 1923 tour. Uday Shankar is credited as dancer and choreographer.

Uday's association with Pavlova had not lasted more than a year (she actually encouraged him to concentrate his attention once more on traditional Indian rather than Western arts), but he remained in Europe for another five years. He lived first in London and then for three or four years in Paris, where he found the bohemian artistic climate more receptive to his Eastern artistry.

Then, after a period spent struggling to make his name, his stars suddenly seemed to burst open. He met two women who gave him great encouragement: young Simone Barbier (or Simkie, as she was known), originally a talented pianist from Paris, but who soon became his dance partner; and the sculptress and artist Alice Boner from Zürich, who was genuinely devoted to nurturing Uday's creative talent and used her considerable wealth to help him establish his own troupe of Indian dancers. In 1929 Boner accompanied him when he returned to India in order to realise the dream he had developed of touring the West with his own dance troupe. He needed to assemble a group of dancers and musicians, and he also wanted to prepare thoroughly by studying in greater depth the arts and history of the various regions of India, before returning with the new troupe to Paris.

This was the first time in his life that Ravi had seen his eldest brother.

When Dada came to India with Alice Boner, for about one year they travelled all over India, especially the South, where there are two old classical dance forms. The oldest system is known as Bharata Natyam, which is from around Madras in Tamil Nadu, and then there is the famous dance-drama enacted by people from Kerala (or Malabar, as it was then), known as Kathakali. To Dada and myself, Kathakali was – and is – the greatest form of combined dance and drama anywhere in the world. It evolved from Bharata Natyam, but developed its own style of presenting the stories of *Mahabharata* and *Ramayana*.

Kathakali is performed outdoors all night, with huge oil lamps on both sides (no electricity), elaborate costumes and highly stylised make-up that takes eight to twelve hours to dry on the face. The roles are enacted by artists, each of whom mostly specialises in one particular character, such as Krishna, Arjuna or one of the other Pandava brothers, Rama, Ravana or Hanuman. The parts of the female characters are played by men. It is a dance-drama, with acting, expressions, eye movements and gesture language. Anything can be said with its hand gestures and facial expressions.

Dada stayed in the South for about three months, just watching. He learnt fifty or sixty basic words and phrases in gesture language, such as: 'come here', 'go', 'who are you?', 'a beautiful woman', and 'king'. He picked up the basic body movements, the steps, and the eye and hand gestures, along with the Nava Rasa (nine principal moods, the expressions of which are a central feature of most performing arts in India) which have a great importance in Kathakali. He assimilated as much as he could in the short time he was there, without really going deep into learning.

Then he travelled around India to observe some other dances, visiting Madras to experience the best of Bharata Natyam; the regions of Bihar and Orissa for Chhau; and the north-eastern part of India for the beautiful Manipuri style, as well as seeing various folk dances, and even some aboriginal ones, including Bheel and Santhal. He also spent many days visiting his dream lands: the ancient caves of Ellora, Ajanta, Badami and Bagh, and the great sculptures carved at Konarak and Mahaballipuram. With his childhood impressions of dance, plus all that he saw during this year, he was enriched and inspired; and with his painter's vision he evolved a dance style of his own, which he started teaching to us when we came back to Paris with him the next year.

Dada was mostly self-taught. It was only much later on, when we were in Calcutta for about six or seven months in 1934, that he had his first guru, Sankaran Namboodri, who came from near Trivandrum in Kerala. That was the time when Dada choreographed, with help from the great guru, his solo piece 'Kartikeya', portraying Kartikeya (the younger son of Shiva and brother of Ganesha) preparing himself before going to slay an evil demon. I too had a few months of proper basic training from Sankaran Namboodri, which is why I have a good idea of Kathakali. Dada's only other period of training came later on in Almora, at the cultural centre he founded in the Himalayas. To tell you the truth, he was not that good a student – he actually took longer to learn than we others did. Sitting down and practising from basics was not his strength. But from watching one single movement, he could create ten different ones himself. He was such a creative genius. Unfortunately the 'art-politicians', snobs and pseudo-connoisseurs in power labelled him (and still label him even today) as neither 'classical' nor 'traditional' – and accused him of being Westernised!

By the time that Dada came to form the troupe, in 1930, he had already started his own dance techniques, creating wrist, palm, finger and hand gestures as well as neck, shoulder, waist and hip movements, many new leg movements and steps. His eye and facial expressions were highly influenced by Kathakali. His speciality was moving the whole arm like a wave (as you can see in his 1948 film *Kalpana*). He devised new dance pieces of his own, such as *Indra*, *Gandharva*, and *Snake-Charmer*, performing solos (and always having to do encores); and he did semi-ballets and group dances, too – for instance, *Gajasur Vadh*.

After touring the South, Dada went to Calcutta, where he met Haren Ghosh, who later became a famous impresario. Anything Haren presented succeeded, his name alone being the crucial factor (except when Dada's name was there, too). He had already started presenting dance in Calcutta and nearby cities, and had heard about Dada and luckily met him. He wanted to present Dada in the best theatre in Calcutta, the New Empire: principally a cinema hall but with an excellent if compact stage, which was usually restricted to the foreign performers who came to Calcutta. Dada didn't have any musicians, though he did have some costumes with him, and Alice Boner improvised to make some more; so Haren Ghosh managed to persuade Dada to perform.

It was in Calcutta, too, that Dada met Timir Baran, the first classical musician to impress me. He was a man of great character, and was very masculine-looking: dark, with long, curly hair. He had just come from Maihar, where he had learnt sarod for about four and a half years from Ustad Baba Allauddin Khan, the great musician who later became my own guru. Inspired by Baba's Maihar band, Timir had created a small chamber orchestra consisting of his family members and students. When Dada heard it, he was very impressed, and asked Timir to take care of the music for the show.

Dada performed a few solo dances, mainly *Gandharva*, *Indra*, *Snake-Charmer* and *Nautch*, for which he used to dress up like a woman, with a big Rajasthani langha (skirt). He shook up Calcutta with his sleek presentation and personality – it was something the city had never seen before. Dada's background was written about in the newspapers: how he had been with Pavlova and taught her Indian dancing. He became a superstar – indeed, the first Indian performing superstar in those days.

Uday went to Benares to explain his dream to his family. He wanted them to join him in fulfilling it; and at length and after some difficulty, he convinced them. Success was far from guaranteed, but they decided to take the gamble and uproot themselves to the other side of the world.

Rajendra abandoned his studies for a master's degree, and Debendra for his bachelor's. Likewise, Ravi's cousin Meena (also known as Kanaklata) agreed to join, as did her father, Uncle Kedar Shankar, a drum-player who sported a French-cut beard. He was known to the brothers as Kaka (which means 'father's younger brother'). Their maternal uncle Brija Bihari, known as Mama (and later as Matul), was another recruit to the emerging troupe. He was actually a distant cousin of Hemangini but had been brought up by her from childhood. Several amateur musicians were also enlisted, and Timir Baran was appointed as musical director; and then Uday invited his mother to accompany them to Paris to look after the household – which meant that ten-year-old Robu had to go as well. He was thrilled at the prospect. At the end of 1930, he was leaving for a new life in Paris.

*Uday Shankar,
Ravi's eldest brother.*

TWO: BAIRAGI

बैरागी

'Robu, Robu! Ot! Ot! Dushtu chhele!'

I heard this through my deep sleep in a wonderful dream, that I was having a bath or a hot shower, or sitting in a hot tank... but then I felt my mother shaking me, and I woke up to realise I had wet my bed and she was trying to get me up!

It was almost early morning and the place was, of all places, Paris. I felt so bad. I was ten, and I had this weakness; once in a while it would happen. In fact, I remember that in Benares, before I went to sleep every night, my mother used to make me recite a couplet in Bengali, almost like a mantra:

'Ghawrey shoton bairai moton
Shoton moton dui bhai'

and then knock the pillow on the left side, before going to sleep. It meant: to sleep inside the house and go to pee outside the house, though the sleeping and the peeing ('shoton' and 'moton') are like two brothers. Then knocking the pillow was a charm, or something like that.

It was ridiculous in a way. It was so cold outside, below zero, with snow on the ground. And after the wonderful warmth that I'd been experiencing in my state of sleep, to wake up in the cold and have to go through the change of bedsheet and clothes... really I felt so miserable!

Being in Paris was like a dream. When we arrived in 1930, I had a slight fever, which had begun the moment we left Benares on the train, and continued on the boat, with all the excitement and newness of everything.

From birth I had been surrounded by all the magic of Benares, and from there I took the train journey to Bombay. For me Bombay was already unbelievable. To see all of the cinema houses – I saw my first sound movie there, of course – it was too much for me!

Then came the boat journey. The ship, an Italian one, the *S. S. Ganges*, was like a whole city. For a few days I so much enjoyed running on the deck, and the small cabins with four berths. It was such fun to see a basin with hot and cold water, and the toilet was so different. Everything thrilled me because it was new.

The only problem we all had was with food. Some days they had rice and curry, which was all right, but on other days they had spaghetti with tomato sauce. Dada, who was so loving and at the same time was a hard taskmaster, wanted us to get used to the way of life in the West, so he would force us to eat pasta, and meat cooked in a Western way rather than the Indian style. I was not enjoying that aspect of the journey. I forced myself to eat it, but by the third day the ship started rolling because the sea was rough, and all of us became sick. From early childhood I had been very weak when travelling; I used to get car sick and sea sick (although not from trains). The moment the sea began to get choppy, then out came all this spaghetti with tomato sauce! I felt so terrible. Even after three or four years, when I had become used to everything else in the West, I still couldn't take spaghetti and tomato sauce!

We passed places like Aden and Port Said. We only stopped for a few hours in Port Said, but it was spellbinding, because immediately on arrival we saw some of the local people performing magic, producing sparrows and pigeons. To me it looked like a charmed land, even though we were warned that the greatest 'magic' would be that our purses or other valuables would 'disappear' if we were not careful! We arrived at Brindisi in Italy, ten or eleven days after leaving Bombay, and from there we went by train to Paris via Venice. The train journeys were wonderful; the carriages were so different from ours, so clean and exciting.

(below) Ravi, shortly after arriving in Paris.

(opposite, left to right) Vishnudas Shirali on tabla, Annada Charan Bhattacharya (known as Bechu) on taus, Ravi on sitar, Timir Baran on sarod, Rajendra Shankar on flute. In the garden of the troupe's Paris home, early in 1931.

Venice was like heaven: the fabulous San Marco Plaza, with thousands of pigeons. It seemed like an enchanted city, with no roads, only water, and no cars, just gondolas – and the gondoliers singing 'O Sole Mio' in tenor voice. The houses were fantastic and the Italian language sounded like music to me, as it still does. I have a great love for the Italians. Their ancient culture is wonderful and their cities are beautiful, but more than that, what I really adore about Italians is that they have a very childlike quality: the men are impish, full of fun, always laughing, and they are the pinching-bottom type. They can get away with murder! And on my first arrival the ladies really made me gape, with all their make-up, perfume and beautiful shapely legs – I started having my fever all over again!

At last we arrived in Paris at the house where we were to stay, 121 Rue de Paris, in Paris seizième. We had an attractive old house which resembled a mini-mansion, with small grounds and eight to ten rooms, including a big hall downstairs. I was to share one of the rooms with my mother.

Everything was brought from India. My brother and Alice Boner had

brought over on the boat with us all of the instruments and textile materials
they had collected during their travels around India; there were huge trunks
full of them. We all loved Alice very much; she had really helped my brother
so much to create this troupe.

Within a few days we had two or three seamstresses, who embarked on
the costume-making. I saw yards and yards of silver and gold brocades that
would be made into costumes and headdresses, and we had ornaments for the
body. Everything was fashioned in the ancient style, thousands of years old,
that one sees only in the sculptures and the caves of Ellora, Mahaballipuram
or Ajanta. Amidst all these colours, I was in a magic land.

Then out came the musical instruments. There were a hundred and fifty
varieties, mostly folk ones, but we also had classical instruments: the veena,
sitar, sarod, sarangi, sarinda, flutes, shahnai, classical and folk drums, with
aboriginal drums from the far North to the far South. Even though I was
Indian myself, I had never seen such materials. Not even in a museum have I
ever seen such a collection.

All sorts of friends of Dada came to greet us, and there were also famous
artists and newspaper and magazine people keen to know more about the
exotic new arrivals. We had a deadline. We arrived at the end of 1930 and the
first show was fixed for 3rd March, 1931, at the Théatre des Champs Elysées.
The work was going on apace, and before long began the rehearsals. Dada had
a number of dancers, and the show was really taking shape. I was
participating in it but not seriously, because they were planning to put me in
a school in Paris.

My school study had gone to the dogs after leaving Benares, where I had
been in school for those two years. I was lucky that my brothers, especially

Mejda and Sejda, were giving me tuition in English, mathematics, geometry and a little algebra; those continued, but this was really the end of my academic career. For a further period of almost two years I went to L'Ecole St Joseph, in the Michel Ange Molitor district of Paris, although I had to enter in a lower class because of the language problem. The only thing I benefited from was learning French. It was a Catholic school and we had to say prayers in French, which I learnt like a parrot. But that was all; there was not much education. In the beginning the boys ragged me a lot, but I was a year or two older than the others in my class, and could run very fast. I used to hit them and run away, and they couldn't catch me! After some time there was peace.

It was about two miles to school, but I enjoyed the walk, with a satchel on my back, a beret on my head and wearing plus-fours. On the way I loved sucking *sucettes*, those flat and round bonbons of different colours and flavours. At the outset my brothers showed me how to cross the road at the lights, and then it was easy.

Paris was the art capital of the world at that time. It seemed that all the foreign artists either lived there as expatriates or visited it. There was a big influx of people from America, and I seemed to meet them all – I recall Gertrude Stein very well, and Henry Miller and Cole Porter vaguely – but without realising who they were or how famous. It was also the period of Gurdjieff, Rudolf Steiner and Dadaism. Hash and other drugs were

around, but were restricted only to elderly, matured achievers!

I had a wonderful life at this time with jazz and classical musicians, ballet and flamenco dancers. Alice Boner's aunt was married to a friend of ours, an American who used to play cello, whose house was like a salon. I saw so many of Paris's famous musicians in that house.

Having heard so much about Pavlova and seen her films, I felt as if I knew her. Sadly, however, she died a few months after we reached Paris, and I never did meet her. But we did see the Spanish dancers Argentina and Escudero, Krieger (the German who danced with a shaved head), and Teresina. I was going to the opera and the ballet with my brothers, and gradually seeing and hearing such great musicians as the guitarist Andres Segovia, the cellist Pablo Casals, the pianist Paderewski, and Shalyapin, the basso at the Paris Opera. When Shalyapin sang I felt a strange rumble in my stomach, and it was as if the chandeliers were shaking! Then there was Jascha Heifetz, Fritz Kreisler, Georges Enesco, Stravinsky and Toscanini.

To have seen all these pheno-menal artists, and met some of them, and heard them again and again in different parts of the world was wonderful. In spite of the fact that I never had any proper training in Western music, apart from some piano lessons while at school in Paris, I heard so much classical music, live and recorded, that I felt very much at home. It was within me; I knew about good music and the famous composers and their pieces.

Some of these celebrities used to come to visit us, too: Segovia, Enesco, the actors Georges and Nudmilla Pitoeff, and Michael Chekhov (Anton Chekhov's nephew). I was being flooded with all these famous people, in our own house – at Rue de Paris and then, after we moved early in 1932, at 17 Rue de Belvedere.

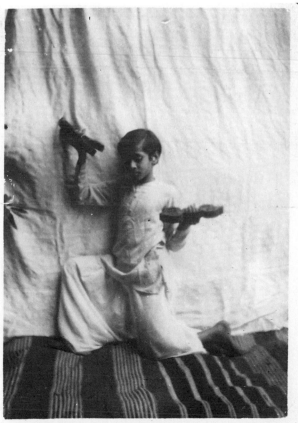

(opposite) The troupe rehearsing music in their Paris home, 1931.

(left) A double-exposure photograph of Ravi, taken by Uday.

(below) Posing with kartal, a wooden percussion instrument.

Very few are fortunate enough to have had all the excitements and wonderful times that I experienced in my childhood. Yet although I knew these people were great, I was not really aware at the time that I was so lucky to have all of these luxuries. I took it for granted. Only now, looking back, can I appreciate what I've gone through.

I used to see a lot of French films. The comedian Georges Milton was my favourite, and I loved Gaby Morlay and Jean Gabin, too. I had a good collection of Western classical music on 78rpm records: flute, cello, symphony orchestra. I also had a lot of jazz and French accordion music, and popular and film songs: Edith Piaf and so on. I didn't see Josephine Baker or Mistinguette at that time, but I saw them much later, when I (and they, too) were a little older. Josephine Baker, the beautiful black American dancer at the Casino de Paris, had a château-like place very near a friend's house I used to visit. She adopted many children. She was renowned for her dance with the bananas to 'Yes, We Have No Bananas'. The French dancer Mistinguette was equally well known. She was famous for her legs – even in her sixties, when I saw her.

What really excited me in those days were the women. I feel they used make-up and perfume much more then than they do now. The lipsticks were deeper, the eyes more often had mascara, the rouge and the scents... and with those curvaceous legs they all drove me crazy. I wanted to be near them, smell them and touch them – I couldn't resist. And they used to love me! They used to fondle me and kiss me, thinking I was a young and cute little boy, of course, but little did they know that I was not feeling like a little boy! I was very excited all of the time!

Our friends Georges and Nudmilla Pitoeff, husband and wife, had about five daughters, aged between ten and eighteen, and two sons. I was very friendly with them, had such fun going to their house in the Bois de Boulogne, and I was in love with all of the daughters! They were Russians, and beautiful, with names like Nadya, Nudmilla and Svetlana.

That period in Paris is still so vivid in my mind. It is so exciting, even now, thinking about meeting those famous and beautiful people; being enveloped in sight, sound, smell, music and dance; being loved and praised by everyone; and, of course, being constantly in love with almost all the little girls and grown-up women that I saw or met.

The result of all this was that I grew up so fast, as you are bound to in show business – as George has told me he did, as one of The Beatles, only I was even younger. I feel that I did not really have much of a childhood. From the very beginning in Paris I was thrown together with older people, like my brothers. Work time was fine, but there were times when they relaxed and some of them drank and had girlfriends. Sometimes they went to some performances and took me, not realising that there would be nude scenes or erotic sequences. All that was very embarrassing for them. They would take me out immediately if such scenes came on, but you can take it from me that by then I had seen enough!

From the start I had been singing, dancing and playing a few instruments in the troupe's concerts in Paris, but by the time I was twelve and a half they began taking me touring. They started to involve me more, as both a dancer and an accompanying musician.

We used to travel by bus all over continental Europe: France, Switzerland, Italy, Germany, Holland, Belgium, Czechoslovakia, Austria, Hungary, Yugoslavia – even as far as Romania, Bulgaria, Estonia, Lithuania and Latvia; everywhere except Russia and Greece, although I visited both a number of times later on.

In its hotels Europe still displayed the ravages of the First World War. The rooms had water jugs instead of basins; or if there were basins with hot water, there were certainly no bathrooms. In those days it was only luxury hotels that had rooms with bathrooms, and then in only a few suites; we had to go down the corridor. It was the same in London, which I first visited in 1932. None of the hotels we stayed in – such as the Imperial Hotel, or the Royal Hotel on Russell Square – had any en-suite bathrooms. This inconvenience meant that one could only take a bath once or twice a week, and usually one had to pay separately for it, too. Even away from the cities, when we went to a restaurant or a cafe the toilet would be outside in a little hut, with a foul-smelling open latrine. We would have preferred going in the field, as in India!

In spite of their lack of luxury, my personal estimation for the French was that they seemed almost perfect. At least they had a bidet in some hotel rooms! And they had such good taste – for food, wine, perfume, women and love. Their attitude for life was (and is) so artistic, romantic and confident. I loved the wonderful morning smells in the streets from the croissants, brioches and baguettes, and of course from the women, too. (I wonder why I mention the women so often...) I have always loved French food, and especially French food in France. Eating it elsewhere is different; maybe it is the water, or perhaps the butter, but *something* makes haricots verts or pommes frites so different from English- or American-cooked beans or chips. I have such a weakness for La Cuisine Française – even a simple omelette with potatoes, a salad, or baguettes. I have frequented many of the very famous big restaurants in France – the Rotonde, Coupole, Maxim's and others – but I always preferred the smaller restaurants in out-of-the-way streets, where the dishes were not only cheaper but also much tastier.

I was so deeply in love then with France and its culture and language that I am still not free from it. But I do realise the other side: the snobbishness, the looking down on others – American and British people, especially the former. It is an irony to see many years later how the French too have been influenced, like the rest of the world, by the American culture of Coca-Cola, jeans, burgers and MTV.

After Paris and Amsterdam and Brussels, London seemed depressing. Those were the days when its 'pea-souper' fogs were prominent, as you can see in the old black-and-white films set in London. All the houses in each street looked identical, and all the buildings were full of grime because of the

DANSES et MUSIQUE HINDOUES

UDAY SHAN KAR

1931 ET SA TROUPE ALICE BONER

SALLE PLEYEL – MERCREDI 6 et MARDI 12 JUIN

(overleaf)
FOREGROUND: *Simkie dancing as Radha, Uday Shankar as Krishna.*
SEATED BEHIND: *Kedar Shankar, Vishnudas Shirali, Ravi, Rajendra Shankar, Timir Baran, Bechu (hidden), Kanaklata, Matul, Debendra Shankar – all the members of the troupe as it was originally assembled in 1930.*

*The whole troupe
outside Cologne
Cathedral, 1932.*

smog and smoke and coal dust. The Royal Hotel, where we were staying, was like a barracks. There was also a strange relationship with the average Londoners then. There were always cases of children running after Indians shouting, 'Blackie! Blackie! Blackie!' and if an Indian was walking alone he had problems. But I had been thrilled at encountering the gorgeous pronunciation of the King's English when it was spoken, and London itself as a city, with its celebrated sights – Hyde Park, Kew Gardens, the British Museum, Madam Tussaud's, the Tower of London – was naturally very impressive. It seemed huge. What most bowled me over was the Tube, because back then compared to the Paris Metro and some others in Europe it seemed the cleanest and most attractive: nice, round and colourful.

Food was another matter. Fish and chips were my favourite, and the breakfast, of course, I liked very much, because it was filling; one didn't need to take lunch as well after all the varieties of dishes for breakfast – bacon, eggs, porridge and fish, or sometimes even mutton chops. The Lyons Corner Houses were the biggest and best restaurants. I don't know where they have gone now. Our favourite was in Leicester Square, where they used to make fried chicken with eggs on top, like batter; served with potato chips, that was delicious. We often used to go out around that area, between Piccadilly and Leicester Square, in the brightest spots of the West End, with all its cinemas and even Indian restaurants. Although there were very few Indian restaurants, as frequently as possible we ate at them. But most other restaurants served poor food and, believe me, in general London didn't seem very exciting at that time.

I love the countryside of the British Isles. Its dark green colour is quite different from most other places, its plants being so healthy because of all the rain. When I am touring, I usually make a point of travelling by train, which is delightful. But we didn't have much luck in seeing the English countryside on that initial trip because we didn't perform in many places outside London. In fact, though Dada was a great success in London, the rest of England was relatively unmoved. It was something about the British in those days: why wasn't Dada invited to Birmingham or Manchester or Leeds? Because most of the country was not interested in Indian culture.

Then I knew the Germans also. The Germans that I remember were different from those of today. They were really in a bad shape then, owing to the after-effect of the First World War, with not enough food to go around; but I was impressed by the intellectual and cultural side of the people. Germany was the first country where we found people shouting to us, 'Gandhi! Gandhi! Tagore!' We went all over the country, travelling by bus to small towns and remote villages as well as the cities – to eighty different places in all. They had excellent theatre, and their knowledge about India was far ahead of that of the French or Italians – or the British, for that matter. It made us feel so appreciated that they had such adoration for our country and people.

The most welcoming country next to Germany was Czechoslovakia. All of my impressions there were good: such a small country, but again the people knew so much about India – even about the *Mahabharata*, for they would call out to us, 'Gita! Gita!' We couldn't believe it in those days. Poland was another country with high cultural awareness, where we found the people so much into the arts and having fun. Nevertheless it was probably Germany that excited me moſt, because of its wealth of music and the people's breadth of knowledge.

During the Second World War, many people in India harboured a secret desire that Hitler should win, because in our heart of hearts we did not like the British. We were politically suppressed. We loved everything from Germany; it was solid. (Japan, in contraſt, was tinny and weak. Everything from there was so flimsy – we knew that whatever Japanese toys we bought would break within two days.) Apart from Germany we thought that British goods, such as their cars, were ſtrong. In spite of our anti-British feeling we had respeét for British solidity and integrity. The King's English and correét manners were very much in vogue, and copied by the Indian civil servants and small elites.

The British influence in India had begun in Calcutta, then India's major city; it was the earlieſt centre of trade, and aétually the capital until 1911 (when it moved to Delhi). Being Bengali, I knew about the golden period, running from the late eighteenth century through to the early twentieth, when Calcutta was the main city and there was a Renaissance in Bengal – Tagore, Ramakrishna, Vivekananda and almoſt all the famous writers, scientiſts, doétors, lawyers and teachers came from there. This gave Bengalis a glow of pride and a snobbish attitude (much like that of the French): 'What Bengal thinks today, the whole of India thinks tomorrow.' Unfortunately for Bengalis, since the middle of this century things have changed, and we are no longer predominant in every field. India's leadership is now shared equally by the peoples of all its ſtates.

(left to right) Uncle Kedar Shankar, Ravi, Debendra, Kanaklata. In St Mark's Square, Venice.

My mother had come to Paris with us in 1930 in order to manage the household and cook for the family. There were very few Indian restaurants then in Paris, and no Indian grocery shops; but in Place de la Madeleine, near the big church and the Thomas Cook office where we would go every week to collect our mail from India, there was a Greek shop called 'Hediard' (still there today) which sold all sorts of spices and exotic fruits. This was our favourite shop, and it was so good to smell all those spices again, and to see mangoes or lychees. My mother used to cook very simple dishes. She couldn't get many Indian vegetables, such as okra or eggplant, so mostly it was potatoes, peas, haricots verts, cauliflower and cabbage. Dals (Indian lentils) were not possible, and instead she would cook the lentils which were available. But to just these few vegetables, chicken, fish, mutton and the limited spices at her disposal, she would add onion, garlic, ginger and some chillies – and what she would make was still so delicious!

She mostly stayed in the house, especially when I was going to school. We were very close. Sometimes my brothers and I would go with my mother or some friends to the park and the zoo in the Bois de Boulogne, and I enjoyed those places immensely. I loved our visits to the Louvre Museum, the Tuileries Gardens and Versailles. I was equally struck by how different the European summer was from the winter, which was so white and cold.

That was also when I started reading more. I would read anything that was to hand: our mythologies, the *Mahabharata* and *Ramayana*, the great literature of Tagore, and various plays in Bengali. I was also reading a great deal in French, from children's comic books through history books, detective books, serious books and geographical magazines, to Jules Verne, Victor Hugo and Emile Zola; even the erotic stories of Balzac. Until I was fourteen or fifteen, my brothers continued to give me tuition in English handwriting and spelling; but it was getting less and less, and my education was really obtained through seeing, hearing and reading. I learnt from life more than anything else.

After almost two years in Paris my mother returned to India. She couldn't take it any more. She had travelled on some of the less demanding tours – she went to Monte Carlo, and did one short bus tour in Germany, for example – but nowhere very far away really. She never went to London. Mostly she had stayed back in Paris to look after me – because I was going to school there – but in 1932 my brothers started taking me on the tours.

So she went back to India, accompanied by Alice Boner, who was going to get some more materials. Mother went to stay in a rented house in Benares, alone; but she had a servant who took care of her, and her next-door neighbour was Mejda's friend and almost part of our family. She was happy there, and safe.

After she went back in 1932, I did not see her for the next year and a half. Meanwhile we went on our first trip to the United States, and then eventually we toured India itself in 1934, when I spent some time with her in Benares, which was really nice. We were always the greatest of friends, very frank and close.

In France I had come to understand my father's behaviour more. When he was based in Geneva with the League of Nations, he had visited us in Paris for two or three days, and then I had observed the hostility on my mother's side. By that time she was very bitter. Though she tried her best not to show it to others, she was curt to him and we felt a strained atmosphere whenever they were together. It was very sad.

Then he had invited my mother, my cousin Meena and me to Geneva, where he had a huge apartment. Madam Henny kept it, and Miss Jones was there, too. It was a mystery to me how he managed that. Was it a ménage à trois, or was Miss Jones merely taking care of them? Maybe that was it, because frankly she didn't look that attractive! It was a huge apartment, and that's where I saw how well he lived. We three all stayed in one room.

By then I knew how to use a knife, fork and spoon, so I had fewer problems; but Madam Henny was still very haughty. Naturally that sense of possession was there: she was the boss. But even so I liked her; she was buxom and cute, and very nice to Mother also – she was not catty. We stayed there for about two weeks, which was the longest period I ever spent with my father. Apart from this occasion, there were three or four visits to Paris, a couple of meetings in New York, and that first short visit to Benares. The total time that I spent with my father in my life would not even add up to one month.

Rajendra, Ravi, Debendra, Hemangini and Uday, outside the family home at 17 rue de Belvedere, Paris, 1932.

My brothers had something of the same hostile attitude towards my father, because they too were pained by my mother's suffering – except for Dada, who had spent so much time with my father when he was studying in London. The two of them would argue; Dada was more forthright than the rest of us, because he was the eldest son, and he would talk back to my father. Living in the West himself, Dada could understand him much better, and especially his love of women – that was natural, because Dada was a champion at that, too!

But gradually, through my brothers, I learnt other things about my father – about the things he had achieved through the Maharajah of Jhalawar for the welfare of the people, and his efforts to arrange one of the best libraries of the native states in India. They told me of his knowledge, and that he was a good person.

(top left) With Alice Boner in Zürich, 1931.

(top right) With Rajendra (left), Debendra and their father, in Paris.

(above left) STANDING: Bechu, Kanaklata, Rajendra. SEATED: Hemangini, unidentified friend of the family, Ravi.

(above) Father and Mother, on one of the former's few visits to Paris.

Arriving in New York harbour in December 1932, dressed up as maharajahs: Uday, Ravi and Kedar.

Apart from heralding my initial tour in Europe, 1932 was also the year of my first trip to the United States. That was another experience completely. Up until about thirty-five years ago the cultural shock on going from Europe to America was almost the same as when arriving in Europe from India, with suddenly all the glitter and glamour and the change to modernism. Today cities around the world have become almost the same as each other – Paris, Tokyo and Singapore are nearly as advanced as New York – but in those days it was not like that.

Every step of the journey was proving more exciting that the previous one. There had been the difference between Benares and Bombay, then the contrast of Bombay and Paris, the City of Light! Each time it was becoming more dazzling, with more electric light – but when I arrived in New York, at the end of 1932, it eclipsed everything that had gone before.

I will never forget the excitement of the moment we reached the port. The approach can never be the same arriving by plane: on a boat in the early morning, with the new Empire State – then the tallest building in the world – and the Chrysler Building gradually emerging through the fog and the haze, and the foghorns of the ships... I tell you, I had my fever again! Whenever I became excited I felt that fever.

We were all dressed like maharajahs, in very formal attire with sherwanis and turbans, and before we docked the newspaper photographers came with the pilot boat to take our pictures. That was so exciting! It was the idea of Solomon Hurok that we should all be dressed like that. He was our impresario, and the greatest of all time – like a super showman. As with Haren Ghosh in India (only more so), the title 'Solomon Hurok Presents...' was enough in itself to ensure that people flocked to his shows. He was such a box-office attraction.

From there we were whisked away by car to the St Moritz Hotel, facing Central Park, on the corner of Sixth Avenue and Fifty-Ninth Street. At that

time the St Moritz was glorious, one of the best hotels in New York
– almost on a par with the Waldorf Astoria and the New Yorker.
Our rooms were on the thirtieth floor, overlooking the park, and I
couldn't believe them – and, lo and behold, we had an attached
bathroom! That whole lifestyle was so different from London and
Paris. The rooms used to be so cold there, but we arrived in
America in the month of December and yet we were just wearing
banyain (undershirts) indoors.

In the morning a waiter would bring in the breakfast on a
pushcart: cornflakes and cream, with hot golden toast. I loved
fried eggs sunny-side-up, with sausages or bacon. This was
something I had already had in England, but for years it remained
my all-time favourite food! I always had a special weakness for the
English breakfast, if not for their lunch; I didn't care for pale
sliced mutton (sometimes undercooked and bloody) with green mint sauce, or
rhubarb pudding. Though I did love, and still do, the English fish and chips!

The first visit to New York was altogether unforgettable. I loved Times
Square, with its lights that dazzled me, and all the cinema houses –
especially the Paramount cinema house! I have never seen so many films, one
after the other, and we went to so many theatres, too. Everything was
so exciting.

And then there were the skyscrapers! We all got bad necks looking up at
them, as everyone does. There was an apocryphal story told to me by an
Indian gentleman in New York which you might like. It concerned a brother
who first visited the States in the days when they had trams, and was
enchanted by the skyscrapers. When sitting in the tram he would lean his
head out of the window and look up, and as he was doing this one day
someone shouted, 'Hey man, look out! Look out!' So he stretched his neck
further out and was hit by a tram coming the other way!

On later tours when we went to the States, most of our troupe members
stayed in second-class rather than first-class hotels, or sometimes even
cheaper ones, because we wanted to save money to spend on other

entertainments. Once or twice, when there was no
other accommodation available (and there were no
motels in those days), we had to stay in a quite sleazy
hotel. Nevertheless, no matter how cheap, each room
had central heating and an en-suite bathroom. That
impressed me the most. The only thing I did not like
was when the heating had central control and it became
too hot; if it was below zero outside we could not open
the window, because then the wind which would blow
in was freezing, so we would have to wear T-shirts
inside; sometimes I would be perspiring and barely able
to breathe.

We also went to Chicago on that first visit. Chicago
is, of course, the windy city, and its tall buildings

51

seemed to be made of elastic, so that they moved in storms. We stayed in a hotel on the twenty-sixth or twenty-eighth floor, and I was terrified when we arrived on our floor. The room was moving so much that I shouted, 'Let's go down – there's an earthquake!'

We mostly stayed beside the lake at the Congress Hotel, which in those days was highly expensive and prestigious. It was ten or fifteen below zero Fahrenheit – so cold that as we walked to the Symphony Orchestra Hall a few blocks away we felt we were almost dying. In the blizzard we had to walk bent forward, with ice forming under our noses. It was the coldest weather I had experienced. Later I encountered -36°F in Quebec, Canada. Then we would get solid ice under the nose in the few seconds it took to walk from the hotel to the taxi, or from the taxi to the concert hall. We were warned never to stay in that weather for long, as our noses and ears might fall off through frostbite – and especially not to pee outdoors while travelling on a bus!!

My passion for the world of films was at its peak on those four trips to America with Dada in 1932-33, 1933-34, 1936-37 and 1937-38. It was something unique to America that the movie houses opened at eight or ten o'clock in the morning, and some of them even went on through the entire night. So began my cinema adventures, going along with one or two friends from our troupe to see up to three movies on a free day when we had no performance. Sometimes we would even go at night after our show. I had all the photographs of the movie stars, some of them autographed, and bought the movie magazines like *Photoplay* and *Movie Mirror*. What massive and beautiful cinema halls there were, as there had been in Paris, London, Berlin and elsewhere. Cinema was the king. Television hadn't yet taken the edge off it.

In the world of cinema the emperor and king of all was Charlie Chaplin. No one can but admire him, and I always remember what Jean Renoir later said about him. It was at a cocktail party I was attending at the Paris home of my friends Jean Riboud and his wife Krishna, with many famous people present from the French film, literary and art worlds. Henri Cartier-Bresson was there, for instance. Listening to all these people's conversations, I heard someone ask Renoir, 'Can you tell us the names of the ten directors you think are the best in the world?' He didn't hesitate: 'Absolument! Charlot, Charlot, Charlot, Charlot, Charlot, Charlot, Charlot, Charlot, Charlot, Charlot!' – Charlot being the French name for Charlie. And that coming from one who was a great director himself! Chaplin is my all-time favourite too. There is no one among the great directors of today who has been free from his influence.

What attracted me most, after the movies, were the vaudevilles. I have been so lucky: I have seen Will Rogers, Eddie Cantor, Ed Wynn, W. C. Fields – all these famous entertainers, and a host of other comedians and musicians. In each theatre there would be a combined cinema and vaudeville show, incorporating a main film, maybe a cartoon, the news (Movietone or Pathé), a comic short by Charlie Chase or Laurel and Hardy, and then about one hour's vaudeville show, which consisted of a famous star, a chorus and then a brief act by a comedian. The vaudeville concept was fantastic. In all there would be three hours of entertainment, or if it was a long film it could be almost three and a half hours. Many of the finest names in films came out of vaudeville. Among the film comedians who attracted me the most were Chaplin, Buster Keaton, Eddie Cantor, the Marx Brothers and Harold Lloyd. Much later on, Danny Kaye became my favourite.

I greatly admired The Rockets, the beautiful tall dancers at the Radio City Music Hall – so many of them to fill the enormous stage, all wearing their short dresses to do the cancan! From the mid-Sixties I started seeing the mind-boggling shows in Las Vegas; but in the early Thirties it was the stage shows at Radio City that excited me so much, with all those curvaceous, scantily-dressed girls. (Of course, that was before I discovered – four years later – 'Minsky's Burlesque' shows, nightclubs on 52nd Street and the complete exposés of the Paris nightlife. I saw the striptease shows, and even Sally Rands, the queen of fan dance in New York.)

Over the next few years I also encountered jazz musicians – Louis Armstrong, Duke Ellington, Count Basie and even Cab Calloway at the Cotton Club two or three times! In later years I heard Charlie Parker. I was becoming so attracted to jazz music. The old jazz of that time is still so deeply ingrained in me, because I found so much innocence, life and soul in it. Their music was not as intellectual as the atonal, modern and avant-garde varieties you hear today, but it appeals to me more.

With our success Dada was becoming extremely famous. In the Thirties and maybe even at the beginning of the Forties, 'Shankar' was actually the best-known Indian after Gandhi and Tagore. Dada was a superstar. He had been so popular in Europe that anyone in the arts, dance or show business circles on the other side of the Atlantic already knew about him and our celebrated troupe before we even arrived; but America was by that time already well advanced in its legendary promotional expertise, and Solomon Hurok had done his homework – he had arranged magnificent publicity campaigns for us.

With Dada so famous now, Sol Hurok could fix it that whenever we went to film studios we met the top stars. Being a movie buff, I found the Hollywood experience intoxicating. For me, fever was my principal barometer of excitement; and as I went around the Paramount and MGM studios I was overheating once again! Meeting Joan Crawford, Myrna Loy, Clark Gable, John Barrymore, Lionel Barrymore, Ethel Barrymore, and all the others whom I used to dream of – it was too much for me.

There we were in Hollywood, having a marvellous time, and one day we went to a tea party arranged by the actress Marie Dressler, who was a friend of Sol Hurok. She was already in her early sixties by then, a very famous comedienne and a box-office star. The films she made along with Wallace Beery were

extremely popular: *Tugboat Annie, Min and Bill, Dinner at Eight*. All the top stars were at her party, and it was a dreamlike experience, meeting them, having tea and talking with them. Some of them were touching me and saying things like, 'He's so sweet!' and, 'Isn't he cute?'

Then I saw Marie Dressler sitting with my two brothers and talking very seriously about something. My brothers were saying, 'No, no! Sorry, it is not possible.' As I went nearer, I learnt that Marie Dressler was saying to Dada that she was so attracted to me that she wanted to adopt me. My brothers were refusing. I was so angry! I asked, 'Why won't you permit it?' I had to go away somewhere and cry it out. I could have stayed in Hollywood, lived with the film stars... what a life! I might have become the first Indian star in Hollywood – even before Sabu! At this time, that was what I wanted more than anything else.

Hypnotised by the sparkle of Hollywood, and bowled over by the material riches of America in general, Ravi was living life to the full, in an environment as different from that in which he had dwelt only a couple of years previously as could be imagined. It was the start of an enduring love affair with America that continues to this day. However, at that tender age it was painful to encounter more chauvinistic attitudes.

(top) With Uncle Kedar.

(above) The troupe meets the high priestess of modern dance, Marie Wigman (with her arm around Ravi's shoulder).

I have a special love for France and French people, but I have always had this special feeling for the USA, too, and it wounded me to hear the French and English frequently criticising Americans for being uncultured, bullying, loud, money-minded and materialistic, and for their pronunciation – 'distorting the King's English'. I would feel hurt by such remarks, just as I would if anybody criticised France. People would say the French were snobs who arrogantly believed their culture to be the highest. Of course they have so much to be proud of: their food, perfumes, wines, champagnes, manners and diplomacy, literature, architecture, the way they live. But this is what happens when you travel from one country to another: you see both sides of each place. It is those who don't travel much who always talk more about the negative aspects than the positive. I could see the good points, too.

It was an extraordinary way to be growing up, spending his formative years travelling the world, meeting the celebrities of the day, and being acclaimed at a young age as a star in his own right – for both his music and his dancing. After the debut concert in New York in December 1932, his 'fine performance' was noted by the dance critic John Martin in his New York Times review. Ravi seemed to take the sudden transformation in his stride, relishing the opportunities, and there is no doubt that being so young made the adjustment that much easier.

The Rozrich Mus[n] Apts.
310, Riverside Drive
23-12-33

Every thing froze here on 23, and the temperature went down to 10°; it is mild now.

My dear Robin,

I am very glad to receive your letter of the 12th from Los Angeles, and also to know of your thrilling experience of a visit to the Hollywood Studios & your meeting with so many stars. The best use you can make of it is to be resolved to work hard that you may become a star or a sun (সূর্য) someday. Nobody can become great without working hard.

I am in good health and look forward to have you here from Jany 19. With love and blessings,

Your affte. Father

---

151 Gaylor Road
Scarsdale
(New York, USA

14.7.34

My dear Debu & Robin,

I am very glad to receive your letters from SS. Victoria before reaching Naples.

As the times are very bad in the whole world I pray to God for your protection and welfare. Take good care of yourselves, proceed economically and very circumspectly. Remember that there are constant ups and downs in luck and no one wishing happiness can afford to be reckless. Have concerted plans to make some money in a respectable way — failing which, try to save what you have and work very hard for progress in your career.

For Robin dancing comes first, music second, correct knowledge of languages third. He must work very very hard to master the art of dancing and become the world's best dancer some day. Give my love and blessings to your mother — Same to you —

Your affectionate Father

My best wishes for Timir & Shishir.

I don't know the exact movement of the Empress.

[illegible]

[illegible]

Vidya Vibhushana, Pandit Dr. Shyama Shan-kar

Sanskrit Scholar – Philosopher – Statesman

of Benares

NEW YORK 1933

TRANSLATIONS TO LETTERS ON PAGES 55-57 AND PAGE 60

PAGE 55
Two letters from Shyam Shunkar to his sons:

(top) To Ravi; the word in the brackets following 'Sun' is the Bengali term for sun – 'Ravi'.

(bottom) To Debendra and Ravi; the Bengali message at the end of the second page is a separate letter to Mina (Kanaklata). It reads:

'Darling Mina, I send my affection and blessings to you. Please convey the same to the others. It is a hard time. Always strive to improve yourself – Your affectionate Uncle.'

PAGE 56
(top right) Excerpt from a letter to Debendra from his father, dated 9th May 1933:

'… It is satisfying to note that, having come to England, you, Meena and Rabin have not lost your balance and have retained your sense of respectfulness towards parents and elders. I pray to God that your allegiance to God and commitment to religion remain undiminished. Never be prey to laziness and addiction, and be a most distinguished personality by dint of your hard work. Let God fulfil this wish.

'With blessings, Your affectionate Father.

'P.S. Please ask Brija to take care of the velvet materials which I use for theatre. As your aunt needs them, ask him to return the materials after his use.'

(bottom left) Letter to Debendra from his father:

'8 Green Croft Gardens, London, NW6

'My dear son Debu,

'Having received your letter I was delighted, but I must say I was a little concerned too.

'I was pleased to know about your resolve that you want to continue to be part of the family, while at the same time you want to keep away from any excessive ties. But I am concerned whether you will be able to live up to this resolve and will suffer mentally in consequence of some lapses.

'However, I bless you that God Almighty and the Mother Goddess, who have given me their continued protection, will fortify you two brothers, so that you can be happy and famous in the future. I wish that this divine power will also protect Mina and Robu.

'Son, I also renounced earthly pleasure at your age. I started meditating in the care of Abou Mountain (first near Adhardevi, and later on the other side of Akan…). Following that, I spent night after night on the sea beaches of Bombay. I kept no money with me and was determined not to beg. I always contemplated God and nothing else. By the grace of God, people from high walks of life used to coax me to have food.

'But even at that stage I used to keep in regular touch with my mother, brother and wife (Uday was only just born). I did not take to asceticism in the formal sense, but was only testing myself. I was convinced those who remain immersed in the worship of God do not suffer from any deprivation. But it is very difficult to remain firm with resolve at a tender age. Those who are able to get better of the daily struggle by reconciling religion, money and carnal desires (by harmonising matter and spirit), that is to say, those who can remain unattached to the pleasure of life and conquer the base emotions, are the true sannyasi.

'I only pray to God that he showers his favours on you four brothers and Srimati Mina.

'Your affectionate Father.'

PAGE 57
Letter to Debendra, from his mother in Calcutta:

'19th May, Elgin Road

'My dear son Debu,

'It was nice to have your letter. Though Rajen reminded me four days ago, I could not get round to writing a letter earlier. Please don't take offence for my lapses. Uday has gone to Puri. He will come back on Monday. Keshta is in Benares. Only we are here.

'How are you? Try to go out as much as possible. Drink plenty of green coconut water to refresh yourself. Please write to me before you come back. I will send the measurement of my feet. If possible bring a few, at least four to six, Madras saris. The borders should be different and made of silk and cotton. Bai will take a few. She asked for it. I will be looking forward to your letter. Your uncle and auntie are keeping well. All the elders of the family send you their blessings. The younger ones send you their regards. There is no other new thing to say. Keep in happy spirits and try to gain some weight. I will be waiting to hear about your well-being. Please accept my blessings.

'Your Ma.'

PAGE 60
Letter from Shyam Shankar to Debendra, 12th October 1934:

Ravi's 'recent illness' which is referred to is his attack of typhoid. The Bengali quotation on the fifth page of the letter translates as:

'For the sake of kinship with other human beings'.

The four Bengali words on the sixth page (at the top and the bottom) are repeated uses of two terms as follows:

'They do not even correspond with such important people except for self-interest. This is not what is called integrity… Try to re-establish integrity and don't impress self-interest.'

12ᵗʰ Oct.   Scarsdale, N.Y.

My dear Debu, I have received your letter (by Air Mail), dated 10th Sept. and enclosing Rajni's post card. Evidently the letter missed the Air-Mail and lost a week in its transmission. I am glad to know that Rabu had been gradually recovering when you wrote; but I cannot be free from anxiety until I receive the news of his complete recovery. I was really shocked to hear of his serious illness, which may keep him too weak to do any work for months, just when I was building hopes

(2)

for his solid progress in Dancing and lessons in languages, etc. "Man proposes God disposes". However, my thoughts are with him and May God keep my Robin in His protection!

I was also wishing great things for Rajni, you and Mina — but I feel so severely disappointed! First time when you were all coming out to India in the hottest months I called it a mad project, and I still hold that the programme for visiting India before Mid-Septr. or October is not at all the result of a safe or sound policy.

(3)

Such a programme ought to be avoided in the future.

I am deeply concerned about the future prospects of Uday and you all. Let me know if you can have a definite idea.

As regards your mother's pension, I already said in a previous letter that I did not think of going so low as to beg. I lost all I was given in Jhalawar without any regret and the last tie

(4)

that bound me to Jhalawar is now snapped. Nevertheless, I would have written to His Highness had I been sure that my letter would be attended to by His Highness himself. I know that our Darbar has got a heart of gold; and he would never interfere with the state-action taken, if myself, or your mother would personally approach him. He was complaining of Uday's omission to pay Jhalawar a visit. He wrote to me that he would be very pleased to receive me and my wife when I communicated to him the possibility of our returning to India together.

(5)

But your mother went alone and did not visit Jhalawar. That must have wounded his feelings. Let your mother could go on a wild goose chase to Lahore to see His Highness only then her money was stopped.

"[Bengali text]"

Neither your mother nor Uday studies anybody who is of vital relationship, or who has done something substantially. They do not even correspond with such important

(6)

people except for [Bengali]. This is not what is called [Bengali]. Even Swamiji, who is the Guru of your mother and is revered by myself, complained that none of you cared to see him when you were there last time!

I do not advise your mother to go out on another wild goose chase to Jhalawar. Try to send Uday by a definite appointment or, Rajni or you should work your mother, only on a visit, and not (partially) for an appeal for the restoration of the pension. Try to re-establish [Bengali] and don't impress [Bengali].

I saw my father again in New York, when he was with the Roerich Foundation. The founder of this institution, Nicholas Roerich, was a Russian count, a great savant, aristocrat and painter. His son, who lived in India, was also a painter. Twice when we performed in New York, Sejda, Mina and I stayed with my father in his apartment in the Roerich Museum building on Riverside Drive. At that time he was alone – there was no more Madam Henny – but he always had lovely women coming to visit him, and plenty of male guests also. He had been invited to give a lecture series on Indian philosophy at the Roerich Museum and later at Columbia University, and he was like a teacher to his visitors. He really seemed to be a changed person, and I grew to like him for what he was.

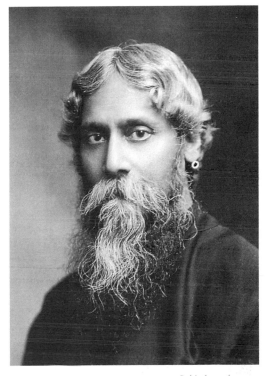

The more I learnt about him, the more my resentment lessened and my respect and regard for him grew, and now I see the whole situation in its true perspective. I understand his behaviour, and I don't blame him. He was a great man, but unsung. He never cared about that renown; if he had, he could have manipulated it to his benefit. He was involved in so many important events in law, philosophy and politics, including the League of Nations; and while he was in Benares, when the Hindu University was being built, he was helping the great Madan Mohan Malaviya, who later on joined Gandhiji in politics. Then he was around with W.B. Yeats and the Maharajah of Jhalawar in the committee that was formed to help Tagore become a Nobel Laureate in 1913. But my father always remained in the background, indifferent to personal fame.

Rabindranath Tagore.

In 1933 we toured India for the first time and went to Calcutta, and that was the first time I saw Rabindranath Tagore. We all went to Santiniketan ('The Abode of Peace'), the university that he founded in Bolpur, West Bengal, where he spent half of his life. It later grew to become a big campus, known as Vishwa Bharati. Tagore conceived Santiniketan in the ashram style, with classes under the trees, and emphasising music, dance and fine art, although there were regular studies, too. There were dancers from the Kathakali and Manipuri styles (Tagore's favourite dance styles, and incidentally Dada's too), and he was the first person to get these dancers at such a cultural centre. With his personality, it was a unique place. I was highly impressed.

Even after having seen so many remarkable people around the world throughout my life, I still have not come across such a personality as Tagore. It was like looking at the sun; he was so dazzling. To me, who had read his poems, novels and essays, and sung his songs, he was already a myth, a legend. Seeing him was like seeing the Taj Mahal or the Eiffel Tower: you see countless pictures and hear so much about them that you feel you already know them, but it is still mind-boggling when you actually see them. An artist to the core, he knew how to dress, to look and to sit – he used to wear a long robe and positioned himself in a high chair. He seemed perfect in appearance: his body, his height, his features, his beard, his hair. He spoke in a very high-pitched voice, which in anyone else would have seemed ridiculous; but after a while one even became used to that.

Meeting him was an electrifying experience, especially when he blessed me with his hand on my head. He remembered my father – whom he used to call 'Pandit Shankar' – and my brother was famous by then; so the words he used to bless me were, 'Babar mauto hawo, Dadar mauto hawo,' which means, 'Be like your father, be like your brother.' At that instant, I felt something magical was happening to me – as if electric currents were running through me.

Being Bengali, of course, makes it natural for me to feel so moved by Tagore; but I do feel that if he had been born in the West he would now be as revered as Shakespeare or Goethe. Even though he did win the Nobel Prize for Literature and is widely translated, he is not as popular or well-known worldwide as he should be. The Vishwa Bharati are guarding everything he did too jealously, and not doing enough to let the entire world know of his greatness. To all of you who are unfamiliar with his writings and his songs, I do recommend that you go out and discover them for yourselves.

Ravi playing the esraj, taken while in Calcutta during 1934.

By the time of this first return trip to India, Ravi was becoming increasingly drawn to music. Already an admirer of the troupe's sitar-player, Vishnudas Shirali, and sarod-player, Timir Baran, when Ravi heard the latter's nephew Bhombol (real name Amiya Kanti Bhattacharya) playing sitar in Calcutta he felt inspired to become a student of the young man's own guru, the celebrated Enayat Khan.

Ravi arranged that when the troupe returned to India the following year, 1934, he too would become a shishya (disciple) of Enayat Khan. However, the night before the formal ganda ceremony he had an attack of typhoid and was taken to hospital. He was forced to abandon the ceremony, which seemed to be a clear sign he was meant to have another guru. Destiny is a concept of paramount importance for an Indian musician.

His interest in the sitar was reinforced by the sitar-player Gokul Nag, who made a strong impression on him when he joined the troupe for a short while in late 1934. Around the same time he and Uday attended the All-Bengal Music Conference in Calcutta. There Ravi met for the first time the acclaimed classical musician Ustad Allauddin Khan, master of the sarod and pioneer of modern Hindustani instrumental music, the man who would later become his guru. The late, great Allauddin Khan, or Baba (literally 'father') as Ravi terms his guru, was performing there with his son, the young Ali Akbar Khan.

I first saw Baba and Ali Akbar in Calcutta in 1934, on 3rd or 4th December, when I was fourteen and Ali Akbar was twelve. Baba had come to participate in one of the music festivals (known in India as conferences) and all the most notable performers were there. They were mostly musicians from Northern India, except for two dancers from the South whom Dada had brought: one was the all-time great Bharata Natyam dancer, Bala Saraswati, a young and beautiful girl of eighteen with whom I had already fallen madly in love; and the other was Sankaran Namboodri, the finest Kathakali dancer and our dance guru at the time. It was probably the first time that these two, each the supreme exponent of a style, had performed for the public in Calcutta.

Among the well-known musicians were the famous Ustad Faiyaz Khan. He was a singer from Baroda who belonged to the Agra gharana – the distinctive tradition of musical style centred on the city of Agra. (I will consider the gharana system in more depth in Chapter Nine.) Very masculine and bold, he had a tremendous voice – almost a basso baritone, which was very unusual for an Indian singer in those days. He was a vigorous and versatile vocalist, performing in all the different styles: alap, dhrupad, dhamar, khyal, thumri, and even ghazal at the end. He used to dress like a maharajah, with a turban, a long tunic made of brocade, and in the old style he used to wear all his medals like an army general. He looked magnificent. People were affected by his merely coming on stage and sitting down; when he then sang – what an effect he had!

Baba had two items on the programme. The first was with the Maihar band. When Baba had been appointed as the court musician in Maihar, about 160 miles southwest of Benares, the Maharajah had told him that he was keen to build up a small orchestra, as existed in other native princely states. Maihar was absolutely barren of musicians, so what Baba had done was take little boys (some of them orphans) who were not at all musical, and gradually force them to become musicians by beating them up! It took him three or four years to knock them into shape and make them play in unison.

The Maihar band was marvellous. Baba composed many pieces for them in the classical format, and a few in light or semi-classical styles to be played by popular demand at the end of his show. At the music conference they were all aged between eighteen and twenty-two, and I was amazed at how he had managed to teach them so many instruments, both Indian and Western. One of them was even playing an instrument made out of steel household pipes, rather like a xylophone. Another of Baba's home-made creations was the sitar-banjo: banjo on the lower half and sitar on the upper half. Baba

1ST ST.
→ 700 W.

WORLD-PACIFIC
PACIFIC JAZZ/AURA

(first page of colour section) On the 1964-65 tour of the USA.

(opposite) With Zubin Mehta outside the Los Angeles Philharmonic Hall, 1965.

(opposite below) At the offices of World Pacific, Los Angeles, with Dick Bock (in spectacles) and others.

(below) Savouring German passion for Indian music, late 1958.

ASIAN MUSIC CIRCLE

(President: YEHUDI MENUHIN)

presents

RAVI SHANKAR

Jitendra Arya

with **CHATUR LAL** (Tabla accompaniment)

Conway Hall, Tuesday, 23rd October, at 8 p.m.

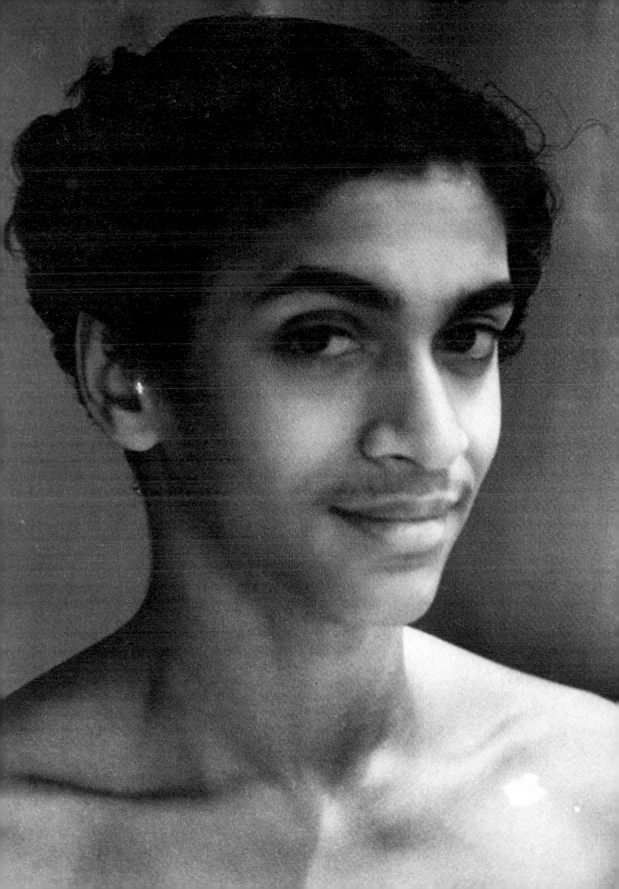

Timir Baran's insights into Allauddin Khan's nature were fortunate indeed, for after that music conference in Calcutta, Uday Shankar managed to persuade the revered sarod-player to join the troupe for a year as a soloist on their European tour. The foreknowledge that there was another side to this extraordinary musician who lashed out at his pupils on stage helped Ravi to establish an early rapport with his future guru – of infinite value in the long term.

It was arranged that Allauddin Khan would meet up with the rest of the troupe at the end of 1935 for the performances in Europe, after they had been on a world tour. So Ravi set off on a trip that would take in Burma, Malaya, Singapore, Hong Kong, China, Japan and the USA. The tour was, however, to be cut short in a tragic manner.

In 1935 my father gave up his lectures on Vedanta and left Columbia University and the Roerich Foundation. All of a sudden it seemed that he was moving into a new phase. He had received three offers simultaneously, including two wonderful jobs in India, both of them paying a tremendous amount of money.

He was invited to India to become the Diwan of Baroda State – today part of Gujarat, but then about the fourth-biggest princely State, and tremendously rich. The Maharajah was a connoisseur of art and literature, whom my father had met in his Jhalawar period and again in London; so he was very attracted to this job. Strangely enough, at the same time he was also offered a legal position by the government in Delhi, which offered one of the highest salaries paid to a civil servant in India at that time.

The third offer was a legal case in England, which he agreed to undertake en route to India. This was the famous case of the Pakur brothers, two very rich zamindars from Bengal who were fighting a legal battle against each other, which went to the Privy Council in London because it could not be solved in Calcutta or Delhi. It was one of the longest cases in history. There was much scandal, money and murder involved. My father was offered a large fee by the one of the brothers to take the case, and so he went to London. There he stayed in a hotel, and used to go to the Privy Council every morning for the case.

All the details we learnt afterwards, mostly through the Indian High Commissioner's office in London, and one can't be sure whether they were true or false, but what we were told was as follows. After three or four days of hearings, the case was going very well for my father. Apparently during previous hearings of this case, when a barrister appeared to be winning he would be murdered. On this early September morning, there were very few people about as my father crossed the street outside his hotel, but there was a policeman who came round the corner at that instant – and saw one man hitting another on the head with a weapon, and the victim falling to the ground.

The policeman rushed forward, but by the time he reached the wounded man, the attacker had run off. My father had a bad gash on his head and he was taken to an Intensive Care unit in a nearby hospital. He knew English better than the average Englishman, but oddly enough in the hospital he was only able to blabber away in Bengali so nobody could understand what he was saying. The hospital phoned the High Commissioner, who was a Bengali and knew my father very well. He came immediately to the hospital, but my father died before he arrived; so the High Commissioner formally identified him and then arranged the cremation. His office sent a telegram to us immediately, care of Haren Ghosh, who was then our agent in Calcutta. We were in Singapore at the time, about to leave for China, Japan and the United States – a long tour by ship – but my brother cancelled everything and we went back to Benares, where my mother was.

Despite the High Commissioner's efforts to put all the pieces together, still the details were so vague and the evidence so elusive that it was impossible to make a case out of what had happened. There was no firm proof of who was involved, and it remains something of a mystery.

Uday and Ravi spent some time in mourning with their mother in Benares. As a result, the tour plans had to be completely reorganised. It was eventually decided that the troupe would make its way to Europe via the Middle East instead. They gathered in Bombay for rehearsals a few weeks before the departure date, and there they were joined by a new female dancer, Zohra. Shortly before their departure, Baba Allauddin Khan and Ali Akbar also arrived.

The second time I saw Baba was just before we left Bombay in November 1935. We were staying in a hotel in Bombay for almost two or three weeks, rehearsing as well as preparing for the trip, because we had had to rearrange everything. Baba joined us about fifteen days before our departure, and brought Ali Akbar along, insisting that his son would also come on tour with us.

That was where I came to know Ali Akbar, almost one year after I first saw him. He had a very sweet hand on sarod, but still had quite far to go at that time. He was docile in front of Baba, even scared. So you can imagine my astonishment when one day he fished a packet of Gold Flake cigarettes out of his pocket and offered me one. It was shocking! It was not that I had not already smoked any cigarettes; I had tried them but I never liked them. (I had also tried beer just for the heck of it and had not been that moved by it.) But Baba's son... only thirteen years old... I tell you, it stunned me!

I was hoping we could become friends, since I knew we had to spend time together. But after a week or so in Bombay, Ali Akbar decided he did not want to travel with us, because he was frightened to go with Baba and be beaten up and scolded all the time. He talked to my maternal uncle, Mama – whom we had renamed Matul. (Matul is another Bengali name for a maternal uncle, which was chosen when we were in Paris because the more correct Mama is French for 'mother'. Similarly Uncle Kedar Shankar ought to have gone by the Bengali name of Kaka, but in France we could not call him that! We changed it to Chacha, the Hindi and Urdu term used in the rest of Northern India.) Matul was friendly and loving with everyone, young or old. He was very cool-headed, a wonderful mediator; anyone who had a problem would talk to him – even Baba became a close friend of Matul.

Trying out a South Indian Saraswati veena, Calcutta, 1934.

Ali Akbar went to Matul almost crying, and said he had had a dream about his mother, and didn't want to leave her to go on tour with us. Though it was all just a pretext for not wanting to go, Matul repeated what he had been told to Baba, who became very sentimental, because he really believed it. He told Dada that he had to leave behind Ali Akbar, and he didn't know whether or not to go himself. In the end he decided to, because he had given his oath and the Maharajah had said he should go. Ali Akbar was sent back home, and we prepared to leave.

My mother had come to see us off, and spent those two weeks in Bombay with me. When we were standing on the dock, preparing to board the ship, I felt extremely sad, and my mother was very emotional, too; she seemed to have a premonition that this was the last time she would see me. She turned towards Baba, who was standing nearby, and said, 'Baba, though Robu is a bit chanchal' – overactive – 'he is still so young and recently lost his father. As I am not coming with you and do not know whether I will see him again, please look after him as your son.' Saying this, she took both my hands and put them on his.

Baba was a very emotional person, and he started howling, crying, 'Ma, Ma! You are ratnagarbha!' – a special term that means someone who conceives a jewel (referring to Dada). 'You have a son who is an incarnation of Shiva. Until now I had only one son, Ali Akbar, but from today I have two sons, and Robu is my elder son.'

All three of us were crying. It was a really dramatic situation! We walked onto the gangplank and went on board the ship, and I saw my mother sobbing there on the dockside, slowly fading away into the distance. That was the last time I saw her'.

oday London is my favourite city in the world, but I grew up hearing about and feeling the crunch of the oppressive British colonial attitude to India. The relationship had become serious and India was on the verge of being a terrorist country, with a very strong anti-British feeling, which influenced me. After spending some time in England, though, I felt differently. It was in 1936 that my attitude changed, during an extended stay at Dartington Hall in Devon.

After Baba had joined us in Bombay, we came to Europe via Egypt and Palestine (now Israel). Baba had already started teaching me on the ship while we were travelling. He really did accept me like a son, although I still used to be scared of him. The way he behaved throughout this period touring with the troupe was so sweet. Never did he show his temper. Well, hardly ever... While in Tel Aviv, at the time of King George VI's coronation, my friend Dulal Sen (the troupe's sarod-player, who was also learning from Baba) and I bought an expensive pipe and tobacco pouch for our new guru, since I knew how much he was missing his Indian hookah. But when he saw the gift, Baba's eyes became big and scary and his hair almost stood up on end. 'Have you come to do the mukhagni to me?' he demanded furiously. (The mukhagni is the moment at a traditional Hindu cremation when the eldest son lights the funeral pyre.) After that we were always careful to assess what mood Baba was in!

We came through from Israel to Greece, and then via Yugoslavia, Bulgaria, Romania, Czechoslovakia and Austria, a little of Germany, to Paris, and from Paris to England. This was when I spent my longest period at Dartington Hall.

We had already been to Dartington Hall once, a year or two previously, for a visit of a few days. That time, we stayed in the small but quaint nearby town of Totnes. After London, this had been a great relief. The hotels in Totnes were in charming little roads, and the Devonshire cream was too good to refuse: with no fear of cholesterol in those days I had guzzled as much as I could, with a little added sugar. We had met the wonderful Elmhirsts – Leonard, his wife Dorothy and her daughter (by a previous marriage) Beatrice Straight – and had gained an idea of what Dartington Hall was like as an institution. Leonard Elmhirst was a prodigious creator, and a true devotee of Tagore. (He had modelled Dartington Hall on Santiniketan, where he had in fact lived; he had also helped in building its adjacent sister institution, Sriniketan, which represented the rural side of education, teaching and researching agriculture.) Dartington Hall is still there today; and if it has changed and become more academic, it is still blessed with the joys that

(above) A bearded Ravi as an old man in Bhil Dance, with Nagen Dey, the troupe's flautist and occasional dancer. (The Bhils are a semi-aboriginal community from India.)

(overleaf) A peasant dance.

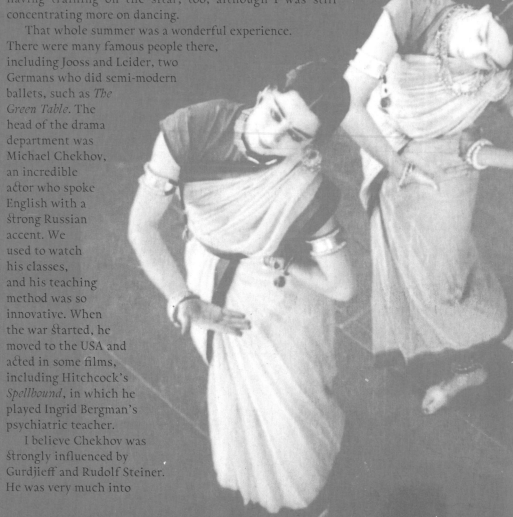

Leonard created. The college is set amongst beautiful green hillside and meadows, with an open-air theatre. Like Santiniketan, Dartington Hall had general education classes; but greater importance was given to dance and music, and especially to drama – even more so than at Santiniketan.

We stayed there for almost three months that summer. Accommodation was allocated to us, and we had a studio to work in, where Dada began devising some new numbers. First we had the beautiful big Redworth House in Totnes, where we all stayed together; it was said to have been built by Mr Singer (the sewing machine man), who gave it to Isadora Duncan, I believe. Later on we stayed in a boarding house within Dartington Hall.

The real excitement for me was in having Baba with us. I was so excited about learning from him. He taught me mostly traditional songs, but also ones he had composed himself. He was so creative: every day he wrote four or five instrumental gats (fixed compositions) or songs. I was having training on the sitar, too, although I was still concentrating more on dancing.

That whole summer was a wonderful experience. There were many famous people there, including Jooss and Leider, two Germans who did semi-modern ballets, such as *The Green Table*. The head of the drama department was Michael Chekhov, an incredible actor who spoke English with a strong Russian accent. We used to watch his classes, and his teaching method was so innovative. When the war started, he moved to the USA and acted in some films, including Hitchcock's *Spellbound*, in which he played Ingrid Bergman's psychiatric teacher.

I believe Chekhov was strongly influenced by Gurdjieff and Rudolf Steiner. He was very much into

psychic forces and
Dadaism. I came to
know that his circle
also experimented with
drugs, although maybe
only soft drugs like
hashish. Nevertheless I felt Chekhov had
some psychic power; he was not only an
actor. When he looked at you there was a
hypnotic quality in his eyes. At that time he was about forty-
five, but when I saw him once playing a fairy-tale prince of
seventeen or eighteen I couldn't believe it: he looked like a
young boy. I believe that this wasn't merely acting, but
something more than that; because I had seen the same thing in
Kathakali dancer-actors.

Kathakali dancers are religious people who meditate very deeply and
practise yoga and meditation extensively, and thereby cultivate their powers.
Some have what we call siddhi, or attainment – here signifying the
attainment of a power in the art for which they have been meditating. About
seventy years ago there was a Kathakali artist who specialised in the part of
Hanuman (the Monkey-God in *Ramayana*), and he had siddhi in this role. It
is established fact that while enacting the part, wearing all the heavy dresses
and make-up and other paraphernalia, he used to take leaps that should not

be humanly possible. He once jumped backwards onto the first-floor roof of an adjacent building. I do believe that, with a terrific concentration, one can become someone else in this way.

Dada himself had that kind of psychic power, that deep strength within him. When he was on stage he was transformed completely. If he was playing the part of Shiva, people would be mesmerised and believe that he really *was* Shiva; especially Indian people, who knew the tradition and felt such respect. I know that, while waiting in the wings before going on stage, he used to close his eyes and take deep breaths to bring out the full spirit of his role – whether it was Krishna, Shiva or whoever. Simkie was also very good at this; under Dada's training she became an amazing dancer. Although French, she adapted and learnt Indian dancing from Dada, and also had a lot of Kathakali and a little Bharata Natyam instruction separately. Together they would look like a real Krishna and Radha, or Shiva and Parvati.

Chekhov's classes were so different from ordinary acting classes. He would tell his students to concentrate on a door so as to open it, and I was told by some of them that they were able to do so; or similarly they would move a piano – by psychic force alone! These exercises were part of the training. The department used to be wonderful, and I know that Dada was strongly influenced by Chekhov.

Beautiful Beatrice Straight was a disciple of Chekhov. She looked like a Greek goddess. When Dada first met her she was only nineteen, and then when we returned to England in 1936 she must have been twenty-one. They were very much attached to each other, and Beatrice later did so much for Dada in helping to found his Himalayan cultural centre, mainly through financial support; in fact, all the Elmhirsts helped him out. She is still acting on Broadway, and has also been in many movies, such as *Network* (for which she won an Oscar) and the Spielberg production *Poltergeist*.

I went back to Dartington Hall three or four times in later years (after 1956), performing in the Barn Theatre. There was actually a very good music department there, but in 1936 I didn't know much about it; I was more familiar with the dance and drama departments, and participated in the new numbers that my brother was creating, such as *The Dance Competition Between Shiva and Parvati*.

Let me tell you about this dance: the story concerned a dispute about Narada, a sage who was renowned for creating friction between different gods and goddesses. He provoked an argument between Shiva and Parvati about who was the greater dancer, stirring up each of them by saying he had heard the other claiming to be better. It sounds a childish tale, but that is the beauty of our Hindu mythology: in all our stories, from as far back as the *Puranas*, *Mahabharata* and *Ramayana*, we have a tremendous devotion and respect for our gods and goddesses but we treat them like human beings also, with their love lives, jealousies, anger, pettiness and injustices.

A competition was arranged to decide the issue. Whatever Shiva did, Parvati had to show she could do also. So the enactment of the Nava Rasa began. In Indian performing arts, every artistic creation should express one of

the nine rasas, and Shiva and Parvati danced each of them in turn. First he danced the shringara, which is the erotic. Then the second, hasya, which means the comic, and the third, karuna, or the sad, and all the other different rasas in turn: raudra, (the furious), veera (the heroic or glorious), bhayanaka (the frightening), vibhatsa (the grotesque), adbhuta (the bewildered), and finally the ninth, shanta, which means calm. At the end Parvati was still doing as well as Shiva, if not better, so he thought there was only one thing left to do: he took off all his clothes and, stark naked, started to perform the powerful style known as urdha tandava, dancing with one leg raised up and jumping around! (Of course Dada did not really take his clothes off on stage – that was illustrated in gestures only.) Modesty got the better of Parvati and she gave up. It was so sly of Shiva!

(left to right) Matul, Nagen Dey, Dulal Sen, Allauddin Khan, Simkie, Madhavan, Uday, Sisir Sovan Bhattacharya, Zohra, Vishnudas Shirali, Ravi, Mr Gordon (manager) – the troupe in Budapest, 1936.

At that period for the first time I choreographed a dance myself, which I called *Chitra Sena*. It was a piece of about four and a half minutes, with a lot of movement in the Kathak style (a North Indian dance form), and plenty of footwork and expression. When I returned to America, I received a fine review for it from John Martin in the *New York Times*.

Dartington Hall was a beautiful experience. From morning until evening there was dance and music, meeting the students in the drama and music departments, making lots of friends from different countries all over the world. I was particularly pleased that the beautiful Uzra, younger sister of our dancer Zohra, joined our troupe that summer. She and I became very good friends right from the beginning. Together with all this, of course, there was my newly discovered world of Indian classical music, and my mentor Baba Allauddin, whom I loved and was loved by as the father I had never had. It was a memorable part of my life.

At the end of the summer we left to tour a few places in Europe, including London and Paris, and then Baba's stint of almost one year with the troupe was over. Dada's contract with the Maharajah of Maihar was coming to an end, and now Baba was due to return. There were still two months left of our tour, however, and we were planning to add an extra one or two months in order to go to America. Baba was excited about the prospect of this; but he was also very worried about his son, Ali Akbar.

Today Ali Akbar is one of the world's great musicians – the master of the sarod – but back then Baba heard reports that he was not practising properly, and was scared that he might go astray, alone with his mother in India. A letter came to Baba from the Diwan of Maihar, suggesting that he should return soon, for the sake of Ali Akbar. That really shook Baba up, and we had to let him go back. We embarked on our third trip to the States in January 1937, without Baba, and toured all over for about three months.

One morning towards the end of November 1936, a few days after Baba had left us to return to Maihar, I was in my room at the Hotel des Acacias in Paris, very near Etoile, when there came a phone call. It was Dulal, my friend who was sharing the room with me. Though he was about six or seven years older, we were great buddies and he took good care of me like a brother. He said, 'Robu, can you come down? We are all in Dada's room.'

Sometimes we would have meetings in Dada's room to make plans; but somehow, maybe from the tone of his voice, I felt something was wrong. I came down immediately and saw Dada, Simkie, Zohra, Uzra and the rest of the group sitting there. They were all looking extremely glum and strange. Usually everybody would be happily talking away, but when I entered they all went very quiet. Dada moved forward to hand me a letter. I looked at him and everyone else, and just said, 'Ma?' The letter said that she had died.

She had been building a little house on a plot of land in Nasrathpur, where my brothers Mejda and Sejda had gone to stay with her. Sejda's marriage had been arranged, and my mother was going through all the marriage-ceremony preparations, which involved much strain. She also wanted to finish building the house before the ceremony, so she was working around the clock along with the masons. But it was the end of the rainy season, and she was getting wet most of the time in the rain. The house was completed in time, but by then she had developed a fever, which she didn't tell anyone about. She had a severe pneumonia, and in the village the medical facilities were almost nil. A few days after Sejda was married to Krishna[1], my mother died. The news was heartbreaking for me, because I was so close to my mother.

The house is still there today, and Sejda lived there till recently with Krishna-Boudi. He is the only one of my brothers still alive. At almost ninety, he is fantastic for his age, so alert – he moves like a spring. He lives in Allahabad now, with his wife and daughter. When he was younger he had a wild temper, but he has become so mellow, funny and loving. I love him so much.

After Baba left our troupe I was in serious confusion. Under the circumstances and in the short time available, I had gone so much more deeply into music, and for the first time I realised the greatness of Indian classical music. For a while after he went I actually took up the sarod because I had been so impressed by him, although he wanted me to continue with the sitar as I was already familiar with it. On the other hand, I was becoming a young man and getting a lot of kudos for my dancing, especially when I became a solo dancer. I was in turmoil as to what to do. I wanted to learn Baba's way. He had told me repeatedly: 'This life you are living is not the way. You will be the jack of all trades and master of none.' His Hindi expression was, 'Ek sadhe sab sadhe. Sab sadhe sab jaye,' which essentially means: 'If you concentrate on one thing, then everything else becomes easier. But if you concentrate on many things you achieve nothing.'

1. Here Krishna is not the male name, pronounced with a short 'a' (as in Lord Krishna, the favourite incarnation of Vishnu), but the female, with a long 'a'.

He would not ridicule me, but would chastise me strongly about the particular life I was leading. I was fond of good clothes and being a dandy, and he sensed my weakness for girls. Though I was very circumspect in front of him, he knew; and he was worried that I would be growing up as just a

Taken on the *S.S. Lafayette* 5-1-1937 8

BANQUET
IN HONOR OF
UDAY-SHAN-KAR AND HIS HINDU BALLET
TENDERED BY THE HINDUSTAN ASSN. OF AMERICA
CEYLON INDIA RESTAURANT-FEB. 5TH 1937

PHOTO BY
E. J. KELTY
CENTURY
110 W 46
67

(top left) The troupe in Prague, 1933.

(top right) Rajendra's marriage to Lakshmi, Almora, 1941.

(right) Aged about fifteen or sixteen.

(far right) In front of 17 rue de Belvedere, the troupe's Paris home, in 1931 or 1932. Ravi stands with his mother to the left of the doorway on the right. Two places to the left of his mother is Amala, later to marry Uday.

dancer and ruining my life. He said, 'I will teach you, as you have all the talent, but you must leave everything and come to me.' After he left we remained in touch through letters, and again and again he told me this. It was ringing in my ears all the time.

In the period from 1936 to 1938, I went to most of the places in Paris that I hadn't been able to visit in my childhood. It was in this period that my curiosities and unfulfilled desires were satisfied.

Along with a few of my friends in the group, I used to visit special nightspots like the Panthéon, or the Sphinx. Sometimes we would see the Minister of Culture or the Minister of Commerce there, openly being served drinks by girls who, except for a ring or a chain, wore nothing. There were floor shows with everything, live love-shows – in natural and not so natural ways. Five English pounds was the maximum spent for a complete night's fun and thrills! In a way it was amazing that one didn't feel uncomfortable at one of these clubs, but everything was so open; it was not sleazy or dirty. When I came back after the Second World War everything had changed, and Paris had become like Amsterdam or Hamburg. That openness no longer existed. There are still nightclubs and cabarets in Paris, but it is not the same thing; they are like any other striptease club. In those days they were special – particularly the Sphinx. I need say no more!

A year and a half went by, and we were still touring. We went back to the United States in December 1937, and once again I was getting good reviews for my own dancing. Although I was never attracted to hard drink, I began to enjoy drinking beer and wine sometimes. I had many experiences with girls, but never very permanent ones; except for Uzra, to whom I was very much attached.

With the approach of the war in Europe, Dada decided to go ahead with his plan to establish a cultural centre back in India, and after that fourth American tour the troupe was disbanded and we returned home. I knew that this was the time to make a decision, and I chose to go to Maihar.

Today I can proudly inform you that. among Indian musicians living today, I was the first to come to the West (in 1930) and to tour extensively in Europe, the USA (in forty states!) and elsewhere – I even played sitar and esraj on the first album, which was recorded by the troupe in New York in 1937 and issued on RCA-Victor Records.

Ravi had spent nearly eight years of his youth touring the world with the troupe, and was accustomed to the thrill and glamour of life as a star in the West. Yet by the time these years were drawing to a close, he found that he was torn between two very different paths. On the one hand there were the delights that he knew, and a promising career as a dancer. On the other was the prospect of devoting himself to the rigour of traditional guru-shishya (teacher-pupil) instruction, a long process with an uncertain outcome – and a million miles away from the worldly life of this self-confessed dandy. Yet destiny was at work.

THREE: RANGESHWARI

रंगेश्वरी

It was May 1938 when we returned to India, and by then it was clear that there would soon be a full-scale war in Europe. In the meantime Dada had planned to open his cultural centre in Almora, so everything was happening together. I had told Dada that I was going to join Baba in Maihar. Dada assumed I would just go for a few months and then return to join his centre as a dancer, so he did not mind. I kept quiet, but I knew I would go for good, and not continue as a dancer, for I felt the pull of music.

First I went to my mother's house in our village, Nasrathpur. I felt sad being there, missing her all over again, but I was happy to be reunited with Mejda after almost four years. (Sejda was in Benares with Krishna-Boudi.) I stayed there for a month, during which I had my sacred thread ceremony. Along with marriage, this is one of the most important ceremonies in a Brahmin's life. It is usually held by the age of twelve, but I was late, being eighteen by then – the delay had been inevitable as I had mostly been out of India during the previous few years. I went through the ceremony along with a maternal cousin and an uncle, both younger than me. We shaved our heads and underwent all the rituals that admit the Brahmin to full spiritual adulthood. It felt as if I had cleansed my body and mind by going on to an almost monastic life.

I had already been in correspondence with Baba, asking his permission to come and learn from him as a disciple. He was very happy and had offered me the house next door to stay in, saying it was ideal. Originally he and his family had lived there, but Baba had built his own home adjacent to it and fortunately the original house was now empty. We had fixed the dates and arrangements.

So in July 1938, a few weeks after my sacred thread ceremony, I was taken to Maihar by Mejda. He was my favourite among my brothers. He was the most educated of us – highly intelligent – and took an interest in everything; full of humour, and always punning. I really loved him. He never treated me like a little boy; we were more like friends, even though he was fifteen years older than me and I was a baby in the midst of all my brothers.

In my years as a dancer I had developed a fantastic collection of suits and all sorts of other clothes, even elegant kurtas (Indian shirts or tunics); but for going to Maihar I ordered some unembellished coarse, white, hand-spun khaddar kurtas, pajamas of the same material, and simple vests, along with bedding consisting of ordinary sheets and pillows. They were all contained in a cheap tin trunk, which I had also bought specially. That was how Baba saw me – plainly dressed and equipped – when we reached Maihar.

Maybe all this was a sort of play-acting, but I wanted to please Baba because he had often told me I was a dandy. He would say, 'You only like to wear fancy clothes and dress up,' When I arrived I still had my head shaven – just a little stubble growing – and with my sacred thread around my upper torso and those plain clothes, he could not recognise me. It was the first time we had met since my mother had died, and he cried. He became so emotional, seeing me like that. 'What have you done to yourself?' he asked, but I knew also that he was secretly pleased. I could sense it. He embraced me in tears. In front of my brother and me, he repeated what he had said that day in Bombay: 'I promised your mother that I would accept you as my son, and that is what you are going to be.' He continued, 'I wish you could stay in my house, but I suppose you want to stay separately.' We insisted that we didn't want to be a burden on Baba. Mejda stayed with me for about a week in my new house, to settle me down, help me buy some necessary items and arrange a servant to cook for me.

After he went away, I was frightened being all alone in that house. Apart from feeling lonely, there was also the discomfort: the khatia (bed) was made of coarse coconut coir tied on a wooden frame. It was extremely hard, even with my thin cotton mattress on top. I had to use a mosquito net for protection and there were so many flies, cockroaches and lizards too; while in the night I used to see snakes and scorpions crawling around, and hear wolves and jackals howling near the house. It was an experience I had never had before. I was terribly spoilt, being accustomed to staying in four- or five-star hotels all over the world.

For Ravi, his stay of nearly seven years at Maihar represented a total commitment to music and to his guru. Day after day was spent absorbing the music, beginning from the basics and attaining mastery through a regime of relentless practice. For a boy who had done much of his growing-up in the West, away from his roots, and at a time when respect for traditional values was starting to be questioned in India, it was an uncommonly deep reverence that he had for his guru. It was undoubtedly the most important phase in the development of Ravi Shankar the Musician. As he himself said in the film Raga: 'Taking a guru was the biggest decision of my life. It demanded absolute surrender, years of fanatical dedication and discipline.'

The guru-shishya relationship is an exceptionally powerful one, at the centre of which is the one-to one oral teaching method. In order to gain the benefits of the received wisdom of the ages, the student must yield completely to the demands of the guru in a submission of the ego, must accept without question what he is taught. Even more important than achieving technical proficiency (though that is vital as well) is the process of imbibing direct from the guru the essence of each raga, and the essence of the music as a whole; without the feeling for these, his potential for authentic improvisation will always be limited. The relationship is as much spiritual as worldly, for the guru leads the pupil into the euphoria that results from true mastery of the music and appreciation of its transcendental potential.

Allauddin Khan and his disciple, Ravi, strolling outside the Uday Shankar India Culture Centre in Almora.

My relationship with Baba had started with a great awe on my side, but after that memorable incident on the Bombay dock when my mother had tearfully implored him to take care of me like his own son, things had changed dramatically. He really gave me the love and affection I never enjoyed from my own father. Then when he became my guru, it developed into a fantastic relationship and a beautiful bond.

Musically, Baba was a giant. The amount of knowledge he revealed even as a public performer was incredible, though I felt that he was not really cut out for that role. In private he was astonishing. I heard him hundreds of times while learning in Maihar, alone with him, or sometimes with his son and daughter present also, and in that little room he could make us cry with his music within two minutes. He had such a deep touch and pure style, and such patience to dwell on a raga, to do progressions for hours while teaching us or even when practising alone himself.

We always realised how much he had suffered, having run away from home at the age of eight for the sake of music. He had joined a group of travelling musicians in Shibpur, a village in Tripura, the extreme north-eastern part of India. It was a troupe of various musicians, not just classical in style but folk too, but being extraordinarily talented he learnt a lot from them. They came to the city of Dacca, now the capital of Bangladesh, and after a long period there eventually reached Calcutta when he was fourteen or fifteen. By then he had learnt to play drums – including the tabla, pakhawaj (the traditional two-faced drum of North India) and Bangla dhol – as well as the shahnai (the oboe-like reed instrument), clarinet, cornet and trumpet.

He had a passionate desire for music. He always stayed away from everything else, never wasting time playing around and forcing himself not to be interested in sex. Even when he had lived with those musicians, who drank heavily, took ganja and went to prostitutes, he was fanatical in controlling himself. He held the old Indian belief that one must preserve the semen to enhance power and energy in the training period of yoga, meditation, wrestling, music, dance or any other vocation that demanded tremendous stamina and concentration to master.

Fanatically maintaining this rigid practice through the years had brought out a hardness in him. Basically he was a very kind person, with such a feeling for serving people – he would embarrass any guests at his home by his concern to see that they ate and slept well and had all comforts possible. Yet if something unfortunate happened, he could get so angry with the same people that they could never believe it was the same Baba!

I was amazed when I heard Ali Akbar playing sarod in Maihar: after November 1935 in Bombay, what a change! It was only later that I heard the whole story about what had happened since I had last seen him. Baba had returned from our tour to find his son in a bad shape, not having practised. When Baba saw all the light music and film records that Ali Akbar had bought, it made him so angry that he started beating him. When he was angry Baba was a crazy person. He bound Ali Akbar to a tree and whipped him, and kept him there for two or three days – such cruel treatment! Then Baba began teaching him, getting up at about three o'clock in the morning to wake him up and make him sit and practise for twelve to fifteen hours a day.

What happened to Ali Akbar in those two and a half years was like a miracle. I couldn't believe the difference: Baba had transformed him musically. He had grown up; he was now sixteen, musically mature, and full of virtuosity. He had run away from home once because he couldn't take the strictness any more, but he returned, and in the meantime Baba had arranged his marriage according to the old system, at the age of fifteen. But Baba was so strange in some ways! He was so paranoid – about sex and drugs and drinks – that he got Ali Akbar married but expected him to practise celibacy and sleep separately from his wife. He was supposed to stay pure and take part in music only! (Although Ali Akbar told me, in strict confidence at the time, that he disobeyed whenever he could.)

Ali Akbar had music, rhythm and melody in his blood, but he was not interested in the hardship it takes to be a musician. Even now he says, 'I was always wondering why Robu took it so seriously.' Today Ustad Ali Akbar Khan is the greatest master of the sarod; but I feel that had Baba not done what he did, it may have been a different story altogether. Ali Akbar was *forced* to be a musician, but rightly so. All the hardships that he went through became a blessing from Baba, in making him such an outstanding musician.

From the time I arrived at Maihar, Alubhai (which is how I always address Ali Akbar – 'bhai' means 'brother') and I became close friends. He used to come over every day, and we would go for a walk to visit the temple, the centre of the town of Maihar, or some of the beautiful spots nearby. I found him to be such a sweet and nice person, and he never displayed any temper, unlike Baba. Though terrified of his father, he remained cool on the outside. He was ignorant in the ways of the world, and naturally so, being in Maihar and not having had many friends or much schooling – only some basic education through private tutors.

In his own domain Baba was so different. During the year when he had toured with our dance troupe in Europe, he had almost always been so sweet and compliant. In Maihar it was as if a fiery aura surrounded him. Everyone was scared of him, including Alubhai, Annapurna (Alubhai's sister), their relatives, and even Ma – Baba's wife (whom I also called Ma). Ma was one of the most gracious ladies I have ever seen in my life, a beautiful soul who also gave me the mother's love I was missing so. Many members of Baba's own family came to learn music from him, but none of them stayed long. Everybody has a darker side, and that was the only dark side I can think of with Baba – his devilish anger.

I had something of a problem with this. It shocked me to see everyone so petrified, and at times to see them lying. With my mother and my brothers there had never been any reason to lie. I was not scared; I was spoilt, never having been told what to do, and having lived such a frank and open life. I knew all about the facts of life – while we were touring Dada even used to tell us how to be careful not to get venereal disease, and how not to be waylaid by the wrong types of girl. My background in the West had educated me well, so it took me a long time to get into the groove in Maihar, though I had accepted that I must go through a hard life of abstinence.

Ravi's training was progressing well, but it was in Baba's tempestuous nature that he would sometimes become frustrated at any inadequacies his pupils displayed. However, his affection for Ravi and the pledge he had made to his mother caused him to refrain from treating him as he did all his other students, including Ali Akbar. Rather than display his anger in front of Ravi, Baba would abruptly end a teaching session. On one sole occasion did he drop this guard and vent his feelings, and the incident serves to highlight how accustomed Ravi was to such indulgence.

One day, maybe three or four months after I had gone to Maihar, I was unable to play a particular toda-with-zamzama passage Baba was teaching me, and he chastised me for having feeble wrists: 'Go and buy some bangles to wear on your wrists. You are like a weak little girl!'

I picked up my sitar and went back to my house. I was not used to being scoffed at like that, and felt so aggrieved. Thinking, 'I cannot go through this,' I packed my bags and planned to take the next train home, which was not till the next morning. Alubhai had heard about the incident, and while I was packing up my few belongings he came to try to persuade me to stay: 'Don't do this. You are the only person he has never laid a hand on or shouted at! You don't know what I have gone through. He used to bind me on a tree and beat me up morning, noon and night. This is nothing!' But somehow I had decided to leave, and went over to their house to bid goodbye to everybody. Ma asked me to go and see Baba, and I went to his small room.

There was a mat on the bed, where he used to teach, practise and sleep. He was sitting there, cutting out a photo of me to put in a frame. 'Have you forgotten that day when your mother gave me your hand, and I promised to her that you would be like my elder son?' he said. 'Go if you want to, but you will hurt me very much.' He said it with a catch in his voice that wrung my heart and filled me with guilt. We both began weeping, and then he took me in his arms.

After that scene I didn't leave, and from that day on he never even raised his eyebrows at my mistakes. He was so kind to me. He would actually go and take out his anger on someone else by beating them up – or if he couldn't find anyone, a stray dog would do.

When Baba had issued an angry outburst at someone, afterwards he again became the humblest and kindest person on earth. It was a sight to see him with his grandchildren, or with any children. He would dance with them, pretend to be a horse and give them piggybacks, tell them funny stories, and let them pull his beard – and enjoy it. When he was teaching the little children, he had all the patience in the world. We couldn't believe that it was the same person who scared the life out of us at times!

I don't remember carrying a sitar when I arrived in Maihar, although it's possible I took one I had kept from my brother's troupe, which had a tin soundbox instead of a wooden gourd. But immediately I arrived Baba ordered a sitar from his younger brother. Ayet Ali Khan was himself a talented musician who specialised in playing the bass sitar (surbahar). He had training from Baba and later went to Rampur for a short while to learn from Baba's guru, Ustad Wazir Khan. In the area between Brahmanbaria and Comilla, Ayet Ali Khan Saheb became well known and had many students in music, but at length he turned to making instruments, and he was a genius in that area. He began by making sarods for his brother – so all the sarods that Baba played after a certain date (in the early Thirties, I believe) were his younger brother's creations – and then he set up a shop and workshop in Brahmanbaria and he started making sitars and surbahars too.

This first sitar of mine arrived within a very short period. It was quite large in size, and instead of a round gourd at the base it had a flat one known as kachhua (which means 'tortoise' – the gourd resembles the shell of a tortoise). It sounded wonderful. Yet one day while I was having a nap in the afternoon I awoke to a peculiar sound emanating from this gourd. Scrutinising it, I found a little hole – and then realized it was full of insects! The gourd was not fully seasoned, as it should be, and it was infested with them. That sitar was sent back and another was despatched to me in its place.

Baba's brother actually made me two more sitars while I was in Maihar, one mid-brown in colour and one very dark brown, almost black. This last one was the instrument I would use most when I was learning from Baba or practising.

I had another large, surbahar-like sitar made by the great Ustad Yusuf Ali Khan of Lucknow, whose sitar-playing was an inspiration to me. He had a shop in Aminabad, the main road in Lucknow, and whenever I visited the city (as I later did regularly, after I started recording radio programmes there) I would spend time watching him at work. He was a wonderful person, so loving. It was this sitar that I played at my debut concert. This memorable occasion took place one morning in December 1939, a year and a half after my arriving in Maihar, at a music conference in the large city of Allahabad. All the best musicians of Northern India were sitting in the front row, including such greats as Ustad Faiyaz Khan, Ustad Mushtaq Hussain and Pandit Omkarnath. It was my first concert on a classical platform and also my first experience of performing in India – and a tremendous success! That was why in 1989 I observed my fiftieth year of performing and now it is the fifty-eighth.

This sitar served me well for a few years, but by 1942 I decided to order a new one from Kanai Lal of Calcutta. Kanai Lal was the eldest of three brothers – the second was Balai and the third was Nitai – who all worked together in a small shop known as Kanai Lal and Brothers, situated on Upper Chitpur Road, the busiest road in Calcutta at that time, with all the trams and cars and people going by and the din of motor horns and hawkers. It bemused me how they could work in that cacophony! Until the early Forties this area also used to be famous for the prostitutes and the singing and dancing girls. If you passed in the night, you could hear the sound of the bells on the legs of the dancing girls or the sound of their singing and instrumental music.

Kanai Lal was like a legend. No-one could make sitars like him. All the great sitar-players in Eastern India of that day, such as Ustad Enayat Khan and Mushtaq Ali Khan, always played his instruments. I had visited him before and we knew each other, so I requested him to make one to my specifications. He and his brothers put their lives into it, and took a long time ensuring it was exactly right. Each of the brothers contributed: Balai was responsible for the woodwork, Nitai carved the design and Kanai Lal fashioned the jawari (the main bridge which produces the special sound of the sitar). Making the jawari is very complex: you have to rub the surface in a certain way, and the strings have to rest on the bridge at a particular angle to get the correct sound, while the buzz of the sympathetic strings has to resonate in the proper manner. There are a multitude of different sitar sounds you can choose from – tinny sounds, buzzy sounds, round sounds – but I had developed in my mind (helped by God) what has become my distinctive sound.

It was around March 1944 that the sitar was finally completed and I went to Calcutta to fetch it. It was fantastic: the first model with that type of ornamentation, that characteristic sound and that particular modification of the strings – the kharajpancham (the third string, literally the 'lower fifth', tuned to Pa two octaves below the middle Sa) was different, and the bass strings were very low and surbahar-like (as on my other large sitars, but this was the first time such a style had been produced by Kanai Lal, and also the first in Calcutta.) That design became known soon afterwards as the Ravi Shankar model, and even today the same name is used. Many other manufacturers have copied its style.

Being basically Muslim, Baba's family observed some amount of purdah. The womenfolk are supposed to cover their faces with a burkha, and not to appear in front of men except those who are closest to the family. But as a Bengali Muslim Baba was not as orthodox as the Muslims are in the rest of India – even more so now, with fundamentalism reawakened. From the first day I was there, he permitted me inside to meet Ma, and I saw Annapurna also, who did pranam to me (touched my feet with a respectful attitude, as a younger person traditionally does in India). I often had lunch, dinner or tea at Baba's house when I went to have talim (training).

Annapurna was very shy when we first met. She was hardly thirteen, although she looked grown-up. I was eighteen. It was the period when she was already practising sitar, and Baba was planning to teach her surbahar but hadn't yet commenced. Once in a while, when Baba was not there, Alubhai brought me inside to his room for a little adda (chit-chat), and sometimes

Annapurna would join us and I would be clowning around and making them laugh a lot! She and I never met separately; it was always in front of Ma or Alubhai.

Annapurna looked very bright and quite attractive, with lovely eyes and a lighter complexion than Alubhai. But I had prepared my mind: this was my guru's house and this was my guru's daughter, and I never encouraged in myself the slightest feeling towards her, except for admiring her quick wit and giggles. Alubhai is also extremely intelligent, but he has such a calm front that it isn't as obvious. Annapurna was bubbly, and it was only later that I realised what a temper she had. In that respect she is like her father. Alubhai, more like his mother, can suppress his emotions.

In 1939, the second year I was learning in Maihar, Sejda, Boudi and their little son Arun came to visit. They stayed in my little house, and Boudi often used to go next door to see Ma, Baba, Alubhai and Annapurna. Baba loved her very much and always called her over for meals, and she became friendly with the family.

Sisters-in-law in our country have always had a uniquely beautiful relationship with their brothers-in-law. It is something not seen anywhere else outside the subcontinent. They are very attached to each other, have fun together and exchange plenty of innuendos, but at the same time it is a beautiful mixture of being a sister and a frank friend, to whom you can tell all your problems and joke freely.

One day Boudi, Sejda, Alubhai and I were sitting having tea, and out of nowhere Boudi said in front of us all, 'Ali Akbar, wouldn't it be nice if we could get Robu and Annapurna married together? What a wonderful thing it would be!' Alubhai agreed with her, but it was a shock to me. I immediately retorted, 'Don't be silly! Don't say things like that.' It upset me because I didn't like that sort of speculation. Marriage never occurred to me at that time; I had a long way to go with my music, and there was enough time later. I was not even twenty.

However, Boudi didn't stop there. She talked with Ma as well, and it reached Baba's ears. Then one day Boudi said it in front of Baba. 'How can it be?' he replied. 'Bamon hoi ki koré chand dhorey?' – which means, 'Being a midget, how can I try to touch the moon?'

This was a reference to the mythological story of Vishnu. Vishnu has had nine incarnations: the Fish, the Tortoise, the Boar, the Man-Lion, the Midget, then Parashurama, Rama, Krishna and Buddha – and finally he will be Kalki (The Destroyer), who has yet to come. What Baba meant was, 'I am a Muslim, while you are a Hindu Brahmin: how can it be?'

Boudi answered, 'No, you are better than a Brahmin. You are such a great person and musician, you are gandharva!' – a celestial musician. So the seed was actually sown by her.

March 1940 saw the Uday Shankar India Culture Centre at last open its doors in the hills of Almora, following the troupe's completion of an eighty-two date tour throughout India. Here Ravi was reunited with his brothers and friends from the troupe, and felt pulled between his old and new lives.

After my constant contact with Dada until the age of eighteen, I had been separated from him because I had gone completely into this different world of music and Baba. Meanwhile Dada had founded the Almora centre. Although it was technically opened in 1939, the first students attended in 1940. He invited Baba to take charge of the music department, and I accompanied Baba. We joined for about four months each year for two years, between 1940 and 1942 – a couple of months in the centre itself at the summer school, and then in the winter of each year touring around India.

Sejda had also been appointed by Dada as a teacher, so Krishna-Boudi was there, as indeed was Mejda. I believe Boudi had already pushed the marriage issue by talking to my uncle Matul there. Matul was the middleman of everything, and by the time Baba and I arrived, it was in the air.

I was not keen on the idea. My focus was on practising hard, and in Almora I was also now reunited with Uzra, to whom I found I was still strongly attracted – and our affair resumed. It was an adventure. Whenever I could slip away in the afternoon, or at night while Baba was sleeping next door, I would go to her and we would spend a few hours of frenzied bliss together. I couldn't stop myself; I was hungry, having been celibate for so long in Maihar, and we were drawn to each other.

While this was going on, Matul and everyone else were talking about the marriage and it was almost settled. When Dada heard about it he was quite happy, and gradually I too began to accept it in my mind. Baba had already taken me as his son, teaching me together with Alubhai, and I was thinking that, with the Indian gharana system (in which musical knowledge is passed on through individual teaching, often through successive generations of the same family), it would be even better if I became truly part of the family. There was no love or romance or hanky-panky at all between Annapurna and myself, despite what many people thought at the time. I do not know how she truly felt about the match before the marriage, although I was told she had 'agreed'. (But on the wedding night I was thrilled to learn how totally she loved me.)

So here I was, emotionally and physically closely involved with one person, and at the same time preparing to marry another. I felt like hell!

The tour with Dada that winter was a strange experience. Dada asked Baba whether he would mind if I joined the group as a dancer, since Baba was himself going along as a sarod soloist. Much to my surprise, Baba agreed, but I felt horribly self-conscious with him there watching.

On tour there was an example of another remarkable characteristic of Baba. He was only supposed to play his solo for fifteen or twenty minutes in the show, but he asked my brother if he could also join in with the musicians playing accompaniment to the dancers. He had done the same on the European tour in 1936. Dada was quite embarrassed, because the musical compositions were not all classical; some were based on folk music, and then there were his modern dance items with social comment like *Labour and Machinery*, which represented the impact of machines on man. However, Baba said he did not mind, and he set about playing the drums, the gongs and the chandrasarang (a bowed instrument of his own creation – part sarinda, part violin and part sarangi). Classical musicians are often such snobs, looking down upon everything – upon dance, any other type of music, or folk

Ravi and Annapurna around 1953.

instruments. But here was one of the greatest musicians of the time having no ego problem, sitting alongside all the other musicians and kids, and playing little instruments like a folk drum, a cymbal or a gong. It was unbelievable!

All the time on tour I was carrying on absolutely the same regime, learning from Baba and practising as much as possible. I used to stay with him wherever we went, but I also carried on my torrid affair with Uzra throughout that winter. It was a complicated situation. At the end of the tour she left the troupe, having heard about my forthcoming marriage, which made me feel both guilty and hurt. It would be many years before we were to meet again, by which time she had been married and sadly widowed, and the magic between us had gone.

When I returned to Almora the next year with Baba, the marriage had been finalised. It was decided to hold it at Dada's centre, and a date was set. Alubhai had also joined the music department and

he was residing in a cottage there with his wife Zubeda and their baby son Aashish. That was where Annapurna and her mother stayed when they arrived in Almora for the marriage.

Baba did many things that bewildered me. He was a strict Muslim, offering namaaz five times a day, and he had been to Mecca and Medina. Yet, at the same time, in his way of life he was remarkably Hindu, because he had been born in a Bengali Hindu village and his customs derived from there. As a Muslim, he never ate pork; but neither did he eat beef, because it is forbidden to Hindus. He took mutton or chicken once in a while, but in that he followed the Muslim custom and it had to be halal. Although he was Muslim, even today if you visit his house you will see all along the walls, together with his pictures of Mecca and the calligraphic inscriptions of the Koran, images of Krishna, Shiva, Kali, Ganesha, Saraswati, Jesus Christ, Mary, Buddha and Zoroastra. You are unlikely to see anything like that in any other Muslim's house! Baba was more of a Sufi (an mystic type of Muslim). I truly wish there was more tolerance and compassion between the Hindus and Muslims today in India, instead of the immense gulf between the two.

Before the marriage, Baba actually suggested that Annapurna be converted to a Hindu. When a Muslim and a Hindu marry, ninety-nine per cent of the time it is the Hindu boy or girl who is converted to Islam. There are some rare cases of a registered marriage in which each maintains his or her respective religion. But our case was unheard of!

(above left and below right) Staff and students at the Almora centre.

(above right, left to right) Uday Shankar with Sankaran Namboodri, Allauddin Khan, Kandappan Pillai – gurus at his Almora centre.

(below, left to right) Allauddin Khan, Sankaran Namboodri, Kandappan Pillai.

So on the morning of 15th May 1941 Annapurna was converted by a reformed and broad-minded Hindu sect called Arya Samaj, and in the evening of the same day we were married according to Hindu rites.

At Almora, there were four great gurus in their different fields. Baba was one. Then there was Sankaran Namboodri, who was in charge of Kathakali. We also had the finest guru of Manipuri-style dance, Amobi Sinha; and lastly, for Bharata Natyam, there was Kandappan Pillai, the guru who taught the famous Bala Saraswati. (Lakshmi, whom Mejda married, had also received training from Kandappan Pillai in Madras.) These four people were the top in their fields and, with Dada at the helm, they made the Almora centre a unique place, appropriately set in an ideal heavenly location, almost six thousand feet up in the Himalayas.

I saw another side of Dada there, as the head, alongside all these wonderful gurus: he with his super personality, creating new dances, taking the general class – and teaching. He devised his technique and ideas influenced by Michael Chekhov, applying to them his own imagination and creative mind. In his younger days Dada used to practise hypnosis and magic,

Rajendra's wedding to Lakshmi, Almora, 1941. Kamala stands at extreme left, Ravi second from left, Uday second from right.

95

and this was another advantage. He added his Kathakali and everything else he had seen, and introduced all of these themes in his general classes in Almora.

He was like an army sergeant, always telling students to stand properly – stomach in, chest out, head upright, with correct body posture and swinging the arms. In these classes he used to teach some remarkable exercises. For instance, he would tell people to sit down, close their eyes and touch the floor, and imagine that they were putting their hands on the surface of icy cold water. Next he would change it to hot water, then change it to hot sand, as though they were sitting in the desert, then turn the sand into a cool dry beach, or ice, and so on – and all the students felt each of these sensations, as I did when I attended a class.

Scenes from Almora: (above) Students in an outdoor dance class.

(opposite) A picnic party.

Another example of his charismatic teaching came during summer school, when there were about a hundred students in the studio. It was quite crowded, but he would tell people to walk quickly all around and make sure that they did not bump into each other. 'If you watch thousands of little ants together,' he used to say, 'you will see they never clash. Just walk naturally.' And the students too never touched, even when it seemed they must collide.

It was unfortunate that the Almora centre had been established during the Second World War. Prior to this there had been help from Beatrice Straight, her parents and other sources (mostly in the United States and Europe), but all this gradually stopped during the war. My brother always thought big, and the centre had been designed in an almost American style, covering the entire summit of a hill. There was a huge studio with a stage, dressing rooms and working places, stores for costumes, a separate music studio, and special cottages for students and teachers. It was a grand affair, with many dancers and musicians, and a large number of staff. If it had survived, it would have become an art centre unique in the world, but because all the financial help ceased Dada could not maintain it. Today our government is spending generously in different fields of the arts, but back then there was nothing like that from the British Raj, even if India was, ironically, still the Jewel in the Crown – though tumbling! Sadly, the centre had to be closed in 1944. Except for a few troupe members and some students who stayed with Dada, all the other students and staff left to launch their own careers.

On leaving Almora, Dada went to make the film *Kalpana* in Madras, taking almost three years over it. It was the first film he had made, but it is fabulous. It was far ahead of its time, technically as well as artistically, and it was highly influential. For many years he and I were separated. I continued learning in Maihar, after which I went to Bombay while he was in Madras.

After my marriage I shifted from the little house in Maihar to move in next door with Baba, who gave us a small upstairs suite of two adjacent rooms. Alubhai was staying in his original room, next to ours.

Being married was a strange feeling for me, because at that time I was still drawn to Uzra. Although I had already had a lot of experience in my life with different women, marriage was different. I knew that I had to change myself and my urges, and be faithful to Annapurna, my guru's daughter, and to my music.

Somehow I began to develop a feeling of guilt about my past life, and it increased as time went on. At the beginning of our married life I was crazy physically. Annapurna too was young and passionate, and at the same time we had our music to practise; so it was a terribly strenuous time in a way, with little sleep or rest for either of us.

And then... I don't know why I did this. Let's face it: I was young and immature – physically experienced maybe, but not mature in mind. I was just twenty-one and Annapurna was fifteen, going on sixteen. By then I felt such love for her, and I thought, 'I will start my life absolutely afresh, and make a clean breast of it.' So I began blabbering to her all about my past life, and especially mentioned again and again about Uzra and how I had loved her, but how that was all finished now. It was stupid of me, as Annapurna was so young and had a romantic mind – she was always reading romantic novels. Evidently it cut very deep and hurt her.

Within two months of our marriage, we realised she was pregnant. I feel sure it happened very soon after the wedding – in spite of all the precautions! Everybody else was happy that she was going to have a child, and we were too, but I had mixed feelings under the circumstances, when we both had to work so hard on our music. I thought it might not be ideal timing to have a child then, and I was thinking of the financial side as well. I had maintained one principle: I was firm with Baba that, except for food, I would pay for everything we needed, all our clothes, food and household goods. It was a difficult period: when Dada had realised that I was not coming back from Maihar, he had terminated the allowance he had been sending me over the previous few months. Shankar the grocer, a friend of mine who loved music, used to provide me with a tab at his shop, but I already owed him plenty. Money was tight.

One source of income was All India Radio, on which I had begun giving programmes in 1940. Usually Baba didn't allow his students to perform until he thought they were ready, but he had already told me in advance that he would permit me to. He talked with All India Radio in Lucknow, where he used to perform, and with his recommendation they invited me to go there every two months to give two programmes on alternate days. Occasionally there would be some other programmes, too, but financially it was not enough. I was quite worried now that the child was coming.

It was at this time, when I began performing on All India Radio, that I started calling myself 'Ravi' instead of Robindra. I was beginning to feel that I was not only a Bengali but an Indian, and trying to be more cosmopolitan or international. 'Ravi Shankar' sounded just right, and that was how I told the announcers to introduce me on the radio. All India Radio was heard throughout India, so people came to know me by my new name. Anyone who was not aware that I was a Bengali always thought I was from United Province (now Uttar Pradesh), Rajasthan or Gujarat. That was what I wanted.

I am proud to be a Bengali, but it made me more international, in the Indian sense.

Alubhai was always so charming. He was the opposite of his father, who brought out everything – no matter how unpleasant – so that he could feel totally clean inside. Baba was honest; he could never keep anything to himself. But Alubhai could not hurt anyone, and suffered dearly through keeping all the pain and anger inside his own heart. In those days we were so near to each other, and he began to confide in me. With my worldly experience and streetwise knowledge I felt much more than two years older than him. I became his confidant and mentor in many subjects.

After I was married there were times when Baba would teach Annapurna and me together, and sometimes Alubhai would sit with us as well. At that time I was playing the surbahar, a bass sitar, as was Annapurna. The sitar and the sarod are tuned to different pitches, so when Baba taught us by playing his sarod, as he sometimes did (on other occasions he would teach by singing), I had to retune my sitar to adjust it to his pitch. That was the germ of my later 'jugalbandi' (duet) with Alubhai.

I went with Baba to many concerts in different cities to perform on stage with him, although I was merely contributing the background sitar assistance to his sarod. It was not a duet; it was more like a student having training on stage with the guru. For many concerts Alubhai sat on the other side of Baba, and he and I became used to practising and performing together.

Actually our first chance to perform properly had come at my debut concert in Allahabad in December 1939. I was using Ustad Yusuf Ali Khan's large sitar, so the pitch of the tonic on my sitar fitted perfectly with that of his sarod. Together we played a morning raga, *Mianki Todi*, and it was a wonderful triumph for both of us.

Alubhai and I were such good friends through these years. In the early 1940s he worked for a few years with All India Radio in Lucknow, becoming the Music Supervisor. On the occasions when I used to go to Lucknow for my programmes, I stayed with him and we performed together in Lucknow and the nearby towns of Kanpur and Allahabad. This continued even after I left Maihar and moved to Bombay at the end of 1944.

Our collaboration blossomed into a wonderful duet. We were both fresh from Maihar and so together. There was so much love between us, and for the next dozen years it was fantastic. It was also something completely novel, because traditionally Indian musicians tended to perform solo, except when the disciple accompanied the guru. There were some vocal duets, but seldom instrumental ones; and it was unheard of to have a duet between two different instruments, sarod and sitar.

The term 'jugalbandi' came to be used regularly to describe our duets. Crudely translated it means 'twins tied', so it was an appropriate word for our close partnership: we were very much in harmony with each other at this stage.

(overleaf) An extraordinary cast list of Hindustani classical music. Seated (left to right) are: Ravi, tabla-player Hiru Ganguli, Allauddin Khan and Ali Akbar Khan.

On 30th March 1942, Annapurna gave birth to our son Shubhendra. An eight-pound child, he was beautiful and we were delighted upon seeing him; he was born with curly hair and lovely features. The birth took place at home with the help of doctors, and I was there, so it was much like the modern system, with the father participating.

After about eight weeks, however, Shubho started crying and crying all night and would not sleep at all. We used to take turns to look after him, but even when Annapurna was caring for him I would wake up. For two to three weeks it continued like that and the doctor could not discover what the problem was. We were getting into a nervous state. Ultimately he diagnosed an intestinal obstruction, a rare condition: food gets stuck in the bowel, and it is exceptionally painful. He gave Shubho a simple laxative treatment, and luckily that opened up the passage and the pain at least was cured.

But because of that trouble Shubho had now developed the habit of not sleeping in the night-time. It continued for the next year or so, and gradually I saw Annapurna's personality changing. For both of us it was extremely strenuous, and our tempers would fray. At that time I too wouldn't stand any nonsense, and we would get angry together. I had not known before, but I found out then that she had her father's temper. She would tell me off: 'You have married me only for music! You don't love me! You had all these beautiful women!' These tantrums were happening more and more.

I came to realise that in some manner her accusations were justified, but by then I felt I had cleansed myself, having told her everything as in a confession. I said to her, 'Now all the past is over and we will begin afresh. I love you!' – which I really did. Yet her temper and tantrums were getting worse, as were my reactions to them. We were living upstairs in Baba's house at the time, so I dared not shout too loud lest he heard downstairs. It became almost a daily ritual – often more than once a day – and it gradually made me feel terribly guilty. Ironically I realised that I loved her deeply, but she was never convinced of it. She was becoming insanely jealous of any other woman I talked to. Whenever I returned from a programme in another city, she would accuse me of having affairs there. It was like an obsession.

Over the next few years I had so much opportunity. I was young, becoming well known, and there were girls flirting and giving me 'green signals' all the time. It would have been easy for me to have an affair, yet even when I went hundreds or thousands of miles away, I tried to be like Baba, as if I were anti-sex and anti-women, always thinking how I must be pure. Thus I was almost killing myself with self-denial, trying to atone for my past, yet whenever I came home I had to go through the storm again!

It became so bad, and with Shubho's sleep problems and our need to practise over ten hours a day on top of that, it was one of the most terrible ordeals that one can imagine. It went on for almost the whole time that we were in Maihar, until the end of 1944, becoming worse and worse.

There was something wrong with Annapurna's health, too, and in 1943 I took her to Delhi for a check-up. An intestinal problem was identified, and she was better after treatment. We stayed in Delhi for almost six months with the great industrialist Lala Sir Shri Ram. His daughter-in-law, Sheila Bharat Ram, was learning sitar from me.

Back in Maihar in June 1944, I developed a serious case of rheumatic fever. My temperature went to 106°F for two to three days; I don't know how I survived. I had brain fever and was delirious. Baba used to visit me in my sickbed, and sometimes I gained a little consciousness, although it was all hazy in the delirium. It embarrasses me even now to think about it, but when he came to see me I would become enraged and shout at him, using the angry words with which he scolded his other students!

I could visualise complete stories in my delirium, some beautiful and some terrifying – it was like seeing movies. I used to recognise people for a second or two and then slip into confusion again. Somehow I recovered; but Dr Maitra, the main doctor who treated me, said that I would have to be careful with my heart in the future, because in later age I might have problems.

In the wake of his critical illness Ravi decided that, after nearly seven years of full-time study with Baba, the time had come to move on from Maihar. In October 1944, he left his guru and uprooted himself with his family to Bombay. The powerful bond with Baba remained, as it always should between an Indian musician and his guru; Ravi would continue to spend around two or three months with him in Maihar every year until 1955. Nevertheless, in choosing to embark on his own career he had begun to step out of the shadow of Baba, beloved as he was, and make his own name.

In our system, we never say we have finished learning, because the process of learning from a guru can never end. However, I was already performing on radio and becoming well known and, although I might otherwise have stayed a year or two longer, after my health trouble the doctor said that I needed a change. In addition, our married life was becoming so unhappy at that time, and with Annapurna's bad health as well, we thought it was best to move to Bombay. Baba reluctantly permitted us to leave. By then Shubho was about two and a half years old. In Bombay we took a house next door to Mejda, who was already there working as a screenplay writer for a film company, Bombay Talkies. I was regaining my strength.

FOUR: MANAMANJARI

मनमंजरी

Mejda had married Lakshmi Śaśtri in Almora in 1941, later in the year of my own wedding. Lakshmi and her younger sister, whom we called Saraswati then although she later took the other name of Kamala, were both dancers at the Almora centre. Lakshmi was about fifteen and Kamala thirteen when they had arrived that year, and on this first meeting Kamala and I were just good friends.

The next time I saw her was three years later, on the short visit I paid to Calcutta in early 1944 to collect my immortal Kanai Lal sitar, and I was absolutely dazzled – not only by the sitar but also by Kamala! By this time she had become a beautiful young lady, and I was very attracted to her. A few months before Annapurna and I arrived in Bombay, Kamala had moved there with her mother to stay with Mejda and Lakshmi in a suburb called Malad. I was overjoyed to see her. Often I went to their house, sometimes alone and sometimes with Annapurna and little Shubho, and we would have some delicious South Indian food and snacks there.

Annapurna's health was still poor, but I was getting stronger and better, and planning what to do next. I took a job in the recording company His Master's Voice in Bombay, as an apprentice in the music department. It was at that period when, although nothing actually happened, Kamala and I became more drawn to each other.

This was the first time since my marriage that I had become deeply attracted to someone else. Annapurna was doubting me with everyone anyway, so it was nothing new for her to doubt me with Kamala – only this time it was true! We never had a chance even to touch each other, but there was some flirtation, and little chits would pass between us inscribed with words written with burning love. We would have brief meetings during which I would say that I was in love with her and she would say the same – that was all. However, Annapurna came to know and – my God! – my brother and Lakshmi did, too, and they were deeply upset. They immediately set about looking for someone to get Kamala married off to. The famous film director Amiya Chakravarty used to come to their house and liked her very

Uday Shankar with his son Ananda during the production of the film Kalpana.

105

much, and a marriage was fixed between them.

Annapurna was furious and wanted to go back to Maihar. After only a couple of months in that house in Bombay she left me, taking Shubho with her. Yet she knew that I wasn't really involved with Kamala, and she came back to me a few months after Kamala was married off. But in the meantime I also left the house and, in January 1945, went to Andheri, a nearby place in the Bombay suburbs, where I joined the Indian Communist Party's 'cultural squad', the Indian People's Theatre Association. It was mostly an artistic organisation at first, and I was delighted to be making music for ballets and short dance items.

Ravi was appointed as the musical director for all the group's stage productions. He was soon composing the score for a ballet, India Immortal *(his first commission), a dance portrayal of the cultural and political history of India since just before the British period.*

I went nearly all out on this because I was in such a bad mental condition, with Annapurna going away and Kamala getting married. It was an excellent opportunity for me to put everything else out of my mind and devote my energy to the creative side. I had a room (with bathroom attached) in a huge house with a big garden; all the young girls and boys in the squad were living in the house, and it was an extremely disciplined life, like an army regime. In the mornings everybody would get up at five o'clock, wash and get ready, have breakfast at six-thirty and then work for eight to ten hours per day. I found that I was again getting the 'green signals' from some of the lovely young girls there, but I had chosen to go into a shell of celibacy.

The IPTA was ideal for me at that time. For about eight months I was inspired and loved the whole place. There was plenty of opportunity to do interesting creative work; indeed that was where I had my first experience in stage productions and film work.

My first experiment with ballet music came in the production of *India Immortal*, which my dear friend Shanti Bardhan choreographed. Shanti was one of the best exponents of the Tiperah style of dancing from the hills of Eastern India, and also an accomplished choreographer. He had joined Dada's centre back in 1940, and we had become friends immediately. I loved him, and had such fun with him while we were touring in India with Dada's troupe in 1940-41 and 1941-42.

The start of my soundtrack music career at the IPTA involved writing the score for two films almost simultaneously, maybe with a month in between. They were K. A. Abbas's *Dharti Ke Lal* ('Children of the Earth'), and Chetan Anand's *Neecha Nagar* ('The City Below'). These were both highly realistic, down-to-earth movies, dealing with poverty and exploitation of the poor – and as such unusual, because the subjects of most Indian films were mythological or historical, or even if social they were quite artificial and lacking in such realism.

The trend towards phoneyness in Indian films had already been established by then. Today it has been blown out of all proportion, almost ninety per cent of them now being based on borrowed and concocted stories, with an unwarranted eight to ten songs and dance sequences. Fighting and violence have always been a feature of these films, and though (until quite recently) kissing and nudity have not been permitted on screen, the dialogue and lyrics have tended to be full of double entendres and vulgarity, as well as there being obscene dances and provocative exposures in costumes. These were (and are) designed as the only entertainment for the large section of the public that is repressed. Of course there have always been some eminent film-makers who occasionally make outstanding pictures. Especially since the advent of Satyajit Ray there have been a few directors in Calcutta, Bombay and Madras who have made some remarkable, world-class films, but usually they are not particularly profitable at the box office.

These two IPTA-backed movies, made in 1945-46, were among the first to be concerned with real people, their lives and problems. They were acclaimed by critics and the intelligentsia, and even won awards and prizes abroad – but naturally they were commercial failures!

They were wonderful for me to experiment on, developing a new style of music for films by placing emphasis on the incidental music, and making the score appropriate to the experiences portrayed – the pain and exploitation. There were a few songs also in both the films, mainly in the folk style but also a few in semi-classical style, as the situation demanded. My sister-in-law Lakshmi sang on these, as indeed she has in many of my stage, film and recording projects since. I tried to use as few instruments as possible and, contrary to the common practice of the time (and today, too), I mostly used Indian rather than Western instruments, with the mere addition of perhaps a violin, cello or clarinet. I felt pleased with these scores, because they were so innovative. I may have been the first in India to use voices instead of instruments as background or incidental music.

At first I didn't feel any pressure at the IPTA, but after a few months I increasingly began to worry about some of the things that were happening. There were directives coming from the Communist Party's headquarters, and our work became almost journalistic in nature. If a riot happened we were told to make a ballet on that subject, or we would have to write a piece about a disturbance in Kashmir, or the famine in Bengal. I was more interested in the artistic freedom that had been there at the beginning. Gradually I saw the boys and girls reading books by Karl Marx, and I realised they were all hardcore communists. At first it didn't matter to me, because I was seeing only the creative side and the freedom to compose music, and that really attracted me. But after a while I saw the deep political involvement, and it became suffocating.

There were incidents that severely irritated me. For instance, the young people were constantly speaking out against Jawaharlal Nehru, which annoyed me because I had always liked Pandit Nehru – at that time he was like a hero to me. It once happened that a famous communist party personality, Rajani Palm Dutt, who was half English and half Indian, had come to visit from England. As I was busy with some music recording in the film studio for one of the films, I was not there to see him at Andheri, and only heard about the episode later. He spent the afternoon there, and it seems that, among other questions, the young people were asking him about his views on Nehru, suggesting that Panditji did not seem to be doing good work for the country. Dutt became angry and said, 'Personally I have enormous admiration for Nehru. He is a wonderful leader and you should all respect him.' He was quite hard on them on this issue. I came back in the evening, after he had left, and found that from that day onward they were all praising

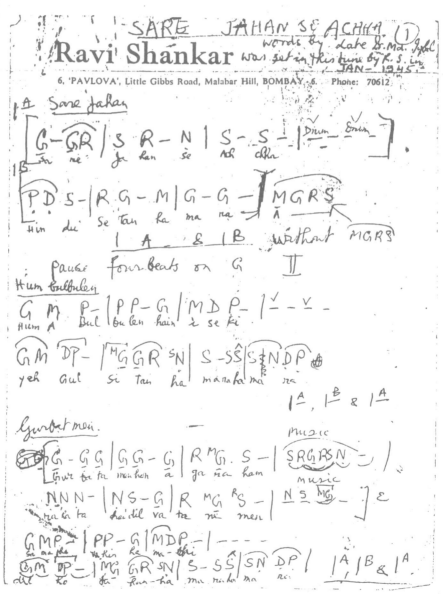

Nehru. You could hardly credit it – they had changed their views just like that, as if a new gramophone record had been placed on the turntable!

We toured late in 1945 with the ballet *India Immortal*, performing in Bombay and Calcutta, and after that, as I couldn't take it any more, I left the IPTA in early 1946. It had been a wonderful one-year period until I felt the crunch of the Communist Party's politics.

It was during that phase at the cultural squad that I was asked to rewrite the tune of a well-known song, 'Sare Jahan Se Accha Hindustan Hamara' ('Our India Is The Best Place In The World'). The original poem was written in 1904 by Mohammed Iqbal, one of the most famous Urdu poets of that time. There was no partition then, so he was an Indian Muslim poet from Punjab, and this was a song for the whole of India. Before I retuned it, though, the melody was long and drawn-out, and didn't have strength; it was sung in a very slow tempo, almost like a dirge.

My new melody was catchy and gave the song a brighter mood. Popularised via the airwaves of All India Radio, it gradually became treated as a national song, especially after independence. The main one was, of course, our official anthem, 'Jana Gana Mana', written by Tagore. There was already another important national song, 'Vande Mataram', but 'Sare Jahan Se Accha' gradually became the second favourite. It was played everywhere in its new arrangement and became extremely popular. It still is today, and features at everything from minor local gatherings to the 'Beating of the Retreat' parade in Delhi every year on Republic Day (26th January).

However, even in India many people do not seem to be aware that the tune is mine. Over the years many different composers have been given the credit for it. I do feel vexed about this issue! Recently I was shocked to read on the inlay card of a cassette brought out by HMV (RPG) India, featuring nationalistic songs by the legendary singer Lata Mangeshkar, that the music credit for 'Sare Jahan Se Accha' was 'traditional'! In India we never had a copyright system for authorship of tunes or musical compositions in the past. This has only started recently, and it is not yet properly organised. It's amazing how much money composers make in the West in situations like this!

In 1945 I had also created my first new raga, my own version of the morning raga *Nat Bhairav*. I started playing it in concerts and radio programmes and it rapidly caught on with other musicians. This was the first of many original ragas that I have created throughout my life.

Ravi was not the only member of the IPTA to have left. Five others (four dancers and a musician), all of whom had earlier been at Uday's Almora centre, had become similarly disillusioned: Shanti Bardhan; Sachin Shankar, Ravi's first cousin, and Narendra Sharma – both fine dancers and choreographers; Prabhat Ganguli, a dance student who was married to Simkie for a few years; and the versatile percussionist Abani Das Gupta, a member of Uday's troupe for many years.

Sponsored by the Indian National Theatre, Ravi formed an artistic group and moved to Borivli, a suburb of Bombay, where he stayed in an attractive large bungalow in which Rajendra and Lakshmi had already taken up residence. The household soon became home to the extended Shankar family and friends, including Ravi's five IPTA colleagues and Matul, who had left Uday after many years. From childhood Ravi had dearly loved Matul, and this band of ambitious artists was immensely helped by his uncle's patience, wise counsel, proficiency as a handyman, and talent for stagecraft, lighting, costumes and mask-making.

New Delhi. 1948.

(above) With Shubho in the late Forties.

The three years or so I spent living in Madgaonkar Bungalow at Borivli were tremendously eventful and brought many changes in my life. It would be the first time that I experienced the joy that can be found in a full family life, living with Annapurna, Shubho, my two brothers (for Sejda joined us later too), their wives and kids, Matul, my dear friend Shanti and the others from the IPTA. A greater joy was derived from creating a new two-and-a-half-hour production based on Pandit Nehru's book *The Discovery of India*, a historical panorama of India from the Golden Period (around the fifth century AD) up to the present day. This was sponsored and supported by the Indian National Theatre, the cultural wing of the Indian National Congress, the main political party which, of course, began the struggle for freedom from the British under its great leaders such as Tilak, Gandhi and Nehru.

We started our rehearsals in the sunken square courtyard inside our bungalow, surrounded by the bedrooms, living room, dining room and kitchen. The quadrangle was covered over with Terpal, a material which gave us shade as well as saved us from normal rain. When the monsoon rains came, which at times went on continuously for up to seven days, we had to stop the rehearsals – the whole yard became like a swimming pool. We even caught some fish for our lunch!

Later on, as the ballet-cum-opera took shape, we had a huge pandal built outside in the garden. This is a huge marquee tent (also known as a shamiana) containing a stage, beside and behind which are dressing rooms divided up by cloth walls. A decorated canopy covers the top and (if needed) the sides. Our sponsors and friends, the press and many other important people visited to see us rehearsing in the pandal. It was thrilling to hear them rave about our new concept of music and production.

I was still having my personal problems and occasional clashes with my wife, especially after the incident with Kamala in Malad, after which Annapurna had of course gone away to Maihar for a long period, while I was with the IPTA. But otherwise she was a wonderful help at this time of preparation for the show, assisting Lakshmi (and later Krishna-Boudi, when she also came) to cook for and serve some thirty-five people.

As well as all this, Annapurna played the sitar, and even joined the chorus in the rehearsals and the shows. Everyone appreciated this wonderful side of her. During that 1947-48 period, she performed a few surbahar duets with me at different music circles. She never wanted to play alone so I had to play along with her. (In this period I was playing both sitar and surbahar – which is like playing both the violin and the cello – but since I had to earn a living by playing the sitar, gradually I gave up the surbahar.)

INT arranged for us to go to Delhi with our production of *The Discovery of India* for the mammoth meeting of the Asian Conference in March 1947. All the great leaders and luminaries were there, including Gandhi, Nehru, Patel, Rajaji and Radhakrishnan. It was such a thrilling experience for all of us, and the show was a grand success.

The production followed the book's narrative of complex historical episodes as closely as was possible in the time available. The sets and props were modest – in the traditional Indian style actors would set the scene by bringing on simple cutouts to represent a certain period – but with the help of Ravi's musical effects the presentation was simple yet forceful, and met with considerable approbation. After seeing this adaptation of his own epic, Nehru is said to have commented that it was a better ballet than book.

Following on from his IPTA work, The Discovery of India *indicated that Ravi's musical compositions were maturing quickly. Still guided by Uday's principles, once again he had largely refrained from using Western instruments, but he had embraced sound effects and some innovative Indian instrumentation.*

Back in Bombay in April we gave seven shows at the Excelsior Theatre, which were also received well. After this, however, poor Lakshmi developed pleurisy, which forced her to give up her promising dance career. Instead she stayed in Bombay and had classical vocal training with Abdul Rahman Khan. Over many years I also taught her a number of ragas and some of my own khyal and thumri compositions. She developed into a magnificent vocalist and has become a favourite of listeners in India as well as in the West, loved for her wonderful voice and the feelings she brings out through it.

At the same time as Lakshmi's illness the INT stopped backing us, and thus we were in a quandary. But we brothers, the other five and Matul decided to form our own group, which we called India Renaissance Artists. For several months we worked hard to improve the show for a further production the following year.

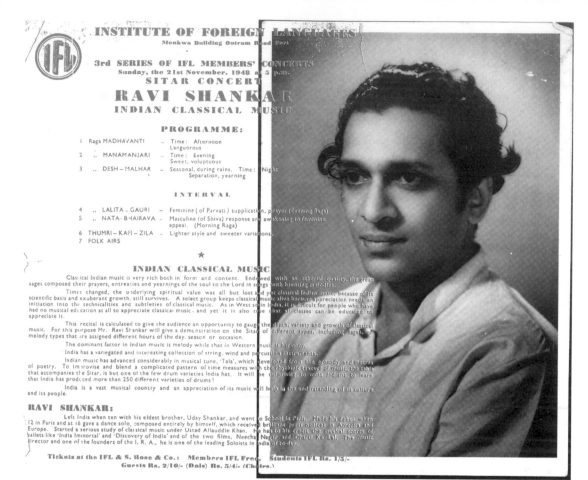

INSTITUTE OF FOREIGN LANGUAGES
Menkwa Building Outram Road Fort

3rd SERIES OF IFL MEMBERS' CONCERTS
Sunday, the 21st November, 1948 at 5 p.m.
SITAR CONCERT
RAVI SHANKAR
INDIAN CLASSICAL MUSIC

PROGRAMME:

1	Raga MADHAVANTI	— Time: Afternoon Languorous
2	„ MANAMANJARI	„ Time: Evening Sweet, voluptuous
3	„ DESH – MALHAR	— Seasonal, during rains. Time: Night Separation, yearning

INTERVAL

4	„ LALITA – GAURI	— Feminine (of Parvati) supplication, prayer (Evening Raga)
5	„ NATA – BHAIRAVA	— Masculine (of Shiva) response and awakening to feminine appeal. (Morning Raga)
6	THUMRI – KAFI – ZILA	— Lighter style and sweeter variations.
7	FOLK AIRS	

★

INDIAN CLASSICAL MUSIC

Classical Indian music is very rich both in form and content. Endowed with an ethereal quality, the great sages composed their prayers, entreaties and yearnings of the soul to the Lord in songs with haunting melodies.

Times changed, the underlying spiritual value was all but lost and yet classical Indian music, because of its scientific basis and exuberant growth, still survives. A select group keeps classical music because appreciation needs an initiation into the technicalities and subtleties of classical music. As in West so in India, it is difficult for people who have had no musical education at all to appreciate classical music. and yet it is also true that all classes can be educated to appreciate it.

This recital is calculated to give the audience an opportunity to gauge the depth, variety and growth of classical music. For this purpose Mr. Ravi Shankar will give a demonstration on the Sitar of different types, including ragas, or melody types that are assigned different hours of the day, season or occasion.

The dominant factor in Indian music is melody while that in Western music is harmony.

India has a variegated and interesting collection of string, wind and percussion instruments.

Indian music has advanced considerably in musical tune, 'Tala', which developed from the prosody and metres of poetry. To improvise and blend a complicated pattern of time measures with the rhythmic texture of music, the tabla that accompanies the Sitar, is but one of the few drum varieties India has. It will be surprising to most Indians to learn that India has produced more than 250 different varieties of drums !

India is a vast musical country and an appreciation of its music will help in the understanding of its culture and its people.

RAVI SHANKAR:

Left India when ten with his eldest brother, Uday Shankar, and went to School in Paris. Made his debut when 12 in Paris and at 16 gave a dance solo, composed entirely by himself, which received brilliant press notices in America and Europe. Started a serious study of classical music under Ustad Allauddin Khan. He has to his credit the musical scores of ballets like 'India Immortal' and 'Discovery of India' and of the two films, Neecha Nagar and Dharti Ke Lal. The music director and one of the founders of the I. R. A., he is one of the leading Soloists in India of to-day.

Tickets at the IFL & S. Rose & Co.:   Members IFL Free.   Students IFL Rs. 1/5/-
Guests Rs. 2/10/- (Dais) Rs. 5/4/- (Chairs.)

Around 1948, in Poona. As the concert programme makes clear, he was already playing Mana Manjari, a raga of his own creation, by this stage.

During this period, starting from May 1947, many great national events occurred and simultaneously most of my major struggles began. It was a momentous time. On 15th August came an enormous milestone, that of India's independence. There was no television to report the occasion in those days, but excellent radio coverage: at midnight our whole family and friends, thirty or forty of us in all, were huddled together at home in Borivli, listening to Nehru's famous 'tryst with destiny' speech to the nation. What an excitement and joy it was! But as well as feeling all the elation of independence, I was deeply hurt by the partition of our country and its consequences – the ruthless communal killings of multitudes and the tribulations of the millions of refugess, uprooted from their homes and forced to cross the new borders. Then on 31st January 1948 occurred the tragic event of Gandhiji's assassination. At that point our show was almost ready for performance, but we chose to bring it up to date by adding some recent events, including the Mahatma's death.

It was after the Bombay shows that Sejda arrived with Krishna-Boudi and their two kids to join our newly formed India Renaissance Artists. It was a tough time, as we had no financial backing except for what I was bringing home from my sitar recitals, what some friends were chipping in, and the immense sacrifices of everyone in the troupe.

I was helped by two dear friends, Shantaram Ullal and Batukbhai Diwanji, and especially Harihar Rao, one of my first disciples – he had begun learning from me in early 1946. As I had no telephone, three or four times a week I had to travel by local electric train the twenty-three miles to Churchgate Station, and then walk two or three miles to the downtown area in order to meet them. All three of them worked in this district, where most of the banks and the stock-exchange market (known as the Share Bazaar) were situated. Usually I would meet one of them on his lunch break, and we would have delicious snacks together – varieties of cut fruit, or the Maharashtrian style of puri, patal bhaji and dudhi halua. Harihar always offered me the best Udipi-style South Indian snacks and coffee. Sometimes I would go to his house, some distance away, where his elder half-brother Taranath Rao (a wonderful tabla-player and teacher) and nephews (all musicians) gave me so much love and respect – and a fine lunch as well!

Tasty though these foods were, my visits were not undertaken for fun. It was through these friends that I was trying to get as many sitar recitals as possible in music circles and wealthy private homes, or in other towns. They were like my unofficial agents – without charging me any commission! I will never forget the love and help I received from these three. This was during what was really my worst period, when I was having to maintain a group and feed so many people. Every night I returned home to Borivli dead tired.

The blossoming of Ravi's creative powers was not in doubt, but under such pressure he went through a deep crisis materially, emotionally and spiritually, and at his lowest ebb resolved to take his own life. He carefully formulated his suicide plan, deciding that he would throw himself under a train, fixing the date and even going to the extent of preparing final letters for Rajendra and the police.

But shortly before the chosen day, he underwent an extraordinary encounter with a man who was to turn his life around. Passing by Ravi's Borivli house one afternoon in 1948, the spiritual guru and yogi known as Tat Baba (so named for his simple robe made from tat, or sackcloth) stopped and asked to use the bathroom. Entranced by the appearance of his visitor and the aura which seemed to surround him, Ravi readily agreed to play the sitar for him, forgetting completely that he had arranged to perform in front of the Prince of Jodhpur that evening – for a generous fee. Yet somehow the yogi knew of both Ravi's missed concert and his suicidal despair, for after the recital he told him, 'The money you missed tonight will come back to you many times over. Don't do anything foolish.' So commenced Ravi's spiritual turnaround.

From my childhood I had much interest and curiosity in spiritual matters, hearing about saints and yogis with special powers performing miracles – some who could materialise objects, who could themselves disappear and reappear elsewhere, or appear in two places at the same time. I believed the stories, because I heard them from people whom I could trust.

For the first eighteen years of my life, I did not have the opportunity to meet any great spiritual yogis. I had met only a few hatha yogis who could perform physical feats. For instance, I saw one chap who could take a bowl filled with half milk and half water, and suck in all the liquid through his penis and then bring it back out – like a straw! He then boasted that he could similarly enter a woman and suck the 'life-juice' out of her through his lingam. Dada, who was there, had asked him, 'Is there a container in which she keeps her "life-juice" for you to do this?' The 'yogi', with his wet, limp dick hanging out, smiled foolishly!

I grant you that sort of exploit was entertaining, but it didn't impress me particularly. Tat Baba was the first great yogi I had contact with, and he came to me when I was in the lowest state of mind and spirit. He had an extraordinary personality and a tremendous power emanated from him. All my problems seemed to vanish from then onwards, and things changed dynamically. I believed in him, and he bestowed such love and strength upon me. He also provided me with the mantras which one chants at times, or preferably all the time inside one's mind.

Everything was fine for almost twenty years, but later on I realised that he was a normal human being in many respects, with weaknesses, rough edges and soft corners like anybody else. He had acquired his powers through sadhana, the traditional Indian practice of sacrificing all materialistic things and working in a disciplined manner under a guru's direction towards achieving self-realisation through spirituality, music or another route. Yogis can, however, lose their powers if they do not stay on the right path and maintain this sadhana. They can fall into the various traps of money, women, sex or power. Similarly in our mythology we have tales about great souls who become attracted to a beautiful apsara (celestial nymph) and lose their siddhi, becoming like any other human being. Though one is not supposed to criticise one's guru in any way, I do feel Tat Baba came down through many grades from the supreme power that he once had. His powerful vibration diminished gradually, like a battery running down.

This made me feel very sad, but I will never forget those wonderful years when he was all-powerful and we were 'connected'. I had felt his presence so strongly, as he was solving my problems and protecting me all the time. I will always be grateful to him for his love and grace of those years.

After Tat Baba died in 1973, for a few years I felt like I'd lost a father. I had been depending so much on him. Even when he was not present, I always had that confidence that he was taking care of me in any dangerous moments. That level of dependence is unhealthy really. One has to have the power within and have full trust in oneself; that is the ideal.

Two or three years later a friend of mine in Los Angeles, Richard Bock, who was a devotee of the great yogi Satya Sai Baba, arranged for me to meet him in Bangalore when I was playing a concert there. I went along to have his darshan (to see him). Satya Sai Baba is one of our best-known and most popular yogis, and I had read books about his miracles and the objects he materialises – lockets, rings, diamonds, whatever; he has that special power – and furthermore his great philosophical and religious teaching. I was absolutely dazzled by his presence. He was so loving. As if he knew me already, he took me aside for three or four minutes and told me almost everything about my life: what I was going to do, my problems, my fears, my hopes. I told him that I was looking only for a blessing, and he said, 'If I am not your guru, it doesn't matter. I am like your mother or your father. Consider me either or both.' He blessed me and gave me vibhuti – white holy ash with a fantastic smell.

That's how it started. For a few years I felt once again that a guardian angel was protecting me, and it gave me a great uplift. A number of times I played for him on his birthday, and he gave me lockets with rubies or emeralds, which he would materialise just like that, as he is well known to do. He also gave me a zircon ring. When in time this became a bit loose, I went back to him and showed him it. In front of many people who were sitting there, watching like hawks, he handed back the ring and I put it on. Although it looked the same, I knew it was different. Not only did it fit me, it was also made of pure diamond and 22-carat gold!

Call him a magician if you like, but this is merely a kind of game – what we know as his Lila (from Krishna's Lila, his game of teasing the gopis). He is more than a magician: whether he truly materialises diamonds or not, and I believe he does, his main ability is that he can talk to you and get inside you. He tells simple parables with profound meanings, and has changed so many people's lives. His other side is curing people. I have met people who have been brought from the dead by him, and others who have had their sight restored. But it is not that he cures everyone – there are many cases where he says he can bring comfort for a little time but there is no way he can prevent them dying; they have to go. Sometimes those people turn against him afterwards, but perhaps that is inevitable. He has a huge university in his name, as well as one of the best hospitals in India, situated next to his main ashram in Puttaparthi, a remote village five hours by road from Bangalore.

He has this tremendous power, and he is growing. His disciples run into millions – in Communist China, Russia, Africa, Mexico, Japan – yet he has never been outside India. He never asks for money, but people send it anyway. His hospital was financed by unsolicited contributions from Non-Resident Indians – Indians living abroad. I truly respect him for not being anxious to go abroad and impress the Westerners with his miraculous powers. He doesn't have to, as millions of devotees have come to him in Puttaparthi, and continue to do so. Two million of them attended his 70th birthday celebration in 1996!

Satya Sai Baba is a musician himself: he sings beautifully and creates bhajans. He loves and understands music, especially the Carnatic system (the classical music system of South India), and all the musicians, North and South Indian alike, flock to play or sing for him. We have been apart for the last few years, yet I still think of him and pray to him. When I sense him calling me, I will go to him.

Over the course of my life there have been many other enlightened swamis and yogis whom I have met and been impressed by. I am very pleased to pay homage to them, and often I have played for them too. Mata Anandamayi was one, the lady-saint of enormous warmth and love. I also met the great Kamakoti Shankaracharya of Kanchi, from the Tamil town of Kanchipuram, when he was in his eighties. He was worshipped like God alive. If he wanted he could have lived like a maharajah, because there were multi-millionaires all over the world devoted to him, but he never travelled in a car, train or plane, only on foot or on an elephant, and he never even had a house to live in – he lived outdoors under the trees as much as possible, or if it was cold there was a place near the temple where he sat. He always ate simply, and just wore a loin cloth or, in the cold, a cotton garment like a shawl. His eyes exuded such love. Seeing him was like taking a cold bath in an extremely hot weather. I met him about four times and I played for him three times; once in Madras, unforgettably, outside underneath a mango tree, with his elephant standing nearby. Despite the scorching midday heat, neither my sitar nor Alla Rakha's tabla went out of tune. I felt such a beautiful feeling – I don't know how time passed.

The big name in the West around the time when I ventured out was Maharishi Mahesh Yogi. He established Transcendental Meditation, or TM, which became popular with many people, even in the government of the United States. He was very charismatic and attracted many followers. Today he is maybe the best-known yogi in the West. He has followers everywhere – even a university in the Midwest of the USA.

Many followed him, like the Hare Krishna movement led by Swami Bhaktivedanta. The Swami was a very good, simple fellow from Calcutta but such an ardent follower of the Krishna cult. From out of nothing he built almost an empire of the Krishna people, known as ISKCON (International Society for Krishna Consciousness), and it is a great credit to him. Westerners became devoted and have built beautiful clean temples everywhere. They sing bhajans and have fantastic food. Some people feel they hustle too much, but there is so much that is positive about them.

Of course a number of other yogis made a bad name for themselves through their collections of Rolls Royces, and in some cases a strong emphasis on taking the sexual route to becoming spiritually pure. But there are people who believe in all that. If they have helped others, which is the most important thing, I never say anything against them. That's fine. But from the outside some of the stories do sound strange.

What unfortunately can happen is that, though the swamis themselves are good and genuine people, in somewhere like America sooner or later their devotees turn their efforts into a corporate operation. They build huge ashrams and it becomes almost like a bazaar. The wonderful souls, who are really not bad at all themselves, get waylaid by it. And after seeing the American televangelists, I have come to realise that there is no business like religion – not only in the USA but everywhere else too, including India. It is unbelievable how commercial it has all become. More than anyone else, the Americans are so naive that you can convince them of anything. It is what makes them so open and dynamic, but it makes them vulnerable as well, especially in the field of religion and spirituality. They are seeking something else. After their whole materialistic enjoyment – 'seen it all, done it all' – they want a deeper experience. So they are easy targets for conmen to exploit. For each of these few great saintly people I have mentioned, you can count at least one hundred quacks. It is very sad. And the USA is the biggest market. You don't yet find this as much in Europe, but it is starting to happen there as well.

There is another group of yogis or saints who have been an influence on my life – those I have only read or heard about. In my childhood I was always eager to learn about the miraculous feats of such spiritual masters as Lahiri Mahasai or his famous friend Trailanga Swami, who was reputed to be over 300 years old and certainly weighed over 300 pounds. Lahiri Mahasai's guru, Babaji, is a legendary and very powerful yogi who is reputed to be a few hundred years old. He does not show himself in public, but is supposed to be alive still, dwelling in the Himalayas. Then I was particularly fascinated by the stories of Ramakrishna Paramahansa, a great saint and yogi from Calcutta, and his disciple Swami Vivekananda.

Vivekananda belonged to an important Calcutta family but he chose to renounce the material world and become a sannyasi. His teachings were derived from a combination of the ideas of Ramakrishna and his own doctrine based on the age-old Vedanta philosophy. His *Raja Yoga* and *Hatha Yoga* are unique books. Blessed with a dazzling appearance, as you can see from photographs, and a tremendous personality, he was the first swami to bring the distillation of the Hindu religion and philosophy to the West and present it in a form that could be understood by Westerners. In 1893 he arrived, unknown and in his late twenties, at the World Congress of Religions in Chicago. He had been allotted just a few minutes to speak, but the moment he stood up and uttered the introductory words, 'Brothers and Sisters of America', it was like magic: he instantly electrified the audience and was allowed to speak for three days!

He founded the Ramakrishna Missions (also known sometimes as Vedanta Societies) in all the main American cities. Gradually they spread all over Asia, Europe and Africa too. His approach was intelligent: he didn't try to convert Westerners to Hinduism. He didn't make them utter old mantras all the time, or force them to learn Sanskrit or worship Krishna. The Ramakrishna Missions had chapels which resembled churches, with photographs of Ramakrishna alongside images of Jesus Christ and Buddha. And his followers don't hassle. Vivekananda saw that it was vital to make sure no one felt threatened. He became extremely successful and popular, and I have always had the utmost admiration for him.

At the end of 1948 All India Radio offered Ravi the position of Director of Music for the External Services Division, with the additional role of composer-conductor of its new instrumental ensemble. This was a singular honour: he was by no means the only musician employed at the national radio network, but never before had one been appointed to a level of such seniority – and at the age of twenty-eight. He uprooted himself to Delhi and took up the post in February 1949.

Instrumental in my joining All India Radio was Dr Narayana Menon. I had first met Narayana around 1946, when he was with the BBC in London. He was a good amateur veena player in the Carnatic system, and also had an excellent knowledge of both Western music and the Hindustani system of North India. In Maihar I had heard some of the BBC programmes he presented introducing Indian music with demonstrations, and he had impressed me greatly.

Before independence some of the large native states had their own radio stations, and when Narayana left the BBC he became the Director of Baroda State Broadcasting Station. At his suggestion the BBC asked me to take over his post in London, but Annapurna created such a tantrum that I had to refuse it.

Ravi with Narayana Menon and the French writer, musicologist and Indophile Alain Daniélou.

Narayana was the first to notice and appreciate the creative side of mine, and when he joined the headquarters of All India Radio in New Delhi it was again at his suggestion that I was invited to join as Director of Music. We became close friends. He and his lovely wife Rekha became extremely popular among the Delhi highbrow socialites, and especially with the foreign diplomats.

It is terribly sad that an intellectual, energetic savant like Narayana is today, in his mid-eighties, suffering with advanced Alzheimer's disease in Delhi. Charming Rekha, though frail and aged herself, is still taking loving care of him. Bless her!

The period of almost seven years while I worked for All India Radio was a most eventful one. There were so many ups and downs, exhilarating successes and frustrations, joys and sorrows. That was when I gradually developed in stature and fame into a personality, with demands for me to perform all over the country growing continuously. Every day there were tourist-cum-visitors to look around All India Radio, and I became one of the star attractions, especially later when I was rehearsing in the No. 1 Studio (the largest one) with my chamber orchestra Vadya Vrinda. It puffed up my ego, but I did feel like a freak at times.

Out of my many compositions for All India Radio, I remember some outstanding ones, such as *Purnima Trayam*, or 'The Three Full Moons' – a short tone poem on Buddha's life, so named because he was born, attained enlightenment and achieved Nirvana (died) on full moon days. There was also *Nirjharér Swapna Bhanga*, an orchestral version of Tagore's famous poem, and *Shishu Tirtha*, based on another celebrated poem of Tagore. I worked hard on a radio feature which I produced on the life of Mian Tan Sen, whose name stands out as the most highly respected in the entire Hindustani tradition, and who was said to be nada-siddha (which means that he had complete yogic mastery over sound). A friend and wonderful drama producer, S. S. S. Thakur, helped me with the drama and dialogue and general production. The feature

was much appreciated. For me it was a special event personally since Baba's final guru, Uŝtad Wazir Khan, was a direct descendant of Mian Tan Sen, and I had therefore been fortunate enough to learn the Senia Beenkar ŝtyle, as it is known, from Baba.

There were some characters at All India Radio who were terribly envious of me and tried to malign me in any way they could. Moŝt of the time, though, my ŝtars were shining bright, and I survived!

(above) Vadya Vrinda, the National Orchestra, which Ravi founded while at All India Radio.

(below) Ravi's 1953 orchestral composition for Vadya Vrinda, based on Raga Tilak Kamod.

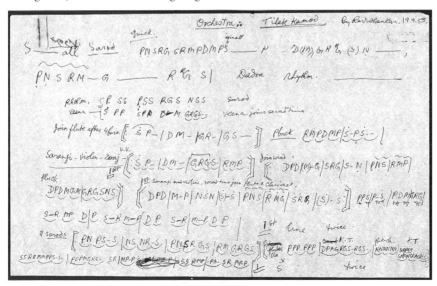

After three years in the External Services Division, Ravi switched to the Home Services, where he was given the opportunity to take his orchestral work further in Vadya Vrinda (the National Orchestra), an expanded ensemble. Relinquishing his Uday-inspired aversion to Western instruments, he now began to explore their possibilities, still retaining an Indian music base and employing predominantly Indian instruments, but opening his ears to other sounds that could be generated. This openness to the Western sound clearly foreshadowed many later musical adventures on the other side of the world – of which more shall be unveiled later.

Vadya Vrinda was a national chamber orchestra I founded, which mostly employed Indian instruments (sitar, sarod, veena, flute, sarangi, shahnai), but also a few Western ones – mainly violin, cello, double bass and clarinet. In a way I was pioneering as a composer, creating a style. Naturally I was inspired by the sound of Western classical, jazz and flamenco music I had heard during my youth; and there was also the influence of the old, simplistic orchestration in India, with all the musicians playing the same melody in unison; and more than anything there was the example of the experimentation of Baba in Maihar. All these ideas had been in my mind, but I wanted to do something different – to find a new way, without aping Western orchestral music, and at the same time not merely playing in unison. I undertook much innovation, and today those particular experiments are still being followed by many composers, while others have expanded them further into new ideas.

My employers gave me plenty of freedom. All the while I was working there, I was continuing to give sitar recitals. All India Radio is a government concern and it was usually very difficult to get leave whenever one wanted it, but they were relaxed with me and I was allowed to give concerts, write film scores in Calcutta, and travel all over India.

The government also gave me quite a comfortable house in Delhi. I converted the servants' quarters into two bedrooms, and for the first time I took in two or three disciples according to the old gurukul system, allowing them to live with me while I provided them with talim, food and lodging. (I have continued to do this ever since, at times having as many as five or six students with me simultaneously.) Shubho was growing up, and the home front was quieter... sort of, anyway! At All India Radio there were many attractive women, and plenty of 'green signals' again; but, though provoked, I was playing 'hard to get' to the utmost!

In late 1953 or early 1954 Tat Baba stayed for a week or so, and while there he encouraged me to drive the car he had brought. I hadn't previously been interested in cars but, after his driver had given me three or four lessons, I decided one day, emboldened by my puffed-up ego, to show off my new passion to my colleagues. I chose a terrible time to do so – about 5pm, when thousands of Delhi office workers were cycling home. All the cyclists were cleverly dodging the traffic – all except one, who flew straight towards me as I was entering the main gate at All India Radio. Immediately I reached for the brake, but in my inexperience hit the accelerator instead, and the car lurched forward, crashing into the corner of the gate and striking the gateman a glancing blow on the leg. What a commotion! In my shock – and terror at how easily I could have killed him – I don't know what happened next, but the poor gateman, a hefty fellow whom I knew very well, was hospitalised for two weeks. I paid for his hospital stay and even ended up buying a goat for him so he would have a healthy goat's-milk diet during his recuperation!

My paranoia after this incident put me right off cars for a long while, and I did not actually attempt driving again until I was in Los Angeles at the end of the Sixties, when I had proper lessons in a rented Oldsmobile Cutlass. Even then I never drove anywhere outside California, where the roads are so good, and since my licence lapsed in 1983 I have never renewed it.

While at All India Radio I returned to giving music to films. They were mostly Bengali movies made in Calcutta, starting with Satyajit Ray's *Apu Trilogy*.

I believe I first met Satyajit Ray in Bombay, some time at the end of 1944. He was a relative of a family friend, a wonderful Bengali lady singer. Extraordinarily tall (six foot four) and at that time very lean, with Grecian features, he was a striking figure. We became known to each other, though not close friends. He admired my music, although at first he had only heard me on the radio; but at the end of 1945 I had given my first major concert in Calcutta – I will never forget the thrill of that tremendous success. He and I would meet when I was visiting Calcutta, and onward through the years we came to know each other a little better each time, as he came to most of my programmes.

Meanwhile he also studied films in London, and became the art director of an advertising company in Calcutta. For a couple of years around the late Forties and early Fifties I used to stay in one of the grand old hotels in Calcutta, the Great Eastern Hotel, which was near his office, and many times on his way there, or at lunchtime, we would meet for a short while. We became quite friendly. That was about all, until he approached me regarding his first film, *Pather Panchali* ('The Song of the Little Road').

Ray's classic debut feature was based on the popular book by Bibhutibhushan Banerjee, with which he had fallen in love when he was providing woodcut illustrations for an abridged edition for children. (Ravi too had read it, in the early Forties, and also adored it.) Ray was spurred on by the encouragement of Jean Renoir, whom he had met in 1949 during the French director's visit to Calcutta prior to filming The River. *For Ray, it became an obsession to make his own film of Banerjee's story about Apu, a young boy growing up amid deprivation and tragedy in a small Bengali village.*

(below) Ravi, Pandit Nehru, Satyajit Ray.

(overleaf) Directing the music for Pather Panchali: *Satyajit Ray reclines to the left of Ravi.*

Dr B. C. Roy, the Chief Minister of Bengal, had given considerable support towards the making of *Pather Panchali*, but Satyajit was still having financial problems. Nevertheless, it was almost finished and he wanted me to provide the music for it. He showed me the rushes of the film, and as I watched them I was inspired; I immediately said I would love to do it. While watching the screening, in my head I could already hear the theme music, which I sang to him later and he liked.

I think it was on my next visit to Calcutta that I recorded the film score, all in one session of at least eight or nine hours into the night – with just me, my assistant Aloke Dey (a brilliant flautist, and an arranger as well) and five or six other musicians. I would watch a section of the film, roughly time it, then sing the music or play it on the sitar, and Aloke would transcribe it into Indian notation for the musicians. We would record it there and then in the studio. This is the style of scoring I prefer, and to some extent still use. Though there is so much facility now with video, computerised timings and time-clicks, I have done all my best work by watching the film in a traditional screening, and only writing down a few notes during it, since my purpose is to absorb the spirit of the film. I compose immediately, we rehearse two or three times and then we record.

Pather Panchali was released in 1955, and within the next few years I did music for three more films by Satyajit Ray. The Apu Trilogy continued in 1956 with *Aparajito* ('The Unvanquished'), and third part was *Apur Sansur* ('The World of Apu') in 1959. In 1958 I also contributed the music to Satyajit's *Paras Pathar*, or 'The Philosopher's Stone', so in all I gave music for four of his films.

But for me *Pather Panchali* is the best film he made, and one of the best I have come across by anyone, because there the entire work blended: the powerful story by a fine writer, and superb direction, editing and acting. I felt inspired, too, and I think that was one of my best works ever. It is an immortal film; even years later, when I see it on television stations around the world, it still touches me deeply. It was a stupendous critical triumph, winning prizes in many festivals, and Ray became a world-famous director from his first film alone. He went on to make an even greater name for himself, and technically he made better films maybe, but still I feel that *Pather Panchali* stands out. It had something very special: that innocent simplicity, straight from the heart without any ego.

Pather Panchali *was a landmark in Indian cinema, earning the prize for Best Human Document at the Cannes International Film Festival in 1956, and is widely considered the most important movie to have come from the subcontinent, a rival to any film anywhere. Its director, like its music director, became a cultural icon and a hero to Indians and, more particularly, to Bengalis, remaining so all his life.*

Satyajit Ray had a powerful personality, and God had given him the stature and booming voice that made him appear even more impressive. A man of extraordinary versatility and culture, he belonged to a family of brilliant writers, wrote many books for children, and before moving into films was already famous as an illustrator.

He had a good ear for both Western and Indian music, and later on he decided it would be better for him to do the music for his own films. We had a slight misunderstanding. I was quite hurt because he wrote somewhere that I was unique as a writer of music for ballet and the stage, but he thought film was something else. He also wrote to me once to say that it was a pity that I couldn't give more time for making the music for films. This was true – it was a hit-and-run affair whenever I recorded the score for anyone: I arrived in the city, saw the film, then went to the studio and did the music. I never had time to stay for editing, mixing or improving it. Yet I do believe that whatever came first was always the best, and when I tried to redo a score it was not as good.

I believe in the saying, 'There are many roads to Rome.' If you take the ten best music directors from all over the world, and tell them to do music for the same film sequence, they will all produce different music. some will have jazz, some electronic sounds, others will use the synthesizer, Western classical, an Indian touch, just sound effects or even 'silence'! And if you ask different audiences to judge each one dispassionately, most of them will say they liked it and the music was well matched. If Satyajit thought he was suitable to do the music for his own film – and people did like it – then he must have been. The director is the boss – and especially when he has the stature Satyajit had earned worldwide.

He made such sublime films. *Pather Panchali*, *Charulata*, *Kanchenjungha* and *Jalsaghar* will always stand out in my memory.

At the time of Satyajit Ray's death in April 1992, Ravi was making an album in Delhi. He received the news when he arrived home late one evening from the studio. The following day he spontaneously improvised a piece he titled Farewell, My Friend *(included on the HMV India album of the same name).*

Not long after *Pather Panchali* I was invited to contribute the score for a film by another wonderful director, Tapan Sinha from Calcutta. *Kabuliwala* was based on a short story by Rabindranath Tagore. The touching tale is set in Calcutta, and concerns a native of Afghanistan. As luck would have it, around the same time I was invited to Kabul to give a sitar recital for His Majesty the King of Afghanistan, and there I heard a great deal of original Kabuli folk music. I used this knowledge to create the aural background of the central character.

The film won the Silver Bear award at the Berlin Film Festival in June 1957, while at the same festival Ravi Shankar was chosen as Best Film Music Director of the year.

Apart from these films and All India Radio, there was plenty of variety to my other activities in Delhi. In 1949 I formed a music circle called Jhankar, which I ran with the support of my friend Mrs Sumitra Charatram, a very wealthy lady, and Harihar Rao. It was Harihar who, having moved from Bombay to Delhi in 1950 to continue to learn from me, helped me the most in organising these music ventures. I began with weekly recitals, usually on Saturdays, in a big mansion that belonged to Sir Shankar Lal, the brother of Sir Shri Ram. Most of the time I performed alone with a tabla-player, although I regularly asked some of my musician friends to perform too, which they did. Our audiences consisted of a limited number of friends and music-lovers, and we didn't charge any entrance fees, the idea being to create an appropriate musical atmosphere.

After about a year or so we gradually managed to invite a number of famous musicians to give a recital for the Jhankar circle while they were in Delhi. With the help of Mrs Charatram we were able to give them a token fee, and although it was much less than they usually charged, they enjoyed it because they had a wonderfully knowledgeable private audience.

Gradually the music circle grew, and after it had been going for about two years we had big three-day-long music festivals, with from ten to fifteen musicians appearing – including some leading names. Many others were musicians who had not performed for mass audiences in Delhi before, and I was inviting them there for their first time. These programmes would be staged in a pandal – with the sides covered because they were held in the winter season, between December and early February. We even had heaters all around the audience.

Delhi had long been known for producing excellent musicians, but to earn their living they had always had to go away to perform in other towns and cities. There had never been much of an audience for music in the city after the Moghul rulers had left and the remaining few aristocrats had dwindled in number. For many decades it had been like that, and it was still true when I first went there in 1949. There was a music school called Gandharva Maha Vidyalaya which occasionally hosted performances, but apart from that there was nothing for large audiences. The presentation of live music in Delhi was really started off by the Jhankar Music Circle.

Later on I suggested a few other music patrons should join, and a committee formed. And soon (as is common in India) a 'musical politics' emerged in the committee. I was disgusted with the atmosphere and left. But the music circle grew, and it still exists today under the name of Bharatiya Kala Kendra, filling me with pride for having originated this activity and organisation. Sumitra Charatram and her daughter are still carrying it on successfully, and have added an institution of dance and music by the same name.

Another activity that led me to come to the West relates to my wonderful friend Louis de San. He was a minister in the Belgian Embassy, very rich (with his own private plane), and a fine piano-player. He used to hold piano concerts at his home, and when any Western musicians came to Delhi he would invite them to perform.

I met him after I joined All India Radio. He was such a music-lover, and we became great friends. I played a couple of times at his place in front of a small group of his Western friends from his and many other embassies. It was not only the ambassadors or the ministers who were present, but also lower officials. Some of them had been in India for two or three years but still had no idea of Indian music; even if they had heard it, they were not that moved. They would say things like, 'It just goes on and on,' or, 'It sounds like cats miaowing' – the same comments as I had heard in Paris and elsewhere in the 1930s! In spite of being lovers of their own classical music, they didn't know what to listen for in our equivalent. I would feel angry, thinking, 'It is a pity that they don't understand the greatness of our music.' But I realised why they felt like that: they missed all the elements that they were used to in their Western music.

The first time Louis asked me to play at his place, he gathered together about thirty-five of his friends. Before I began playing for them, I talked for about five minutes to explain the music. I compared it with the Western system: where the differences lie, and why it is so different. I introduced its simplest characteristics, such as how we don't change the key (modulate) by shifting the 'Sa' (tonic) in a performance, even if we perform numbers in different ragas. I explained that there are no chords, counterpoints, dynamics or harmony, all of which are fundamental to Western classical music; that we dwell more on the melody and the complex rhythms, with extempore improvisation based on the ragas (melody forms) and the talas (rhythmic cycles). I clarified what ragas are: their shapes, the ascending and descending structure of the notes they use, and their connection with different times of the day – ragas of the morning, afternoon, evening and night – or with seasons and special occasions; and their expression of the moods (rasas). I explained about talas, and the divisions of the beats in each cycle. By way of example my tabla-player would beat out some cycles as examples: Rupaktal of seven beats (divided 3-2-2), or Jhaptal of ten (2-3-2-3). I illustrated how with finger counts and handclaps we show these divisions.

Our whole approach is different: it is individual music. The elaboration of a raga may last for hours, whereas those in my audience that day were not used to any musical item (except for a few symphonic movements) being longer than twenty or twenty-five minutes. Unless they were interested and tried to understand, it was natural for them to feel confused and bored.

I explained these basic ideas, and they seemed absolutely charmed. They were like children, getting right into the spirit. They would say, 'My God! We have been trying to listen to Indian music but we couldn't get through to it, and you have made it so much easier for us to understand.' They felt the emotional context and the spiritual quality, appreciated the virtuosity, and discovered that it can be entertaining at the same time: as exciting as jazz, they would say. Soon a few Delhi socialites (Indian friends of Louis and myself), who were equally ignorant of Indian music, joined this exclusive group.

From these early days Ravi set expectations for his audience as well as himself. He required from them an appropriate level of respect for the music. He insisted that during his performances no one present should, as was common in those days, smoke, drink, talk or otherwise behave inappropriately; and he preferred to sit on a raised dais with the audience on the floor below him.

Learning from Baba, I had always heard him say how sacred music is, and how it should be kept that way when you perform. It applies not only physically, to yourself, but also to the atmosphere, which must be amenable. My earlier association with Dada also influenced me in this direction. I became even more fanatical than Baba about never playing in places where there was a bad vibration, and was extremely stern if ever any such problems arose.

I liked to have a little dais. Louis de San's house was a small venue and I didn't insist on it there, but I did when I had a larger hall. I always demanded that everyone stop smoking and drinking, and I would ask them to sit properly on the floor. (Of course older people and those who had problems with their legs were given the chance to sit on a chair.)

Problems occurred more often with rich Indian people and royalty. On two or three occasions I was invited (and paid a fabulous amount) to perform, yet I would arrive to discover that everyone present was drinking, and the hall was messy, with a mass of chairs arranged in a huge room and an ordinary carpet on the floor. I would politely refuse to play unless a dais were erected. Usually I had to tell this first to the aide-de-camp, who always said 'no' – that previously they had invited some eminent musicians to perform and none of them had ever made any fuss. It was like saying, 'You're a young musician and you're making unreasonable demands!'

I had to say, 'Excuse me. I want respect to be given, not to me as a person but to the music itself, which I learnt from my guru and his great tradition. I don't want my audience drinking or smoking; they should be just sitting quietly and listening to the music. And if the audience is to sit on chairs, I want to be put on a raised platform or podium covered with a carpet.'

This happened a few times, and luckily every time the host would come over, and I could then explain the situation to him in English. He could see my sincerity, and the difference between me and the meek musicians he had dealt with in the past, who agreed to anything that was suggested.

Throughout my career in India I have made a big point of the need for appropriate behaviour on my listeners' part. It used to be the case that audiences at home could be such a pain! Many people would arrive late, talk to each other, buy tea, cold drinks or peanuts from the snack-seller and then munch them throughout the concert, or get up to go to the bathroom whenever they wanted. It was the height of disrespect to the music, and disturbed my concentration. Fortunately things have changed greatly now, especially in the large cities like Delhi, Bombay and Calcutta, where the audiences are so much better-behaved. But I really had to make a lot of commotion in the beginning, saying in press conferences that we must have more discipline and decorum. For this I was criticised very forcefully. Many commented: 'Does Panditji expect us to sit like statues?' Yet in the West audiences observe the decorum. Admittedly Westerners, with their long history of public musical performances, have had more years in which to get into the ritual of classical concerts, and this sort of thing is quite new in our country. Similarly in South India things are much better because they have a long tradition of large crowds going to performances in temples, although I have had problems sometimes in Madras, when some people arrive late and leave before the last item.

Recently I even insisted on certain arrangements in a performance I gave for the Queen of England. In April 1990, during the official visit to London of Mr R. Venkataraman, then the President of India, the Queen gave a reception banquet in his honour, and the President wanted to respond in kind. It was decided not to hold it in the Indian High Commission, but rather in St. James's Court Hotel. Since I am friendly with Mr Venkataraman, the High Commissioner requested me to perform at the banquet.

It was a huge honour and pleasure for me, but I asked if it could be arranged that the recital was not held during the actual banquet, since I will not perform when there is eating or drinking going on. At my request, the organisers of this special occasion set up a dais for me and the accompanying musicians, and arranged for Her Majesty and the Royal Family to be seated on chairs along with our President and his wife. I played for about forty-five minutes, and felt the vibes of great appreciation. Sukanya, Anoushka and I then had a private audience with the Queen, Prince Philip, Princess Diana and Prince Charles for the fifteen or twenty minutes before the banquet. Prince Charles, who learnt to play the cello, was especially enthusiastic. We had met before when he had attended performances of mine in Westminster Abbey and the Royal Albert Hall.

Until the Forties or Fifties, the Indian attitude to musicians was reminiscent of the stories you hear about Mozart and other legends a couple of centuries ago, who were permitted to eat only in the kitchen! I rebelled against this, and at length such troubles ended. Never did I have a problem after that.

The only comparison I can give from my own experience were the jazz musicians in America as they were up till about forty or fifty years ago. Although admired for their art, they were social pariahs. I came to understand why it was that most of them were spaced out with alcohol and drugs. While performing they had to shut themselves out from the uninspiring, noisy and smoky atmosphere in order to be able to bring out such beautiful music. Until forty or fifty years ago many of our greatest North Indian musicians – the dharis, mirasis or kathaks – were like those jazz musicians: most of them uneducated, and alcoholic or addicted to drugs. They had to put up with much that was demeaning to them and their great music.

Because of all that, I was known as a rebel. I didn't belong to that musician class, and thus it was easier for me to bring about major changes in attitudes towards musicians. Now things have changed, I am glad to see. All these musicians are better educated and well mannered, and have changed their habits and approach. They are socially accepted as well as respected.

My private concerts at Louis de San's house were becoming increasingly popular. The audience grew to savour even the alap and jor parts of a raga, the initial slow, serene and spiritual sections played on solo sitar without tabla accompaniment. At length Louis and some of his other friends started asking me, 'Ravi, why don't you go out and make our people in the West understand Indian music? You're the first person we've seen who can do it.'

That's when it struck me: the idea of going to the West. I was confident that I could do it. At that time there were no quality performing artists who could speak fluent English and were capable of articulating the nature of our music to a foreign audience. It was a challenge: a responsibility that I took upon myself, with my previous experience of the West in my childhood, and my knowledge of the Western mind.

My first tour of Soviet Russia was in 1954, when I went with the huge, prestigious first cultural delegation sent by Pandit Nehru, just as the Bolshoi Ballet and Russian folk ensembles came in delegations to India from the USSR. We were given red-carpet treatment everywhere. There were a large number of musicians on the tour, as well as Kathakali, Bharata Natyam and Manipuri dancers. I had a segment of only fifteen or twenty minutes to play, but we performed at the Bolshoi Theatre and Tchaikovsky Hall in Moscow, and went to Leningrad, Kiev, Tbilisi in Georgia, Yerevan in Armenia, the Black Sea resort Sochi, and Tashkent in Uzbekistan.

It was a wonderful experience, an unforgettable trip. I was astounded by the Hermitage in Leningrad – one of the greatest museums, of similar stature to the British Museum, the Louvre and the Metropolitan – and the palace of Peter the Great. Leningrad had the appeal of a European city, having maintained all its culture and beauty, although the general standard of comfort and service everywhere was poor in comparison to Western Europe. It was fascinating as well to see all the different regions of the USSR such as

The Cultural
Delegation arrives
in Prague, 1954.

Ukraine or Armenia, where they had retained their traditional music, even if
they had polished it up, removing the earthy crudeness which is the beauty
of folk music. I had a pleasant surprise in Georgia, where one of the music
ensembles that we went to see – a chamber orchestra with local instruments
(including the balalaika) – played one of my compositions, *Caravan*, a three-
and-a-half minute orchestral piece, which had been recorded on a 78rpm disc
in India. It was surprising to hear them play an Indian piece quite so well.

Funnily enough, it seems that back then I looked very much like Pushkin,
the great Russian poet. Of course, at 5'3" I am much smaller than he was
supposed to be, but he also had a dark complexion. Wherever we were
travelling people would call out to me, 'Pushkin! Pushkin! Pushkin!' I was
even offered a role by a film director who was making a film about him!

We were also shown the very impressive pioneers' schools. Starting from
the crèche, children were being introduced to acrobatics and gymnastics and
watched closely to see what tendencies they had towards dancing, music,
handicraft, art, painting or whatever. From about the age of five those chosen
would attend the Palace of Pioneers, where they were encouraged in their
specific talents as well as receiving general education. The aim was to ensure
that every individual was doing what he was capable of. That was something I
liked. Children all over the world have talents, but often they are not
recognised and encouraged.

However, there were many things that made me uneasy, and there was a
down side to this great pioneering organisation of education. We felt that
everybody was suppressed, especially in the region of art. All the artists,
writers and musicians were regimented. They were told what to do, rather
than being allowed to express their creative power and freedom. The stifling
atmosphere was quite apparent.

(overleaf) On the
streets of St
Petersburg, then
Leningrad, during
the visit of the first
Indian Cultural
Delegation to the
USSR in 1954.

(below) Performing
with tablá maestro
Kishan Maharaj
(left) in Benares.

(bottom, left to
right) Chatur Lal,
vocalist A. Kanan,
Yehudi Menuhin,
Ravi, sarangi-player
Ram Narayan and
Dulal Sen – upon the
occasion of the first
meeting between
Menuhin and
Shankar, in Delhi in
1952.

We met Bulganin and other political bigwigs, and also such greats as Shostakovich, Khachaturian and the ballerinas Galina Ulanova and Maya Plisetzkaya. (I met Maya again in February 1996 at the World Economic Forum in Basle – she was delirious at recalling our visit in 1954!) I also remember how, in spite of all the pomp and ceremony, the long lunches and dinner parties, the caviar, vodka and champagne, and the beautiful interpreters (one might flirt a little – but never touch!), we were forewarned to be very careful in whatever we said (even in our mother tongues) and whatever we did (even within our closed rooms). We were advised that we were being bugged or on 'candid camera'. It was a very stifling and discordant feeling in the midst of so much talk of 'mir' (peace), love and friendship between the USSR and India.

On the tour I was accompanied on tabla by Kishan Maharaj. From the mid-Forties onwards, Kishan performed with me in many concerts all over India.

Today he is the doyen of the Benares style of tabla-playing. I have hugely enjoyed playing with him, especially in the less common talas like Dhamar (fourteen beats), Pancham Sawari (fifteen) and Shikhar (seventeen). He is extraordinary in calculative rhythmics, and at playing in Khulabaj – the virile open-handed style of pakhawaj-drumming. Three years younger than me, he is still a handsome personality and we remain such good friends.

In those days it was said that people came to see Ravi Shankar and Kishan Maharaj as much as to hear them.

After Soviet Russia we went to Prague, Warsaw and Poznan, and we saw the birthplace of Chopin, near Warsaw. It was a happy experience after many years to step out of India and return to places I had been to in the West, and it was even more exciting for me to visit the USSR for first time.

Performing in Bombay in the mid-Fifties with Ali Akbar Khan (sarod) and Chatur Lal (tabla).

(overleaf) The legendary jugalbandi partnership of Ravi Shankar and Ali Akbar Khan.

In 1952 Yehudi Menuhin visited Delhi, and I met him at Narayana Menon's house. By now Narayana was the Director-General of All India Radio. He invited Yehudi one day for breakfast and arranged a morning session in the drawing room, and enquired if I would like to play. I was delighted to be asked, and performed along with a young tabla-player, Chatur Lal, whom I was training as my accompanist and who was working in my orchestra. Something happened from the very beginning. It was the first time Yehudi had heard Indian music, and he was so moved – absolutely entranced by it. Our friendship started then. Though I had seen Yehudi in my Paris days, when he was hardly fifteen (and wearing shorts) and I was a mere eleven, we did not know each other then. My brothers and I were well acquainted with his teacher, Georges Enesco, who came to our house in Paris a few times, but this was the first time that I had been introduced to Yehudi.

YEHUDI MENUHIN: *It is interesting that Ravi should remember seeing me in Paris, because that passed me by – I didn't take it in. But it must have laid the seed of something, because at that time Enesco had already insisted that I go*

1913 Coburn

Ravi (right) with
the Indian painter
K. S. Kulkarni and
American contralto
Marian Anderson
(second from right),
at the house
of Sundari
Shridharani,
director of Triveni
Kala Sangam.

to the *Exposition Coloniale* in Paris to hear the Balinese and the Vietnamese music, and then when I once played for him an African record he was absolutely fascinated.

It is amazing to look back and to see how seeds were planted and that now I am just fulfilling their destiny. Whether it was my father's preoccupation with social circumstances of people, my mother's with teaching and with children, or Enesco's tremendous interest in exotic or unknown musics, I can see so clearly I am simply the living product of these impressions. So it's very interesting that I should have encountered Ravi in Paris.

But the great impression he made – unforgettable! – was the first time I heard him play, with Chatur Lal, in Delhi. That was a music-making that I could have only dreamt of, because it was nothing to do with scores. It had everything to do with this internal passion that the player obeys, and which carries him, on the basis of an extraordinarily exacting discipline – far more disciplined than anything we learn in the West. Because in Indian music you learn enough to master the scales and the rhythms, but you learn to create out of that, out of a given number of formulas. In Indian music it is very obvious: the musician who plays still within the formulas makes about as dull a music as you could wish to hear! But then when you break the shell of the formula, and it emerges as a living work...! When Ravi plays, that is what happens.

Yehudi went back from India, and once in a while he wrote to me, offering his thanks for the wonderful gift of music that I had given him. I found him to be such a remarkable person: kind, humble and full of love.

It was sometime in 1955 that a telegram arrived from him saying that the Asia Society were holding an India Festival in New York, which he was hosting. He asked me to come and perform at the Museum of Modern Art as part of the Festival. The prospect was exciting, but at that time, with all the problems in my marriage, I was having such restrictions from the home front, and with these tensions I decided not to go. However, I could not tell this to anyone; it would be such a stupid reason to have to give, that family pressure was the reason.

I sent Yehudi a telegram explaining that I would love to come, but regretted that, due to a commitment, I could not. However, I thought that someone else should go, so I suggested Ali Akbar Khan playing sarod. A reply came back saying, 'Who is Ali Akbar Khan, and what is sarod?' It was not Yehudi's fault that he didn't know, and neither was it putting down Alubhai; but that's how it was. I explained that he was my guru's son and one of the greatest Indian instrumentalists – definitely the greatest sarod-player – and that I was sure he would be the best person. It was duly fixed up and I also arranged for Chatur Lal to go with him.

That was how Alubhai and Chatur Lal came to perform in the USA in 1955. Their performance was a big success in New York, and especially for Chatur Lal who became something of a celebrity. There was a hungry look to him, and when he smiled his white teeth would shine. The Americans who heard and saw him went crazy about him, and at that time he was what Zakir

Hussain later became: a truly charismatic young idol with tremendous sex appeal. Chatur Lal appeared on Alistair Cooke's *Omnibus*, a TV programme shown all over the nation, on which he played with a jazz drummer. Yehudi introduced Alubhai before the performance, and also on the recording of his first L.P.

For some time now Ravi had been gently propelled by various factors towards taking the big gamble in the West: his understanding of the Western mind; experiments with Western instruments in Vadya Vrinda; the music he had scored for ballets and films; his success in introducing Indian music to the peoples of the Soviet Union, and to Louis de San's circle of foreign diplomats; his friendship with Yehudi Menuhin, who had displayed such joy at discovering Indian music. All these factors, and no doubt other less tangible ones too, were edging Ravi Shankar, a man filled with a sense of the beauty of his own country's music and the respect due to it, towards a mission to help others experience it.

Everything happened automatically after Annapurna left me, at the beginning of 1956. When she had left me in Bombay in 1944, it had not been that serious; but this was something else.

Annapurna's departure was the catalyst for Ravi's first tour of the West as a solo musician, and the dawn of a new international phase in his career – a personal crusade to bring Indian music to the peoples he had seen in his youth. He was confident of success.

Looking back, it may seem inevitable that such a supreme musician, such an eloquent and cosmopolitan man, should have sought new horizons for Indian music. But in 1956 a move to the West was a leap in the dark, however sure he himself felt about his prospects.

FIVE: SURANJANI

By 1956 there were many problems in our marriage, and in January there was a serious breakdown. It would be in bad taste to spell out the details; suffice it to say that it was a major issue and I was shattered! Annapurna went back first to her father in Maihar and then to Calcutta, where she stayed with Alubhai for almost three years. It was traumatic for Shubho, who was then fourteen and going to school. Because I was touring regularly in India, he moved to Sejda's house in Delhi, where he was able to continue his schooling and do plenty of painting and sketching. It had already become clear that he had artistic talent.

Around the same time I resigned from All India Radio. I was getting tired of it, and although I knew I had developed considerably through my experiments with Vadya Vrinda, there was nothing more to be gained and it was time to leave. Alone at home, I was also very unhappy and had had enough of Delhi at that point. It seemed to be a suitable moment to get out of the country, and I had a simultaneous stroke of luck. My friend Jamshed Narielwala, a wealthy Parsi socialite and lover of Western music who resided in Bombay, had introduced me to an impresario from London by the name of John Coast, who then sent me a proposal for a tour. So in September 1956 I departed for Europe. My initial destination was London, where I was to stay with a friend while taking my first steps as a solo artist in the West. On this first solo tour I was accompanied by Chatur Lal and also Nodu Mullick.

I had first met Nodu way back in 1943 when he used to come to the house of my dear friend Dulal Sen, the sarod-player in Dada's troupe. Nodu was a very shy-looking man, an instrument-maker, so I was told, although at that time I had not seen any of his creations. He had never received a proper training, only what he had gleaned while watching Kanai Lal and some others from the old school of sitar-makers. But Nodu had a real talent, and he specialised in that particular sound that I had developed, emphasising the bass notes and the alap sound. We saw each other often and became good friends. By the early Fifties he had showed me a few instruments he had made, and when I came to leave for the West in 1956 I asked him to join me.

JOHN COAST ARTISTS REPRESENTATION

55 ENNISMORE GARDENS, LONDON, S. W. 7

Licensed Annually by the L.C.C.

KNIGHTSBRIDGE 4

9th August 56

Miss Divall,
E.M.I.Ltd,
3 Abbey Road,
London. N.W.8.

Dear Miss Divall,

Could you possibly pass this letter on to the
right person in the Columbia Gramophone organisation, to see
whether the idea in it is of any interest.

Last year, Angel made a record of an Indian sarod
player who was visiting America, named Ali Akbar Khan. I dont
know how this record sold in America, though I've written
Nelson Lansdale to find out; but I think I have seen what I
presume to be this record listed somewhere recently on a
Columbia Coming Records announcement, or something of that sort.

The artist who should have gone to America and
Europe last year was Ravi Shankar, a brother of the dancer
Uday Shankar, who is a friend of Yehudi Menuhin. Mr Menuhin
apparently had long wanted him to go abroad, considering him
to be one of India's finest musicians and perhaps her best
younger Sitar player. The Sitar is said to be a more popular
instrument than the Sarod.

At any rate, as you'll see from the enclosed, I
am booking this artist in this country in October-November, and
just in case you could be interested in him, am sending you
his publicity material. He does 3 Third Programme broadcasts;
appears on "Music for You" in November; and gives about 5 recitals
in London and elsewhere, besides going to Germany in that time.

Best wishes,

Yours sincerely,

John Coast.   27118

*(above) John Coast's
letter of
introduction to EMI
in London.*

*(opposite) Back at
last in London, late
1956.*

He was to play the tanpura (the drone instrument) in the concerts and to take care of my sitar, adjusting the jawari whenever it needed it. Venturing away from India together was to give us a special nearness.

As he set about building a following in the West, Ravi had to eke out a living playing at the size of venue he had long ago left behind in India. But the glitter and good times of stardom were not the object now. After all, seasoned international artist that he had been in his adolescence, Ravi had already experienced all the glamour the West could offer. He had a different aim.

My first concert was on 12th October, presented by the India Arts Society at Friends' House in London. On that British trip, I had to perform in small halls such as Conway Hall and Wigmore Hall. London welcomed me warmly, but its Indian population then was smaller than it is today, and on this first venture back to the West it was clear the British people were still behind Germany and the United States in the appreciation of Indian arts.

Unfortunately the British had never taken any interest in our performing arts during the days of the Raj – though they left them alone, which was good in a way. But the comparison with Holland, another major colonising nation, was not favourable. The Netherlands' empire included Java, Bali and Sumatra (the Dutch East Indies), and it was tremendous how the Dutch loved the culture of the people that they were governing. When I was hardly twelve I was lucky enough to visit the huge Exposition Coloniale in Paris. There the Dutch had built a beautiful pavilion and pagodas typical of Java and Bali, and brought a complete Balinese gamelan troupe, which we heard for the first time, as well as the Javanese shadowplay and fabulous Balinese dance. Museums were built in Amsterdam and The Hague to house all the treasures of their colonies. The British had nothing like this, except for the Indian sculptures, works of art and old manuscripts in the British Museum.

Nevertheless it was in 1956 that I fell in love with London, as a result of the bombardment by the Germans! Compared with before the war, there were so many clean new buildings and the fog had gone. Cosmopolitan restaurants had sprung up everywhere, and not only Indian: any country, you name it.

*(below and overleaf)
In performance at the
Woodstock Festival,
1969.*

*(all other images)
George Harrison's
photographs of India
in September-October
1966, featuring Ravi,
George, Kamala,
Pattie Harrison,
Shambu Das and a
cast of children and
animals.*

people, and especially the younger generation. They were all working hard to stand on their own feet and regain their self-esteem. In the years since then, like the French and the Japanese (and even the British), they have achieved phenomenal economic affluence, but I do find them more materialistic now and noticeably more under the spell of the USA, even though they outwardly affect to despise the pull of Americanisation.

An aside: the same influences in turn reached Asian and other Third World countries. They have also reached India, along with the new economic developments and the arrival of the multinationals. The worst effect is the widening gulf created between, on the one side, poverty, hunger and overpopulation, and on the other, the excesses of the nouveaux riches (many of whom seem to gain their money through the black economy). The onslaught of the hamburger, Coca-Cola and MTV culture is quite apparent in India now, but this way of life is suitable only for the small elite in our big cities. The priority for the rest of India is to have food, shelter and a way of life that maintains their health, self-respect and identity. To top all this, at present we are unfortunately also going through the troubles of political upheaval, violence, terrorism, separatism, communalism, pollution and corruption, with the worrying additions of drugs and especially Aids, which has crept in with a fearsome magnitude. It's a turbulent time for India.

Back to 1956. Upon completing the German tour in November, and before heading across the Atlantic, I returned briefly to London to play a couple more recitals and cut my first long-playing album in the West. Featuring the ragas *Jog*, *Simhendra Madhyaman* and *Ahir Bhairav*, EMI released the LP the following April under the title *Ravi Shankar Plays Three Classical Ragas*.

After my happy days spent in America in the Thirties, and the frustration of having missed out on the previous year's invitation, it was with tremendous pleasure that I arrived in New York, for a tour presented by Beate Gordon and Ann Laughlin – two ladies from the Asia Society – and sponsored by John Rockefeller III. Isadora Bennett was the agent who had arranged the tour, which was mostly focused on campuses. In New York my first concert was for the Young Men's Hebrew Association, at the large Kaufmann Auditorium. There weren't as many Indians in New York then as there are today, but I established good friendships with a few (including Karuna Maitra, whose Riverside Drive apartment I stayed at, and Gopal Sanyal), and the show was a splendid triumph. We played in a few more places in the region, including Boston and Philadelphia, before heading out to California.

The Sunshine State appealed to me instantly. My principal home for most of the year at present, it is enormously attractive, mainly because of the weather and the scenic beauty. It is very inspiring: the ocean, the green hills, the mountains and the desert, all within about an hour's drive. You can have the Riviera, you can have the Himalayas, you can have anything. It is a blessed area.

By phoning and talking to a few friends, in advance of my arrival on the West Coast I had arranged some concerts there myself. The first performance, in January 1957, was held at the Self-Realisation Fellowship

(SRF) in Los Angeles, at their centre on Sunset Boulevard. They had a small hall in the basement, and about 200 people attended for a very enjoyable evening.

The SRF was established by Swami Paramahansa Yogananda, who wrote the famous book *Autobiography of a Yogi*, which I later gave to George Harrison, whose life it changed greatly. It is a most unusual and very well written book which gives an understanding of the spiritual side of India, penned by a man who had self-realisation and did so much to bring to the West an awareness of and respect for India's great spiritual heritage.

India's original spiritual pioneer in America was Swami Vivekananda, who established the Ramakrishna Missions. It was in a similar though less spectacular way that Swami Yogananda came to the West in 1920 and established his SRF centres, including three in Los Angeles and others in several locations around the States – one in what is now my home town of Encinitas, California. I was fortunate enough to meet him a couple of times in the States in the Thirties, although at my tender age I had not realised what he was worth. He had behaved so normally and simply that, apart from being impressed by his looks, I had thought him no different from the man next door. Later on, as my knowledge grew (and through knowing his family in Calcutta), my appreciation of him blossomed.

The Ramakrishna Missions and the SRF centres are very dear to my heart. Their low-key followers are not into selling the Hindu religion, uninterested in earning millions of dollars through exploiting the appeal of its yogas, mantras, tantras, kundalinis and chakras. It is a joy to visit the SRF centre at Encinitas, which is about three and a half miles from our house, situated on the shore of the Pacific Ocean in a serene and spiritual setting with beautifully landscaped grounds. All the monks (known as Brothers and Sisters) are radiant and sweet, and seem to be so much at peace. The Swami himself died in 1952, but his principal disciple, Shri Daya Mata, now aged eighty-three, succeeded him as the head of the organisation. Sukanya, Anoushka and I are very close to her. She is gracious and beautiful – love just flows out of her! She resides at the main SRF headquarters in Mount Washington, near Los Angeles. The present local head in Encinitas is Brother Mitrananda, a dear friend of ours who is learned, witty and down-to-earth.

At the Sunset Boulevard SRF in 1957 I met Richard Bock, a great connoisseur of jazz music who had recently formed an independent jazz record company called World Pacific. Dick was interested in recording me for his label, and he soon did. After the SRF I was off to San Francisco, where some further concerts had been arranged in two small auditoriums, before returning to the East Coast.

Back in New York again, it was time for some recording. Upon my arrival in the Big Apple a couple of months previously, my attention had been caught by a happy face with an honest smile, that of George Avakian, Director of the International Department at Columbia Records and another ardent jazz expert. We became great friends immediately. George's family are Armenians who until recently had a huge wholesale oriental-rug business, and for years

Chatur Lal, Ravi and Nodu Mullick meet Gene Kelly at a Hollywood film studio, 1957.

they supplied the carpet or rug for the podiums I sat upon in all my New York recitals. His wife, Anahid Ajemian, was a well-known concert violinist. Between March and May he recorded my three sessions at Columbia's old 30th Street studio, yielding my first two LPs to be released in the States. Chatur Lal accompanied me, and I gave short spoken introductions to the ragas and talas we played.

Apart from these two releases with Columbia, for many years almost all the records I made in the USA were on Dick Bock's World Pacific label. Right from the outset I had these two terrific friends in America, one on each coast.

Keen to spread appreciation of Indian music, Ravi was the first to not only perform it but also explain it intelligently and fluently. Being able to communicate in English or French whenever necessary enabled him to bridge cultural barriers more easily and hugely aided his progress as a pioneer.

With Dizzy Gillespie, 1957.

Although there were only a few concerts on my first solo foreign tour, they created such a level of interest that my future was already well established in Europe and America. I met many musicians, especially in the jazz field. There were certainly a few Indophiles too – every city had them: Paris, London, Berlin, New York – but most of them were not particularly knowledgeable about our music. Back then jazz musicians and jazz-music buffs were the major part of my audience.

Owing to the improvisational factor common to both Indian music and jazz, many people take it for granted that our music *is* like jazz – which is far from the truth. The improvisation in jazz is based on Western chords, harmony and a particular theme. In Indian classical music one improvises on a theme, either in the form of a song or in a gat based on a chosen raga (one of thousands!), being bound by rules and observing the complex rhythmic structures and time cycles, in each of which there can be anything between three and 108 beats. It takes twelve to fifteen years of training with a guru in the oral tradition and a strict adherence to the traditional discipline before one can reach the ultimate aim, which is to improvise with the sky as the limit, and even then the percentage of improvisation in any performance of our music depends on the creativity of the artist'.

During my stay in New York a lady by the name of Rosette Renshaw had come from Montreal to meet me. She was teaching an Indian music course at McGill University. While we were talking in the hotel lobby, she said she had seen *Pather Panchali* and that the film score was one of the most beautiful pieces of music she had heard. Tears were coming into her eyes and it touched me to meet someone who appreciated it so deeply.

She told me about Norman McLaren, a celebrated man who was then with the Canadian Broadcasting Corporation. Norman was a sheer genius: an innovative animator who made unique short films, employing numerous original audio and visual techniques while conveying social messages. Hollywood made him fabulous offers but never could lure him away from Montreal. Apparently Norman wanted me to do the music for his new short film, *A Chairy Tale*. Anything in the line of music composition always interested me, so I journeyed on to Montreal and met him.

He demonstrated for me one of his new techniques, taking an ordinary pin and making perforations on some film, so that when it was played back it produced a ticking sound He could control the pitch and the rhythmic pattern through the size, numbers and separation of the holes. It was something completely novel – he was such an expert that way.

He then showed me *A Chairy Tale*. This will always be a personal favourite among the films I have scored. It was a fantasy without dialogue, hardly ten minutes long but both touching and comical, and a beautiful metaphor for relationships. Claude Jutra plays a man who wants to sit on a chair. Time and again the chair refuses to allow it, yet every time he walks away it coyly flirts with him, encouraging him to try again – but when he tries to sit, once again it moves away and he falls down on his derrière! The poor man is bewildered until he has a sudden realisation: maybe the chair wants to sit upon him? So he crouches down on the floor like a seat, and the chair joyfully jumps on him. Satisfied now, it gets down and at last permits him to sit.

This was not a standard animation; it was live action – Claude Jutra actually walks on the stage in front of a black curtain, and there is a chair. Clever techniques were employed – including variable-speed shooting,

'pixillation', and invisibly manipulating the chair with a cord like a puppet – and it was all so beautifully done that the chair genuinely seems almoſt like a human being.

I watched it a few times before recording the music, as always composing and performing spontaneously along with the film – using only the sitar, tabla (inſtruᴄting Chatur Lal what to play) and a cymbal (played by Nodu Mullick). It came over so well that it won prize after prize in different countries, shown as it was in feſtivals all over the world. It was a marvellous experience working with such a talented man for whom I had tremendous regard. Even today the film seems so fresh and new.

Little more than a year after embarking for the West, Ravi was displaying the full range of his talents and already attracting considerable attention. A Chairy Tale *was nominated for an Academy Award for Best Short Subject in 1957-58. It also won a Special Award from the British Film Academy, and further prizes at Venice, Rapallo and the Canadian Film Awards. At the same Venice film festival Satyajit Ray's* Aparajito, *featuring Ravi's music score, collected the Golden Lion.*

In May 1957 Ravi returned to Europe from North America for a tour lasting three months, taking in Britain, France, Italy, Belgium and Holland. He made further recordings with EMI in London before heading home to Delhi. Intrepid traveller that he was becoming, though, he was back in Europe before the end of the year.

There was one more film soundtrack I recorded in Europe that year: *The Flute and the Arrow*. Late in 1957, I went to Sweden to discuss it with the director, Arne Sucksdorff. Shot in central India, it was about a tribe called the Murias, an unspoilt people who have peculiar old customs and a collective lifestyle, living in a gotal (commune). I made the music using a few musicians available from London, my tabla accompanist and my own sitar.

My activities outside of India did not prevent me from still being very busy at home, and as time passed I only grew more ambitious in my ideas for artistic ventures there. Apart from all my concerts, I was contributing the music for documentaries and feature films, mostly in Calcutta, and then in Delhi in March 1958 I staged my first magnum opus – *Melody and Rhythm*. In

152

this I was aided by the cultural organisation Triveni Kala Sangam, the director of which, Sundari Shridharani, had been a student of my brother in the Almora Centre and was a dear friend. She helped me to put on the production at the Arts and Crafts Hall. It was my idea to present a complete musical without any dance, something that had not been done seriously in India prior to that. The whole conception was new, lending a progressive touch to the music while still catering for the traditionalists and the lovers of devotional songs. *Melody and Rhythm* featured the combination of a choral group and a medium-size orchestra, perhaps sixty boys and girls in all. Instead of the singers being seated, as is traditional in India, they were standing in different tiers, as in the West, and there were about eight bass tanpura-players sitting on the floor at the front. It was visually striking: I took care that the girls were dressed in attractive saris and the boys wore kurtas and pajamas. Lighting and decor effects were harnessed to complement the overall effect, and the entire production was very sleek. Harihar Rao was the Production Manager.

One day while we were rehearsing in an old building in Delhi, there came an important Member of Parliament and other distinguished persons to watch us. At the end he announced that earlier the same day in Parliament Pandit Nehru had mentioned me by name, apparently saying that young Ravi Shankar was doing a fine job as a 'cultural ambassador' projecting India in the West through music. My jaw dropped! I was touched and delighted – it felt like the most amazing tribute of all, coming from the great man himself whom I adored so much.

The programme of *Melody and Rhythm* was made up of a variety of items, but I had kept one theme: it covered the entire history of Hindustani music, starting from dhrupad-dhamar singing, going all the way through to contemporary forms, including khyal, tappa, tarana and thumri, followed by folk songs and then modern compositions, with some orchestral pieces in between.

There was one lullaby number, where Lakshmi Shankar was singing to a baby (a doll, actually). With the effect of a little blue light, it was a charming, peaceful number. One night Pandit Nehru came to the performance. In those days he was always exceptionally busy and active as Prime Minister, either travelling or spending long hours in the Parliament and his office. He was like a superstar at that time; wherever he went people wanted to look at him, touch him and talk to him. Although we had invited him, we never thought he would have the time or energy to come to the show. But surprisingly he did, and sat in the central box. That was a unique incident! Usually there was plenty of applause after the lullaby, but that evening there was almost total silence. All day the poor man had been harangued in Parliament, and as he had a hot temper he used to flare up a lot – and after such a tiring day the lullaby had sent him to sleep. He was snoring! The whole audience became aware of it, because it was quite a compact hall of about seven hundred people, and though they had begun clapping gently they stopped. They didn't want to disturb him! It was so sweet, the love and respect people had for him.

After the show finished – awake now! – he ran up by himself (in those days, there was rarely anything like the security of today) onto the stage and hugged me. He was very moved, and he gave generous compliments to me and the rest of the group.

Fresh from such a triumph, Ravi was, however, not one to relax and take stock. It is not in his nature to be particularly concerned about the past, and in any case he didn't need to reflect; the flame of music burned inside him and this filled him with passionate self-belief. Over the next few years he established a frenetic pace of international travel, mixing time spent in India with frequent trips abroad for concerts, recordings and festivals.

Attending a show in Japan during the Cultural Delegation tour in 1958. In the foreground, with bouquets, are (left to right) Kamala Lakshman, Ravi, Damayanti Joshi.

In late April I visited Japan for the first time. Once more I was part of a cultural delegation, although it was smaller than the Russian one of 1954. This time, however, I was leading the party so I was in an exalted position, especially as such official delegations had previously always been led by bureaucrats. Alla Rakha accompanied me on tabla and Harihar Rao on tanpura, and there were other musicians to accompany the two female dancers in the delegation, the charming Damayanti Joshi, who specialised in the grace, beauty and softer elements of the Kathak style, and the young Bharata Natyam danseuse Kamala Lakshman. The fantastic Kamala Lakshman actually looked quite plain, but once on stage with her costume and make-up – my God! She transformed into such a dazzling personality, and what a dancer!

In my childhood the flimsiness of its toys had left me unimpressed by Japan as a nation, and naturally the war had enhanced my negative feelings.

But when we went there and performed, my view changed completely. The Japanese bowled me over. To see how they were catching up with the whole world economically and technologically, with their cameras and cars, was fantastic. They were not merely copying the West but actually improving on its achievements. What I really fell in love with, though, was the people's passion for nature (the month-long tour occurred in the middle of the Japanese cherry-blossom season), their love of etiquette, and their thriving traditions amidst all the ultra-modernism of the younger generation: the people were maintaining their old way of life, wearing their kimonos and constructing their houses from bamboo and other light materials – comfortable and yet scientific. Such beauty in their tradition.

We visited the cities of Tokyo, Nagoya, Tokushima, Hiroshima, Fukuoka, Kobe, Osaka, Nara, Kyoto, Hakodate, Sapporo and Asahikawa. Initially I was terrified of how we would be received, this being my first visit, yet everywhere there was such a warm reception and it was an exhilarating experience performing. Japanese audiences tend to behave in a highly respectful way, but they are actually extremely appreciative of Indian music. From their faces you wouldn't necessarily know whether they are moved, but sometimes Japanese people have come to see me after a concert and they simply cannot say anything to me; that shows how deeply they have felt the music. I have kept one memorable if gruesome letter from a Japanese fan, a very long one written in English, which perplexed me when I received it because the ink was a peculiar colour, neither blue nor red nor brown. With heartfelt enthusiasm she described how much she loved my music and how deeply she felt towards me spiritually, but the final line gave me goose-bumps: 'the music reached my inner depth and so I am writing with my own blood...'

On the way back from that first visit I returned to India via Hong Kong, completing a memorable trip. Since then I have been back to the Land of the Rising Sun regularly. It amazes me how the Japanese have an audience for everything. They embrace not only rock and pop, which have become almost a universal language, but all varieties of music: from Western classical music and opera, through jazz, folk and country-and-western, to medieval music. And Indian music too. You name it, they have it. Their food is delicious – the tempora, sushi and teriyaki! – and their manners are refreshing. There are some Japanese who have broken free from traditional formal behaviour codes and are internationalised, and through them I have come to learn that the clash of cultures is causing considerable problems now. Westernisation has seeped into their society to such an extent that the younger generation are almost rebelling. But it has not yet completely changed, and I find it charming that the emphasis on etiquette still exists.

After my first solo tour in the West, which had lasted almost twelve months, I returned to perform almost every year, or sometimes alternate years, and each time the audience was growing larger everywhere. For the next year or two the arrangement of my British concerts was split between John Coast and the Asian Music Circle, a London-based organisation founded in 1953 to promote in the West music from throughout Asia, headed by Yehudi Menuhin and run by Ayana Angadi. Within two years of my first arrival, John Coast presented me in the Royal Festival Hall, on 4th October 1958, accompanied by Alla Rakha. This was my first really big concert in the West, and the first time an Indian performer had appeared in the main Festival Hall – and it was packed!

After a three-day recording session for EMI at their Abbey Road studios in London (generating the material for a further release in EMI's ground-breaking Music of India series), Ravi crossed the Channel for a gala concert staged at UNESCO's Great Hall in Paris on United Nations Day (24th October). Held as part of Les Semaines Musicales de Paris, a five-week music festival organised by UNESCO and the International Music Council, the programme featured the Chamber Orchestra of the French National Orchestra with four illustrious soloists from around the world.

With the great film director Jean Renoir and Nikolay Nabokov, cousin of the Russian author Vladimir, while in Paris for the UNESCO show in 1958.

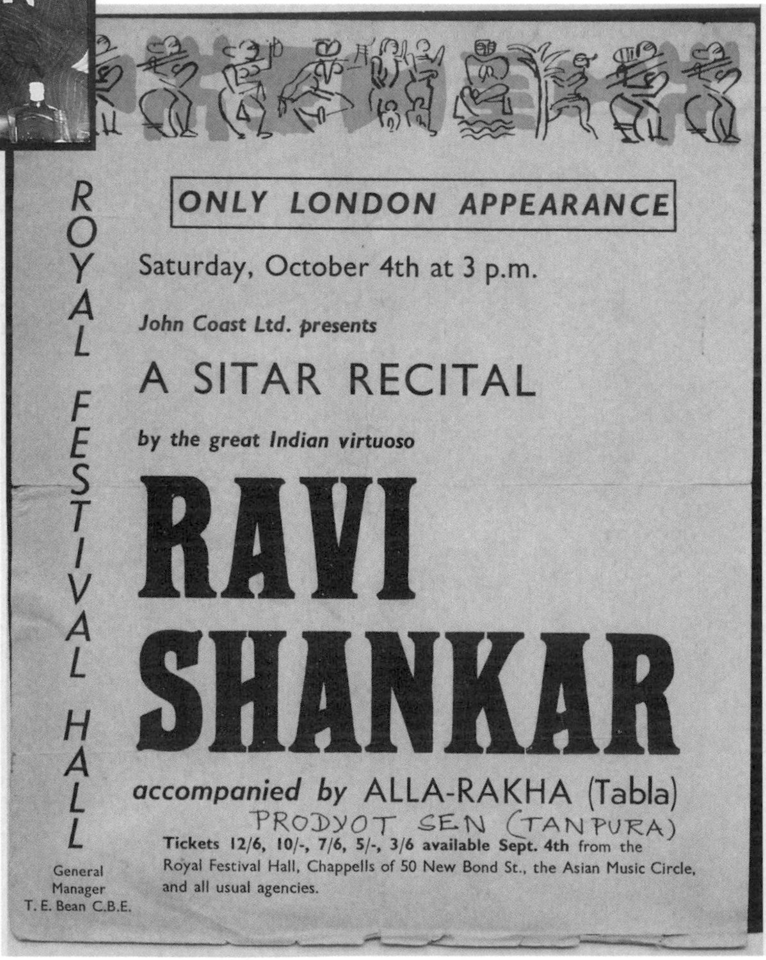

ROYAL FESTIVAL HALL

ONLY LONDON APPEARANCE

Saturday, October 4th at 3 p.m.

John Coast Ltd. presents

A SITAR RECITAL

by the great Indian virtuoso

RAVI SHANKAR

accompanied by ALLA-RAKHA (Tabla)
PRODYOT SEN (TANPURA)

Tickets 12/6, 10/-, 7/6, 5/-, 3/6 available Sept. 4th from the Royal Festival Hall, Chappells of 50 New Bond St., the Asian Music Circle, and all usual agencies.

General Manager
T. E. Bean C.B.E.

London, 1958: Alla Rakha (tabla), Prodyot Sen (tanpura), Ravi (sitar).

From Japan came Shinichi Yuico, the celebrated blind koto player, and then from Russia there was David Oistrakh, one of the greatest violinists of the time, as well as Yehudi. David and Yehudi played Bach's *Concerto for Two Violins*, and Alla Rakha accompanied my sitar performance. I was only allocated a short time slot, but appearing along with all these celebrated names was very exciting for me and a great experience for all present.

My 1958 tour did not go to the United States, so I returned to India in November, and it was then that Annapurna came back to me in Delhi. Thereafter all three of us stayed together in a house I had recently secured in Haily Road. Still at school, Shubho was by now very much into fine art, but it was from that period onwards that Annapurna herself took more interest in teaching him the sitar, although his attention was divided between the two pursuits, art and music. Though Annapurna and I tried hard, something had snapped between us, and by now I had established a stronger relationship with my old flame Kamala, who had been widowed in 1957. We met as often as we could and wherever possible.

In 1960 I left Delhi and bought a flat in Malabar Hill, a very posh area of Bombay. Early the next year Annapurna and Shubho joined me there, but by this point my relationship with Annapurna had completely deteriorated. She remained with me in Bombay till I left her for good in February 1967, but it was all finished between us. After moving to Bombay I was spending even more time with Kamala, feeling closer to her than ever; although admittedly it didn't stop me having torrid affairs almost everywhere as I travelled frantically all over the world.

My next trip to the West after the UNESCO gala was in late 1959, when a tour was fixed up in the USA, to include many of the large cities. Colleges, universities and theatres were the most common venues, and I gave a few lecture-demonstrations in museums too. Once again I also toured all over Europe, appearing at the 1960 Prague Spring Festival for a sitar recital, accompanied by Sashi Bellari on tabla.

I was also still doing film work in India. Mostly the scores I contributed were for Bengali films produced in Calcutta, but two Hindi films made in Bombay stood out as memorable experiences for me. *Anuradha* received rave reviews upon its release in 1960 and won the President's Award in India. It was a song-orientated film, with about five or six of them all becoming hits, magnificently rendered as they were by the legendary playback singer Lata Mangeshkar. (In Indian films, traditionally all the songs are sung by professional 'playback' or 'ghost' singers, rather than the actual actors on screen.) Hrishikesh Mukherjee, a fine director, was sympathetic and musical, and the lyricist was my favourite, the late Shailendra. Making the music with such talented colleagues was satisfying and highly enjoyable. I was partly instrumental in their choosing my dear friend and passion, the beautiful Leela Naidu, as the heroine of the picture.

  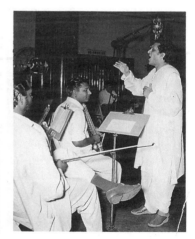

Anuradha: Ravi with the incomparable Lata Mangeshkar, vocalist on the film's soundtrack, and directing the ensemble.

Within the next couple of years I was asked to provide the score to another notable film, *Godan*: a classic story written in the early part of this century by Prem Chand, a great Hindi writer from Lucknow. Set in rural India, it concerns a landlord's oppression of a poor farmer, and how the latter's family are ruined; a sad but beautiful tale. Unfortunately the picture, made by a new director, was not up to the mark, though happily the music was much appreciated. For this I chose to emphasise the folk-music element of that region in Uttar Pradesh, near my own birthplace, Benares. Lata Mangeshkar, her sister Asha, Geeta Dutt and the famous male singers Rafi, Manna Dey and Mukesh all sang as playback singers. Lata told me later that she liked the music of *Godan* very much!

By the late Fifties I had used my Kanai Lal sitar for so many programmes that it had really been overplayed, so I had decided to order a new one, to be crafted by Nodu Mullick. Kanai Lal's model was sounding a little light and the kharaj (the last bass string), though good, was no longer at the standard I wanted. It was in 1961 that Nodu presented his new creation to me at my new Malabar Hill apartment. He actually made two of them at the same time, the other one being for Amiyo Das Gupta, a senior disciple of mine who was with me in Delhi and then Bombay. These two instruments were almost identical, but every sitar is nevertheless unique. Nodu told me to choose whichever one I wanted, and after playing mine for a few months Amiyo and I exchanged because I preferred the sound of the one given to him. That sitar is still my master sitar today, with which I perform most of my concerts.

The style of jawari Nodu made had great characteristics: it gave a bold sound, and my bass strings were like thunder. But, as Nodu would explain it to me, 'You can't have it both ways. If you have this sound – which is *your* sound – you have to sacrifice something.' And the deficiency with this sitar was that it restricted me in the meend, that is, pulling the strings sideways to merge from one note to the other. For instance, pulling from the tonic (Sa) I couldn't raise the pitch beyond about four and a half notes. On most other sitars you can pull five or five and a half notes higher. So I had to restrict many of my meend phrases, which were a special element in my performances.

Nodu did not make many sitars because he did everything single-handedly, from the main work to the ornamentation, never using an assistant, and always making them from only one piece of wood. He made two more sitars for me over the years, and a surbahar as well. One of the sitars he gave me didn't really sound that great, and when I told him so he got very angry and took it back – he nearly broke it himself! But the other one did sound good and I kept it. After many years it was skilfully repaired and I then gave it to my daughter Anoushka. Two more of Nodu's sitars were handed on to me by students of mine, including Amiyo's one which I was given after he died. So I now have four of his sitars. They are very valuable to me.

All Nodu's passion was directed into working on sitars and conducting research on the sound. He never married, and never seemed to have any interest in sex. I used to tease him about it, addressing him sometimes as 'No Do'! In some places I even introduced him as my father-in-law, and people were shocked until I explained the logic: I treated my sitar as my wife, while Nodu felt that the sitars he made were almost his children!

He was temperamental and could be very obstinate, so we had a tough little time occasionally! But he was really a wonderful person, and a great friend. He toured with me continuously up until the early Eighties, travelling as my tanpura-player and looking after my sitar. I was extremely fond of him; he died some years ago, and I miss him very much.

I hadn't had much contact with Dada since his centre had closed. A few months after my marriage in Almora in 1941, he had also got married there, to Amala. We had first met her in 1931-32 when she was an attractive young dancer in Paris. She is a year older than me, and we had become good friends back then – I developed a childhood crush on her. Later she had joined the troupe in Almora when the centre opened, and it was Dada who fell in love with her seriously then.

Over the years Dada and I only met by accident when I visited Calcutta, or Madras for a few days, and it was not until 1961 that we worked together again. By that time he had mellowed somewhat. He had some problems with his heart and other health troubles that had gradually slowed him down, from that level of super-superstardom when he was treated like a god or a king. He still had the troupe, and continued to tour America up until 1968, but it was not quite the same. He had settled down in Calcutta with Amala, their son Ananda and daughter Mamata, and was not doing so much creative work. Dada seemed frustrated throughout the Sixties and Seventies; as he had always been a superstar and a creative person with a turbulent personality, this tame life of being mainly a family man didn't quite fulfil him.

Whenever I went to Calcutta I would suggest that we do something new together; and eventually, after much persuasion, he agreed to do a ballet with my music. I poured my heart into it, and it was a wonderful experience. The production was staged to celebrate the centenary of Tagore's birth (1861), so Dada and Amala chose to make a ballet called *Samanya Kshati*, based on one of Tagore's poems, a simple story of a beautiful but spoilt and haughty young queen, played by Amala-Boudi. It depicts how she takes a bath in the river in wintertime and comes out feeling chilly. She tells her companions she needs some warmth, and insists they dismantle the poor people's huts nearby to make a big bonfire. Her husband, the Maharajah, is enraged and banishes her from the kingdom for one year. In exile she suffers greatly, for she has never before seen what it means to be poor and without any money or position. A wise yogi whom she meets helps her to learn humility, and then after a year spent working for the poor people she returns chastened and the Maharajah takes her back.

'Samanya kshati' means 'a little harm' – that's how she dismisses her decision to burn all the huts simply to warm herself. The Rajah says, 'Do you know what you have done? You have burnt these people's homes?' But she replies, 'What's the big deal? It is only a samanya kshati!' – just a little harm. 'Build them new houses!' she exclaims, in a manner reminiscent of Marie Antoinette's 'Let them eat cake!' when she heard that Paris's poor masses had no bread to eat. This is what particularly angers the Rajah and incites him to banish her.

Lakshmi was again featured as a singer, and she assisted me also, along with the flautist Aloke Dey. The Kathakali dancer Raghavan, an assistant of Dada's, did a great job helping with the choreography. The musical emphasis was on voices and Indian instruments for the production. It was one of my works where I felt most inspired, trying major innovations with the melodies and with the effects music as well – for example, making the voices mimic instruments.

An ingenious reversal of roles – since all Indian instrumental music is based on the imitation of the early vocal music, from the Vedic chants onwards. This was a historical connection which Ravi had of course explored previously in Melody and Rhythm.

Dada and I planned to undertake more projects together. I wrote some music for his shadowplay, *Life of Buddha*, but unfortunately it was never staged with my music, and we never did work side by side again.

At dress-rehearsal time for *Samanya Kshati*, we had been paid a visit by George, Lord Harewood, who at the time was the Chairman of the British Council's Music Advisory Committee. He and Marion, his lovely first wife, were visiting Calcutta, and they saw a special rehearsal we put on in a film studio floor. He was moved by it. 'You must bring it to the West,' he told me, but unfortunately it was too big a group and therefore financially not feasible.

Sisters who have been central figures in Ravi's life: Lakshmi Shankar, his sister-in-law, and her sister Kamala Chakravarty, who was for many years Ravi's partner.

I had first met George and Marion in London, when I visited their Orme Square home several times, even performing for a small exclusive gathering there once. He is the first cousin of the Queen but nevertheless such a down-to-earth and charming person, and highly respected by musicians for his knowledge of their field. Marion was a wonderful pianist and the main force in organising the festivals at Aldeburgh. Through them I met and became friends with the great composer Benjamin Britten, such a sweet person, and his friend Peter Pears, who had an angelic voice which touched the heart immediately.

In 1963 I appeared at the Edinburgh Festival, of which George Harewood was the artistic director. There I met Julian Bream, Larry Adler and many other notable musicians. At a dinner Isaac Stern kept us all in stitches with his funny stories. Larry Adler was hilarious, too; he twisted our names around so that Ali Akbar became Ali Snackbar, Alla Rakha was Al Rocker and I turned into Rabbi Shanker!

On a later occasion I was a guest at George's ancestral mansion, Harewood House. By then he was divorced from Marion and married to Patricia, whom I found warm and full of humour. The Harewood mansion was more like a palace, actually. The ground floor resembled a museum, with its ancestral

Arriving home to an overwhelming welcome from a trip to the West.

tape&tries, ornaments, furniture and other fabulous family heirlooms. Staying there was a delightful two-day experience. The bed in my gorgeous room was supposed to have been slept in a few times by Queen Victoria. I don't know how the great queen managed it, but I had enormous difficulty getting up on that high bed! I was also kept awake all night with an eerie feeling that ancient spirits clothed in period dresses were lurking in the shadows.

I came to America again in late 1961 for a coa&t-to-coa&t tour, sponsored once again by the Asia Society Performing Arts Program, bringing Kanai Dutt, a superb tabla-player from Calcutta. (After this tour Alla Rakha and I began our close association. The fir&t times I had brought him on tour were for the Japanese trip and the UNESCO recital in 1958, and after 1962 he became my regular accompani&t abroad right up to 1985.) Dear Nodu Mullick was also with us.

This 1961-62 tour was even longer and larger than before, and included my fir&t programme at Carnegie Hall. My music was increasingly reaching beyond the confines of the jazz scene, and attra&ting an audience with varied musical ta&tes. Yet although the audience for me was getting bigger each time, &till very few other Indian musicians were coming to the We&t.

Alubhai did teach at McGill University for some time, and later he came to San Francisco, invited by Sam Scripps and his wife Louise, who had &tarted an in&titution featuring Balinese and other Asian music, where the great Bharata Natyam dancer Bala Saraswati also taught. Alubhai became e&tablished and since then he has remained in the Bay Area, where he has been successfully running his own Ali Akbar College of Music.

Unlike him, I didn't join any particular teaching e&tablishment, although I was later persuaded to open the Kinnara School of Music in Bombay and Los Angeles (as I will discuss shortly). In early 1965 I ran some short workshops in the University of California at Los Angeles (UCLA), and in the fall seme&ter of 1967 I was Visiting Professor at City College, New York; but apart from these positions the way I chose to educate the public outside India about our music was through touring, giving concerts and demon&trations, appearing on TV and radio talk shows, providing plenty of interviews for newspapers and magazines – and ultimately, in 1968, writing the book *My Music, My Life*.

It was at this time that I was fir&t drawn into fighting again&t the &tudy of Indian music being subsumed under the heading of 'Ethnomusicology', along with the music of many other parts of the world. To us, Indian music is the only original classical music apart from its We&tern counterpart. It is over 2,000 years old, with an unbroken hi&tory of development, and above all it is a living tradition that is &till in the process of evolution. I even recall a music scholar from the South of India once proposing that, since Indian music is the older, it should be We&tern classical music which is categorised as 'Ethnic Music'! We&terners have always had this snobbish and patronising

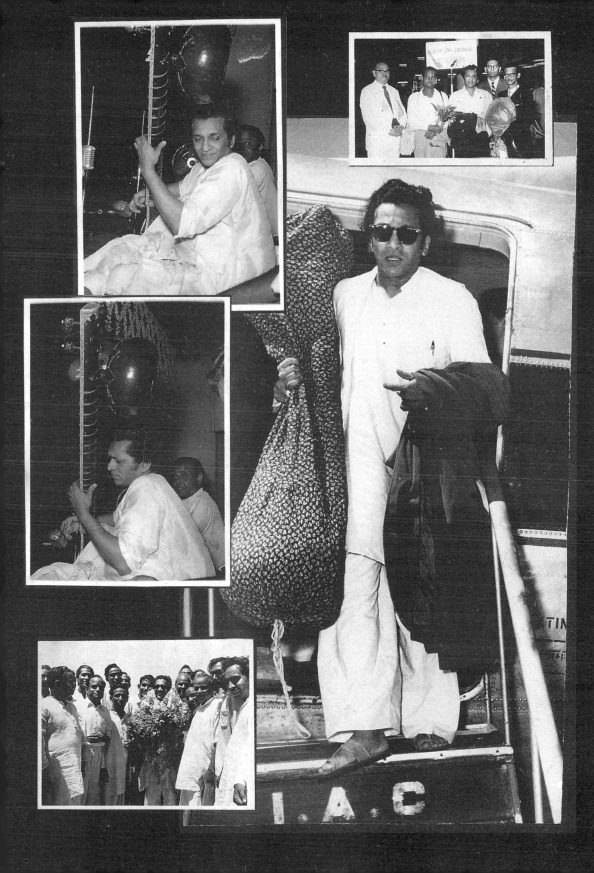

Snapshots from around the world in the early Sixties:

(top right) In recital in Bangalore with Kanai Dutt (tabla), Ravi's disciple Rama Rao (tanpura) and Ali Akbar Khan (sarod).

(right) With King Mahendra and the Queen of Nepal, 1960.

(below) With Alla Rakha at the start of their long collaboration.

(Below right) On the dancefloor, in the Philippines.

PRESENTED BY
AKHIL NEPAL KALA NIDHI
2ND OCT 1960

Snap Shot Studio

At the Edinburgh Festival, 1963, with (top left) Julian Bream and (left) Larry Adler.

(top right) With Martha Graham.

(above) Signing autographs after a show in Rome.

(below left) Edward Kennedy and Robert Kennedy Jnr in the audience at a recital in Calcutta.

(below) Imelda Marcos looks on.

attitude of segregating off Western classical music from every other, and classifying Indian classical music under the banner of Ethnic Music, together with all the non-Western styles, folk music, aboriginal music and traditional music – which may have ancient backgrounds but *not* living, developing and growing traditions. (Of course, China, Japan, Indonesia and some Middle Eastern countries are trying their best to keep their traditional music alive.) I am happy to see that – perhaps influenced by my little crusade! – most such music departments in the West have now changed their name to that of 'World Music'.

When I arrived on the West Coast in November 1961, Dick Bock had assembled several jazz musicians for an East-West recording: Dennis Budimir on guitar, Gary Peacock on bass, Louis Hayes on drums, and the famous jazz flautist Bud Shank. Although Kanai Dutt (tabla), Harihar Rao (dholak and kartal – an electrifying type of wooden percussion that sounds like Spanish castanets) and Nodu (tanpura and manjira) performed, I didn't play on the piece myself. I wrote the main melody theme, based on the scale of *Raga Dhani* (which resembles the blues scale), and conducted as each musician improvised. It was my first experience of collaborating with non-Indian musicians in the jazz style.

In Western American states such as California, there are brush fires on the hills in the summer. There had been a catastrophic one which had devastated large areas of Los Angeles a week or two before I arrived, and people were talking about it – so I called this particular piece *Fire Night*.

A second collaborative piece followed: on Improvisation on the Theme Music from Pather Panchali, *this time Ravi himself took the lead with an improvisation in three different rhythmic cycles on his own celebrated soundtrack. Bud Shank, on the Western flute, performed the part played in the film on the Indian bamboo flute, and the ensemble was completed by the other jazzmen, Kanai Dutt and some of Ravi's disciples – once again including his student Harihar Rao.*

Harihar had remained based in Delhi throughout the Fifties, continuing to learn from me, helping in all my musical activities, teaching at the music and dance school Triveni Kala Sangam, and accompanying me in the delegation to Japan. In 1961 he had won a Fulbright scholarship and moved to the States to study at UCLA. Though very talented he chose not to concentrate on sitar alone, instead distributing his ability between a range of spheres, taking in sitar, tabla, rhythmics, musicology and teaching. He taught some young jazz musicians, such as Tom Scott, Don Ellis and Emil Richards, and even formed an Indo-jazz combo with them.

We linked up again when I settled in Los Angeles in the late 1960s. Together we founded the Ravi Shankar Music Circle there in 1973. This was established on an unofficial basis at my Highland Avenue residence in Hollywood, before starting to hold formal programmes mostly in a chapel at Occidental College, where we featured visiting Indian musicians. To encourage attendance and membership, I gave a number of free recitals in the first couple of years. Today, under the stewardship of Harihar and his wife,

Paula, the Music Circle (as it is now more simply known) is still successfully staging regular programmes and annual festivals, featuring top artists from India.

I am so fond of Harihar, with his warmth and his sense of humour. He is one of the rare disciples who has not changed his colours or attitude through almost fifty years!

The Kinnara School, Bombay:

(right) Staff and students.

(below, left to right) Leading Hindustani violinist V. G. Jog, Kamala Chakravarty, Ravi, Penny Estabrook, Alla Rakha, Lakshmi Shankar and Ravi's flute disciple Vijay Raghava Rao – at the opening, 1962.

(opposite) The second production of Melody and Rhythm, *staged by Kinnara in Delhi, 1962.*

In July 1962 I opened Kinnara,[1] my own music institution in Bombay, first of all on the premises of Breach Candy school, then after a couple of months shifting down the same street (Warden Road) to the building known as Bhulabhai Desai Memorial Institute. This Institute was run by Soli Batliwala. In his younger days he had practised law and was a fiery communist; but subsequently he had joined the famous lawyer, politician and Congress leader Bhulabhai Desai, who had set up the Institute complex adjoining his residence. After the great man's death, Solibhai (as we called him) was given complete charge of running the Bhulabhai estate. The titular head was Bhulabhai's widow, the beautiful grand old dame Madhuri Desai, who was fabulously rich with a superlative private collection of old sculptures, paintings and artefacts; but Solibhai looked after everything.

1. The school was named after the Kinnaras who, like the Gandharvas, are mythological celestial musicians (mainly instrumentalists). They are known to be half human and half bird.

RAVI SHANKAR'S
MELODY & RHYTHM

PRESENTED BY KINNARA

IN ASSOCIATION WITH BHARAT SANGEET SABHA

MELODY & RHYTHM, as it has been named, is a concert first of its kind in this country which combines chorus and orchestra and having over 90 distinguished artistes as participants. In vocal it will include vedic hymns, dhrupad, dhamar, etc. and the instrumental music will consist of classical ragas, thematic orchestral compositions, folk music, percussion ensembles, etc. Apart from these, as an added attraction, the chorus will offer some delightful compositions from different parts of the world.

ABOUT KINNARA—The Kinnara School of Music was opened in July, 1962 in association with the Bharat Sangeet Sabha. It is the realisation of a long cherished dream of Ravi Shankar to start an institution of music where its multifarious branches could be more thoroughly studied and taught in a scientific way. "Melody & Rhythm" is the first elaborate production of KINNARA.

★   ★   ★

AT BIRLA THEATRE ON 17th & 24th NOVEMBER   AT 9 P.M.; 19th to 23rd NOVEMBER AT 7 P.M.

TICKETS: Rs. 100/-, Rs. 50/-, Rs. 25/-,   Rs. 15/-, Rs. 10/-, Rs. 5/- and Rs. 3/-

Solibhai was one of the most unusual and remarkable people I have ever come across. Like most Parsis, he was big-hearted and kind. Though not rich enough himself to be a philanthropist, he donated all his time and energy over almost forty years to helping hundreds of painters, sculptors, dancers and musicians, giving them space in which to work and create, or letting them take classes in the building, and many a time supporting them financially through the institution or even personally. I have always been indebted to him for his invaluable help. He allowed me to use the premises of the Institute not only to run the Kinnara classes, but also in 1964 to rehearse our second musical show *Nava Rasa Ranga*, for which he furthermore helped me to find a promoter. He also assisted me in presenting a series of lecture-demonstrations on Indian music for Kinnara.

My intention was to make Kinnara a very special place, concentrating on teaching sitar, sarod, flute, tabla and vocal music. Some of my advanced students such as Shamim Ahmed, Kartick Kumar, Shambu Das and Sachdev took instrumental music classes, while vocal music was taught by Tulsi Das Sharma. (Shamim, who belongs to Agra gharana, became my disciple when he was in his teens. His love and devotion towards me touches my heart.) Following many requests we also introduced dance classes, obtaining the excellent Kathak dance teacher Hazari Lal, an exponent of the Jaipur gharana who came with his dancer wife Sunayana, and for a short period Sumati Kaushal, a young Kuchipudi-style dancer. I was supervising everything, but could not take daily classes because most of the students were beginners, and moreover I was touring so much. Once in a while, though, I took a special class.

Amiyo Das Gupta was also teaching at Kinnara from the outset, and with me away so much I appointed him the senior teacher at the school. When in 1967 I opened a second branch of the Kinnara school in Los Angeles I put him in charge of running it, and when we closed that institution he joined the newly-founded California Institute of Arts, concentrating more on teaching, along with some composition work. In the latter he remained faithful to the style of my own Bombay productions like *Melody and Rhythm*. He died in 1994, and he is another whom I miss greatly. He had such dignity. He was the gentlest of men and a very patient teacher. Everyone who knew him admired and loved him.

As soon as the original Kinnara was opened I began putting together a revised production of *Melody and Rhythm* (which had previously been seen only in Delhi), and by November 1962 it was ready. We performed the same items as in the original show, and in the same way we covered the whole history of music, how it developed through the various voice styles from dhrupad onwards. It was, however, a much improved production, with a larger group and better musicians – ninety of them in all. Premièred at Bombay's Birla Theatre, it was a grand success.

After *Melody and Rhythm*, I composed the musical score for the Bombay stage show *Chandalika*. This was a major production put on by the South Indian actress Vyjayanthimala, who was then the top movie star of India. She was beautiful, a mesmeric dancer blessed with a gorgeous figure. This was the period when she wanted to come off the screen and return to performing more classical Bharata Natyam on stage, so she choreographed and took the lead role in this production.

Chandalika was a ballet based on the geet-natya (song-drama) of Rabindranath Tagore. Originally it was a Jataka story (from the Buddhist period), concerning an untouchable girl who becomes blessed by Ananda, one of Buddha's main disciples. The story is enchanting, but we decided not to use any of Tagore's original songs. Tagore's version is often performed, and I thought of presenting it differently. It would also not have been possible to do justice to his songs with the style that we were employing, so we took only the storyline from his play.

There were new ideas for me to try out. Since forming Vadya Vrinda I had been using certain basic Western instruments, including the violin family (violin, viola, cello, double bass) and the clarinet, because they added more body, more bass and a wider octave range to the orchestration. Our Indian instruments are more or less like Indian people: we are very individual, and seldom agree with each other! Similarly our instruments are meant mainly for solo purposes, and because we use a lot of resonating sympathetic strings, which give an extra buzzing sound, it is not ideal to play them together. I have tried; I have done work with eight or ten sitars, sarangis or sarods, but always this problem occurs, especially when a recording is made. It is the same with the playing: no matter how well the musicians play, all of them have a different approach, touch and sound production. The basic sound is not uniform and regimented as it is with Western instruments like the violin. Therefore in *Chandalika* I again incorporated a few Western instruments along with the Indian ones.

The music had influences from different parts of India. Apart from our own Hindustani forms, I added a little from the Carnatic system, some folk melodies, and some special effects where the character Chandalika is performing a Puja (worship) of the snake god Naga Devata.

Ravi kept up a furious pace of work during this period. In 1963 he returned to Europe to perform at three major music festivals – Leeds, Prague and Edinburgh. That the profile of Indian music was gradually rising in the West was apparent at Edinburgh, where there was a special focus on the subcontinent that year. Ravi's artistry met with critical and popular acclaim, as did that of Bismillah Khan, M.S. Subbulakshmi, and Ali Akbar Khan. Offstage, Ravi built up a friendship with the folk-singer Rory McEwan, who was also appearing at the festival that year in tandem with his brother Alexander.

Following this European trip, and before his fourth solo tour of America in late 1964, he returned his attention to India. His passion for creating elaborate productions for the stage was by no means satiated, not even by Samanya Kshati, Chandalika *and a double dose of* Melody and Rhythm.

(top middle) Ravi's niece Manju, daughter of Debendra.

(bottom left) With Debendra, Harihar Rao, Amiyo Das Gupta, Chatur Lal, three other students and Rana, Ravi's golden cocker spaniel.

(bottom right) Ravi and Alla Rakha being seen off at Bombay Airport for a foreign trip. Among the well-wishers are Lakshmi Shankar (to left of Ravi), her daughter Viji (in front of her mother) and the young Zakir Hussain (in front of Ravi).

The other three shots portray Ravi, Shubho and Rana in various combinations.

In 1964 I wanted to do an even bigger production, so we assembled a larger group, and called it *Nava Rasa Ranga* (which translates as something like 'Entertainment Through the Nine Moods'). It was a completely new production with original compositions, but it followed essentially the same format as *Melody and Rhythm* in that it progressed through all the musical forms from history, with the difference that we started from further back this time. Opening the main show were the spoken words, 'In the beginning was sound...' and then we commenced with man's earliest experiences of sounds: birdsong, the chirping of crickets, the clapping of hands, the stamping of feet, the first blowing of a reed to produce pitch, and the tones of the voice; this gradually developed into Vedic chants, the Jati Gana and Chhandra Prabhanda in Sanskrit, followed by num-tum, alapana, dhrupad, dhamar, khyal, tappa and thumri, plus orchestral pieces and modern songs.

The production was put on a few months after Pandit Nehru had died, so before the first item we paid homage to him. A beautiful painting of a rose was placed on a chair in the centre of the stage to symbolise Nehru, who always wore a fresh rose in the buttonhole of his tunic, and a short instrumental hymn-like piece (which I had composed in *Raga Hem Kalyan*) was performed. The audience appeared very moved by the tribute.

Nava Rasa Ranga contained a variety of items, including dance, magic, and a puppet show featuring Madhav Lal Masters, the finest puppeteer in Bombay. Many little features were introduced that were exceptionally uncommon. For one section we made it look as if the characters on stage were flying. Against the backdrop of a black curtain on a darkened stage, we erected a platform (also draped in black) for the dancers (dressed in light colours) to run up and over. With their platform invisible to the audience, they appeared to be

The Hindu
14 October,
Madras

RAVI SHANKAR'S PERFORMANCE

AMERICAN CRITICS ENTHRALLED

NEW YORK, Oct. 12.
New York's music critics to-day
hailed the performance of Ravi
Shankar and Alla Rakha who on
Saturday last drew a packed audience at the start of a coast-to-coast
tour through 48 cities.

Robert Shelton of the *New York
Times* said : "At the hands of Shankar, the sitar, a 700-year-old member of the lute family, created a
whole new aural landscape. There
were cascading runs of great dexterity, overtones co-mingling like
strands of hair and tufts of weight-
less curling resonances."

"It was evocative of a musical
mystique, rich in religious and phi-
losophic traditions, symbol and
meaning. Even if not all that meaning is accessible to the Westerner,
the gossamer tapestries Shankar
weaves galvanise the attention."

On the accompanist Alla Rakha,
he wrote: "At his magically gifted
hands the drums were melodic. He
helped Shankar provide an almost
hypnotically engrosing evening".

GREATEST MUSICIANS

Alan Rich of the *New York
Herald Tribune* called Ravi Shankar and Alla Rakha as "the greatest musicians of any sort of music
in the world to-day".

Writing under a three-column
heading "Enchanting, exciting Indian classical music". Rich noted
common points and differences between Western and Indian music
and said that while in its improvisations Indian music might resem-
ble Western baroque style, virtuosity of improvisation reminded one
more of Beethoven and Paganini.

"But beyond these intellectual
considerations there is the timeless
and international consideration of
creativity at its purest which can
relate any listener, however, casual,
to excitement of the event. The
emotional outburst at the end of
Saturday night's concert, which
swept the cheering capacity Town
Hall audience to its feet, almost
with a single impulse, was hardly a
response to something distant or
esoteric. It was rather a response
to the display of stupendous virtuosity plus magnetism in complete
exuberant and inventive interlock-
ing of the performers techniques;
it was a reaction, in other words,
to the kind of giddy, dizzying,
breathtaking kind of idealised
chamber music".—PTI.

soaring through the air. A simple technique in magic shows, but it was so effective!

After the interval there was a comic item, one of my favourites, with the spotlight turning on a small booth for the puppet show. It was a story of mine about another haughty princess, this time called Madhu Goolgooli. ('Madhu' means 'honey' – and can also be the name of a person – while 'Goolgooli' is a term of affection, which we call little cuddly dolls, for instance.) She had big eyelashes and could have been a cross between Betty Boop and Miss Piggy!

Madhu Goolgooli's father, the Maharajah, wants her to get married, so they have what is known as a swayamvara (literally 'self-choice of a mate'), where a group of princes arrive in hope of being selected by her; she is supposed to place a garland around the neck of her chosen one. But Madhu does not like any of them, and discards them all. Then one day while hunting she gets lost in the forest and a woodcutter saves her. Instead of being grateful to him, she behaves as if it had been his duty, and treats him like a servant. A proud man, the woodcutter will not tolerate her behaviour, returning her rudeness with interest. She is shocked, since nobody has ever stood up to her before – but for the same reason also finds him attractive. Her father is so happy at her safe return that he offers the woodcutter whatever he wants; but he declines everything, which further impresses the Maharajah. Meanwhile the princess tells her father, 'I am in love with this woodcutter – I want to marry him!' At first the woodcutter refuses: 'She is too haughty, too proud,' but then she falls at his feet. Seeing how she surrenders her pride, the woodcutter agrees to marry her, and the show ends in their happy celebration.

There was another unusual feature in this piece. In those days one of the best tape-recording machines was the English Ferrograph. The dialogue was recorded in advance at a blind school, which had a little studio with two Dolby Ferrographs. Since I owned an identical machine, I knew that it could do double-speed recording. Although I had little experience of using double speed, I tried it out instinctively for the story, recording the three main characters' voices myself in three different pitches. I even spoke Madhu Goolgooli's lines and sang her thumri song myself at a very slow speed, and then played them back in double speed. It sounded so funny! One hears this technique in cartoons but it was not common then, especially in live performances. Quite an experiment for me! Each character was recorded in a different voice, in a dramatic style similar to that of old Hindi stage dramas. It was so rewarding to see the audience enjoy it so much; they roared with laughter.

The whole conception of the show was mind-boggling! Even when I think of it now, I can't believe it. There was such a range of items, never matched by anyone else in India, even today. Yet although it received some sensational reviews, and people who saw it were extremely impressed, it did not become a box-office hit. Ironically this was mainly because we could only afford to mount five or six shows. By the time it was catching on with the public we did not have enough money left to continue this gigantic production.

Throughout his career, it seems that almost everything Ravi has created, whether compositions, stage productions or film scores, has been done before its time. Rarely were his creative works fully comprehended by the Indian general public at the time they were unveiled, for many of the conceptions involved were too advanced. Critics recognised the extent of his originality, but it took another ten or twenty years for such innovations to become widely accepted, by which time there were other artists doing exactly the same things and gaining credit for them. Many of Ravi's older pieces and productions are more appreciated in India today than they were at the time of their creation.

Assisting me for *Nava Rasa Ranga* was Dr Penelope Estabrook. I had first met Penny in 1960 when I visited Sri Lanka, one of my favourite countries. It has a wide variety of scenic beauty, and the people are generally so likable – live-and-let-live, happy-go-lucky types, fond of music and the arts. It reminded me of our own South Indian state Kerala. Lionel Edirisinghe, the late principal of the music college in Colombo, was a friend of mine who did much for the teaching and popularising of Indian classical music there.

Penny and I had met just when I was leaving for India. She was a good piano-player, with a doctorate in Western music and well trained in ballet and tap-dancing. Though mainly a theoretician and a mere beginner on sitar, she was very interested in Indian music and was undertaking a short training course with Lionel. I told her that if she wanted to pursue sitar she would be welcome to come to Bombay. Within a year I met her again in Delhi, and we became close to each other. At the time my plans for the Kinnara music school and some other projects were taking shape, and I asked her if she could help me. She came to Bombay and was closely involved in opening the school, while Kamala took care of the administrative side. The two of them became great friends, and remain so today. Penny and I published a booklet together, *Music Memory*, which contained musical information for students,

(top) On the long American tour of 1964-65.

(above) With the folk singer-songwriter Pete Seeger, his manager and Nodu Mullick.

175

half on Indian music and half on Western. She also gave worthy assistance on several other ventures: the second production of *Melody and Rhythm*, a monumental series of lecture-demonstrations that I gave on the history and development of our music (Amiyo Das Gupta helped me with the graphics), and this mammoth production of *Nava Rasa Ranga*. She then toured the USA along with Alla Rakha, Nodu Mullick and me in 1964-65.

Our close and meaningful relationship lasted for four or five years, even while Kamala was there prominently too. What I appreciate most in Penny is that, although we drifted apart long ago, she is still such a good friend, full of warmth, still ready to learn, and always ready to offer help whenever needed. She is also friendly with Sukanya, and loves Anoushka, whom she helped with her early piano lessons.

In the West, Ravi's progress was unfaltering. In 1965 he was elected to the American Society of Composers, Authors and Publishers. As his reputation and popularity gradually rose, he nevertheless continued to diversify, venturing into new areas. Many and varied were the fields of Western music that fell under the spell of his artistry.

His desire to experiment seriously in new and different musical spheres is probably the most controversial aspect of his career. By following his curiosity in this way, he has laid himself open to accusations that he is cheapening his own music, polluting it with the influences of the West. It is a measure of the purity and sacredness of Indian music that feelings run so strong, but, as he will say himself, there have always been two distinct sides to him: the performer, maintaining as a classical sitar-player the great tradition handed on to him by his guru; and the composer, the innovator of world music, experimenting with music and dance styles from all over the world. Although he has demonstrated that the two roles are compatible, it has been hard to satisfy both camps at once, especially given the rigidly exclusive attitude of many of his Indian music contemporaries. The ensuing controversy has dogged his entire career, but not dissuaded him from the path he has chosen.

Dick Bock had often spoken to me about John Coltrane over the previous few years: about how he was fascinated by India, had become a fan of mine, and had all my records. At some point during the winter of 1964-65, when I was back in America giving something like forty-two recitals on another coast-to-coast tour (once again with the support of the Asia Society), Dick brought him to meet me in New York.

Coltrane's approach was different from that of most jazz musicians I had

seen or met over the years. To hear good jazz, I mostly had to go to jazz joints in the big cities like New York, San Francisco and Los Angeles. At these venues, even as all these brilliant musicians were playing, people would be drinking, smoking, eating and talking. Once in a while when a musician played an exciting solo the audience turned their attention to him and showed their appreciation by clapping with real gusto. But the venues used to be so thick with smoke (almost like the London fog of the old days) that my eyes burned and watered and I couldn't breathe. In spite of some of the most dazzling music that one could hear, the atmosphere was disturbing.

When John Coltrane came to me, he looked different from his contemporaries: so clean, well-mannered and humble. About six months earlier he had apparently given up drugs and drink, become a vegetarian and taken to reading Ramakrishna's books. For a jazz musician to go the other extreme, especially in those days, was a pleasant surprise. He was intrigued by Indian music and asked me all about it. As a jazz artist, he was amazed by our different system of improvisation within the framework and discipline of fixed melody forms, by the complexity of our talas, and more than anything by how we can create such peace, tranquillity and spirituality in our music.

We met a few times and I taught him the basics about ragas and talas. He never sat with an instrument, but I would demonstrate with my voice and sitar while he wrote down a few notes and asked me questions. We had three or four sessions, at the end of which he said he was waiting for a chance to come and spend six months with me studying. We met again the next time I came to New York, for a short tour in 1966, when we fixed a date the following year for him to come to LA for a few weeks to learn properly from me. Sadly he died before then.

Coltrane's regard for his Indian music tutor was evident: he named his own son Ravi.

After the American tour, and another long trip to play concerts in Australia and New Zealand in early 1965, the next stop was Paris. There I contributed the music for the cult film *Chappaqua*, made by the director Conrad Rooks. Conrad based the story on his own life and took the lead role himself. It also starred the hippy gurus William Burroughs and Allen Ginsberg. I had first met Conrad in New York, and found him to be a most unusual person. He had earlier been into drugs and had come out of it by drying out in a clinic in Zürich; his character in *Chappaqua* goes through the same experience. Indeed, to me, Conrad seemed like he *had* just stepped out of a Hollywood film: handsome, suave, quick-witted and amusing, as well as temperamental. We became friends and roamed about in Greenwich Village and its jazz haunts.

In Paris he had a fabulous apartment and a striking white convertible Thunderbird with a loud musical horn. He actually behaved like a film star there. We had plenty of fun in the Paris nightlife – champagne and caviar at the Ritz and so on. He had a gorgeous black girlfriend and I had a lovely French companion. One day Conrad was driving us at high speed down the Avenue des Champs Elysées from Etoile in his Thunderbird. Soon we heard blaring sirens, and two police cars stopped us. The police officer was fuming at our going so fast over the speed limit, and the two girls and I were quite scared – but Conrad was not fazed. Exuding confidence and innocence, he pretended not to understand French. From underneath his ten-gallon hat, there came a loud and fast Texan drawl: 'Look here, aahfisser! Ah didn't know the speed limit and ah was drivin' like we do back home. Ah'm sorry!' Whether the policeman understood any of it was anyone's guess, but with the traffic piling up behind and passers-by crowding round he gave up, said, 'Alors, allez-y! Faites attention la prochaine fois,' and signalled for us to go.

Conrad originally planned to ask Ornette Coleman to take care of the music, but changed his mind and offered it to me. It was a bizarre film with many sequences of hallucination and fantasies about India, meditation and spirituality. Though I found it a slightly disturbing subject to provide music for, it was nevertheless a challenge that I relished. For the recording, which was held in a Paris studio, I used Alla Rakha and six or seven local musicians. That was where I met Philip Glass for the first time.

Philip had graduated from the Juilliard School in New York and, like many talented American musicians, had come to Paris to acquire some advanced training from the high priestess of music, Nadia Boulanger. Meanwhile he was earning some extra money as a session artist, and had obtained work as one of the musicians on *Chappaqua*. We clicked from the moment we met. He was so interested in Indian music. Within the several days that we worked together, apart from helping me to transcribe my compositions into Western notation and conducting the other musicians, he spent many hours asking me all about ragas, talas and the way we improvise. He was fascinated with our advanced mathematical system of rhythms.

In 1967, back in New York, I arranged for him to have a few tabla classes with Alla Rakha. I lost track of Philip completely for a few years, but sometime in the Seventies his name came to my attention again, for his Minimalist music system was becoming well known. I was pleasantly surprised to read of his mentioning that meeting me in Paris had influenced him and changed his musical thinking.

PHILIP GLASS: *When I met Ravi it was my first contact with the classical music of a culture other than my own: the traditional classical music of India. In 1965 Indian music still had a very esoteric feel. It was a taste that was not shared by many people; and when I went to work with him, I didn't know a thing about it. There were several things that were very impressive at that first meeting.*

What most impressed me was to meet a man who was a composer and a performer, who brought these activities together in one person. Up till then, though historically there have been lots of composer-performers – we can go back to Mozart, Beethoven, Liszt, Chopin, Rachmaninov, Bartok – in recent years that has not been true in contemporary Western music. We were not encouraged as young composers to develop ourselves as performers. And when I met Ravi, I saw that this separation didn't exist at all. It was unimaginable for him not to be a performer of music, though of course he was writing, and has done sitar concertos and other things since then, and has emerged in more recent years as a composer apart from his playing. But at that time he really appeared as the composer-performer.

The second thing was the actual way Indian music is organised. Briefly, in the West we talk about melody, harmony and rhythm as being the three elements of music. In Western music, melody and harmony take the dominant role in terms of creating the structure of the music, with the rhythm being more of a decorative element. But in Eastern music, and in non-Western music generally, the harmonic function is almost not there at all, and is sometimes completely absent. The rhythmic and melodic functions operate in tandem to determine the overall structure – and this was a very important theoretical and practical idea.

Being a young composer, I was looking for a new way of organising my music. I wasn't happy with what was then considered contemporary music, which was Boulez and Stockhausen and Elliott Carter – very good composers, but it was music of another generation from mine. In conjunction with some other experiences I was having in the theatre, this contact with Indian music pushed me towards a whole new way of thinking about music, in which the rhythmic structure became the controlling function and I reduced a lot of the harmonic to almost nothing (although the melodic material was also much reduced). This was the beginning of what a few critics called Minimal music. The word stuck around long after anyone was writing that kind of music any more, but in the music I wrote in the late Sixties and early Seventies the rhythmic structure was really what was carrying the piece – and I got that from Ravi.

The third thing that was so impressive about Ravi was him as a person: an extremely warm, kind person, but not only that – someone who was genuinely interested in young people and young composers. We talked for hours and hours about contemporary music, about modern music, about his music. He was curious about everything – and still is. He was very open: he encouraged me to keep in touch with him, and when, a few years later, he and Alla Rakha were teaching for a short time at City College, New York, I did get in touch again.

Before he met George Harrison in 1966 and knocked the popular music world into an Indian orbit, Ravi had already been embraced by an early incarnation of the hippy movement in the folk-music boom of the early-to-mid-Sixties, one of the leading lights of which was Rory McEwan, whom Ravi had known since the 1963 Edinburgh Festival. Rory lent him a cottage on Cathcart Road in London's West Brompton district, which was Ravi's base for a short while.

Rory belonged to an important family from Scotland, his father being a baronet. Along with his handsome brother Alexander, he took up singing beautiful old English folk ballads with guitars. They became well known in the period of the new folk-song movement. Rory was a very good friend of mine, and I played maybe twice at his house in London, enjoying it enormously. He and his lovely wife Romana would invite about fifty or sixty serious Indian-music lovers, and it was a rewarding atmosphere. He also introduced me to an attractive young American folk-singer, Caroline Hester, for whom I arranged and wrote some lyrics to a Bengali boatman's song, 'Majhi Ré', which she recorded for one of her albums.

Along with the craze of rock music, with The Beatles and The Rolling Stones, these folk and folk-rock groups were also becoming popular. In late 1965 and early 1966, a new folk movement was springing up in the clubs all over Britain. Basil Douglas (then and for many years my manager in Britain) booked me into a few such venues. I was not very happy, because that was the first time I had been introduced to the hippies. These clubs were full of peculiarly dressed people, flamboyant in their Renaissance or Louis XIV-style clothes, the men in their long hair and beards, with beads around their necks, and the women wearing long old ornamental dresses.

Then there was the marijuana and hash, and so much smoke, along with the sweet odour of patchouli incense to hide the smell. I had to stop playing, and insisted that Basil Douglas ensure there was absolutely no smoking during my performances. That was the birth of my campaign against drugs. The hippies listened attentively, but they were mostly stoned. I couldn't tell how much they were into LSD or harder drugs, but the hash and marijuana was more obvious. It was my first experience of seeing these strange young weirdos!

It was not that I did not understand these hippies. Back in the early Sixties, I had met a few of the beatniks in San Francisco and LA. Those beatniks were mostly artists: leading poets, painters and writers, mostly aged above forty – mature people who had already achieved something and reached somewhere, so in spite of the drugs I admired them. I had discovered more about the whole scene then, and learnt how people like Aldous Huxley were experimenting with drugs. Going back even further, I remember the grandfathers of the hippies in Europe, who were present in Paris in the early 1930s – the Bohemians. Like the beatniks, they too were mature achievers, mostly well-known painters, writers, actors and choreographers. Hashish and cocaine seemed to be their main stimulation. In the forefront was Gurdjieff. Originally a dancer, he had popularised the mystic cult of Dadaism. Rudolf Steiner had been the guru among these people, and I had read some of his books and found them interesting.

Nor was it the case that I had never tried any drugs. I had experienced bhang (cannabis) a few times in India, mixed into a tasty drink of milk, almonds, rose petals, sunflower seeds and other ingredients. It scared me, though, and I always tried to take very little. Usually it just makes one laugh a lot, eat a lot and then sleep, but on one occasion someone mixed too much bhang into my drink and that gave me such a bad trip! I had terrible palpitations, and felt as if I had been thrown high in the air and fallen with a thud on the bed. My brain was on fire with frightening hallucinations, my

With Yehudi
Menuhin on various
occasions during the
Sixties, including
(second from top)
recording the first
West Meets East
album, and (third
from top)
performing at the
United Nations
Human Rights Day
celebration in
December 1967.

cheſt felt tight, my throat was parched and I wanted to drink gallons of water – I thought I was going to die! This experience filled me with a dread of ever trying any harder drugs. Some friends in New York once pressed me to take a few puffs of marijuana; but, as I don't smoke, I didn't inhale and felt nothing except a big headache!

The firſt time I heard of LSD was in 1965. Dick Bock, who had an experience once, wanted me to try it. He said, 'Ravi, it really expands the mind. You can do so much more with your imagination.' But it did not lure me, and I said I didn't need it. However, a lady he knew had produced a short film with Timothy Leary on the theme of a person who takes peyote mushrooms and has a hallucination, firſt enjoying very erotic sensations but later experiencing a bad trip. I met Leary and her, and when she and Dick asked me to provide the music for the film I agreed. It became popular on campus as it seemed to promote drugs. But I felt I was pushed into the projeƈt. It's something I never felt happy about and I've never been proud of having done. I have ſtrong feelings againſt hallucinogens.

For me, it is performing that generates a deep ecſtasy, physically, mentally and spiritually. Through years of sadhana, I have developed this built-in 'ſtimulator' or 'inspirator' which, once I have tuned my inſtrument and closed my eyes, immediately ſtarts working – shutting out the world, gradually giving me a sensation of great peace and power, together with either sadness or extreme joy. I have a real feeling of being high, sometimes 'higher', or even 'higheſt'! It may not happen each time to the same degree, but when everything works out well – the audience, the venue, the sound, my sitar behaving properly and my mind completely attuned to it – the raga comes alive and it performs some miracle in me. It's hard to explain; one can achieve a similar feeling at the height of meditation or sometimes when making love. I feel so near God when deeply involved in music.

I love to enjoy some champagne, wine or cognac occasionally, but I am not a regular drinker, and when occasionally I do indulge it is only after a recital, *never* before one – and I do not go beyond a limit. It is so disagreeable when people get drunk, sloppy, out of control, violent or obscene, and become a nuisance – as unfortunately many artiſts do, whether in India or Europe. A number of people whom I loved dearly have behaved abominably through drugs or drink, deſtroying our beautiful relationship, and some have died early because of them.

As well as a cross-over influence on Western jazz, film, folk and pop music, Ravi was still a classical musician at heart, and this was as apparent in his activities in the West as it had always been in India. To this day he has maintained his commitment to the performance of live Hindustani classical music with an endless round of recitals worldwide.

This dedication to his tradition was perhaps reflected in the flourishing of his partnership with the first Western classical musician he had met who seemed to understand the depths of Indian classical music. It was in 1966, even as Ravi began to set alight a myriad of other domains, that they played their first duet together.

Yehudi Menuhin and I had remained in contact over the years. We had met when I came to London on my own in 1956, although he was very busy. (He is one of the busiest artists, even today.) We would see each other briefly when we were in the same city, attend each other's concerts when we were free, and write or phone once in a while, and that was how we kept up our relationship.

I had once suggested to him that it might be interesting if we were to play a duet together, but it was not until 1966 that we did, at the Bath Festival, which he was directing – indeed he had founded it back in 1959. He asked the well-known German pianist and composer Peter Feuchtwanger to write a violin-sitar duet specially for the occasion. It was an interesting piece in which he had used the skeletal scale of the Indian *Raga Tilang*. But somehow, from the point of view of the sitar and Indian music in general, it seemed quite

strange to me – especially if I had to perform it. I told Yehudi this frankly, so he said, 'In which case, why don't you write a new piece?' I was hesitant, not wishing to hurt the piece's composer; but Yehudi was so enthusiastic that I agreed and did a completely new composition based on the same raga. This was transcribed into Western notation for Yehudi by John Barham, a brilliant young pianist who had studied with me for some time.

It featured a few cadenzas for Yehudi written in such a way that, although it was not a free-improvisation piece, it sounded as if it was. Our duet was warmly received at the festival.

YEHUDI MENUHIN: *My wife Diana and I went to India very often during the Fifties. So many of my colleagues had been thrown against mountains by airlines that we decided to travel only by train and boat until radar was installed in civilian planes. So we went twice to India by ship from Genoa and Venice – and it was delightful. On each occasion I saw Ravi, and came to know a little more of the Indian classical music.*

But it took me a long time before I could accept Ravi's invitation to play with him, because I felt that I was in no way worthy. At last there was the great moment in Bath, when I had finally said I would play with him. I was terrified, but we worked night and day, and

Diana brought food from an Indian restaurant for us while we worked. Whenever we stopped we ate or slept, but otherwise we continued for about a day and a half – and always with the incense burning. Finally I was able to play a few pieces with Ravi, and then we performed. I assure you I was never more nervous than that! It came off so well that we had to repeat it, the very same day – and then I was initiated.

EMI immediately wanted to record the duet, and in due course a revised form entitled Swara-Kakali *appeared on the Grammy-winning first album of the ground-breaking* West Meets East *trilogy. In a pattern that would be repeated on the second LP, this featured a solo by each principal artist as well as the duet pieces. This first volume also featured the haunting opening track* Prabhati, *based on the morning raga* Gunkali.

Yehudi had wanted me to write another short piece for him, and we named this *Prabhati*. I wrote it for Yehudi to play in pizzicato style. It has a Japanese flavour to it, as they use a similar scale to *Raga Gunkali*.

The *West Meets East* record was so popular that EMI urged us to do a second one. This was to feature a work based on *Raga Mishra Piloo*, which we also performed in the big hall at the United Nations in New York for the UN Human Rights Day on 10th December 1967, to celebrate the twentieth anniversary of the UN's Declaration of Human Rights. The concert was filmed and televised all over the world.

These collaborations with Yehudi were my first top-notch ones with a foreign artist. After this it seemed better for me to record only with classical musicians, and it convinced me that I should always be the composer. Moreover, whatever music we chose to play, whether based on ragas or folk tunes, it had to be Indian. I was reluctant to play anything like Bach or Handel because I doubted I could do justice to them. There are many technical difficulties involved, like playing different parts on separate strings at the same time, which is foreign to Indian classical music.

In 1976 we recorded a third record under the same title of *West Meets East*. By then I had met an outstanding flautist, Jean-Pierre Rampal. Earlier he had come to Los Angeles for a concert, and I had invited him to dinner. He is such a remarkable musician; I have heard other exceptional flautists, but he is my favourite. He was keen to play along with me or to perform one of my compositions, so I wrote two pieces for him. *The Enchanted Dawn* was a composition based on *Raga Todi* (a morning raga), scored for just him and a harp. Since there was no tabla player, I thought of shaping the piece so that it had a short alap and jor, and a gat; while the harp, played by the late Martine Géliot, was used at some points as if it were the drone of a tanpura and at other times, emphasising its percussive effects, like a tabla. This all sounded exhilarating, with the combination of different tans (brilliant fast passages) and the exchange between harp and flute.

The second piece, *Morning Love*, was a spontaneous composition for flute and sitar, accompanied by Alla Rakha on tabla, with Kamala playing the tanpura. I used the second note on my sitar, Re, as the Sa, so D sharp became the tonic. *Morning Love* was based on the Carnatic scale of *Nata Bhairavi*, but it was my own version composed in a light classical style, referring to other ragas and folk melodies using the Western modulation system. (Although modulation is not commonly practised in Indian music it does exist, enabling us to play different ragas by shifting the Sa to different notes. This is known as swara bheda.) Jean-Pierre played so beautifully, and I personally have a weakness for that piece: it is one of my favourites among the collaborations I have done. Since then he and I have played together two or three times in recitals in Paris and London, including the Royal Albert Hall concert on my 70th birthday, when Yehudi also performed.

For the other side of that third record, I composed two pieces for myself and Yehudi Menuhin, *Twilight Mood* (based on *Raga Puriya Kalyan*) and *Tenderness* (based on my own adaptation of *Nata Bhairav*). They too were very interesting as far as composition is concerned. Again there were a few places where I wrote a cadenza to sound like improvisation when performed, and by then Yehudi was more at home playing Indian music, too.

(opposite) Jean-Pierre Rampal.

(below) Yehudi Menuhin performs namaskar behind his back, one of his less publicised talents.

❧

Yehudi travels all the time, conducting more than performing nowadays but still giving ten to fifteen concerts a month, even now he has turned eighty! Thankfully he is highly organised and takes good care of himself, which includes practising hatha yoga. We still manage to meet regularly, and our musical connection continues to this day. I have performed three times with Yehudi at his famous summer festival in Gstaad, and we both played

TITLE &
DATE OF RECORDING

w/Y.MENUHIN - STUDIOS
EAST MEETS WEST
PRABHATI
RAGA: PURIYA KALYAN
SWARA: KATALI
Recorded: 24.4.67 25.4.67
3/4.7.66

w/RAKHA/CHAKRAVARTI
RAGAS
RAGA TILNAJ
RAGA LALIT
Job 1096-6H
Recorded: 24/25 April 1967

w/A.RAKHA/L.CHAKRAVARTI
RAGA: NATA BHAIRAV
RAGA: MISHRA PILOO
Job. 1095-6H

w/L.S.O./PREVIN
SHANKAR: Sitar Concerto
Job No.1055/71HS
Rec.29-31/5/71

(solo and together) at a special concert in Southwark Cathedral in London. I have also been to his renowned music school in Surrey to give a lecture-demonstration and a short recital. His love for Indian music is as strong as ever: in my 1993 show at London's Royal Albert Hall he was sitting in the front row, and was in tears when he met me afterwards, which touched me deeply.

One cannot think of Yehudi without his beloved Diana. She has a razor-sharp intelligence and an extensive knowledge of the arts, and is full of wit and humour. In March 1995 they invited Sukanya and me to their London residence for dinner, and Diana kept us both in stitches with her droll stories and mimicry. Yehudi also has a gift for fantastic writings and extempore speeches: they are like music itself.

In November 1995 he arranged a festival at the Cirque Royal in Brussels called 'From the Sitar to the Guitar', focusing on the art, culture, music and dance of the gypsies, tracing their history back to India and illustrating how they migrated from there through the Middle East to Europe: one group travelled north of the Mediterranean to Russia, the Balkan countries and beyond; while another group went through Morocco to Spain, where their art blossomed to become the great music and dance form flamenco. The proceeds of the two marvellous shows went to the International Yehudi Menuhin Foundation, which does valuable charity work promoting international understanding through the meeting of cultures via music.

I was co-hosting the event along with Yehudi, who spoke beautifully when presenting each item. After his introductory speech at the start of the show explaining the whole concept, I initiated the proceedings with my short sitar recital, improvising on two new raga patterns of mine, one on each of the two nights: *Raga Banjara* on the 24th and *Piloo Banjara* on the 25th. ('Banjara' is the name by which the nomads in India are known.) I was accompanied by the fantastic tabla virtuoso Kumar Bose, who had been my regular tablist everywhere I toured in the years 1985-91; Sukanya played the tanpura.

I had specially secured the participation of a Rajasthani music-and-dance group from India, and they continued the show: the Manganias and Langas, with their fabulous singers, instrumentalists playing drums, kartal and bowed instruments, as well as two fiery young girls dancing in the Kalbelia style. After twenty minutes of their thrilling short items, on came the nomadic gypsy performers: a cymbalum solo by Ludovit Kovac from Slovenia; three terrific Russian gypsies, the Trio Loyko, consisting of two violinists and a guitarist who all sang as well; followed by a group of Algerian musicians led by Abdelli the Kabyl. To conclude the main section there was the sensational Spanish dancer Blanca Del Rey and her flamenco group of three singers and three guitarists. Blanca's footwork is quite remarkable, and although in a different style it reminded me of Fred Astaire, Eleanor Powell and some of the great black American tap-dancers I heard and saw in my younger days.

Lastly there was a grand finale, which I conducted and organised with Blanca, her group, two of the Rajasthani singers, their dholak- and kartal-players, the Russian gypsies and Kumar Bose. I arranged a sawal-jawab ('question-answer') section of quickfire exchanges between Kumar's tabla, Gazikhan Barna's kartal and Blanca's Spanish-style tap-dancing. As a climax the whole flamenco troupe joined in. This finale brought the house down, and we were obliged to perform many encores!

Apart from my love, regard and friendship for Yehudi, I have a real admiration for him. He embodies the ideal Indian quality of vinaya, which broadly means humility, he is fascinated by all our intricate ragas, rhythmic structures and improvisations, and he openly talks everywhere about my teaching him, which is truly refreshing. Many musicians and conductors of Western music have a superiority complex, but not Yehudi. Nor, I must add, do my friends Zubin Mehta and Philip Glass.

Yehudi is not only a great musician but also a great human being; I have always felt so and said as much. He may appear frail now, but in spite of being at the age where most musicians slow down, he is as busy and productive as ever. He is unique in his humanity and his love for other musicians and types of music everywhere in the world — always curious, wanting to learn, trying to do something for the cause of other musicians. As well as the many honours and awards he has received from all over the world, in England he was first knighted and then in 1993 had the title Lord Menuhin bestowed upon him – indeed a great achievement for a classical musician, but one which he has fully deserved.

We now return our attention to 1966, the time when Ravi was first collaborating with Menuhin on an Indian piece. In the same month of the Bath Festival, June 1966, he had just met George Harrison and was about to unleash the phenomenon of Indian classical music – until recently utterly alien to most Western audiences – becoming the fashion among America and Europe's youth, one focus of the flowering creative mélange of the day.

SIX: KAMESHWARI

कामेश्वरी

I met George Harrison for the first time in June 1966, one evening in a friend's house in London. At that time, although I had heard of The Beatles, I knew only that they were an extremely popular group. Something clicked from the very beginning with George. The other three I met on different occasions through the years, and Ringo especially was always very warm and friendly, but I never really had anything much to do with any of them.

From the moment we met George was asking questions, and I felt he was genuinely interested in Indian music and religion. He appeared to be a sweet, straightforward young man. I said I had been told he had used the sitar, although I had not heard the song 'Norwegian Wood'. He seemed quite embarrassed, and it transpired that he had only had a few sittings with an Indian chap who was in London (a student of the late Motiram, my disciple in Delhi) to see how the instrument should be held and to learn the basics of playing. 'Norwegian Wood' was supposedly causing so much brouhaha, but when I eventually heard the song I thought it was a strange sound that had been produced on the sitar! As a result, though, young fans of The Beatles everywhere had become fascinated by the instrument.

Then George expressed his desire to learn the sitar from me. I told him that to play sitar is like learning Western classical music on the violin or the cello. It is not merely a matter of learning how to hold the instrument and play a few strokes and chords, after which (with sufficient talent) you can prosper on your own, as is common with the guitar in Western pop music. I told him this nicely, getting him to understand the seriousness of Indian music.

I said, 'I have given so many years of my life to sitar, and by God's grace I have become very well known – but still I know in my heart of hearts that I have a long way to go. There's no end to it. It is not only the technical mastery of the sitar – you have to learn the whole complex system of music properly and get deeply into it. Moreover it's not just fixed pieces that you play – there is improvisation. And those improvisations are not just letting yourself go, as in jazz – you have to adhere to the discipline of the ragas and

Letter from George Harrison to his parents, written while he was in Bombay for his extended stay with Ravi, September 1966.

189

the talas without any notation in front of you. Being an oral tradition, it takes many more years.

'And there is more to it than exciting the senses of the listeners with virtuosity and loud crash-bang effects. My goal has always been to take the audience along with me deep inside, as in meditation, to feel the sweet pain of trying to reach out for the supreme, to bring tears to the eyes, and to feel totally peaceful and cleansed.'

Then I asked him if he could give time and total energy to work hard on it. He said he would do his best, and we arranged a date then and there. It was not practical for him to come to my hotel, so he invited me to visit his house in Esher soon afterwards. I went twice within a week or so. Initially I gave him some basic instruction – how to hold the sitar properly, the correct fingering for both the hands, and some exercises. I also wrote down the names of all the notes in the sargam (Indian solfeggio) to make him familiar with them. That was all. We fixed it that he would come to India for a couple of months to learn in more depth.

I felt strongly that there was a beautiful soul in him, and recognised one quality which I always have valued enormously and which is considered the principal one in our culture – humility. Considering that he was so famous – part of the most popular group in the world ever! – he was nevertheless quite humble, with a childlike quality which he has retained to this day.

GEORGE HARRISON: *Ravi was very friendly and easy to communicate with. By this time The Beatles had met so many people – prime ministers, celebrities, royalty – but I got to a point where I thought, 'I'd like to meet somebody who could really impress me.' And that was when I met Ravi. He was the first person who impressed me in a way that was beyond just being a famous celebrity. Ravi was my link into the Vedic world. Ravi plugged me into the whole of reality. I mean, I met Elvis – Elvis impressed me when I was a kid, and impressed me when I met him because of the buzz of meeting Elvis – but you couldn't later on go round to him and say, 'Elvis, what's happening in the universe?'*

Ravi came to my house in Esher, and then he had arranged that we should sit in the afternoon for an hour or two, and he showed me how to get started on the sitar. After that he'd arranged for Alla Rakha to come, and they were going to give a little concert, so John and Ringo came, and they played for us for an hour and a half. It was really nice.

The moment we started, the feelings I got were of his patience, compassion and humility. The fact that he could do one of his five-hour concerts, but at the same time he could sit down and teach somebody from scratch the very basics: how to hold the sitar, how to sit in the correct position, how to wear the pick on your finger, how to begin playing. We did that and he started me going on the scales. And he enjoyed it – he wasn't grudging at all, and he wasn't flash about it either.

One thing he said was, 'Do you read music?' I said 'no', and my heart sank – I thought, 'I probably don't even deserve to waste his time.' But he said, 'Good – it will only confuse you anyway.'

Ravi and George in June 1966.

*(right and below)
together with Pattie
Harrison, Lakshmi,
Kamala and friends,
in Bombay,
September 1966.*

It was at that meeting that we arranged for me to go to India, at the next convenient break we both had, to start really learning – and also to enjoy India itself, to experience it. On the way back from The Beatles' tour in the Philippines in July I stopped in Delhi and bought a good sitar from Rikhi Ram, and it happened that I got a break after we finished our last tour of America, so I went back and stayed in Bombay, and had about a six-week trip in India.

After meeting George I found out about how popular he was as a Beatle, even without the other three. I also heard some of the group's records, and acquainted myself with what they stood for as artists. Many of their songs and melodies were beautiful. All my young nieces and nephews were gaga about The Beatles, and when they heard I had met them they were so excited! I knew about Frank Sinatra and Elvis Presley creating such a frenzied atmosphere wherever they sang – especially from the footage of girls shrieking before Elvis even started a song – and I was told there were the same situations, only much more crazy, with The Beatles.

When George and his first wife Pattie came to Bombay in September, they

came under the name of Mr and Mrs Sam Wells. George had also grown a moustache and cut his hair, and they passed unnoticed through Customs and Immigration. He was booked in a suite at the beautiful Taj Mahal Hotel; it was all kept quiet and nobody knew about it. I visited him in his hotel and he also came to my apartment on a couple of occasions. The training got under way. In ten minutes I could show him so much but he needed to practise, and for this reason I

THE MATERIAL WORLD CHARITABLE FOUNDATION

PRESENTS

RAVI SHANKAR'S
MUSIC FESTIVAL FROM INDIA

 PRODUCED BY GEORGE HARRISON

(previous page) The concert programme for Ravi's 1974 European tour, designed by Jan Steward.

(opposite top) In Vrindavan in 1974, by the banks of the Yamuna river, with George Harrison (behind, to left of Ravi), Sripad Maharaj (to left of Harrison), Kumar Shankar (behind, partly obscured to left of Sripad Baba) and others.

(opposite middle) The performers on the Music Festival From India album, assembled for the recording, 1974.

(opposite bottom left) Jean-Pierre Rampal and Ravi at the latter's Highland Avenue home in Los Angeles, around 1970.

(opposite bottom right) Philip Glass (front) in attendance for Ravi's recording sessions for Passages in Madras.

(this page) The wedding of Ravi and Suhanya, 3rd January 1989.

(above) Leading Anoushka through her first lessons on sitar, April 1989.

(right) With baby Anoushka.

(below) The inauguration ceremony for the new family home in Encinitas, February 1993.

brought along Shambu Das, an advanced student whom I put in his service to guide him as he practised the lessons I gave him, and to help him with fingering problems.

By the second or third day, George felt that no one had recognised him. He became overconfident and went down to the hotel lobby to see or buy something, but when he was coming up again he was recognised by the young elevator attendant, who happened to be a young Christian boy and an amateur musician.

GEORGE HARRISON: *Ravi had written to me saying, 'Maybe you could disguise yourself? Maybe grow a moustache or something?' The idea that a moustache could be a disguise – it was all pretty naive in those days. And anyway a moustache on a Beatle was kind of 'unexpected'...*

That was when the big hullabaloo erupted, with thousands of boys and girls on the street outside the hotel shouting, 'We want George!' It was impossible to learn anything like that, so we ran away to Srinagar in Kashmir. There we stayed in a beautiful houseboat which had two different rooms with attached bathrooms. I took Kamala along and we stayed in one room, while George and Pattie stayed in the other. Pattie was very beautiful, childlike and innocent.

I had already introduced George to Yogananda book's *Autobiography of a Yogi*. He was totally enchanted by it, and he also had brought some other books on Indian philosophy, including Vivekananda's *Raja Yoga*, which my brother Rajendra had given him. He also had the *I Ching*. All the time we were there he was reading and studying and asking me questions. I had brought many Indian classical LPs, so we were playing plenty of music, vocal as well as instrumental, and I was of course teaching him. He was also particularly interested in the whole area of yoga – and not only hatha yoga, the physical exercise which trains you up to concentrate and have control of the body; but also the mental yoga, or meditation, which hatha yoga prepares you for.

My heart melted with love for him. His quest was beautiful, although at the same time it was more like a child's; he wasn't fully matured back then. Nevertheless his interest in and curiosity for our traditions, mostly in the fields of religion, philosophy and music, was quite genuine. And he adored Indian food!

We were there for some weeks before he had to leave. That was the only long stretch of training he had from me. He was willing to practise, and he was good at learning, but owing to his commitments he couldn't stay as long as he wanted to. The disagreements had already emerged a little bit within The Beatles, but still they were together, and the entire group came to India again in 1968 to go to Maharishi Mahesh Yogi's ashram in Rishikesh, George having persuaded them into coming. He tried to encourage the other three towards Indian philosophy and religion. I don't think they were really interested, but because of George they did try to find out for a short period.

GEORGE HARRISON: *When I went to India, I had a desire to know about the yogis. So it was like a parallel interest for me: Indian music and the yogis of the Himalayas were both high on my agenda at that time – and they still are now. The great thing for me is that I latched onto that when I was twenty-two years old, and it's been consistent right through for the last thirty years. A lot of people might have thought it was a trendy thing – and for some people it was only a trend – but for me, I knew it had a certain intensity, and there was a certain intensity to my desire to pursue that.*

In retrospect there's a good chance I had a connection with India somewhere in the past, in a past life. In 1965 something happened that opened the door, or lifted the veil, and allowed me to realise: 'Yogis of the Himalayas – and what's this music?' One by one we get awakened by the sound of Krishna's flute. His flute works in many ways.

So I went to India, and I said to Ravi, 'I want to know about the yogis.' His brother Rajendra and he gave me all these books, and one book Raju gave me that was a great influence on me was Raja Yoga by Swami Vivekananda. Vivekananda says right at the beginning:

> *Each soul is potentially divine. The goal is to manifest that divinity. Do this through work and yoga and prayer, one or all of these means, and be free. Churches, temples, rituals and dogmas are but secondary details.*

As soon as I read that, I thought, 'That's what I want to know!' They tried to bring me up as a Catholic, and for me it didn't deliver. But to read, 'Each soul is potentially divine. The goal is to manifest that divinity' – and here's how you do it! – was very important for me. That's the essence of yoga and Hindu philosophy.

Ravi also gave me the book Autobiography of a Yogi. The moment I looked at that picture of Yogananda on the front of the book, his eyes went right through me and zapped me, and to this day I have been under the spell of Yogananda. It's a fantastic great truth.

When we were on the houseboat in Kashmir, owned by a little old guy with a white beard called Mr Butt, it was really cold in the night because it was on a lake right up in the Himalayas. Mr Butt would wake us up early in the morning and give us tea and biscuits and I'd sit in bed with my scarf and pullover on, listening to Ravi, who would be in the next little room doing his sitar practice – that was such a privileged position to be in.

What I'm getting at is that pure essence of India. You could easily be diverted in India by the smell or the dirt or the poverty, but I was fortunate to have Ravi as my friend. The Indians I saw were the ones who got up early in the morning, had a bath and put their clean dhoti on, did their prayers, and then practised their music for a couple of hours before they had their breakfast. The ones who had all the respect for the past. With the temples and the incense and the music, the whole thing – it was like I got the privileged tour. All the people I met were the best musicians, and I didn't have to go through the rubbish to find the gems. That in itself was worth a few years of saved time. And that's what a guru is, anyway – the word 'guru' means 'dispeller of darkness'.

A few days after George left I also flew to London, to spend a week doing the music for a black-and-white BBC Television production of *Alice in Wonderland*, directed by Jonathan Miller. It featured many famous actors, including Peter Cook, Alan Bennett, Peter Sellers, Michael Redgrave, John Gielgud, Malcolm Muggeridge and Wilfrid Brambell. *Alice in Wonderland* itself is a story that has nothing Indian about it, yet apart from the oboe (played by the great Leon Goossens) all the instruments used were Indian: flute, sitar, tabla, other drums, and a little vocal effect.

Jonathan was courageous to have thought of me to do the music for *Alice*, and no doubt many people were thinking, 'Why these sounds?' Perhaps some of the film crew were scared that it might not come out right, but it did – thanks to the fantasy nature of the film. I saw it again after many years, on a video copy I obtained with great difficulty, and I was amazed; it has a remarkable surreal effect.

In 1968 I was to supply the music for another film whose subject had nothing Indian about it: Ralph Nelson's *Charly*. On both occasions it was strange to be providing Indian music for non-Indian films, but I did try to match them up, and in both films the combination seemed to have worked.

I was planning to leave India again in February 1967, for a long, long tour. I had already become well known by then through my classical career and the recitals I had given at some folk clubs, even before my contact with George. But from the Bombay incident onwards there was such a big flash all around the world in the newspapers connecting him and me, about how I had become George's guru. It was like wildfire, creating such a big explosion of fascination with the sitar that there was a tremendous demand for my concerts. I became a superstar! Usually I used to go on tour for only two or three months, but with all the requests this time I planned to stay longer and take up a house in Los Angeles. In my absence Kinnara was to continue to be run under the guidance of a few of my disciples, although it gradually diminished in activity and was closed down a couple of years later.

This was the first time that I had travelled with Kamala as my companion. We had been deeply involved with each other from 1958, and we had spent time together whenever and wherever we could. My wife was still with Shubho in our apartment in Bombay, but Kamala and I had been meeting each other very often, especially whenever I travelled to Calcutta, where I had kept another apartment.

We left along with Alla Rakha and Nodu Mullick. We had arranged a few concerts *en route* to America – first of all in Soviet Russia. This was my second trip there, but it was a disaster and such a let-down, simply because of the Indian and Soviet bureaucrats who messed it up. If I had been aware of the plans earlier, I would not have gone.

On a few other occasions I have been abroad as part of a cultural exchange programme sent by our government to foreign countries, including Afghanistan, Japan and three times to Bangladesh. These trips are not organised for professional gain, but usually I have been fortunate enough to be shown terrific governmental respect, and have enjoyed the finest VIP treatment and the satisfaction of performing for huge and appreciative audiences. However, this time, thanks to some people in the cultural ministries of both India and the Soviet Union, only two performances had been arranged: one in Moscow and one in Leningrad, to be held in the House of Composers in each city! They were small halls with a capacity of only 150 to 200, and the audiences were made up mostly of old musicians and composers, with no outsiders. I was given no chance to play for a public audience, or to young people.

Twenty years later I returned to Russia to an overwhelming reception from the public, so I know the 1967 disaster was not the fault of the Russian people themselves. By and large Russians are very emotional and musical people, but at that time they never had the opportunity to hear any classical musicians from India. All they knew of were the Indian commercial films, which they lapped up. Indian film music was extremely popular there, especially the song 'Awara Hoon' (from Raj Kapoor's celebrated film *Awara*), which was almost as well-known as the Soviet national anthem.

After a few more concerts on the way, in London and Paris, we arrived in Los Angeles, where I established myself in a South Vista rented house with Kamala. (Later I brought over a chef from India, Vasudevan, to cook for us.) There were already plans to establish a school of Indian music, Dick Bock and a few other friends having talked me into opening a Los Angeles branch of Kinnara. Students enrolled in droves, and before I realised it I was waylaid by the crowd. At first it seemed like a good idea and I was swept along; it took me some time to realise that the approach of most of the young students was quite superficial.

At the Kinnara School, Los Angeles; Kamala on tanpura.

By then the whole scene was happening together: the hippy movement was already in full swing, with the Vietnam war protests, the drugs scene, meditation, the fascination with India, the encouragement to take drugs by Timothy Leary, Allen Ginsberg and Alan Watts (the three big drug gurus)... and in among all this were sitars and Indian music. It all became so mixed up. What really irritated me, and I started talking about it, was that some people took the name of India as the House of Drugs. They would say, 'Everyone takes drugs there – and you can't do music, meditation or yoga, or even make love, unless you do.'[1] These young people had no reason to take drugs – they already had their own in-built fountain of youth as stimulation, and had no need for over-stimulation through drugs. By taking them so many lives were ruined. Unfortunately even today, though perhaps it is less apparent than in that era, so many are still being destroyed, like a cancer – and now there are additional perils with the frightening advent of Aids.

My manager in the United States naturally took full advantage of my burgeoning popularity, booking me wherever a lucrative offer came from. So it was that in June 1967 I played at the Monterey Pop Festival, which was a completely new experience for me. It was the peak of the hippy scene. Some good vibrations were in the air, with the flower children, their clamour for love and peace and their interest in spirituality.

However, I had to change many of the arrangements for my performance. For instance, the organisers had wanted me to play in an evening section along with some of the rock and pop stars. I insisted my slot be changed to the Sunday afternoon, with nothing else going on immediately before or after, so that the crowd would not be influenced by the rock atmosphere. Therefore, in spite of a lot of people there being into drugs, they did concentrate on my music. It was daytime and the atmosphere was so beautiful – one of the most rewarding experiences. I played for over two and a half hours, sitting on the stage under the cloudy sky... a few drops of rain came but stopped... and it was truly magical. I became inspired and gave a very good performance that afternoon.

The festival organisers had arranged for thousands of orchids from Hawaii to be placed on the stage for Ravi's appearance. And the elements were apparently blessing his performance too: it had been raining all day, but about half an hour before he came on it stopped and brightened up – and after he finished it poured with rain.

Monterey also gave Ravi an ideal opportunity to view the stars of the rock and pop firmament, until then unfamiliar to him. Here was a dynamic and powerful world into which he was being welcomed with open arms – yet only twelve months earlier he had hardly heard of The Beatles.

I had arrived in Monterey on the Friday, two days before my own programme, so I had the chance to listen to some of the famous names and get to know a complete new scene.

---

1. This was not true in 1967, but unfortunately in more recent years India has also been having problems with its level of drug abuse.

Already orientated by their music in the film *The Graduate*, I was impressed by Simon and Garfunkel's performance and became extremely fond of them. Paul Simon wrote such beautiful music, and Garfunkel had an angelic voice; indeed that's what I miss among rock and pop singers. Most of them go sheerly by their talent, their presentation and their lyrics (and also, I think, a lot of luck), but few of them have a good voice with accurate pitch. Donovan was another exception, as was Joan Baez – as well as her striking looks and a beautiful personality, she had a lovely velvety voice.

There was a lot of talk about Janis Joplin – that she was addicted to drugs and wild as a person. In spite of all that, at Monterey I was struck by the emotion and the electricity, the passion and the fire, which blazed from her so prominently. She sang from her guts, like some of the olden-days jazz singers. A fantastic but quite different singer who made a great impact on me was Otis Redding, whose melodic voice I remember vividly. He had a clean and handsome appearance, too. His death in a plane accident six months later was a sad loss.

However, there were two performances on the final evening that upset me very much. I had heard plenty about Jimi Hendrix, and the moment his name was announced there was crazy applause. When he came on, at first I couldn't hear him at all because the girls in the audience were shrieking so loudly. A fabulous performer on guitar, he could have been a solo guitarist throughout a long career. I was really enjoying his tremendous power and virtuosity, but after the second or third song he began all the antics for which he became famous. First he was almost making love to his guitar with obscene movements, and that upset me a little because in our culture we have such a feeling of respect for the instrument. We treat it as something sacred. Worse was to come: towards the end, like a ritual, he poured some petrol on the guitar and set fire to it. It seemed a sacrilegious act, and I was so angry that I felt like getting up and going away.

Later on came The Who. I had no idea who The Who were, and I didn't find their sound any different from those of many other rock groups. I was exhausted by then and planning to sneak away afterwards, but because of what happened next I almost ran from there! If Jimi Hendrix's antics were too much for me, this was even worse. Towards the end, as part of their act, The Who started meticulously banging, breaking and shattering their instruments on the stage. That was the limit! I couldn't take it any more, and left with disturbing sensations in my mouth, ears and heart – although I still have some wonderful memories of some of the earlier performers.

There were a few other groups I listened to at Monterey who belonged to the different American school of hard rock, including Jefferson Airplane and The Grateful Dead. Out of all the American groups The Grateful Dead were the ones that lasted, still commanding respect in the Nineties. I met Jerry Garcia at Monterey, and Mickey Hart has long been an enthusiast of Indian music. (It was a joy to see Mickey at my October 1995 concert in San Francisco, which took place at the Masonic Auditorium. At the invitation of Zakir Hussain, who was accompanying me on tabla, Mickey had brought his own sound equipment and he was in charge of the sound engineering for the whole performance.) But at Monterey the Grateful Dead's sound was too loud for me, hurting my ears with the pounding rhythm – although the young audience seemed to go crazy about these hard-rock groups, and never stopped shrieking!

Every art form has a spectrum of styles. In literature there are some works that enlighten or delight you when you read them; and there are others that are more realistic, make you appreciate the trials of life. There are suspense and 'whodunit' mysteries, which lead on to horror stories and then those sickening ones punctuated by gory details of inhuman creatures with raw flesh, blood and all the secretions of the body flowing freely. There can be romantic and erotic writings that are so beautiful, counted among the highest literature – and then there can be sheer pornography, perversion and sex-and-horror stories all mixed in with disgusting details. In the same way I believe that in music you find all the different layers of feeling. In India these are vital elements of our music – we call them rasas. With many groups, such as The Beatles, I never had any disturbing feelings about rock music, but gradually what I was to hear later was different. The loud and pounding sound of hard rock, acid rock and punk rock, with the ear-splitting amplification of shrieking voices and the metallic steel sound, created a feeling of violence. The kids would get into a violent sexual frenzy, with musicians and listeners both high on drugs. I expected that 'this too shall pass', since everything seems to come and go in pop music (as in life), but I am appalled that this has not been the case. Even some of the MTV programmes magnify devilish, violent feelings, not only through the music but also through what you see.

Causing a commotion in Haight-Ashbury, 1967.

After meeting George, I was curious about The Beatles' music. I was not that attracted by their voices, since they mostly sang in a high falsetto pitch, which seems to have remained in vogue ever since. I also had trouble understanding the words they sang! But I do like a number of the songs they wrote, especially George's 'Here Comes The Sun' and 'My Sweet Lord' and many by John and Paul. There was definitely a lot of music in them, and the chords and harmony in the orchestration and also the instrumentalisation are great (for which I believe part of the credit goes to their producer, George Martin). Around the same time I heard The Rolling Stones, who were so lively and exciting, and from Eric Clapton's Cream days onwards I also appreciated his wonderful musicianship.

After Monterey I performed at three or four more festivals. My manager had booked me so I couldn't avoid them, but I hated myself for being there! People in the crowd were shrieking, shouting, smoking, masturbating and copulating, all in a drug-crazed state – it was a horrible experience. I would ask myself, 'Why am I here?' I felt as if I had soiled and dirtied my music. At times I walked offstage with my sitar because it was too unruly, and would only come back again when they had calmed down.

I used to tell them, 'You don't behave like that when you go to hear a Bach, Beethoven or Mozart concert.' (Admittedly most of them probably never went to one.) 'Many of you are the same people, merely dressed differently and behaving differently. Be whatever you are – all I expect from you is to be sober, behave properly, concentrate on the music, and don't mix it up with sex and drugs. To me, my music is sacred, and it can make you high on its own! You don't need this extra stimulus. Give me a chance!' I had to tell them this again and again. It was an unpleasant experience, but by and by it began to sink in and work to some extent.

At rock festivals Ravi was caught in an unhappy situation. Such wanton behaviour disturbed him, and the atmosphere created was completely inappropriate for a performance of Indian classical music. The temptation to walk away was overwhelming at times. But he felt love for these young people who were searching for enlightenment, and persisted with his appeals for respectful conduct. The missionary in him also felt a sense of duty to persuade them that their conduct was wrong – and moreover unnecessary, for he could offer an alternative route to a spiritual bliss.

I had to go through this identical scene many times over the next couple of years, not only in America, but also in Europe, South America, Japan, Australia... even at a Mardi Gras Fest in Madras! Those few years were extremely testing in that way. My name was like magic, and there were such large crowds that I had to perform in stadiums rather than halls. But it was a crazy time.

Monterey did open my eyes to the rock'n'roll world. Afterwards I saw the Haight-Ashbury scene in San Francisco, and I was very much shaken by the effects of the music's drugs association. All these young and beautiful people, and some of them so talented, all waylaid in the same manner by this destruction I was seeing. And with all the sexual freedom... thank God there was no Aids in those days, otherwise half of the world's population might have been obliterated!

Then there was the shallowness of the hotch-potch of ideas. I felt offended and shocked to see India being regarded so superficially and its great culture being exploited. Yoga, tantra, mantra, kundalini, ganja, hashish, Kama Sutra – they all became part of a cocktail that everyone seemed to be lapping up! This was bugging me, especially upon the opening of my school. Of all the hundreds of kids who were enrolling at Kinnara in LA, I found only one or two of them genuinely interested in the music and working hard at it. Most of them were doing it simply because it was the fad or the vogue.

Within a few weeks of its opening I had realised that the school was not going to work, but I couldn't stop it at that point (it remained open for about two and a half years). Amiyo Das Gupta and a few other advanced students of mine were engaged to run it, so I wasn't giving that much time; I would show my face once in a while to supervise. But the kids all expected me to be sitting there like a guru, giving some spiritual guidance and discoursing on life and meditation. Maharishi Mahesh Yogi was doing very well in this area of our great heritage, but my main language is music. I did my best to make them understand this.

I believe it was on my trip to Paris at the end of 1967 that I heard some musicians called Les Structures Sonores, who had invented a special type of sound with bowl-like glass structures, which produce the type of sound that you get from rubbing the rim of a glass with a moistened finger. There was a wide variety in pitch between the structures, which were objects of diverse shape and size producing several different scales – weird sounds, but beautiful, celestial, spacey. The French musicians would all play together, and they took up plenty of room because so many of the instruments were needed to produce the range of sounds. I was inspired by them, and when I was asked to compose the music for the British art film *Viola* I chose to use their sound together with Alla Rakha on tabla, Kamala on tanpura and my own sitar. It was not until 1973 that the recording was issued as an album under the title *Transmigration Macabre*.

The *Festival From India* ventures had a much higher profile. In 1968 I invited to the USA Shiv Kumar Sharma, Sabri Khan, Miskin Khan (tabla and various percussion), Sharad Kumar (shahnai and flute) and my disciple Shamim Ahmed, as well as Lakshmi Shankar. For all of them this was, I think, their first break in the West (though Lakshmi had been to the West once before with Dada's group in 1962, to direct my music for *Samanya Kshati* and give a short solo vocal recital in each performance). The ensemble was completed by Alla Rakha, Aashish Khan, Palghat Raghu (mridangam), Jitendra Abhisheki (vocals), Taranath Rao (Harihar's half-brother, on tabla), Fakir Mohammad (dholak and tamboura) and Kamala (vocals). Nodu and Amiyo played drone instruments. We made a double-album set in Los Angeles at the World Pacific Studio of Dick Bock, who produced it and then issued it as *Festival From India*. It was a highly satisfactory recording because there were many varied items, ranging from classical to folk in style. There was a beautiful cover jacket for the album, designed by Jan Steward, a dear friend and a wonderful artist who has since designed fantastic artwork for a few more albums and booklets of mine. After the recordings we set off on a coast-to-coast tour. Some of the artists also took classes at my Kinnara school for a few weeks.

Fame opens doors, this is well known, and great fame opens greater doors. Ravi's new profile was accompanied by the type of lifestyle reserved for a major Hollywood celebrity. It was a situation he had been prepared for by the tours in the Thirties, and mostly he took it all in his stride, enabling him to enjoy the opportunities thoroughly. A wise head helped him through the pressures of this fame thrust upon him suddenly – although not that suddenly, considering he turned forty-seven in 1967, and had been touring on his own in the West for over a decade.

As far as superstardom and popularity went, I was absolutely at the height of it! I appeared on numerous TV talk shows, including Johnny Carson (twice), David Frost, Joey Bishop, Dick Cavett and Mike Wallace. I couldn't walk in the street without being mobbed, with fans following me shouting, 'Hi Ravi!' or even, 'Hi Rav!' It was unbelievable – though I was enjoying it, I won't deny that.

I was so busy at the time that I couldn't think properly. Everything was happening at once: moving so fast, giving concerts and making appearances, I don't know where the next two years went. It was as if I was completely in the hands of my managers, with all the dates fixed by them. Everything was a blur. However, at forty-seven I was mature enough to cope with it. I would have gone completely bonkers if I had been younger!

Between 1967 and 1970 I rented a succession of four houses in Los Angeles. We were living in the first one when Kinnara was opened, and after that I moved into a huge house in the Hollywood hills which had its entrance on the fourth floor. A few showbiz parties and dinners were held there, with Marlon Brando, Peter Sellers, Terence Stamp, all four of The Beatles and many others present on various occasions. They loved the Indian food, and we would have some Indian music too. Peter Sellers became a very good friend while he was shooting his film *The Party*, in which he was to portray an Indian who plays sitar. He was having problems, so he requested me to help him with the appropriate posture for holding the sitar. We used to meet quite often. In real life, as in performance, he was extremely funny, warm and charming, but he was very moody as well; he could just turn off, become sour and want to be alone. At a musical party at his home I met Henry Mancini and his son, who were very enthusiastic about my music.

In 1968 I moved to a third house in LA, which I remember as being my residence when I was taking my driving lessons. In early 1970 I stayed for a couple of months in the fourth rented house, which was on Dorian Avenue, before eventually buying and moving into a beautiful Spanish villa-style three-bedroomed house on Highland Avenue in Hollywood.

Instructing Peter Sellers on how to look like a sitar-player, for his role in The Party.

I recall Marlon Brando phoning one day and coming round to my first house to invite me to perform at a UNESCO charity show in Paris, held in December 1967. There was a lot of public interest because George Harrison and John Lennon were attending the show. I performed along with Alla Rakha, for a mere fifteen minutes. At the show I met Elizabeth Taylor, Richard Burton and all the other participants that Marlon Brando had persuaded to appear. We were all staying at the George V Hotel in Paris and it was quite an occasion.

A new level of Hollywood stardom. Ravi pictured below with Richard Burton, in Paris, December 1967, and opposite with: (top left) Bismillah Khan, master of the shahnai, during Ravi's rehearsals at the Hollywood Bowl, 1968; (top right) Zubin Mehta, at the Los Angeles Kinnara School, May 1967; (main picture) Dizzy Gillespie; and (bottom left) Marlon Brando. Accepting (bottom right) the Grammy Award for Best Chamber Music Performance of 1967 for West Meets East.

A few more times I met the rest of The Beatles, but George was the one to whom I felt closer and closer. He visited my Kinnara school, as did Yehudi Menuhin and a few others. I also met Bob Dylan a few times, including at the Bangladesh concerts in 1971. Like John Lennon, he commanded a special respect from everyone, but we never became close – I could not tell whether he was aloof or merely shy. Another rock musician I encountered was Jim Morrison of The Doors, who attended a couple of my sitar lessons in Los Angeles.

In the same period of Hollywood parties, I came across Zubin Mehta, although not for the first time. Zubin is a dear friend. He belongs to the Parsi community, which is descended from the Zoroastrians who migrated from Persia many centuries ago and settled in the western part of India surrounding Bombay. Most Parsis are Westernised, many of them being wealthy industrialists. Zubin's father, Mehli Mehta, was a fabulous violinist in the Western classical domain, maybe one of the best that India has produced; today Mehli is the beloved conductor of the American Youth Symphony Orchestra in LA. Zubin has been into Western music all his life. He was born in Bombay and was introduced to music by his father, but I think Mehli felt that his talented son would be better off receiving further training in the West, and Zubin was sent to Vienna at the age of eighteen. He soon shaped up to be a fine conductor.

The first time I met him was in Montreal in the early Sixties, where he was conducting the city's symphony orchestra. I was highly impressed by him, but also found out that he didn't have much idea about Indian classical music. We met again in Los Angeles when he was being given great acclaim because he had been appointed as the Music Director of the Los Angeles Philharmonic. Young, handsome, and getting all the fanfare, he was the sought-after 'Zubie Baby' of all the Hollywood parties. He was charming and funny and, although he was years younger than me, we became good friends, as we remain.

Zubin is truly international: he spends much time in Israel, where he is the principal conductor of the Israel Philharmonic Orchestra. The people there love him and consider him as one of their own. It is wonderful to see an Indian attaining such a prestigious position in the Western classical field as one of its top conductors and, despite his involvement in music that is so completely Western, still maintaining his innate Indianness: in his way of talking, his manner, and his love for his homeland and its culture.

Receiving an honorary doctorate from the University of Santa Cruz, California, 1968.

At the same time as being feted in the West, I was also experiencing the effects of false propaganda formed in India. I was in the news all the time, but along with much praise there was also condemnation of me for having become a 'hippy' – or even a member of The Beatles – and for being sacrilegious toward our music: 'commercialising', 'Americanising', and 'jazzifying' it, not playing 'pure music' for Westerners. Those were the terms that were repeatedly used.

Another accusation was that my performances of ragas were too short. Some people were saying, 'In the West he plays a raga for no more than half an hour.' That sort of comment is stupid and has no meaning. It's not the length of time that is important, because our music is not written down: there is no such thing as a 'twenty-minute raga', a 'one-hour raga' or a 'two-hour raga'! For a long time great Indian musicians have been making recordings of all different lengths, from 78rpm records of three and a half minutes through EPs to LPs of up to twenty-one minutes, and performing on radio for fifteen to thirty minutes – and they have given great performances, whatever the length of piece.

Such criticism was hurting me immensely, because I was doing exactly the opposite: trying to make our music understood. I was fighting all the time against what was being said in India, and when the feedback from India started to hit the West many of the conservative listeners thought that I had sold my soul to the Devil or something like that! Many serious musicians and solid admirers of our music, even in Europe and America, thought I was a goner. I recall Pierre Boulez saying in an interview for *Time* magazine that, whereas I had once played sitar well, what I was playing now was 'Neapolitan banjo'!

Many critics, particularly in India, assumed Ravi had found the lure of American wealth too tempting and had sold out. 'From Ragas to Riches' ran the headlines, seeking to bury him by misrepresentation. To Ravi, though the money was naturally welcome, it was not the point.

The question might fairly be asked: why was I making all this effort in the West? I was doing it because I felt I had a mission of sorts, a self-imposed responsibility to enlighten the people about our music. There was a tendency at the time for India to be represented inaccurately, and for our music to go in the wrong direction. There was undoubtedly a stubbornness about my behaviour, but I wanted to ensure that Indian music held its rightful place. Even though I was sometimes made impatient by the eager young Westerners, the music deserved to be played to them, and to be understood and appreciated in the proper manner.

I was not doing it for the money, although it was coming in large amounts. Despite enjoying life as a star, I didn't take as full material advantage as I could have taken. I have always felt that Americans in general are the most childlike, innocent, naive and impressionable people in the world. The good side of this is that it provides so many opportunities for people with talent and new ideas. But it is also why, along with all the greatest talents who have ventured to America, done great things and found appreciation and success, there have been an equal number of quacks, showmen, people with the gift of the gab and conmen, who have reaped their harvest in so many different fields, including religion. If I had wanted to become a billionaire, I would have had every chance by posing as an ochre-robed swami and a raga-rock king combined.

I was trying to be faithful to the music. I did make objections about the attitude and behaviour of some of the fans, and I am glad of it. Gradually all the superficial members of the audience were weeded out, and many of those who remained are still there today, free from drugs and with genuine reverence for our music.

Meanwhile I saw many Indian musicians taking full advantage of the chances which now opened up for them as a result of my success. Indeed many of the same people who had earlier been criticising me for commercialising our music now flocked to the West to make hay while the sun was shining! I did my utmost to create interest and respect for our music among Western listeners. The floodgates were opened for many of our musicians, from those of great seniority to the young and promising, to come and find a large and appreciative audience. Yet some of these musicians persisted in criticising me, still claiming that they were the traditionalists, the guardians of 'pure sitar', while I played 'Beatle sitar'!

The controversy and his own ambivalent attitude were discussed in his book My Music, My Life *(published in 1968), in which he also elaborated the roots of Indian music, the great masters, and his own life up to that point, as well as providing an introductory manual on playing the sitar.*

Ravi also alluded to the same themes in the film Raga, *a stirring document of a man both creating and caught up in a unique cross-cultural maelstrom. Shooting commenced in 1967 and went on until the end of 1968, following Ravi around India as well as the*

In Maihar with Baba Allauddin Khan and three other students of his: 'Kabul' (Nalin Mazumdar), 'Biloo' (Suprabhat Pal) and (seated) Bindu Mukherjee.

States; although delays due to financial and technical problems ensured that it was not until the end of 1971 that the movie received its première. Raga captured the intensity of the performer and the adulation of his American festival audiences and, during the exquisite scenes shot in India, further reflected on the ancient sources of Indian music and dance.

Along with everything else that was happening at this time went the filming of my movie *Raga*. This film was beautifully made, but it was financed with my own money, which was rather sad because it cost a large amount and I only realised this later! George Harrison also provided some final help to see that it was released.

When I was in India in 1968 the film unit followed me all over, including a visit to my guru in Maihar. There was plenty of other footage from America, such as the Monterey Pop Festival and the UN Human Rights Day performance with Yehudi Menuhin. The film-makers adapted some of my text from *My Music, My Life* and recorded me narrating the lines to go along with the sequences they shot.

The *Raga* shooting also went to Big Sur on the Californian coast in June of the same year. Big Sur is a wonderful place with hot springs. I used to go once in a while to the Esalen Institute there, a retreat where people could stay for a few days and relax and take a bath in a hot spring. Always there would be some eminent cult guru there to give talks. It was very hippy-orientated: all love and peace, with quite a bit of free love. There were also some weirdos there who related to me how many times they had seen UFOs landing, and how they had met the extraterrestrials – some even claimed to have had sex with them! At the same time there were some good things going on – yoga and meditation classes, lectures on Buddhism, Hinduism, Sufism. George visited and a scene was filmed of my teaching him and some other students.

Apart from showing a few of my sitar recitals, *Raga* featured some incidental music by me. There is also a rapid visual collage sequence which reflects all the distortions in that period – Indian music mixed up with rock, hippies and drugs. The music for that section was put together in a modern style with a profusion of electronic sounds by an American disciple of mine called Collin Walcott. He was with a group called Oregon, and learnt sitar from me and some tabla from Alla Rakha. Sadly Collin died in an automobile accident in Germany a few years later.

Raga is a good documentation of Indian music and culture in America and Europe in that period, and the role I played. It was not and could not have been a box-office success, but it is still available on video today through a company in New York called Mystic Fire.

The narrative for Raga does provide a lasting record of Ravi's feelings of the time about everything that he was witnessing, and for this glimpse into his mind it is worth citing some of the narrative here. Both exhilarated by and wary of the cultural changes being forced upon India by the modern world, Ravi ponders the future for the traditions of the old India and then, in a pensive final scene filmed on a windswept Californian beach, he reflects on whether he has been entirely judicious in his efforts to enlighten America:

'To be received like this in a foreign land – my God! It is overwhelming! I have never felt so much love for our music. It inspires me so. But I wonder how much they can understand, and where all this will lead to. There is so much in our music that goes back thousands of years: the prayers in our temples, the pain and struggle of life, the sound of the rivers, the timeless chants. So many things that are within me whenever I play, whatever I do.

'I wonder if I tried to do too much, if I took on a false role in America. Somehow I simply could not let it go. I keep asking myself if all this terrible distortion could have been avoided. You cannot just brush the surface of a culture and pretend that you have found an answer. We must turn inward to the deepest of our own roots to find the very best of who we are. But it is a constant search, trying to reach something that I can see and feel, that I can almost touch but never hold on to.

'Music is the only language I really know, for I believe in Nada Brahma: "The Sound is God".'

My few experiences at the rock festivals continued until Woodstock, in August 1969. This was a terrifying experience. If Monterey was the beginning of a new movement or beautiful happening, I think Woodstock was almost the end. We had to go by helicopter from the motel where we stayed many miles away, and landed just behind the stage. I performed with Alla Rakha accompanying me on tabla, in front of an audience of half a million – an ocean of people. It was drizzling and very cold, but they were so happy in the mud; they were all stoned, of course, but they were enjoying it. It reminded me of the water buffaloes you see in India, submerged in the mud. Woodstock was like a big picnic party, and the music was incidental.

(below and overleaf) During his performance at the Woodstock Festival, 1969.

I wish I hadn't performed there, but because of my commitment I had to. The thought of my instrument getting wet and spoilt was worrying me so much that it was not a very inspired performance, although I did my best. When I looked out there was no way of communicating to the crowd – it was such a vast audience. I learnt that, apart from the abundance of drugs, there was violence, theft, robbery and raping at Woodstock. It was not what people try to glorify it as today.

What a great difference and pleasure it was when I was performing at the conservative indoor venues, such as Carnegie Hall or the Royal Festival Hall, where the unruly element was absent! In the

darkness of these auditoriums, I could see if even one single cigarette was lit faraway up in the balcony, and I would put my sitar down and say, 'Please don't smoke.' If there were catcalls, I would give a glare and ask for some quiet so that I could concentrate. I did that constantly and it worked; being in that atmosphere, the younger audience felt guilty if they behaved disrespectfully.

Despite my determination, the negative criticisms did lead to doubts weighing upon my conscience, and after Woodstock I began to want to get away and cleanse myself. Since around 1966 most of my concerts had been handled by pop or rock promoters, and eventually I left my managers and cancelled many of those concerts that had not been arranged through classical promoters. All along I had been returning to India for at least a couple of months every fall (except in 1967), but in the mid-Seventies I stopped playing for a year and a half in the USA, and waited until I found a proper classical agent. For a while the classical impresarios did not seem to be interested in me, because they associated me with rock and pop only.

In India I went back to playing concerts featuring only two or three ragas stretched out over never less than four or five

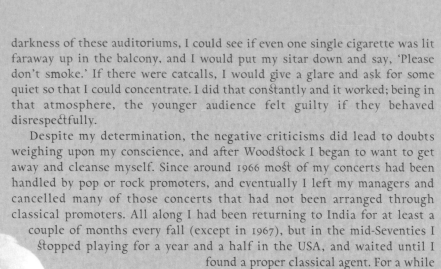

hours, just to prove myself to my denigrators. I had to do this for several years, putting myself through such physical strain. After I restarted concerts in the West, now arranged through classical agents at classical venues, it took a few years but by the beginning of the Eighties people were back to accepting me as one of the top classical musicians, a traditionalist. They knew that I had not gone astray, and my music was still there.

With hindsight, not only is Ravi's reputation as a classical musician safe, but the effects of his activities in that crazy period of superstardom seem much more beneficial now. Far from damaging his ancient music, by plugging it into the mainstream of Western culture he was bringing enlightenment to a large number of young people who had no prior experience of India's treasures. These were the fans who were persuaded to treat the music with respect and discover the depths of its roots. After all the hype and nonsense had died down, it was clear that Ravi had impacted on many people's lives.

He doesn't like labels, but if anyone can lay claim to the title 'Godfather of World Music' it must be Ravi. Time and again he has showed it is possible to introduce an apparently alien art form successfully into the heart of another culture.

For the sake of convenience, Ravi's solo career in the West can be divided into three phases since 1956. Initially his appeal was restricted to the classical field, but from 1966 onwards the second period began, when he attained the centre of the youth consciousness. After several years, he decided to retreat from this kind of life back towards the classical fold, and in the third phase, which has been his favourite one and has lasted ever since, he has enjoyed the synthesis of the benefits of the first two phases: the public acclaim built up to extraordinary levels in the second, and the security of knowing that his base is firmly fixed in the traditional classical camp, giving him the freedom to roam in all the fields he chooses.

At the time, I was irritated because I had developed a complex from being so severely criticised in India. A bit of paranoia set into me for those few years. With all the fuss, I started believing some of the propaganda being levelled against me, feeling that I must be doing something wrong. Always being known as the Beatle-guru didn't please me; if that was all I was admired for, it was not right. My love and affection for George was always the same, as it is now, but I absolutely never wanted to cash in on his name.

In withdrawing from those heights of success which I achieved in the late Sixties and early Seventies, I went overboard somewhat in attempting to disassociate myself from my new fans in the West, even from George to an extent. In endeavouring to please one camp, I hurt the other. With some justification, the young faithful in the West objected to what must have seemed like my ingratitude in turning my back on those who had made my name and fortune. I was excessively harsh at times, and trampled on some feelings.

(above, left to right) Lakshmi, Kamala, Ravi, Pablo Casals – meeting the legendary cellist at Tanglewood summer festival, 1968.

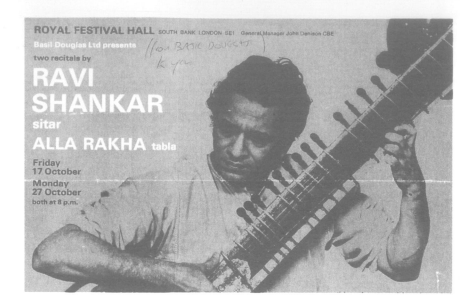

It was a unique situation to be in, and at times it was not easy. I feel I was always something of an enigma, since few people really comprehended what I stood for. The public usually like things to be clear-cut. Perhaps only Leonard Bernstein among contemporaries faced the same sort of troubles as I did over categorisation, between traditional and modern, classical and popular/jazz, or composer and performer.

Yet I myself didn't realise how deep I had penetrated into people's minds. In the world of pop and rock music, most artists live for only a few years. I was particularly aware of this because the classical field is so different. You remain known all your life, and even after you die. Though the classical artist rarely enjoys as much popularity or money as the star of pop, rock or film, people will never forget Bach, Beethoven and Mozart, Segovia, Casals and Heifetz, or Tagore and Tyagaraja. Of course, modern recording technology will keep alive some of the pop and rock greats, such as The Beatles; but there remains a big difference between classical music and pop in this respect.

Though I have always been fortunate enough to occupy an enviable position in India, I have also been lucky in the West, where people did not forget me. Even today I am reaping the harvest of those years. Wherever I go, I meet people whose eyes light up and they kindly say how I have made an impact on their lives. I feel the same thing everywhere, not only in the United States but all over the world – and it could be anyone: a plumber, a taxi-driver, an porter, or someone in the street or an office. It constantly surprises me and makes me feel grateful to God to realise how deeply I have affected some people.

Sometimes it is embarrassing to be recognised, to have to reply to strange questions such as, 'Do you remember me? Twenty-five years ago I took your autograph after your recital in Timbuktu?'; or to be caught in the men's restroom by some admirer who oozes praise and doesn't want to leave you even after you have finished what it was you came there for! On the other hand, it is of course great to be recognised by immigration or customs officers and, in exchange for providing an autograph, to be released quickly and with courtesy, instead of being grilled for a long period!

I went through some mental agony in those years, but I have changed my views now. What happened was for the best, and not only for me: it has helped Indian music itself. All our wonderful musicians who have been able to come to the West today and perform in front of enthusiastic audiences, they too are enjoying the fruits, and their success is a testament to the benefits of what I did then.

It might still be easy to misinterpret what I was doing in that hectic period, but there was always a balance between my various activities. For some time I had been enthusiastic about the idea of working with a Western orchestra; and in 1970, amid everything else that was going on, a commission came from the London Symphony Orchestra to write and perform a sitar concerto. This employed a new approach, consisting of orchestral sections separated by sitar pieces that I improvise during the performance, ending each sitar passage with a prearranged cue for the orchestra to come in again. There are also some cross-combination sections, in which the orchestra and I play simultaneously. At least three or four rehearsals are always needed with this piece, because of the novel approach, but the different elements blend well and I remain happy with it today.

For the Western notation an American student of mine, Fred Teague, transcribed the parts for all the different instruments from my Indian notation. Intricate details, or sections spontaneously composed, I demonstrated to him on either sitar or piano.

(above) With the eminent vocalist and musicologist B. R. Deodhar.

(opposite below) Signing an autography for Edward Kennedy.

Dedicated to Ustad Allauddin Khan, the concerto features what is essentially an Indian composition written for a Western orchestra, with the part of the tabla being taken by bongos and a host of other Western percussion instruments, while the tanpura's drone sound is imitated early on by two harps and later by the strings. The emphasis is naturally on melody and rhythm, and the scales and sounds are unusual to the Western ear. However, Ravi allows modulation between movements, with the key changing as the orchestra proceeds from the opening movement based on the raga Khamaj, to the second in Sindhi Bhairavi, the brief third in Adana, and the closing movement in Manj Khamaj. He also made limited use of harmony and chords, without losing the essence of each raga (what is termed the 'Raga-Bhava').

Composing the piece took two and a half months, and it was premiered to considerable acclaim on 28th January 1971 at the Royal Festival Hall, London, conducted by André Previn. It was the first time that anyone had attempted to write such an ambitious piece based on Indian ragas and talas, and his presence as performer too was a first. Since 1971 Ravi has accepted many invitations to perform it all around the world, most recently in Mexico (October 1993), Singapore and Angers, France (both as part of 1995's 75th birthday celebrations, and at the Barbican Hall, London in March 1997. However, such performances have not always been free from complications.

When I play in one of my own sitar concertos with an orchestra, I feel enclosed within my own prison. It's all fixed: I have to enter at a certain point and, after my improvisation, play the cue and make eye contact with the conductor for the orchestra to come back in at the right moment. Whatever I improvise is not scored, but it is within some limitations, some time value.

My biggest problem comes when I hear the slightest error, a wrong intonation or a wrong note, or a rhythmic mistake by even one single individual, especially when I'm playing a cross-combination piece. I get so disturbed that I forget my own part and make a mess of it!

Many Western musicians also have problems. For instance, when they try to play the meend it sounds so out of tune, because they touch all the microtones in between notes; and that's not how we do it. Our meend takes years to master; it is not merely a glissando or a slur. Rhythmically also there are problems, because of the complex Indian cycles of sevens, elevens and other odd talas. The younger musicians tend to be much better at grasping it because they are orientated to jazz, pop and modern music.

I am very fortunate in that, without having learnt Western music technically, I am able to appreciate it – whether it is classical, jazz, country-and-western, folk, or modern pop and rock. During my childhood spent touring the world, I was surrounded by all sorts of music, particularly classical; I had the opportunities to hear the great instrumentalists, vocalists and conductors of that time. As a child you absorb things automatically, so my ears became attuned to such a variety of music.

It should, however, be stressed that my formal knowledge of Western classical music is quite limited. I did start to learn it in Paris in my youth, but did not keep it up for long. I can read Western notation only in slower passages, and cannot write it – when I am composing for Western musicians an assistant helps me to do this.

My tastes are mostly for pre-twentieth century music. I have always been very fond of baroque music, especially the music of Bach, which is much easier for an Indian listener to appreciate, because he finds attractive melodies in it. Mozart is another great favourite of mine, for the same reason. I do generally prefer pieces with solo instruments; I have no trouble in appreciating symphonic music, but it is not always that it affects me emotionally. Beethoven's sonatas and a few of his symphonic pieces touch my heart deeply, and Tchaikovsky is extremely melodic. When it comes to opera, there is so much to admire in Mozart's *Magic Flute*, *Don Giovanni* and *Marriage of Figaro*, Bizet's *Carmen*, and a few lighter operas and operettas, but I still have problems with long Wagnerian epics.

Within the classical framework, I find it difficult to appreciate fully more recent music, beginning from Schoenberg and atonal music, through avant-garde, musique concrète and electronic music. Strangely enough I have great trouble with anything discordant. In Darmstadt, Germany, there is a regular festival of modern music featuring pieces by all the famous modern composers, and I have twice been invited to give sitar recitals there. If I arrive at such a venue one day before my performance, I always make a point of listening to what is going on. On those two occasions in Darmstadt, and at least two other times since, I have noticed that I develop a peculiar problem.

It is mystifying how it happens, but I find that when I start hearing those strange sounds or discordant combinations, within a few minutes I feel a stomach cramp, and from stomach cramp I develop a terrible headache and nausea. At first I thought these physical effects were coincidental, that my suffering was due to some bad food I must have eaten; but it has happened again and again, right up to this day! I feel ashamed of myself, because thousands of people rave about this music. Though I am sure most of them are sincere in their appreciation, one has to wonder whether some are just behaving in a trendy manner, motivated by snobbery. Sometimes I can intellectually appreciate the intelligent combinations used, yet the whole gamut of this modern music, I am embarrassed to admit, is a physical problem to me. I have to try harder, maybe!

In 1971, while I was living in my Highland Avenue house in Hollywood, there developed the big Bangladesh problem. Bangladesh, or East Pakistan as it then was known, wanted its independence from West Pakistan's domination. The trouble originated with the language issue.

Bengali is the mother tongue in what is now Bangladesh, just as it is for the West Bengal people in India; though in Bangladesh the population is mainly Muslim (which is why that region became East Pakistan in 1947), while West Bengal is predominantly Hindu. Hindus remain in a minority of about 10–15% in Bangladesh today. In 1971 the Government in Islamabad (West Pakistan) was attempting to make Urdu the national language throughout both Pakistans. The Bengalis, who already considered that they were treated like second-class citizens, objected strongly.

From the language issue the troubles escalated into a large scale conflict between the Islamabad Government and the huge Bengali-speaking population in the Eastern side. The Bengalis wanted freedom and the war inevitably followed. India then intervened, and unfortunately the bad feeling remains even today between India and Pakistan, with the main issue now of course being Kashmir. The Indian Army stepped in as a liberator, established the Bangladeshi Government and then left. It was admirable that they did not dominate the area, as the Russians did with the countries they liberated in Europe.

While all this was going on I learnt that many of my distant relatives, along with hundreds of thousands of other refugees, were fleeing to Calcutta. I felt very concerned. It was not political or religious feeling on my part; it was more linguistic. Being Bengali-speaking myself I felt sympathetic towards Bangladesh, but even more so for the refugees who had crossed the border into India and were suffering so much, especially the children.

I wrote some songs in Bengali and recorded them as an EP for Apple Records. One was 'Joi Bangla', which means 'victory to Bangladesh'. Another was a lamentation, 'Oh Bhaugowan'. The first line of this was, 'Oh Bhaugowan, Khoda tala.' 'Bhaugowan' is the Hindus' word for God, while 'Khoda' is the word for the Muslims, so it means 'Oh God' to people of both religions. I sang:

> 'Oh God, where are you? To see us suffer like this, in this flood and this fight and this hunger. Why should we suffer so, with all these calamities?'

The idea also occurred to me of giving a concert to raise money to help these refugees – something on a bigger scale than normal. While I was thinking of this, George Harrison was in Los Angeles. He would come to my house in the mornings and spend time there, and he understood what I was going through. I asked him frankly, 'George, can you help me?' because I knew that if I gave a concert myself I would not be able to raise a significant amount. He was really moved and said, 'Yes, something should be done.' That was when he wrote his song 'Bangla Desh'.

GEORGE HARRISON: *The war had been going on for a bit, and I had hardly even heard of it, so he fed me a lot of newspaper articles about it. He was saying, 'I'm going to have to do something to help. Attract a bit of attention to it, raise a bit of money, much more than I could make doing my own concert, maybe like ten to twenty thousand dollars.' That for him was like doing a big one. And so I got involved. The priority was to attract world attention to what was going on. It wasn't so much the money because you can feed somebody today and tomorrow they will still be hungry, but if they are getting massacred you've got to try and stop that first of all.*

I said, 'OK, I'll go on the show and I'll get some other people to come and help. We'll try and make it into a big show, and maybe we can make a million dollars instead of a few thousand.' So I got on the telephone trying to round people up. We pinpointed the days which were astrologically good, and we found Madison Square Garden was open on one of those days – 1st August.

Only one show was originally fixed but there was such demand that eventually two were arranged on the same day, in the afternoon and evening. They were a grand success: George sang 'Bangla Desh' and some of his other songs, while his friends Bob Dylan, Eric Clapton, Billy Preston and a few other musicians all did a couple of their numbers.

The show was started by Alubhai and me playing a duet accompanied on tabla by Alla Rakha, with Kamala playing tanpura, lasting for about half an hour. A funny incident happened at the beginning. After we had tuned up we were silent just before playing, whereupon the audience broke out in applause! So I said immediately, 'If you like our tuning so much, I hope you will enjoy the playing more.'

The Concerts for Bangladesh were made into a Grammy-winning triple album and a film, which along with the proceeds on the night raised huge sums of money for Bangladesh, the money being administered by UNICEF. (At the last count – since the album and video are still selling – the receipts were fourteen million dollars.) Yet arguably the biggest benefit of the night was the international attention it brought to a hitherto remote and unfashionable conflict, and a new country.

Overnight the word 'Bangladesh', the name of the country, was all over the world because of the press coverage. It created such a good wave of publicity for the newborn country.

In 1988 I went to Bangladesh as a state guest of their Government, and was invited back again in 1992 and 1997. I cannot express what a tumultuous reception I was given on those visits, from the President right down to the common people. Everyone showered me with such love and expressed gratitude for helping to arrange the concerts in 1971. On the second visit I brought my wife Sukanya with me, and she was given such adoration by the people. Bangladeshis are so similar to my people from West Bengal: full of love, temperamental and emotional, passionate for poetry, literature, music, theatre, cinema and celebrities. We went gaga over the food, with its tasty vegetables and especially the wonderful variety of fish. Because my ancestors were from Jessore, the people even claimed me as their own – a Bangladeshi!

1972 and 1973 were years of loss for Ravi, with the deaths of first his musical guru, Allauddin Khan, and then his spiritual guru, Tat Baba. In memory of Baba Allauddin, Ravi and Ali Akbar Khan played a famous duet at New York's Philharmonic Hall, accompanied by Alla Rakha, which was released as a double album on Apple Records.

My relationship with Baba had become more complex over the years. At first the beautiful bond between the two of us had remained intact, even after I left Maihar for Bombay, and later still moved to Delhi. It was only in early 1956, when the discord in my marriage reached its peak and Annapurna left me (first going back to her father in Maihar and then to Alubhai in Calcutta) that things changed drastically.

Baba was a great musician and, apart from his terrible temper, a wonderful person. But then he was also a mortal, and blood is thicker than water. He changed from the father and guru whom I cherished so much to a mere father-in-law, and a furious one at that! Many people who were jealous of me joined together in supporting and sympathising with my wife, fanning Baba's ears with their accounts of what had gone on, making a devil out of me. By that time his health was deteriorating and he was becoming slightly senile. He became mad with rage, cursing me. Not believing the truth about the episode (which it would not be constructive to go into here), he accepted everything he was told about me. There was nothing I could do to appease him, particularly since I was living in Delhi, so it had been in many ways a good time to leave India for my first individual tour in the West.

Even after Annapurna came back to me near the end of 1958 he was still furious with me. It was only after some years that he seemed to calm down, although things were not quite like they had been before. The last time I saw him, when I visited Maihar in 1968 at the time we were filming *Raga*, he seemed to be his old self again, the guru-plus-father. Some of this meeting can be seen in the movie.

There was always pain in my heart that he was so prejudiced against me, which resulted in hurting us both. Now, however, I am calm and think only of the years when we had that father-son and guru-shishya relationship. From up there his spirit can see and know that I have loved and respected him from the bottom of my heart, and that I have tried to be sincere and do justice to whatever music I was lucky enough to gain from him. I know too that whatever accolades I have received and am receiving are only due to his great gift of music and blessings.

(opposite) Sharing accolades for the Bangladesh efforts with Ringo Starr and George Harrison.

(below) Allauddin Khan in his sitting room in Maihar; the portrait on the wall above him is of Mohammed Wazir Khan, his own guru.

After the Bangladesh concert had once more publicly confirmed the potential of the collaboration between Ravi and George Harrison, it was perhaps only natural that they would consider their first joint recording project.

The first of my records to be produced by George was *Shankar Family and Friends*. We assembled some Western session musicians, mostly from the jazz field, and then for a few days in April 1973 we hired A&M studios in Los Angeles.

Once again my compositions were done on the spot in the studio. As we assembled, I would start improvising, with the thread of the story for a ballet in mind. The basic theme of this ballet was my favourite one, which I have reworked on a few other pieces since. The first stage is Utopia, when everybody is happy, which we think of as being the state of the world yesterday or further in the past – when everything was good and rosy. In the next stage life slowly becomes discordant, leading to anger, violence and ultimately war and holocaust, when everything is destroyed. Then you hear a voice that says, 'There is a hope... get up again... there is hope for the future,' and everybody is talking about peace and ecology, and calling for positive action.

On one side of the LP was this thematic creation, a whole ballet conception, and on the other side were a few instrumental pieces and songs. I wrote one special song called 'I Am Missing You', one of the few that I have written in English, a simple lyric that just gushed out of me when I was travelling on a plane: 'I am missing you, oh Krishna where are you? Though I can't see you, I hear your flute all the while. Please come and wipe my tears and make me smile.'

There were two versions of this song included. In the original Indian one, sung mainly by Lakshmi Shankar, we attempted to convey the sounds and atmosphere of Vrindavan, the ancient holy city where Krishna grew up. Vrindavan is an astonishing place. Even today people there still talk of Krishna as if he is still a little boy in their neighbourhood. It is said you can still hear him playing his flute in the city, so it seemed appropriate that on the track the flute was featured throughout. Similarly we feel that he is always around. He is thought of as 'purushottam' – a kind of superman. He was so full of every quality possible: childlike, naughty, wise, yogic, erotic. The *Gita* is the greatest proof of his teachings of practicality and the highest form of spirituality.

We included an alternative version on which Lakshmi sang the same song with the music rearranged in a Western pop style by George, who also played the acoustic guitar and autoharp. This further featured Billy Preston on keyboards, Klaus Voormann on bass guitar, drums by Jim Keltner and Ringo Starr, saxophone by Tom Scott, and Emil Richards on marimba and percussion.

For this album, which was to be released on George's Dark Horse label, I had specially secured Shiv Kumar Sharma on santoor, and for the first time I brought Hari Prasad Chaurasia to the USA for the flute. Alla Rakha played the tabla. I also introduced a brilliant young Indian violinist, L. Subramaniam, who was about to receive his doctorate in Western music from the California Institute of the Arts, Los Angeles. He became famous much later on, as a performer and composer, but his first breaks in the West came on this record and the tour we were to arrange the following year.

In 1974 George came to India at the time of the opening ceremony for my new house in Benares, 'Hemangana' (literally meaning 'the Golden Courtyard', but an association to my mother's name, Hemangini). In a beautiful ceremony, eight South Indian Brahmins chanted from the Vedas for almost an hour and a half. Afterwards George and I discussed what to do in the future, and he suggested, 'Why not get some of the musicians you like, and we can have a tour in Europe and America?' I agreed, and proposed dividing the show into two parts, one consisting of myself with the Indian musicians, and the other, George with his band.

We all came over to England, and first of all the album *Music Festival From India* was rehearsed and recorded. George was the producer. For that record it was mostly the same Indian musicians I had used a year before for the LA recording: Hari Prasad, Alla Rakha, Lakshmi Shankar, Shiv Kumar Sharma and L. Subramaniam. There were also a few different artists, including four of my disciples – Kartick Kumar (on sitar), Gopal Krishan (vichitra veena), Satyadev Pawar (violin) and Harihar Rao (percussion and effects instruments) – as well as Sultan Khan (sarangi), T. V. Gopalkrishnan (mridangam and vocal), Kamalesh Maitra (tabla tarang, sarod and percussion) and Rijram

The musicians assembled for recording Music Festival From India *in 1974:*
FRONT ROW:
Viji Shankar, Ravi, Lakshmi Shankar.
SECOND ROW:
Kumar Shankar, L. Subramaniam.
STANDING:
Kamalesh Maitra, Rijram Desad, Harihar Rao, Kartick Kumar, Shiv Kumar Sharma, Alla Rakha, Hari Prasad Chaurasia, Sultan Khan, T. V. Gopalkrishnan.

Desad (various percussions). For the first time I also featured my niece (Lakshmi's daughter), Viji Shankar, who had a soft and lovely voice. (Later she married L. Subramaniam. Tragically she died young, from brain cancer, in February 1995.)

During the recording I was living in Belgravia, where George had fixed up a house for Kamala and me in Eaton Mews. Every day I had to travel by car to Henley, and I actually wrote most of the compositions on the M4!

GEORGE HARRISON: *All the other musicians stayed in the Imperial Hotel in Henley. I had an ex-John and Yoko Mercedes Benz 600 stretch limo, and I arranged for the driver to pick up all the musicians from the Imperial and bring them up to my house. It was funny: the big white car with blacked-out windows would pull up, the doors would open, and all these amazing Indians would get out! It was great.*

Most of the music for the album was played live in the drawing room of my house – we had mikes up to the studio. Ravi would tell everybody what their part

was, and Indian musicians are very good at memorising what they have to do. They would make some notation if they needed to remember something specific or especially difficult – and then he'd say, 'OK, ready?' He'd go to count them in, and I thought, 'This is going to be chaos.' But we'd start playing and it would be like magic.

George has always been very fond of Indian food, and he suggested we invite my former cook, Vasudevan, over from the States. He supplied us with Indian dishes, which were wonderful after our long rehearsals, in spite of the fact that afterwards we felt more like having a siesta than going back to work!

Within a few weeks we finished the recording, and then we toured (without George) in a few places in Europe, performing in Munich, Stockholm, Copenhagen, Paris and finally one evening at the Albert Hall in London. After that we all went to LA. George had a few rehearsals with his musicians in A&M studios and then in November we went on the road.

(top) Harry Harrison (George's father), Billy Preston, Ravi, George Harrison, President Ford, Jack Ford, and Tom Scott in The White House.

(above) With Jack Ford, outside The White House.

This was an extremely well organised tour. George had even arranged a Boeing 707 for us, complete with a big Aum painted on the outside, and the inside rearranged so that the front first-class area was a floor with carpets and throw cushions, like a Maharajah's lounge. The entire plane was ours for the tour. Our musical instruments, cushioned in large protective boxes, were travelling by road along with the sound equipment. After a performance three trucks used to leave for the next city, while we would fly later on, so that when we landed and were whisked off from the plane directly to the hotel (by car), they were there to meet us. One of the trucks was even converted into a full kitchen run by Vasudevan, so that there was Indian food ready for us on arrival at the hotel!

GEORGE HARRISON: *That was great. Everybody really got on well on the plane, all the Indian and the Western musicians. The flights were the best times. It was easier to fly after the show, so we got into the groove of escaping out of the hall, running to the airport and jumping on the plane. Then we'd take off and go to the next city and there would be a little after-show party on the plane, and we would arrive late at night so we would already be in the town for the next gig. Jim Keltner, Emil Richards and Tommy Scott were so into all the Indians – they would be hanging out with Alla Rakha on those plane rides, playing different rhythms. It was fantastic. And with the kitchen truck, it reached the stage where the Western musicians would be eating Indian food and the Indians would all be eating pizza!*

The American leg was known as the Dark Horse tour. The first half of the show consisted of me conducting and leading the Indian musicians, playing short instrumental compositions, and one item with me on sitar along with my group. The second section was George and his musicians, at the end of which we would join in for a combined East/West version of 'I Am Missing You', with vocals by Lakshmi and George (who also played the guitar), while some of the Indian group joined as a chorus, with me conducting.

For two months we toured all over the States and Canada, playing more than forty shows in stadiums and big halls like Madison Square Garden. The concerts were sold out everywhere, but there were one or two problems. George had been working very hard and as a result his voice went hoarse during the tour. He also wanted to perform all his new songs, and was insisting on not singing his old favourites which people were clamouring to hear. So it didn't work out quite as was expected.

There were also troubles with the half-and-half combination of Indian and pop music. I suppose only a tenth of the audience came for me, and the rest of them were there mainly for George. Neither camp was fully satisfied! Of course there was the same type of audience – continuously shrieking young rock fans – that I'd seen earlier. Reviews were lukewarm, but financially it was not a failure, and in spite of the difficulties we all immensely enjoyed the performing and especially the touring together.

GEORGE HARRISON: *During the tour of America we met Jack Ford, President Ford's son. He was studying to be a lumberjack somewhere in the West or Midwest. He said, 'When you come to Washington you can come up to our house – the White House.' He hadn't even been there himself, but he flew in specially for our concert in Washington near the end of the tour, and he arranged for us to visit it. Nixon had just left office, and that's why I was keen to go there. I wanted to see how many of the bad vibes were left hanging over there after all the Watergate scandal.*

They organised our visit in two tours. Billy Preston, Tommy Scott, Ravi, myself and my dad (who was with us on that part of the tour) were all taken in early and we met the President. We were taken up into the private apartments, had lunch up there, came down and went in the Oval Office, and as we came out we bumped into all the others from the Indian band, who had arrived later.

There's a photo of Billy Preston playing the piano in the White House. He was playing 'God Bless America' on the 200th or the 2000th Steinway. There were quite good vibes in the White House, which was interesting – I couldn't believe the place felt as comfortable as it did, after going through that Nixon period.

Unfortunately I had the first alert from my heart while we were in Chicago. I was hospitalised in Intensive Care for five days. Luckily it was not that serious, but I was cautioned to take care of my heart in the future, which reminded me of the warning Dr Maitra had given me in 1944 after I had the attack of rheumatic fever. The cause of the trouble this time seemed to have been the thunderous noise I'd had to endure from the stage monitors for those few weeks on tour. I missed the shows in a few cities, and Lakshmi had to conduct my group instead. Sue Jones, an intimate friend of mine, was with me on the tour and stayed back in Chicago to take care of me during my illness. She took me to rejoin the group for the last shows, and I managed to finish the tour.

There was a view at the time (still sometimes expressed today) that Ravi had been merely a phenomenon of the hippy era. It might be easy to forget that in 1976 he was marking twenty years of solo performances in the West. To celebrate this landmark, in March of that year he played to about 6,000 people in a dusk-to-dawn recital at New York's Cathedral of St John the Divine, the largest Gothic structure in the world and still unfinished today. In the inspiring setting, Ravi's performance of the final raga of the night is said to have sent a wave of goose-bumps around the entire audience as, after a night of drizzling rain, during the final fifteen minutes of the recital the sun rose and its first rays of the morning shone through the stained-glass windows onto his face.

With George's problems over Apple and The Beatles' court cases, and his hoarse voice during and after the tour, he had been going through strange up-and-down moods in this period. His manager was also behaving oddly with me, seeming to imply that I was taking advantage of George financially. After the tour George had said that I could keep the fabulous house in Eaton Mews, but I'd wanted him to know that I did not want to take any advantage of him, so I had gently turned down his generous offer.

There was little connection between us over the next few years. I was spending more time in India and we didn't meet that much, but the strong bond between us remained. We stayed in touch and we did work together again on one number ('Friar Park') on my 1987 album *Tana Mana*, but it's only in the last five years that we have once again been meeting more frequently. He visited me after I had my angioplasty operation in 1992, and he now comes to my homes in California or Delhi quite often. We have become closer than ever.

He has been very concerned about my health in general. My health is actually a very intriguing thing even to myself! I have gone through quite a few operations, and had so many occasional problems with my stomach or heart, yet still within me someone who is beyond the body seems to be very healthy. That carries me through, even when everybody else gives up and thinks I've had it! In a way I'm lucky, up to now – touch wood.

In the last few years Sukanya and I have both become good friends with George's wife Olivia also. She is a strong lady and takes good care of George and, of course, fantastic care of their handsome son, Dhani. I have known Dhani since his childhood. I first saw him on a half-day visit to George's in the middle of my 1978 tour of Britain. He was just a few months old, a lovely baby, and Olivia a proud and beaming mother. On the spur of the moment I wrote a silly little song for him, which went, 'Dhani, oh Dhani, oh Dhani...'!

GEORGE HARRISON: *Shortly after Dhani was born, Ravi and Alla Rakha took the train over to visit us, and I picked them up at Reading. They came over to see the baby, and Ravi wrote a tune called 'Dhani'. The name 'Dhani' actually came from my study of Indian music: from the scale of Sa-Ri-Ga-Ma-Pa-DHA-NI-Sa. So he wrote this song, and Alla Rakha played on one half of the tabla, the bayan.*

We recorded it together with George in his studio, with George himself on guitar. Later he overdubbed it with bass guitar and some other instruments. It was only a private recording for fun, but on my most recent visit, in the summer of 1996, he landed a surprise by playing it back for me, and it tickled me to hear it! Dhani celebrated his eighteenth birthday during that same visit of mine. He has grown up to be a very intelligent, handsome

George, Ravi and Peter Sellers, somewhere in the Seventies.

and funny guy. It seems his passion is being the cox of a rowing eight; he also plays the guitar and is very musical.

SUKANYA SHANKAR: *What probably touches me most about George is the sincerity of his relationship to Raviji. He is familiar with all of Raviji's records and songs and knows how each raga develops. He knows them so well. They have a unique relationship. They are so close.*

It's a deep and strong friendship that George and I have. Sometimes I am like a father to him, and sometimes he takes that role with me, while at the same time we are teacher and student, and along with that close friends. He puts me into a bubbly mood and provokes me into being funny and 'punny', by which I can justify my title of 'Pun-dit' to him!

He has some pronounced characteristics. He is so loving and magnanimous, going out of his way to help those whom he cares for. He also has something of a child in him, and likes to joke and pun too – he has that glint in his eyes, like a naughty boy. He always remembers the jokes I have told him and he repeats them all over, saying that he 'heard it from Ravi'!

Another quality he has is that of a wise old man who likes to advise and teach. He talks about what he's been reading and what he has imbibed from Indian philosophy – especially from Vivekananda's *Raja Yoga* and anything by Yogananda and his guru, Shri Yukteshwar. George is so serious and keen to teach people about this. He always says how much he likes everything Indian: our religion, philosophy, music, culture and food. I tease him sometimes when he becomes very serious talking about Indian philosophy, and bring him down to earth, full of fun and frolic. But I know he genuinely means what he says, and he swears by Indian classical music and all his favourite Indian artists.

He also has his black moods, as we all do – and God help anyone who at that time incites his wrath! He can be very hard, but he's frank like that; he doesn't hide his feelings. He can also completely shut himself off, and be quite indifferent and distrustful. Of course this is understandable, because he has been exploited so much by people he has trusted. It is a wonder that he is not like that all the time, that he still can have such feelings for others, especially fellow musicians.

He has been good to me. It is wonderful to have his regard, respect and love, as I too feel such deep love for him in my heart.

SEVEN: TILAK SHYAM

तिलक श्याम

As his focus shifted away from the West towards reaffirming his roots, Ravi was spending more time in India – particularly Delhi, from the start of the Eighties. In 1978 he published a Bengali-language autobiography aimed at the specialist music audience among his Bengali readers. Whereas My Music, My Life (1968) had been thin on technical detail lest it baffle the Western audience at which it was directed, in Raag Anurag Ravi discussed Indian music and musicians in a depth appropriate for a more knowledgeable public. The book was published by the Research Institute for Music and the Performing Arts (RIMPA), and translated into several languages, although not English.

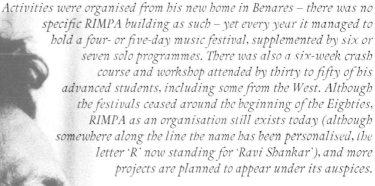

RIMPA was an artistic foundation which Ravi had set up himself. The aim was to provide an opportunity for younger performers to improve themselves and gain public recognition in India. Activities were organised from his new home in Benares – there was no specific RIMPA building as such – yet every year it managed to hold a four- or five-day music festival, supplemented by six or seven solo programmes. There was also a six-week crash course and workshop attended by thirty to fifty of his advanced students, including some from the West. Although the festivals ceased around the beginning of the Eighties, RIMPA as an organisation still exists today (although somewhere along the line the name has been personalised, the letter 'R' now standing for 'Ravi Shankar'), and more projects are planned to appear under its auspices.

Ravi was also responsible for a book-and-triple-cassette set entitled Learning Indian Music: A Systematic Approach, produced with the assistance of Professor Elise Barnett from City College, New York, and issued in the USA in 1979. It was a further extension to his continuing efforts at education about his art form, following on from the monumental Anthology of Indian Music set released on World Pacific a decade earlier. The latter, a personal favourite of Ravi's, had comprised a double album, featuring a spoken history of Indian music with example performances, and an accompanying book with artwork by Jan Steward.

With Uday and his family in Calcutta: (left to right) Amala Shankar, Mamata Shankar, Ravi, Uday, Ananda Shankar.

In September 1977 Dada died in Calcutta. All the government offices in the city remained closed for a day in tribute. People turned out in huge numbers to pay homage to him, in one of the largest funeral processions ever seen in the city.

After *Samanya Kshati* back in 1962, Dada and I had not produced any more finished work together. Gradually he developed more health problems and in 1968, when he came to America for what proved to be his last tour with the troupe, he had suffered a brain haemorrhage while in San Diego and was hospitalised. As I was living in Los Angeles, he'd stayed in my house for about six weeks while convalescing, being looked after by me and especially Kamala.

To see him like that was such a pity. I felt like crying, because I couldn't forget him from earlier years when he was absolutely like fire – this handsome superstar, so strong and virile. Unfortunately, through his bad health he had lost some of that charisma and wonderful blessing, and he was an unhappy and frustrated person during his last years. I used to see him sometimes, but we did not collaborate again.

Both of Dada's children have made a name for themselves. Ananda is a composer and director of his own troupe along with his lovely dancer wife Tanushree. Mamata has likewise earned great success, in her case as an actress in films, including some by Satyajit Ray. She is a fabulous dancer as well, reminiscent of Dada on stage. Amala-Boudi takes care of the Uday Shankar India Culture Centre, which she established in Calcutta. She has taught many young students the Uday Shankar style of dance, and even now is continuing to do so with dedication.

It is a shame that little else has been done to celebrate Dada's glory and what he did for India. I have been talking about him regularly to remind people of his greatness. Even now our government has not built any memorials or statues to him, and it seems it was only recently that the West Bengal Government first named a street after him. The present generation know almost nothing about him. For this reason I became eager to produce a festival in his honour, and in December 1983 I did so. It was a stupendous triumph.

We staged a four-day celebration in Delhi named *Uday Utsav* ('utsav' is the word for a festival). It was a moving experience for all present, including the then Prime Minister, Indira Gandhi, who inaugurated the festival. Amala, Ananda and Mamata participated along with their troupes, as did students of Dada such as Sachin Shankar and Narendra Sharma. Many more admirers and other great artists paid tribute to his memory – including Kelubabu, the ultimate dancer and guru of Odissi style, and Vyjayanthimala, who danced in Bharata Natyam style.

I contributed a few musical items myself, including a special vocal and instrumental composition called *Manoharini* in homage to Dada, using the voices of Lakshmi and others. This piece also incorporated a slide show put together by my American friend Alan Kozlowski along with his companion Sandra Hay. (They married each other the following May.)

Alan had first approached me through Dick Bock in the late Seventies, as a photographer who wanted to take some portraits. Along with his camera, something else clicked between us, and a deep bond was formed. From photography he went through transitions into the audio, video and interactive fields, and he has now, along with dear Sandra, built up a successful production and post-production firm in Santa Monica. He became my disciple in the true Indian style in 1994, his instrument being the acoustic guitar, although he has now started on a new instrument created by Bishandas Sharma of Delhi which I have named the 'pushpa veena'. (Recently I gave one to George also.) Mostly Alan plays flamenco music. He is very dear to me, and I have entrusted him with many of my photos, newspaper cuttings, videos and other memorabilia, which he has organised for a future archive and is temporarily safeguarding for us. Sukanya plans to establish the archive with these and other materials at my future home in India.

In directing my attention away from the West in the late Seventies, I turned my thoughts to the Far East. For years I had felt that there was a possibility of my working with Japanese musicians. I had heard the koto played by leading Japanese performers (at the Paris UNESCO gala in 1958, for example) and was enchanted by its sound: such a beautiful mixture of the guitar and the harp. I also loved the shakuhachi, a big bamboo flute which produces a deep and spiritual sound, the quality of which is finer than even our Indian bamboo flute. The Japanese have some old songs dating back to the fourteenth century, which are based on scales resembling certain of our ragas – such as *Bairagi*, *Gunkali* and *Shivaranjani*, and some of our pentatonic ones (ragas with a five-note scale) like *Bhupali* and *Durga*. It was clear that this similarity would make it easier for me to find the meeting point between Indian and Japanese music in a composition.

Polygram in Japan showed interest, and a project was fixed up in 1978 through my agent in Tokyo, Yoshiro Kambara. So he arranged all this, and I went. Two Japanese musicians were suggested whom I had already heard of: the koto virtuoso Susumu Miyashita, and Hozan Yamamoto on the shakuhachi. They play traditional music as well as modern and jazz styles, and are experienced commercial artists. The idea was very attractive. So I travelled all the way to Japan especially to do this recording, while Alla Rakha joined me on the trip to play tabla. I had a few ragas in mind beforehand and decided on two of them in Japan. For the shakuhachi piece I selected *Raga Shivaranjani*, naming it *Namah Shivaya*. I chose *Durga* for the koto piece, naming it *Padhasapa* after the sargam names of the composition's first four notes: Pa, Dha, Sa and Pa. The Japanese musicians felt there should be one piece in which I performed also, and for that they suggested a beautiful fourteenth-century traditional melody known as *Rokudan*. So I learnt the first and second lines of it, and we began playing the melody separately, then together, and gradually moved on to improvising, returning to the main melody intermittently. For that I played a smaller sitar than I usually use, tuned to D. As for the name of the album, I had done three volumes of *West Meets East*, so I thought of *East Greets East*. Everyone liked the name and we kept it.

In June 1985, the chance arose for me to produce another piece with Japanese flavour at the Japan America Theatre in Los Angeles. For their *Rhythms of the World* festival I devised a continuous piece which developed dramatically over an hour and a half, beginning with Japanese themes and smoothly leading on to the Indian melodies. There was a fine collection of musicians participating: June Kuramoto on koto, Kazu Matsui on shakuhachi, Johnny Mori on the o-daiko drum, plus Lakshmi Shankar on vocals, Aashish Khan (Alubhai's son) on sarod, Swapan Chowdhury on tabla, some folk drums and other folk instruments. Also part of the ensemble was my son Shubho, who at this time was a regular sitar performer. I myself participated in one or two items. Again the production turned out to be quite unlike anything I had done in the past. Alan Kozlowski made a video of the concert.

I brought several of my disciples to the USA for the first time in order to appear in this show: Tarun Bhattacharya (santoor), Ramesh Mishra (sarangi), Daya Shankar (shahnai) and Vishwa Mohan Bhatt on slide guitar. (Vishwa Mohan, a dear disciple of mine, added side strings and sympathetic strings and called his new instrument the Mohan Veena – which drew criticism because, unknown to him, back in the Fifties or late Forties the famous sarod player Radhika Mohan Maitra of Calcutta used the same name for an instrument he created by combining the rabab and the sursingar. Vishwa Mohan is a marvellous virtuoso; in 1994 he won a Grammy Award – only the third Indian to do so – for the album he made with Ry Cooder, *A Meeting by the River*.)

I have long wanted to undertake a similar project with Chinese musicians. Traditional Chinese music is so beautiful. They have fantastic performers and many of their scales are almost the same as the Japanese ones. Maybe I can do it in the future? I would also love to do something with the Indonesian gamelans. Let us see!

In 1979 the Hindi film *Meera* was released, another film featuring my soundtrack. Directed by the celebrated poet, writer, lyricist and film director S. S. Gulzar, it concerns the life of a fifteenth-century poetess and saint from Rajasthan, who was a Maharani. She was a Krishna devotee who wrote and sang beautiful bhajans which are still famous today. Although not a box-office hit, it was a sensitively and beautifully made movie. Some of the songs were much appreciated, and I enjoyed doing it. Lata Mangeshkar was my first choice as the vocalist, but due to some misunderstandings between the director and her we had Vani Jairaman singing instead. Vani did a fine job of it, and since then she has become one of the best-known playback singers in South Indian films.

In the Seventies Ravi remained keen to explore more thoroughly the possibilities of an Indian/jazz hybrid. Although jazz's similarity to Indian classical music runs no deeper than their parallel emphasis on improvisation, such a musical rendezvous was still a challenge. His enthusiasm for the form had been kindled during his childhood days in Thirties jazz haunts like the Cotton Club. Down the years, in addition to his associations with Bud Shank and John Coltrane, he had given basic lessons in Indian music to Don Ellis (who also studied with Harihar Rao) and was good friends with Dizzy Gillespie. For a World Pacific recording Ravi had even arranged and conducted a rhythmic piece for Alla Rakha and the jazz drummer Buddy Rich, which rejoiced in the title Rich à la Rakha.

In 1980, at a specially arranged jazz festival in Bombay, he joined forces with some visiting American jazzmen, including John Handy (alto saxophone), George Adams (tenor sax), Mike Richmond (string bass) and the keyboard-player Louis Banks from Bombay. Ravi composed a series of linked pieces to be played by them along with a host of local musicians playing Indian instruments. He called it Jazzmine.

In the past John Handy had learnt Indian music informally during a few sittings with me, and had also recorded with Alubhai. John came to Bombay along with a number of other famous names for a jazz festival. I was asked to create a special composition, which became a long piece – a kind of variety show – consisting of a number of diverse but related pieces joined together. At the beginning Sanskrit shlokas were sung with orchestral and vocal accompaniment, then I introduced khyal and thumri styles and some folk music, and after that there was a transition from folk to jazz. In the jazz piece some basic motifs were elaborated and then there was some improvisation by those wonderful musicians.

A live recording was made of the event by Polydor. But I couldn't believe what they did: a man had come all the way from Germany specially to tape it, and I found out he was using an ordinary two-track machine from the auditorium! The sound was naturally unsatisfactory, no matter how much we tried to doctor it. Nevertheless a live record, *Jazzmine*, was brought out.

'In this composition, I have tried to explore the meeting ground and the interaction between the classical and folk music of India on the one hand, and jazz on the other. I have named it "Jazzmine". My aim in these pieces has been to extract, that is to say "mine", the spirit of jazz and wrap it in the fragrance of the jasmine flower, which is uniquely Indian. The result is "My Jazz" or "Jazzmine".' *(sleeve notes)*

Ravi's rare degree of versatility enables him to switch between different styles of music, although always mounting them on an Indian base. A lifelong determination to expose himself to all forms of music and life has ensured he is open to the latest advances in music technology – for instance, he was soon to embrace the possibilities of the emulator.

Such curiosity cannot be dismissed as a fondness for gimmicks. Quality and sincerity have always been keynotes of his experiments. Had he been less rigorous, he could no doubt have made more of a killing in the late Sixties. So it was typical of this man with the musical coat of many colours that shortly after working in the jazz idiom he made a happy return to the Western classical field through his reunion with Zubin Mehta.

Since getting to know Zubin Mehta in the Sixties, through the years I had met him once in a while, but it was in 1980 that we came much closer. Having done the *Concerto for Sitar and Orchestra* with the LSO in 1971, by the late Seventies I wanted to experiment with another one. In 1977 Zubin joined the New York Philharmonic as their music director, while I too was spending plenty of time in the Big Apple. Zubin and I discussed the project I had in mind. He was very interested and obtained the commission from the orchestra.

(above) Conducting Buddy Rich in the piece Rich à la Rakha.

(opposite) Mike Richmond, Louis Banks and Ravi, collaborators on Jazzmine, *in Bombay, 1980.*

He suggested I visit the Avery Fisher Hall at the Lincoln Center on the mornings he rehearsed there with the orchestra, so that I could get to know all the musicians and their sound, their possibilities and limitations, and the range of what I could do with them. That was truly helpful for me in formulating my ideas for the composition, and I discovered that among them were some fabulous musicians, including the flautist Julius Baker. After meeting all of them I wrote the piece with particular people in mind for the solo parts. That was how my second sitar concerto came about. We first performed it in April 1981, and I dedicated it to Zubin.

I named it, as I have now named this book, *Raga Mala*, which means 'Garland of Ragas'. I took about forty different ragas, one after the other: with the first ones we played long pieces of each raga, and then gradually each one received a shorter and shorter elaboration, so that in the end they were mere flashes of ragas, eight to sixteen bars each. I am very pleased with it. It employed many instruments which I hadn't used in the first concerto, like the brass section and wind instruments, which made it sound quite different.

However, it turned out to be more difficult to perform than my first concerto, especially the first movement where I deal with the morning raga *Lalit*, which to Western ears has a very unusual pattern. Its scale has the minor second and minor sixth notes, and no fifth, but it has both the normal and the augmented fourth. The musicians had a difficult time playing it!

As a conductor *par excellence*, Maestro Zubin Mehta holds an exalted position and earns much respect in the Western classical world, yet he retains something of the child in him and can be so funny and down-to-earth. He loves hot spicy food (he is even said to carry a small tin of red or green chillies in his pocket to add to bland food!) and before I had composed the concerto he had suggested, 'Let it be something like hot chilli. Make it difficult.' I really made it very complicated – and we had problems. It was not played as accurately as I would have liked. Zubin conducted it wonderfully, grasping the spirit of its rhythmic structure – the pieces in complex cycles like six and a half or thirteen and a half beats and cross-rhythms – but unfortunately the overall result was (as it had sometimes been with the first concerto) that I myself messed up each time I played it, because the discordant sounds or wrong rhythmic accents I heard in the background from the other instrumentalists affected my own concentration.

I'm scared of the second concerto, because it is so much more difficult that the first. Of course, playing with an orchestra is not like giving a solo sitar recital, when I am absolutely the king: leader, conductor and performer. When playing solo I don't depend on anyone else, and as it is all improvised I can do exactly what I want. But with an orchestra it's a very different situation.

I have the highest regard for Zubin, not only because I am proud he comes from my country, but also because I know him personally, and he is a fantastic musician. Since our association began back in the Sixties he has also become more familiar with and fond of Indian music. He was so helpful and cooperative throughout all the work on the concerto, and displayed such love and regard for me.

I spent a few weeks with him again in April 1989, when we toured together with the European Youth Orchestra, which consists of talented young musicians from all over Europe, roughly between the ages of eighteen and twenty-four. We started off in London and Madrid, and then continued on to India, performing in Calcutta, Bombay and Delhi. The arrangements in India were taken care of by the Oberoi hotel group in an excellent manner. We had a memorable experience and a lot of fun. It was exhilarating to be playing and touring with the kids – young and full of life, such fine musicians – while Zubin was so humorous and entertaining. He conducted some Western pieces and then my first sitar concerto, omitting the first movement.

Even though I had written this particular piece in 1970, this was the first time India had heard it. The concerts were televised by Doordarshan (our state TV station) so that people in the places where we didn't perform could also see and hear it, and there were some glowing reports about it. It was quite amusing to receive such late recognition for a piece in my own country. I have always felt gratified for being admired in India as a performer, but to my chagrin much less is known there about my creative side, although gradually this has changed – and better late than never!

Zubin has also caught the public eye and ear in his work along with the Three Tenors (José Carreras, Placido Domingo and Luciano Pavarotti), which is a fabulous collaboration, especially the performance they gave in Rome for the 1990 World Cup. What a treat to hear three of the finest voices together

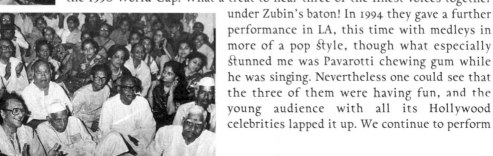

under Zubin's baton! In 1994 they gave a further performance in LA, this time with medleys in more of a pop style, though what especially stunned me was Pavarotti chewing gum while he was singing. Nevertheless one could see that the three of them were having fun, and the young audience with all its Hollywood celebrities lapped it up. We continue to perform together occasionally – most recently he conducted my March 1997 performance of the first sitar concerto at London's Barbican Hall.

ZUBIN MEHTA: *It was really two friends getting together, wanting to be together on stage, that made our collaboration possible. Musicians appreciate one another. It's wonderful to have colleagues from different worlds speak and listen to each other. And my collaboration with Raviji during the second concerto was one that educated me more than anybody else.*

Everybody wants jazz and classical music to fuse, or Indian music and Western classical, but basically on paper it is impossible! With Ravi's first and second concertos attempts were made, though orchestra players can't really improvise, especially in the Indian vein. Ravi, when he plays, is a free bird. He flies in space. He is the soaring eagle. So when he plays with the orchestra he is shackled. During the composition of the second concerto I said, 'Leave yourself space to improvise.' He felt terribly handicapped during the rehearsals because he had to keep to the number of measures allotted to him.

We played this concerto four or five times in New York, and then later in Europe – always to standing ovations. It really filled my heart with joy to see this great, great musician, this Jascha Heifetz of India, being so honoured. I don't think the Indians took to it quite as well, because of the fact that in the West we are just not trained to improvise, although the musicians of the New York Philharmonic surpassed themselves in trying. Indians want the development of the raga – they want to hear the improvisation – which was hardly possible with fusion.

But it is a very exciting piece and it was a unique collaboration. It demands a great virtuosity on the part of the sitarist and the orchestra, and of course in the West it was very well appreciated. And people like Ravi should be encouraged to fly in space and soar above all of us, as he has done all his life.

(below) In Calcutta with Zubin Mehta for the 1989 tour with the European Youth Orchestra.

(bottom) Premiering the second Sitar Concerto with the New York Philharmonic in 1981.

I was excited when I was asked to supply the music for the major film *Gandhi* – one of the most important movies ever made in India – but there was a slightly discordant feeling from the outset because it was never exactly clear how the situation stood. There was supposed to be another music director on the film, George Fenton, and I had never worked with anyone else in that way on a film. Somebody had always been there to help me with orchestration or arranging, but I had never before had to share the role of music director. I explained this to the director, Richard Attenborough, when he, George Fenton and I met in Bombay in 1981. Richard said it was necessary to have orchestral background music for the predominantly Western viewers, which would mostly be

George's responsibility. My involvement would be in composing the original melodic pieces and directing the Indian instruments.

I did insist on having as the theme music a particular raga that I had created a few days after the assassination of Mahatma Gandhi in 1948. At that time I had an afternoon radio programme in Bombay, and I was asked to play some mournful music without tabla accompaniment – an alap only. Arriving about two hours before I was due on the air, I was having trouble deciding which raga to play. Then an idea came to me: thinking of the name 'Gandhi', I took the three sargam notes which approximate to it: Ga, Ni, and Dha (the third, seventh and sixth notes). I flattened both the seventh and sixth, and with occasional use of the second note (Ri) a melodic theme developed. I followed the pattern in my mind and immediately plucked it on the sitar, composing on the spur of the moment while tuning up in the studio. This theme returns again and again as a refrain in the melody. At once it gave me the entire structure that I performed.

My new raga had some resemblance to a popular traditional pentatonic raga called *Malkauns*, which has three notes flattened – the third (Ga), sixth (Dha) and seventh (Ni) – and uses neither the fifth (Pa) nor the second (Ri). When the radio announcer asked what piece I was about to play, I had to think quickly. Gandhiji's full name was Mohandas Karamchand Gandhi, so combining his first name with the similar raga *Malkauns* I arrived at the name *Mohankauns*.

As well as this refrain, I contributed all the other Indian pieces in *Gandhi*. For some of the Western orchestral music George Fenton arranged some of the melody structures I had written, as well as contributing a few original pieces himself. Unfortunately my main section, a piece in which the Mahatma's favourite bhajans were sung, came right at the end when the titles were coming up. Since few people stay to see the titles after the end of a movie, many will have missed it.

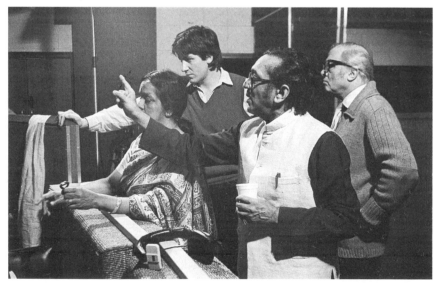

· *Directing the music for the Oscar-laden Gandhi, with Lakshmi Shankar and Richard Attenborough.*

But even if I was not entirely happy with the music, and would have preferred to do it all myself, nevertheless the total effect of the film was superb. Everybody was moved, and I feel it had the desired effect. I saw it being released in London, New York and Los Angeles, and it had a major impact, on younger people more than anyone else. It was tremendous how Gandhi's message of peace and non-violence came over so strongly.

From the point of view of authenticity, there were many flaws. Leading characters who had played an important part in Gandhi's life, such as Rabindranath Tagore and Subhas Chandra Bose, were omitted. And having met in real life most of the characters who were featured, I felt that the actors who played them did not seem suitable; though for people who didn't know them that didn't particularly matter. All the same the overall effect was still extremely satisfactory. As for Ben Kingsley: he did an excellent job as Gandhiji. The film was Attenborough's finest hour, a commercial triumph and the winner of eight Oscars, though not one for the music, which nevertheless was nominated for Best Original Score.

A round the end of 1981, while in Bombay I was approached by General Sethna and General Narinder Singh of the Indian Army, who asked me if I would contribute the musical and artistic direction for the Ninth Asian Olympics (known as ASIAD) which were to be held in Delhi in 1982. This was a highly prestigious occasion and it was a great honour to be asked. My only concerns were that I should have artistic freedom in creating the musical numbers (while following the basic guidelines they gave me), and that I could choose my working assistants. They gave me *carte blanche*. Preparations lasted several weeks, but all the arrangements were extremely efficient. This was the first time I had worked with army personnel, and it was a pleasure to collaborate with people who were so well organised, disciplined and helpful.

I was responsible for the opening and closing ceremonies, some other dance items, and a grand finale piece. All the music was prerecorded at HMV Studios in Bombay and then played in the stadium on huge amplifiers. For the 'Hymn Of The ASIAD', the main theme song, I set to music a lyric by the celebrated Hindi poet Pandit Narendra Sharma, the first line of which was 'Swagatam shubha swagatam' (which translates as something like 'Welcome, good and auspicious welcome'). It was sung in Hindi by a choral group, and later recited in an English version by the actor Amitabh Bachchan, who was for about twenty years the most incredibly popular superstar in Indian films – he possesses a beautiful bass baritone voice. A further instrumental version was played by the Band of the Indian Navy.

Assisting me with the music was Vijay Raghava Rao, my flautist disciple, who has worked with me on many compositions for films and other productions in India, including *Meera*, *Jazzmine*, *Gandhi* and *Uday Utsav*. He is a brilliant composer himself (he has provided the music for many films and ballets) and extremely versatile. He is like my alter ego in some ways: as well as being a musician, he was originally a dancer. He is also a notable poet in English and in his mother tongue, Telugu. For the choreography I brought in my nephew Ananda Shankar and also Narendra Sharma (Dada's student, not the Hindi poet of the same name). Narendra was a student at the Almora centre and a famous dancer, and is now a well-known choreographer.

The success of the events filled me with pride. They were a wonderful spectacle: the boys and girls dancing on the central field of the stadium; the thirty bedecked elephants specially brought from Kerala circling the arena to the accompaniment of the nadaswaram (a loud reed instrument), chenda and maddalam (drums), and cymbals; followed by the Kathakali dancers with their flamboyant dresses and the fabulous folk dancers from all over India with their colourful costumes. It all provided me with one of the most satisfying feelings of achievement I have had in all the big projects I have been associated with.

There were some funny scenes, too. The one that particularly sticks in the mind is the sight of a team of half a dozen people running after the elephants with huge buckets and spades, always alert for one of the creatures emitting any of its elephantine waste. As for people's reactions when a male elephant grew his massive 'fifth leg'...!

Three brothers at 'Hemangana': Ravi, Debendra and Rajendra at Ravi's Benares home.

Just after the ASIAD ended, while I was still enjoying the feeling of euphoria, I received a long-distance call from Kamala in Madras. She told me that Mejda was gravely ill, and that I should come immediately. I took the next flight available, and arrived to find him lying in a coma in a nursing home. It was heartbreaking to see him thus, unable to hear, speak, think or feel anything, and being fed through a tube. He died on the third day I was there. Traditionally it is the eldest son's duty to perform the final rites, but with Kumar being in Los Angeles I took on the role, bringing Mejda to the funeral site.

This was the third death I had witnessed. The first was my brother Bhupendra, the second my mother's father – and now my beloved Mejda. I felt numb and empty after this for quite a long time.

My sadness on that occasion in Madras was compounded by the presence of Kamala, since our connection had been completely severed a year earlier in Calcutta. At length I shall explain to you more about the tangled web of my personal life.

Until August 1983 I had never performed in China. Back in 1935 we had been about to embark on a tour of China when the news came through about my father's death, and that visit had been called off. So when at last I arrived, at the invitation of the Peking government, it was a great thrill to be there. I went to only four places: Peking, Canton, Shanghai and Chengdu in Szechuan Province. I didn't like Canton, and Shanghai, although it was interesting to see the old music conservatoires and the sights that were so familiar from old films and books, still didn't attract me very much. Szechuan Province and Peking itself I found fascinating.

Our hosts showed us some wonderful sights and constantly reminded us that their culture was four or five thousand years old, but as an Indian that only made me love and admire my own country even more. We also can talk about a five-thousand-year-old culture but with ours almost everything is still alive. It is a living culture; our music and dance are living arts. Maybe they are going through a process of development, becoming slightly modified, but they did not effectively cease a few hundred years ago, as was the case in China. All the arts in China appeared to be a matter of heritage only. Nevertheless we did enjoy some of their old traditional music, and I was very impressed with the remarkable Peking Opera, although the best company is actually not in the People's Republic but in Taiwan. The original Peking Opera Group was one of the great assets Chiang Kai-Shek brought with him when he fled the mainland in 1949.

The Chinese people were not really that knowledgeable about India. Indeed they didn't appear to have much regard for any other cultures. They were into their own, which is fine, but their own is nowadays so Westernised, consisting of ballet, opera, symphony orchestras and so forth. The conservatoires were closed down for a long time by the first communist government, but now they have reopened and are dominating. Nevertheless – and I am really very lucky and blessed – I had no problem myself. I gave a few performances in the music conservatoires with large audiences of a thousand to fifteen hundred people, as well as two lecture-demonstrations in Peking, and they were always marvellous successes.

If someone asks me, 'What do you find most important in China?' I say the food. I have always been extremely fond of Chinese food but, having frequented Chinese restaurants all around the world, I have invariably found that the Chinese dishes you find in every city outside China have been influenced slightly by the local cuisine or the taste of the people in that particular country. To have Chinese food in China is something entirely different. I couldn't believe the variety we had – it was like the variety of food we have in India. But India, like Europe, has so many different nationalities with different languages, culture and people that it is easy to explain such diversity. China is a huge country, with a huge population, but with only two principal languages it had always seemed to me to be more homogeneous – until our experiences in its restaurants. I can't tell you – what fantastic food we had everywhere! From very hot and spicy food to very bland, but always with subtle differences and always so tasty.

My master sitar which was given to me by Nodu Mullick in 1957 is still with me even today, but in recent years it has suffered two bad accidents. On a trip to Milan in the early Eighties, after Nodu had stopped touring with me, it was broken into two pieces just below the neck. That was the first time I had carried my sitar in a box on a flight. It seems there was something wrong in the way the case was made, as I discovered when I opened it after arrival – on the day before the concert. All my sitars are very special to me (I am always terrified about them being damaged or exposed to sunlight or damp) but Nodu's was the most important of all. My heart was broken, just like the instrument. There was nothing that could be done, and the concert had to be cancelled.

I brought the sitar back to India, but Nodu was in bad health in Calcutta at that time and I did not have the courage to tell him about the accident. He had always told me never to keep a sitar in a box when travelling, and that's why for so many years I had carried the sitar myself all the time – even buying an extra air ticket so it could occupy the seat next to me. But it was becoming too difficult, especially with more and more security hazards. Everywhere I was having to open the sitar cover and show the instrument to the airport officials, and even then they were doubtful. They would bang on the gourd – which is very delicate – as if there were a bomb or drugs being smuggled inside it, and eventually I had decided to use a case. So in Delhi, without telling Nodu anything, I had the sitar repaired at Rikhi Ram and Son. The two pieces were joined together, and though I feel it has never again produced quite the sound there previously, it is very near to it.

Rikhi Ram was a wonderful instrument-maker, who originally came from Lahore but after partition had settled in Delhi, where he established his shop. His own sitars did not really have the finesse of those from Calcutta, but gradually he trained his son Bishandas Sharma who, after the death of his father, advanced the workshop greatly. He grew much more versatile in repairing and manufacturing various instruments. The repair of Nodu's sitar was my first commission for Bishandas. After Nodu's death a year or two later, however, I had no one else, so I had to use Bishandas more and more. In the beginning he could not reproduce my style of jawari, but he learnt rapidly, and after some time he came very near to it. He's now the person whom I have really chosen to maintain my instruments – and those of my daughter, too, as well as some of my students. With the help of his two sons, Ajay and Sanjay, Bishandas is one of the best now. When a similar accident occurred in September 1996, the gourd being cracked during the flight back from a recital in Philadelphia, once again he repaired it for me, after some emergency patch-up work by my student Tony Karasek in San Diego. Bishandas is also my disciple.

Nowadays when I travel I keep with me another sitar, a slightly smaller one which I had Bishandas make for me, because I have become so scared about anything happening to my main sitar. The spare one is slightly smaller and tuned to D. The higher pitch is ideal for the sitar concerto. My main one is half a note lower, C sharp.

Among the Calcutta instrument-makers, after Kanai Lal and his brothers died there have to my mind been two who have stood out. Hiren Roy became very famous. His style of sound did not suit me, but he made sitars for almost every other leading sitar-player, and with the advent of the sitar explosion in the mid-Sixties there were so many orders from all over the world. All the sitar-makers of India benefited – they made millions. Another leading name was Hemen Sen, a sitar-maker who at Alubhai's request started also making sarods and became a true expert at sarods. These two craftsmen were situated very near each other in Calcutta, on the same road. Hiren Roy died a couple of years ago, but Hemen is still there, and they both had sons who work in the same craft.

On nearly all his foreign tours since the beginning of the Sixties, Ravi had used Alla Rakha as his regular tabla accompanist. They were closely identified with each other, especially outside India (since in India Ravi had continued to work with other tablists as well). Their partnership lasted until 1985, almost twenty-seven years, before they parted ways.

The longest period that I had anyone as my tabla accompanist was that with Alla Rakha: a fabulous tabla-player, a great virtuoso, with wonderful tonal quality and a romantic and humorous context to his playing. As a person, he has such a good nature, almost like a child – and in fact I really had to baby him a lot, especially for the first ten years or so as he didn't speak any English. I had to help him in every way. Early on he was rather fond of a drink or two, but upon my suggestion he restricted this to after a recital or in free time. Instead he became a TV addict! Watching *I Spy*, *Mission Impossible*, *Hawaii Five-O* and *Bonanza* (which were my favourite programmes too!), old epics like *Ben Hur*, *Spartacus* and *The Ten Commandments* (which he liked even more) and cowboy westerns helped him to learn American English.

But by the middle of the Eighties I felt that age was getting the better of both of us. I needed someone younger, not only as an accompanist but also to carry my shoulder bags, fill in all the forms and help in so many other ways. His family and students in Bombay also needed him more. In 1985 we parted company, and young Kumar Bose of Calcutta became my regular accompanist. There was some feeling of hurt on the part of Alla Rakha and his followers for a couple of years, but now we are friends again. He accompanies me in special concerts in India every year.

Kumar basically has the virile pakhawaj style of his guru, my friend Kishan Maharaj of Benares, but belonging to this age Kumar (a left-handed tablist) is very versatile. His personality is as impressive as his playing, projecting a tremendous vigour and excitement. He remained my regular tabla-player everywhere for about five years up until 1991. Since then I have been giving a chance to several different tablists of the younger generation, although whenever possible I like to have Zakir Hussain, Swapan Chowdhury or Kumar.

One finds such a wondrous extension of Alla Rakha in Zakir Hussain, his son. I have known Zakir since his childhood and it is such a joy when he accompanies me in any concert. By the age of three or four he was fascinated by the tabla and already his father had started to train him. At my performances I was amazed to see this child sitting there all night, often on his father's lap, listening and keeping tala, sometimes dropping off to sleep towards the end, but above all loving the music. I was very drawn to young little Zakir and knew that he was going to be something fantastic – and that's what really happened. I saw him growing from a budding artist to a talented prodigy to the full-blown genuine article that he is today.

In addition to the traditional Punjab gharana and his father's own style in which he trained, Zakir is adept not only in all other gharanas of tabla-playing, but also those of nakkara, mridangam, dholak, bongo, jazz, African drumming... the list goes on! He has assembled it all and enriched his tabla to such an extent that he drives his listeners into a frenzy. He is blessed with handsome, youthful looks and sex appeal, as well as manners, intelligence and humour, which have all helped to make him the most outstanding and popular drummer anywhere. With all this he has maintained his equilibrium and humility, particularly in giving due respect to elderly musicians and other people senior to him, in the true Indian tradition. Lately we have become very close and I love him like a son.

Swapan Chowdhury is another fabulous tabla-player. The tone Swapan produces on the right-hand tabla drum is unique. Two other tabla-players whose perfect tuning and sound production I hugely appreciated were Samta Prasad of Benares and Kanai Dutt.

Lately there has been much concentration by tablists on the bayan (the left-hand, bass drum of the tabla pair). This is a vogue initiated by Kumar and Zakir and now followed by most other tabla-players, but it is not new: the most famous tabla-player of olden days was Biru Maharaj, who could play a whole melody in fast tempo on the bayan alone – simply with the pressure of the base of his palm. Benares tabla-players were masters at this. I have also had the privilege to have heard the great Kanthe Maharaj (uncle and guru of Kishan Maharaj), who used to work rhythmic wonders with the bayan.

I enjoyed doing the music for the film *Genesis*, made around 1985 and directed by the internationally successful Mrinal Sen from Calcutta. Although the dialogue (what little existed) was in Hindi and the film was shot mostly in the northern part of Rajasthan, it was financed and produced by a company in Brussels. Starring Shabana Azmi and Om Kapoor, *Genesis* was an excellent film with a simple story, but again (as my luck would have it) not a commercial hit. I recorded the music spontaneously in a studio in Paris, using just a few musicians: Kumar Bose, the extremely versatile Kamalesh Maitra (who lives in Berlin, and had been on the Dark Horse tour with me), and two local musicians on the cello and other instruments.

In 1987 Ravi returned to the Soviet Union. The extraordinary reaction he received from the Russian public was ironic in the extreme, given the cold bureaucratic treatment he had received in 1967. Returning after years spent trying to unload his hippy-guru burden and regain classical regard, he was met by an echo of his past.

My third tour of the USSR was a real surprise. I performed in the Bolshoi Theatre, Tchaikovsky Hall and the best hall in Leningrad. By 1987 more music had filtered through into the Soviet Union, and the public knew all about me and the connection with George. To my astonishment it transpired that there were hippies in Soviet Russia, dressed in the same style as the Western hippies of the late Sixties! At one concert venue they were trying to break the glass roof above the box office, because my concert was sold out and they were not allowed in! When I emerged from the hall afterwards there was such pandemonium – they were screaming, 'RAVI SHANKAR! JAI GURU! JAI

GURU!' I couldn't believe it! It did not seem possible that I was in Soviet Russia, because my memory of it was so different from this. It had obviously taken a lot longer for the music and that fervour to spread there.

After the performance a similar scene occurred at Moscow railway station, where we went to catch the train for Leningrad. A group of fifty or sixty young people was waiting for me in the station itself, and upon my arrival they embraced me, giving me flowers – as if it were the mid-Sixties again. Seeing this in the mid-Eighties, and in Moscow of all places, was bizarre! They followed me into the station, calling out, 'R-A-V-I! RAVI! WE LOVE YOU, WE LOVE YOU, JAI GURU!' We boarded the train with much difficulty, but by now there seemed to be hundreds of them on the platform, shouting. As the train moved off, all the kids ran alongside right to the end of the platform – and I was scared that someone would fall down into the wide gap between the train and the platform edge. But it was a touching and memorable experience to see this happen in Soviet Russia. The performances were sold out, and there were gorgeous reviews.

I have a good friend in Los Angeles called Frank Serafine, one of the funniest and most lovable guys that I know. He has a recording studio, equipped with the latest types of sophisticated synthesisers and emulators, where he makes special-effects music which has been used in many films, such as Walt Disney's *Tron*. It was around 1983 that I sat with him in his studio for the first time and saw all the wonders that could be done through the keyboard with these machines. They are commonplace now, but at that time it was not so. I couldn't believe the techniques he showed me: he recorded one sole note from my sitar onto a floppy disk, put it in the emulator – and then I could play a staccato sitar on the keyboard! We did that with tanpura and voice, and even with a hand-clap sound. I was so inspired by it.

Just for fun I did two or three pieces before I had to go back to India. They sounded fresh and different. I played nearly all of it myself on the keyboard, producing different instrumental sounds and even the voice. Frank chipped in with some chords here and there.

All my musical friends in the Los Angeles area who heard the pieces were extremely excited. A demo was made and there was plenty of positive feedback, but at the same time the problem developed that the record companies didn't know which slot to put it in. They couldn't classify it as jazz, pop, country-and-western, Indian or classical, and at that time the name 'New Age' was not yet in use, so unfortunately my demo was left sitting there waiting for someone to show more interest.

After a few months I returned to Los Angeles, wanting to finish the album with some extra numbers. I got hold of Lakshmi Shankar, my son Shubho, Aashish Khan and Swapan Chowdhury, and added voice, sitar, sarod and tabla to the existing tracks, plus four or five more pieces so that it became a complete record. On one of my favourite numbers, against a background of sitar, sarod, voice and (mainly) synthesiser, I sang one line in Hindi: 'Tana mana dhana chrana pé varoon', meaning 'My body, mind and wealth, I offer thee at thy feet.' It was dedicated to my mother.

In this collection of recordings there was a variety of styles, mostly based on my keyboard-playing, while some had a jazz feel and in some the vocals were dominant, but they all turned out well in their own ways. I was happy and we had all enjoyed the venture. Frank is such a funster: when we were all struggling to think of a name for one of the jazz-orientated numbers, he came up with a suggestion following in the tradition of my previous titles *West Meets East* and *East Greets East* – 'West Eats Meat'!

While touring Europe a few months later I recorded one further piece, at George Harrison's studio at his home in England. Along with my sitar and the tabla played by Markandeya Mishra (a local musician who sadly died soon after), George played the autoharp and Ray Cooper the marimba. We named this piece 'Friar Park', after George's home.

The tracks were sitting around for almost four years, with no one to bring them out. Thank God the New Age was born in the meantime! Peter Baumann, formerly of the German band Tangerine Dream, had recently founded a new label in Los Angeles, Private Music Limited, and when he heard the tape he liked it and said he was going to release it. At last this record, which we named *Tana Mana* (meaning 'Body and Mind'), was brought out in 1987. It had a beautiful cover, my favourite among my releases, with a photograph of what looks like an exotic tree but is actually an underwater coral plant. Peter was thrilled with it, and we agreed a contract for three records altogether.

Ravi's second release on Baumann's label was recorded live on his next visit to Russia in 1988, on the occasion of his stunning aural and visual presentation held right in the heart of the Kremlin. He composed a series of pieces exploring the crossover between traditional Indian and Russian music. The collection was named Swar Milan – literally 'musical notes meeting', but also symbolising the meeting of the two distinct peoples in a harmonious blend.

Once again he achieved a masterly synthesis of the best from each culture, writing music of startling beauty for combined Russian and Indian ensembles totalling more than 120 musicians.

Our government had arranged a special Festival of India, a series of cultural events held first in America and Britain, and then for a whole year throughout Soviet Russia, beginning there in June 1987. The closing celebration was held in Moscow on 5th, 6th and 7th July 1988, in the Palace of Culture within the Kremlin. I was asked to contribute a special musical composition, emphasising the message of peace.

I conceived a number of compositions, orchestral and choral, which in all lasted about one and a half hours. Along with sixteen Indian musicians who came with me, there were three groups of Soviet musicians: the Chamber Orchestra of the Moscow Philharmonic, the Government Chorus of the Ministry of Culture and the Russian Folk Ensemble. You could hardly believe what hard work it was to put everything together! In the performance I conducted a few numbers myself, with my assistant Ashit Desai conducting the rest. In the end there was only one piece on which I played sitar: the last number (based on *Mishra Piloo*) in the grand finale *Bahu-Rang*, with the entire group in the background.

The performance was an experience I shall never forget. Almost 5,000 people attended. At the end we reprised *Shanti-Mantra*, in which the Indian vocalists together with the Russian choir sang in the traditional num-tum vocal style, along with a peace mantra in Sanskrit which was recited towards the end: 'May there be peace on earth-water-sky-trees-air-mind-body and everything throughout the universe.' During that number choreographers from the Bolshoi Theatre added some special effects and mimes by the ballet dancers in the background. This expression of artistic unity was so effective that almost the whole audience was in tears. I couldn't stop myself, either!

The show was recorded live by Peter Baumann, who had come all the way from the States, while the recording unit had driven in a truck from London. The album *Ravi Shankar Inside the Kremlin* was released the next year, with a beautiful cover.

Following the Kremlin celebrations I visited Riga for a concert. Years before, my brothers had gone there with the troupe, but I had not accompanied them. The Latvians were such marvellously friendly people, and so musical – they gave me true joy. Nothing can be more rewarding for a performer than deep appreciation and love from his listeners.

The final part of the Private Music trilogy saw the historic fulfilment of Ravi's 1965 meeting with the young Philip Glass on the film score of Chappaqua. At the suggestion of his company's president, Ron Goldstein, Baumann proposed to Ravi the idea of his working with Glass again. It proved to be another stunning and highly original work on the new age music label, a success only tainted in Ravi's eyes by the weakness of the promotional push behind the album, hard to understand considering the pre-eminence of each of the artists in his field.

Since I had first met him, Philip Glass had of course become very famous. I had heard his stage works *Satyagraha*, based on Gandhi's life, and *Einstein on the Beach*. His music sounded very different, his speciality being those endlessly repetitious passages. I was truly impressed by both the music and him – he has always retained plenty of humility.

Sometime in the summer of 1989, Peter Baumann suggested that Philip and I should attempt some collaboration. At first I told him I was a little unsure. As far as I knew, Philip was not really a performer as such. I understood him to be more of a composer, though he had his own group, and it wasn't clear to me how we could play together. But I was interested in trying because it seemed like such a worthwhile challenge, and I always like undertaking new experiments – why repeat yourself if you can attempt something new? Peter arranged a meeting between Philip and me in Los Angeles, and so after a gap of over twenty years we met again, and spent about three or four days together.

Initially we were both rather sceptical about what we could do together, but then Peter came up with a brilliant idea. He suggested, 'Why don't each of you write two short pieces – like a theme? Then you exchange pieces and each orchestrate and arrange them in your own way.' That struck us both as something we could do. A couple of days later we met again to try out our ideas. Philip played for me on the piano two short passages he had written, maybe sixteen bars each, and I wrote them down. Then it was my turn. To tell you the truth, I had not yet composed anything! However, I had some idea of which ragas to use as a basis, so there and then I decided on two themes. I sang and played them on piano for him, and he noted them down in the same way. We went away to arrange and record them separately. Independently we each did one extra track of our own; mine was *Prashanti*, which means 'peacefulness'. I recorded three tracks in Madras with local artists, assisted by the brilliant musician Suresh Lalwani of Bombay (who has been my assistant on a few of my projects), and Philip did his three in New York with his musicians. The CD *Passages* is made up of those six pieces.

PHILIP GLASS: *The reason why I think* **Passages** *works so well is that when I listen to those four pieces we did together, I don't know whose music I'm hearing. We didn't want one of us to write a piece and the other to embellish it; we wanted to do something that more profoundly linked the process of writing and imagining. When someone says to me, 'Who wrote that?' I actually don't know what to say – except for the two pieces we did by ourselves. I think that was nice, too – to each have a moment on the record where we could stretch out.*

Finding their way through the Passages: *Philip Glass and Ravi at work in 1989.*

Artistically it was a very satisfying project to do. It's been made into dance and used in film; people have enjoyed and appreciated the CD.

It was also a way of stepping up my relationship with Ravi onto another level, because before that I had always been the student. Now we were collaborators, and there was as good a union as we could make between two composers with somewhat different backgrounds and personalities. But still there was a very strong element of teacher-student in it for me, where he was still the master and I was sitting at his feet. It was nearly twenty-five years since our first meeting and our relationship had changed a lot. But once we began working, I found that I was still learning from him. He naturally assumed the role of a teacher, and I naturally assumed the role of his student.

I really think of him as one of my teachers. In fact I used to say that my two most important teachers were Ravi Shankar and Nadia Boulanger. Teaching is a natural function for him, whether you call yourself his student or not. He is very generous with his ideas and skills and technical understanding of music. If there's something you don't know, he wants you to know it. The impetus of his teaching comes from that desire to share knowledge.

In the West we live in a secular society. Our music, our artistic life, our intellectual life, our spiritual life, our religious life – all are separate. With Ravi these kinds of separation are not so hard. That was something I saw for the first time in him. To him they flow together.

Rehearsals for Ghanashyam: (below) Working with Radhika on the choreography; (opposite) with Shanta, Dhananjayan and the musicians.

In 1989 I was given an exciting opportunity to create a 'musical theatre' for the Birmingham Touring Opera Company. It came about in a remarkable way as a result of an initiative from my wife Sukanya – although this was before our marriage. She had already been involved in arranging my performance as the chief guest at Britain's first national festival of South Asian music and dance, held in July 1988 in Crawley, Sussex. The idea of a new stage production was born one beautifully sunny early summer's day in 1988 when we were walking together in St James's Park in London, near Buckingham Palace. We were very much in love, closely attuned to each other, and this inspired me.

I was unburdening myself to her about my feelings of frustration that are constantly with me: 'Sukanya, I have not been able to do even one tenth of the things I want to do.' When she asked me for an example of the ideas on my mind, I spontaneously narrated the story for a complete ballet, mixing fantasy with an old Rajasthani motif of maharajahs, princes and intrigues. To my satisfaction, she was very impressed and said she would endeavour to find a way to have it produced. As luck would have it, after I left London she heard that the Birmingham Touring Opera Company were interested in me doing an opera with them. I was thrilled when she informed me.

It all happened very swiftly. She arranged for the artistic director, Graham Vick, to come to London to meet me, and I explained to him that if it were to be an opera we would need to write English arias to Indian music, which was unprecedented. I suggested that we should attempt more of a mixed production, a dance-drama consisting of dance, ballet, mime, singing and musical dialogue in Hindi, based on Indian themes. We decided to call it a 'musical theatre', and left it at that for the time being.

To discuss the project further, Graham Vick then visited me when I was in Delhi later that year. In our first meeting, with Sukanya and Ashit Desai also present, he asked what the show's story would be, explaining his preference for it to have a theme relevant to contemporary times and issues.

SUKANYA SHANKAR: *It was quite extraordinary the way Raviji came up with the story. First he excused himself and went to the bathroom, and then when he returned after a while he had a smile on his face. He said that he had been inspired, and had just the appropriate story theme for modern-day problems – DRUGS! (He says quite often that many of his most ingenious compositions or brainchildren are born in the toilet!) He immediately started reciting the story of* **Ghanashyam** *onto a tape, while Graham, Ashit and I listened intently – he never once paused! It was like he was reading a story or a finished script. We couldn't believe our ears. In fact my reaction was that I would never believe him again as he could make up stories so instantly and convincingly!*

The story of *Ghanashyam* came to me like an improvisation. That is the way it happens sometimes! I believe in stars. I believe in destiny. I believe in people being in the right place at the right time, and everything working out as a result. Sometimes I have known instinctively that an idea should be pursued, and whenever that has been the case I have followed it and it has borne fruit.

Graham was charmed by my idea, and agreed that was what we should do. Rehearsals were started immediately. I brought in Shanta and Dhananjayan, who are great dancers and choreographers from Madras, to help in choreographing my concept while I was composing and arranging all the music spontaneously. I chose the musicians – mostly my students – and elected to use entirely Indian instruments, except for the violin and the later addition of a synthesiser to create a sound rather like that of a vibraphone. My son Shubho joined at the time of the final rehearsals in Birmingham.

We gave about fourteen performances of *Ghanashyam – A Broken Branch* in Britain in 1989, and in 1991 we performed it in Bombay, Calcutta, Madras and Delhi. I was very satisfied with our creation, from both the musical and choreographic points of view.

For the British shows the main character, Ghanashyam, was played by one of our finest Kathak dancers, Durga Lal of the Jaipur gharana. Durga Lal was strikingly handsome and manly. He had a happy family life, was very pious and untainted by addictions or bad habits, and everybody loved him, one and all, so it was a terrible shock when he died. We were all numbed by his sudden demise, and the eerie circumstances of his death made it even more astounding. In *Ghanashyam* the central character ruins his life by becoming addicted to drugs. After he steals the precious jewel from the village deity Shiva, his action is discovered and he is chased by the people of the village. While running for his life he gets a sudden heart attack and drops dead. About three months after Durga Lal had finished playing this character in *Ghanashyam*, he travelled to Lucknow to give a regular solo programme, and after performing chakkars in the finale he too suffered a massive heart attack and died.

For India we used a young dancer by the name of Maulik Shah, who was commendable, though we all greatly missed Durga Lal. The shows were received well in both Britain and India, and I hope to put on another series of performances one day soon.

᠙

In 1990 I was asked to provide the music for a short film called *The Tiger and the Brahmin*. It was being made by a New York company called Rabbit Ears, which specialises in videos featuring animated versions of folk tales from around the world, mainly aimed at children. *The Tiger and the Brahmin* is a delightful story set in India, about a Brahmin priest who is saved from being eaten by a tiger through the intelligence of a jackal, based on one of the stories from the *Panchatantra*, an age-old book similar to Aesop's Fables.

The animation is achieved through a succession of still paintings, and the story is narrated by the actor Ben Kingsley, whose expressive voice gradually unfolds the tale with the music in the background. Doris Sottnick, the owner of Rabbit Ears, and her husband Mark visited me in Delhi, and I recorded the music in a studio there before the animation was done. I played sitar, and in the closing title sequence used seven other musicians, including a few of my students. All I had to work on when composing was the soundtrack of Ben Kingsley's voice (which had been recorded in Pinewood Studios in England) and the timings of the characters' actions in relation to these lines. The animations were drawn afterwards. I was shown some sketches, but said I was not happy with their portrayal of the Brahmin – he looked more like a Pathan from Afghanistan. So I suggested how an average Brahmin priest might appear, and showed them some animated storybooks of our Indian epics to help.

The film ultimately came out beautifully, and it is broadcast on American television from time to time. In 1994 a video unit was sent by Macmillan and McGraw-Hill to my home in Encinitas, and they recorded me introducing and discussing this series of films for a special course to be shown in schools all over America.

Ravi has made fewer studio recordings since the turn of the Nineties, although there are more in the pipeline. However, he has played an increasing number of special concerts. By way of example: in 1989 he marked the 50th anniversary of his Allahabad debut with a major concert in London's Barbican Hall. Then, after receiving the prestigious Grand Prize at the Fukuoka Asian Cultural Prizes in September 1991, he returned to play there in January 1995, along with a recital to a full house in Tokyo. In 1995 he marked his 75th birthday with a series of celebratory concerts in cities all over the world, including Singapore, Delhi (at the Siri Fort), Pasadena and London, where he performed at the Barbican Centre as the guest of the London Symphony Orchestra. His work rate is remarkable: his 1997 schedule took in Thailand, Bangladesh, Switzerland, Hungary, Turkey, Italy, Britain, Spain and Japan, as well as his twin home countries of India and the USA, and there is no sign yet of any significant scaling down of ambition. Retirement isn't really an option.

For a Bombay concert in 1991 I managed to get the present generation's top stars of tabla-playing all together at the same time on the stage – namely

Zakir Hussain, Swapan Chowdhury and Kumar Bose. For this occasion I composed a piece of about ten minutes with the name *Chhalaktey Ghadey* – 'the sound of a water-filled pot'. The story concerns three pots: one full, one empty and one half-full. The empty pot is sad and cries that he has no water, while the full one is at first very proud; but after the mediation of the half-filled one, the full one pours some water into the empty one, so that all three are happy. I narrated the story to the audience and had the three tablas playing the sounds of the pots, with the tone varying as the water level in each pot gradually changes –

Kumar the full pot, Swapan the half-full, and Zakir the empty one. A simple but effective story, and the audience went wild!

After the intermission, first I performed with each of them separately accompanying me, and then, for the pièce de résistance, I played along with all three at the same time. It is exceedingly rare to have three tabla-players of this standard all together. I played a gat which I had composed the day before, and we had only had one rehearsal of about half an hour; but this gat was in a bizarre rhythmic cycle – I made each of them play a different tala, with the rhythm of all three coinciding on the sum (first beat). One was playing jhaptal (ten beats), another was in ektal (twelve), and the third in pancham sawari (fifteen). All the musicians present were absolutely in raptures, because it was a new conception within the classical framework. It became a bit noisy towards the end when all of them joined in together, but nevertheless it was a tremendous success. Apart from that gat composition, the rest of the performance was improvisation. At the end we all played a long piece together with a final tihai (a musical phrase repeated three times, finishing on the sum). I have more plans for such adventures in the future.

Robin Paul of Calcutta, a man dear to me, has an organisation called Jalsaghar which over many years has successfully arranged concerts for me. Some of the more unusual venues have included the old mansion Marble Palace, the Victoria Memorial Hall and the original home of Rabindranath Tagore.

Some more special shows were arranged in 1993, the series of Concerts for Peace in Washington and London in aid of Rajiv Gandhi Memorial Foundation and drawing attention to the war in Bosnia. Washington National Cathedral was full to overflowing, with about ten thousand people attending (inside and outside) over two days in July! Our great friend Cynthia Thomas gets the credit for organising this peace programme. Then for the next peace recital, at the Royal Albert Hall in November, I played with Zakir Hussain accompanying me. It was a thrilling night – a CD has been issued by Moment Records.

Present on that occasion at the Festival Hall was my friend Dr L. M. Singhvi, until recently our High Commissioner to the United Kingdom. It has been so pleasing to see him in this important post. I have always thought that our Indian Government, as well as arranging a few India Festivals in some countries, should do more to project our country abroad. The foreign missions could do so much by way of public relations to create the correct image of India. Over the many years of my life I have known a few heads of missions who have done commendable work, such as Sardar Pannikar, Mrs Pandit, B. K. Nehru and K. P. S. Menon (to name a few), and some lower officials as well. But these people have unfortunately been rare.

Dr Singhvi is such a dynamic person. He has achieved – and is achieving – so much for India. He is not only highly competent but a very warm human being. He and his charming wife, Kamala, have won the hearts of everyone who has met them. He is an outstanding ambassador to represent our country.

As Ravi's light continues to shine brightly, with the full maturity of age has come the satisfaction of being truly appreciated for his art. Honour after honour has been bestowed upon him. These include the 1999 award of the Bharat Ratna – India's highest civilian honour – as well as eleven honorary degrees at doctorate level, Sweden's Polar Music Prize (1998), Japan's Praemium Imperiale (1997), France's Commandeur de l'Ordre des Arts et des Lettres (1985), and Manila's Ramon Magsaysay award (1992). There has been a wealth of further recognitions from his home country too: Fellowship of the Sangeet Natak Akademi, India's premier institution for the performing arts (1975); the Award of Deshikottam from Vishwa Bharati, presented in December 1982 by Prime Minister Indira Gandhi; the Kalidas Samman Award from Bhopal, and the VST Industries' Spirit of Freedom Award, both in 1990; the Rajiv Gandhi Excellence Award (1991); and an Indian Army Special Award (1985). He was also nominated by Prime Minister Rajiv Gandhi to the Rajya Sabha, India's upper parliamentary chamber, serving as a Member of Parliament between 1986 and 1992.

Yet there have been testing times too. In some ways it is no small miracle that he is still with us, let alone performing. He has long been dogged by heart trouble, having had two cardiac arrests and quadruple bypass surgery, and serious problems with high blood pressure and angina, the latter necessitating two angioplasty operations. In 1994 he had surgery on his right ear and right shoulder, the latter damaged in a fall, preventing him from picking up his sitar for almost ten weeks – a time of almost unimaginable frustration for such a committed musician (his daughter Anoushka said recently, 'If he wasn't able to play music any more I think he would die.'). Add to this the electric shock he received in 1995 while taking a shower in Calcutta, and it seems that Fate is dealing him a generous hand of troubles, while continuing to ensure that, as yet, he survives each trial.

There has been frustration of an artistic nature, too. He is as musically creative and ambitious as ever, but advancing age and health problems have meant that fewer commissions of the sort he is seeking have come his way in the last few years. His latest dream (or 'itching', as he would say) is to bring more grand audio-visual presentations to the West. To date the costs of staging such productions have prevented a repeat of a show like Ghanashyam, *and he has had his fingers burnt too many times in the past to spend his own money. But given his reputation and remarkable resilience one would be foolish to bet against his mounting just that kind of creative extravaganza again in the not-so-distant future.*

Apart from my many plans for the future by way of creative productions, there is one further dream which is still to be realised. I would like to establish a centre in India housing a research department and an archive of all my recordings, videos and written materials, and containing accommodation and facilities for a few disciples, as in the old gurukul training system. It should also be a venue where I myself can undertake creative work for musical productions, ballets, orchestration, films or even work in the new media. We have some land in the Chanakyapuri area of Delhi which we obtained from our government at a very low rate, considering it is a crème de la crème plot in the diplomatic enclave. If it happens that will be great, but with all the governmental bureaucracy it is taking a lot of time to finalise the details.

Sukanya has really been a great strength and force in this, as in everything. I love her so dearly and deeply. She has been working tirelessly to fulfil all my dreams. Some of them have been realised, like the productions of *Ghanashyam*, and I have full faith that with her help and that of a few other very dear people it will be possible to realise this ambition too.

EIGHT: JOGESHWARI

जोगेश्वरी

Shubho, my son. It was heartbreaking to lose him.
September 15th, 1992.

I wish Shubho had possessed a little more drive in him. He had everything else: music in his blood and a wonderful touch on the sitar, especially the left hand. He had benefited from a long period of good training from his mother Annapurna and later from me.

He started music late. When he was little, Baba had introduced him to the sarod, as he did with all his grandchildren, but that was not serious. After we moved to Delhi in 1949 we found out that Shubho had a lot of interest in drawing, and everything he was drawing was very unusual. All my artist friends said, 'This boy has talent! He should be encouraged,' and I felt that if he had talent in another field we should not force him into music simply because he was my son. (I now think that was a mistake.) It was arranged for a fine art teacher to come and give him lessons, and he was also studying at the Modern School. After some time he did start some sitar practice, but it was in addition to his schoolwork and painting.

For three years after we shifted to Bombay in 1961 he studied fine art at the city's famous Sir J. J. College of Arts (where Uday had earlier studied), although he didn't finish the course. I was so busy on tour, concertising or travelling to do the music for films and ballets, that I did not have the time to teach him music. That was the period when Annapurna took over; she was able to give him much more time, and he had some rigorous training. Through her instruction he developed a wonderful left hand, so he became proficient in playing the slow alap with beautiful meends, but his right hand was not developed sufficiently for the other sections of a performance. He also needed to develop control of the multitude of mathematical rhythmic variations – what we call layakari.

When I was staying in Bombay sometime in early 1970, I received an SOS call at my hotel from Shubho, asking me in a feeble voice to come home immediately and take him away. I didn't know what was happening and was terrified by his tone of voice, so I rushed to the flat in Malabar Hill, which I had not visited in the three and a half years since I had left for good. There I saw Shubho lying down and looking ill. He clung to me desperately, like a little boy, and begged me to take him away with me to America, as he could no longer stand the hot temper and harshness of his mother – not only in connection with music, but in general too. Coming from a man of twenty-eight, this both melted my heart and angered me. I did not want to make a scene, however, and managed to control myself even as Annapurna was shouting in fury, 'Yes, take him away! I don't want him!' After we left, I learnt that Shubho had taken eight or ten strong sleeping pills in an attempt to end his life. Fortunately the doctor had arrived in time and emptied Shubho's stomach out completely.

Seeing his desperation, I had to take him away, though I knew that this might later be portrayed as me forcing him away from his mother and harming his musical career – and ultimately some people did put this interpretation on my actions. First I took him to Mejda's house in the Bombay suburbs for a few days, and then to my student Rama Rao's house in Bangalore for some weeks so that he could recuperate, as he was in bad shape. Due to my commitments I soon had to leave for California, but Kamala stayed back with Shubho in India. When he had recovered sufficiently, he and Kamala followed me over to LA. On their arrival at my rented Hollywood house on Dorian Avenue, complete with swimming pool, he was delighted to see his new environment.

Now I have to tell you that I was anxious about Shubho, feeling guilty that I had never been able to do much for him when he had been growing up. He was a mama's boy. Within a week or two I fixed him up with a small apartment and a Ford Mustang to drive. Kamala and I did not stay long in the rented house, shifting after about six weeks to the villa on Highland Avenue.

The first thing I did was to ask him to be really frank about what he wanted to do. I didn't want him to give up the sitar; but if he was keen to continue painting it seemed better that he should pursue that, though he could keep up his sitar practice also. So he joined the College of Arts in Los Angeles, where he studied graphic arts. Unfortunately he didn't finish the course. I had given him the freedom to choose what he wanted to do, and he had taken to the American concept of independence.

In the beginning I persisted in encouraging him to keep up his sitar-playing. Within a year or two of his arrival he had already performed along with me at New York's famous Carnegie Hall and in San Francisco. But gradually he lost interest, seeming to prefer Hindi film songs to classical music, and he practised less. Though I was helping him financially, he also took a job in a liquor store to earn some extra money.

At length he met and fell in love with Linda, and she moved into the apartment. Knowing about the repressive atmosphere that he had grown up in, I did not discourage it. But when after some time he said that he wanted to marry her I was unhappy. I knew that he was not ready for marriage, not having established himself with a career (as either musician or artist) or any financial stability; but I had to give in, as he was adamant. Around the same time he also gave up the sitar completely, after I left Los Angeles to spend more time in New York, India and around the world. I continued to assist him and helped him to buy a house in Orange County, but I was saddened by his lack of drive – especially as he was living in America, where self-reliance goes hand in hand with independence. Wanting to make up for our years spent apart by making things comfortable for him, I had overcompensated when he first came to America. In the long term, this probably reinforced his existing lack of fire and motivation.

After a while he did take a graphic art job for a few years. He and Linda had two children – a boy, Som, and a daughter, Kaveri – and he doted on them. Though in the beginning I was unhappy with the marriage, soon I really started to like Linda, and appreciated her very much for taking upon herself most of the burdens, household and otherwise. I'm happy to say that gradually over the past few years we have become very close.

About eight years elapsed before I persuaded him to return to the sitar. Once again I started to teach him whenever I visited Los Angeles, and was getting him to practise as much as possible. I was giving him long sessions of training, especially emphasising all the complex layakari he needed to turn him into a layadar (a master of layakari), and also a variety of drut (fast) gats, tans, bols and toda (a range of plucked strokes played along with left-hand variations), and jhala (when rapid chikari – side string – strokes are played in combination with the main melody string). These were the aspects he needed to work on more. I also wanted him to play not just in his house or for connoisseurs but also in concert, so he would become a performing artist. I therefore took him on my tours to assist me in recitals, and we worked very hard on performance skills. He was getting much better.

That was the period of a couple of years when we came closest to each other. We were like two friends together, going to films, on walks, and trying out different Thai, Chinese and Indian restaurants in Santa Monica, Hollywood and West Los Angeles. We went to many different parties where he was thrilled to meet people from the film, recording and showbiz worlds.

We shared a rather childlike sense of humour, and had some funny times. I recall the ganda ceremony held in a Hindu monastery by which my American student Steve Slavek was initiated as my disciple. The priest for these formal rites was very learned, but he came from the Eastern part of India and his pronunciation of Sanskrit was strongly influenced by his mother tongue. He was reciting some mantras from the Vedas and Upanishads, and after each couplet he would translate them into English, his pronunciation of which was very Indian too. After uttering the final line, 'Om Shanti, Shanti, Shanti,' instead of translating it three times as 'Let there be peace', he said, 'Let there be piss'! Shubho and I made eye contact and doubled up with laughter! We would often have these fits of giggles together. He had that sweet childlike quality in him.

For a few years he performed on all my tours in the USA, and once in Europe. He also came to India for one year for more intensive training, mostly at my Delhi house where there were a few other students in residence. He played in a few of my studio recordings of creative material, including *Tana Mana* in LA and *Passages* in Madras, as well as at my 50th anniversary concert

at the Barbican Hall, London, and on
the *Ghanashyam* musical theatre tour in
the UK.

The children of famous parents
always encounter the problem of the
expectations they have to live up to,
and Shubho suffered from this burden.
The pressure of being the son of
Annapurna and myself, the grandson of
Baba and the nephew of Ali Akbar
affected his confidence, pride and self-
respect. He was not really a fighter, and he buckled somewhat.

Nevertheless he latterly found his own strong points. He was really
improving and becoming a more rounded musician. In addition, he started
giving music for some Indian stage productions and ballets in California,
including the dancer Viji Prakash's play of *Ramayana*, which all received
great appreciation. He had a real talent for this creative work, composing his
own tunes and songs, and a fantastic voice too, with a timbre and a quality
which touched everyone. I always thought he could have made a fine playback
singer for film music, which is of course so popular in our country. These
successes late in life did boost his confidence.

But in his last few months he cut himself off from everyone, including
me, and when he contracted bronchial pneumonia he didn't bother to seek
proper medical treatment. I didn't know how bad it was until one day I

visited him unannounced, and was shocked to see how sick he looked. I myself was suffering from angina and this was just one day before I was due to go into hospital for an angioplasty, so I discussed Shubho's condition with Linda and had him put in the care of a doctor. I tried to call Annapurna in Bombay, and as she was not there I asked her second husband, Rushi, to inform her how sick Shubho was. Unfortunately she could not come.

A week after my operation, I suffered an acute attack of diverticulitis, and spent six days in Intensive Care. I was in a bad state, but still kept trying to find out how Shubho was. After I was discharged from hospital, George Harrison visited me and a few days later he took me to an Ayurvedic centre in Lancaster, Massachusetts, to rest for a few days; then we went on to London, confident that Shubho was being taken care of. But the day after I arrived in London, 15th September, the news came that he had died.

It was such a terrible shock for me. Shubho was so stubborn; everybody had been ready to help him but he had cut off all his connections. What a tragic shame to die prematurely just through neglecting to take care of his health.

Somehow I felt there was always a child in him. He was so giggly, sweet and full of love. In many ways he was like me in that we both have had a tendency to dodge problems, tolerating situations with which we are unhappy in order to avoid unpleasantness (and, for me, overexcitement, due to my paranoia regarding my hypertension and angina). Ultimately what happens is that one lets things go too far and then makes a mess of it by overreacting. There is a child in me who never grew up, who remains wide-eyed, curious and impish, and Shubho might have inherited that tendency. But he was different in many ways too: he shied away from the burdens of responsibility and discipline and never quite took control of his life. Yet he was very well liked, a man of good character devoted to his family, and a real charmer. Despite having a weakness for junk food and Coca-Cola (and being practically a chain smoker), he was a gourmet too, and taught himself to be a fine cook, especially of Indian cuisine.

It gives me some solace to know that he did eventually find what seemed to be his artistic niche. I was also glad that, after many years of feeling bitterness towards his mother, in the last few years he had grown very fond of her again. Even though this created some distance between him and me once more, I was happy that he found renewed comfort in his relationship with her.

It is all but impossible to add anything significant to a man's comments on his only son's early death. Ravi had always acted in what he perceived to be Shubho's best interests, yet agonising questions continue to nag at the mind of the bereaved father. Could he have done more? Should he have been there more for Shubho when he was younger? Would an earlier training in music have provided his son with a better focus? Should he have tried to be firmer with him?

Death comes to us all, and each of us must face up to it in his own way. Born in the holy Ganges city of Benares, Ravi knows all about the ceaseless flow of the mighty river of life.

*In the years following the breakdown of his first marriage, Ravi's private life had undoubtedly
become complicated. By the early Seventies, his troubled relationship with Annapurna had long ago
left him disillusioned with marriage, and his massive worldwide success had only served to enhance
his magnetic appeal to women. Moreover, he thrived on their attention.*

I t will come as no surprise to many of you to hear that I have always been very attracted to women. Right from my very childhood they have been always a source of great inspiration, spurring me on to do creative work in the field of music as well as providing general motivation and keeping me so active. At various times different women have given me so much, and in return I have also given myself completely to whomever I have been with at the time, however long or short it lasted.

After leaving Annapurna for good I had been through a number of affairs here and there, and had once again become like I was at the age of eighteen – I felt I could be in love with different women in different places. It was like having a girl in every port – and sometimes it was more than one! However, Kamala was there for me all along, and after 1967 we lived together as man and wife.

Ravi's relationship with Kamala was indeed his most durable one. However, in a fateful move in late 1972, Ravi's niece Viji asked her friend Sukanya Rajan if she would like to join her in accompanying Ravi on tanpura at his Royal Albert Hall concert in London the following March. The eighteen-year-old Sukanya hailed from Madras and was well orientated in the Carnatic system of vocal music. She had recently moved to London, and was very close to Viji and her mother Lakshmi, as well as Kamala. For Sukanya this opportunity was like a dream.

SUKANYA SHANKAR: *Before I met Raviji he seemed like one of those unreachable names. He was someone you would hear about and admire, but not in my wildest dreams did I ever think I was even going to meet him. So when I first heard from Viji that he was coming to London, and she asked me if I would play tanpura with him, I almost fainted! I couldn't believe it.*

We first met a few days before the concert. I saw him walk down the stairs, this godlike figure coming down, and I was just dumbfounded. I couldn't even talk! I didn't know what to say, and when he started talking I just smiled. I was honestly so taken aback to see him in person, at such close quarters – and he was such a strikingly good-looking man! That scene has always remained in my memory, him coming down the stairs.

We rehearsed with him at his home in Charles Street, which George had lent him: a beautiful experience. And then the concert itself – for me, it was not a question of being on stage, or the excitement of playing tanpura at the Albert Hall, but the excitement of being with him more than anything else.

I found Sukanya very attractive and giggly, full of life and spirit. At the Royal Albert Hall she and Viji sat either side of me with the tanpuras. Alla Rakha was playing the tabla.

Of course, playing tanpura is no big deal: one just continuously strums it to provide the drone sound in the background of our music. In the early days in the West, it was embarrassing when people would sometimes include the tanpura-player in their congratulations to the musicians after a performance –

the equivalent of applauding a pianist's page-turner! The person who turns the page or plays the tanpura has to know music, but is not really performing. Nevertheless, with Sukanya I was impressed to find that she was very musical, able to follow the correct tala (an intricate cycle of seventeen beats) which I played that evening.

From the beginning Sukanya felt an unusual degree of attachment to Ravi. The relationship became very cordial, but progressed no further at this stage. Indeed in November 1973 Sukanya married, and settled down to working in a bank in London. Her marriage was an affectionate but not a close union. She was content that she and her husband should have quite different interests because this enabled her to live her own life, which included seeing Ravi whenever he came to London.

Mostly we met when I visited London for performances or passed through, staying in Eaton Mews – in the house George loaned me after Charles Street – and later in different hotels after I had given it back: the Cumberland, Bailey's Hotel, the Churchill. Yet there was nothing more at that stage. There was a strong restraint from my side. Maybe with any other person in that situation I wouldn't have resisted the attraction I felt, since by then I had many liaisons in different places. But because she was such a good friend of Viji and called me Kaku (Uncle), I didn't want to yield to a moment of weakness. My self-control over the situation lasted for a few years until finally it was not possible. In 1978 Sukanya came to a performance of mine in Greenwich – and that's where it started.

SUKANYA SHANKAR: *I had a deep crush on Raviji. He touched my heart with his warmth and generosity, while his sense of humour and quick wit impressed me so much. We met many times. I attended his concerts, we went to films, we went to restaurants. Nothing ever happened, but I suppose subconsciously I must have loved him all along, because even then the day he would arrive in London would be the most important date in that year for me. I used to look forward to cooking or cleaning for him. Just washing and ironing his clothes was such a pleasure for me! I didn't want anyone else to do it. I would sacrifice anything to be with him and listen to his divine music when he practised.*

That night in Greenwich he must have had something planned in his mind, because he played Raga Yaman Kalyan *and just looked at me. Ah, that was it for me! If I had had my way I would have left my husband right then, because for me it was absolutely clear that I was in love for the first time.*

However, it was a complex situation. Sukanya was married, living with her husband, and because of my complicated emotional situation I didn't want her to divorce – there was no way that I could cope with that. Also the relationship was not yet as significant to me as it was to her. Marriage was always far from my mind. After my previous experience of it, I had no respect for this whole institution. That reason made me put pressure on her not to divorce, so that not only her husband but, as far as possible, everyone else should remain ignorant of our affair.

Another factor was a dear friend in London (whom I do not wish to name here) who had been a great influence on me for many years. He had become my confidant and adviser, and I really loved him like a younger brother. I was always vulnerable in this respect, dependent on advice and direction from a friend, or a guru like Tat Baba: if I felt that someone really cared for me, what they said had a major influence on me. This particular friend knew about all my various relationships because I confided everything to him. He did not object to my affair with Sukanya, but he did warn me that discretion was essential. He told me about all the dire consequences that would follow if it became known to the public. In India we have a great 'what would people say?' syndrome, especially among those who happen to be famous or in a responsible post. It was always in my mind that I might fall from their high esteem – from that pedestal which I have always enjoyed occupying. So though Sukanya and I had given ourselves to each other, and I couldn't tear myself away from her, at the same time I didn't want her to leave her husband and the news to come out in the open. She even continued to call me Kaku, so people wouldn't suspect anything.

I had an insatiable and burning passion for her, and could never have enough of her. We were so much in love with each other, and yet when I left London I was away for months at a time and there were other people I was involved with, including Kamala (in India then). It became very messy emotionally for everyone concerned, including me, as I suffered the reflected pains of all of them. Now I wonder how I could have loved two or three women at the same time in different cities, as I did then.

SUKANYA SHANKAR: *Raviji used to phone me once in a while, and I used to look forward to those phone calls, and I used to write to him continually even though he never wrote me a single letter in all those years. That's the only grudge I have against him!*

Our daughter Anoushka was born on 9th June 1981. She was a planned child: for the first time in my life I wanted a baby – I wanted Raviji's child and I didn't care whether I was married to him or not. He told me very clearly that he could not be involved as a parent. It was totally my decision, wanting to have her. Being married to someone else, and with Raviji not wanting to acknowledge Anoushka as his daughter then, I had no choice other than to abide by his wish.

At first I was completely happy with Sukanya's wish to have our child but, to my regret and shame, in the turmoil that enveloped me while she was pregnant I allowed the 'what would people say?' syndrome to take over. I was pulled in many directions and became so confused. I first saw Anoushka when she was three months old – such a lovely baby! From then on I would meet the two of them whenever I was in London. Sukanya would bring her to my hotel, but I was forcing myself not to get too involved, not publicly admitting she was my child for fear of the effect on my public image. I was going through a mixed-up phase which was a great strain for me. The mental stress was mounting up and affecting my health, particularly my heart. Nevertheless I realise today the mistakes I made in my behaviour towards Anoushka and Sukanya and truly regret them.

By the time of Anoushka's birth my relationship with Kamala, which had lasted so long, was over. She had gone through all those years tolerating my passion for new exploits, hoping that one day I would stop hurting her – although she never showed her pain. In a way this was the part of her which attracted me the most. I never had to pretend with her. I could be frank, and always went back to her with greater joy after experiences with others.

But then something snapped in her. She could not take it any more, especially when she learnt that I had a daughter in the West, born in 1979. (This was my first daughter. Her mother doesn't want herself or her child to be identified with me or to keep in contact, and I have to respect their wish for anonymity.) Kamala left me at the beginning of 1981. It really saddened me greatly.

Kamala has been an important part of my life. We spent years together, starting from the late Fifties then touring India and all over the world, building 'Hemangana', the house in Benares, and enjoying the glorious period from 1967 when our base was in LA and we settled down together. There was such love and understanding between us. She took great care of me, with true love and devotion, and we shared some very happy times. I will always remember her fondly for all those wonderful years.

Gradually she was able to accept Sukanya and Anoushka with affection, and we meet now once in a while in Madras. Sukanya has always maintained a great liking for Kamala.

After Shubho left his mother in 1970 to go to the USA with me, we were completely cut off from Annapurna. I was soon aware that rumours abounded of what a terrible thing I had done by taking him away. For years I did not see Annapurna but was regularly supporting her, while she lived in the new flat I had bought for her in Bombay, next door to the Bhulabhai Desai Memorial Institute. I had arranged a very dignified job for her, taking master classes in music at the National Centre for Performing Arts, run by the big business house of Tatas. It was also at my insistence that Shubho had travelled to India to receive her blessing before he married Linda.

Annapurna and I did not see each other again until about 1980. While I was in Bombay a mutual friend and sympathiser arranged for me to visit her. She had cooked a wonderful lunch for me, and we had a very cordial meeting, with conversations about Shubho and his family, my health and so on. I then asked her how it was that some of her devotees and students were helping to spread various rumours and lies about me – some of which had even been published in journals – to the effect that I was not supporting her financially at all; that the reason she was not performing anywhere (apart from teaching) was that I had made her promise not to; and that I had practically kidnapped Shubho away from her. She denied taking part in this herself, but promised that she would tell those responsible not to spread such lies in future. We parted amicably.

It was almost a year later that she wrote to me to ask for a quiet and mutually agreeable divorce. This surprised me – because ever since 1967 I had been asking *her* for a divorce, and she had always firmly refused! If she had ever given her assent, I would have married Kamala. Shortly after receiving the letter, we met again when I was in Bombay. I asked Annapurna why she had now, after all these years, done what she should have done so much earlier. Had she found a man? I enquired – in which case I would be happy for her. But she replied, 'No! Men are all the same.' (Actually she said many more things about them!) 'It is just that I feel stifled.' She asked me to give her 'mukti' (liberty). I said that if that was what she wanted it was fine with me, and made arrangements through my lawyer. The divorce came through within a year, in 1982, with my agreeing to a decent financial settlement.

The biggest surprise to me came the following year when I heard that she had married Rushi Pandya, a much younger man who had been a student of hers for many years. I had actually met him in the Sixties, in Montreal, where he resided then, and a few times in Los Angeles, where he had produced a record of the *Bhagavad Gita*, to which Aashish Khan had given music and I had recited a few of its famous verses – translated into English by Rushi himself, if I am not mistaken. He was a good friend of Shubho and Aashish, being about the same age as them, and I too liked him very much. He went on to San Francisco to have sitar lessons from Alubhai, and then I think some time later he had started going to Bombay regularly to learn from Annapurna. He has also studied and specialised in hypnotherapy – he excels at it, and is sought after by all the institutions in India.

Annapurna is definitely the best performer on the surbahar; indeed it is a pity she doesn't perform for the public. Back in Bombay in the late Forties she had of course been a member of our troupe and had played my compositions on sitar for *The Discovery of India* in Calcutta, Bombay and Delhi. Though she was always reluctant to face the public, I had persuaded her to play a surbahar duet with me a number of times in Bombay and Delhi for the music circles. She did once give a solo recital, in Calcutta in 1956, after she had left me and was living in the city with Alubhai and teaching in his college. But she has always been a recluse, not wanting to perform in public, except maybe in front of a few acquaintances and students.

Positive reports have reached my ears about her marriage to Rushi: that he has really been good for her, and that she is happy, in better health and mood, and busy, mostly teaching. After all our years of problems, I am happy for Annapurna now, and thank Rushi for bringing peace and happiness in her life.

SUKANYA SHANKAR: *Even as a young child, Anoushka had an uncanny instinct. One day she was watching a programme featuring Raviji on the television, and her first reaction was, 'Baba looks like me, doesn't he?' I thought: 'What am I going to tell her?'*

She had always respected him like a father, and she knew she had to behave herself with him. He was always the best thing happening if ever he visited us. Somehow, like a magnet, she would only want to go to him. I remember incidents when she was tiny where there were so many people present and she only wanted to follow him or hold his leg. If we were all having some tea, I'd feel so frightened that she might insist on dunking her biscuit in his cup, in front of everyone. She wouldn't listen to anyone! She just wanted to go to him.

From her very childhood Anoushka showed all the signs of being such an extraordinary child: so talented, superintelligent, a mimic and copycat, full of humour and all the rarest qualities. She was always a few years older than her age, even from the time she was a baby, and I'm really proud to say that Sukanya has been such a fantastic mother to have brought her up so well, even in that difficult situation. Apart from her love for me, her whole attention was on Anoushka and she gave her the best of everything under the circumstances.

What I really appreciate so much, which I see the result of now, is that despite being born in England and growing up in an English atmosphere –

even going through English nursery school – she didn't become like so many Indian kids there, who hardly know their language or anything about India and its heritage. Whenever she was home Sukanya (and sometimes her mother) was filling Anoushka with India, teaching her Indian dance and stories, beautiful Sanskrit shlokas on gods and goddesses, reading to her the *Ramayana* and *Mahabharata*, and teaching her songs. Sukanya has a fine voice and an excellent knowledge of the Carnatic system. She even taught Anoushka her own mother tongue, Tamil. Anoushka was brought up with the whole English culture, including very English pronunciation, and at the same time she was being fed with fantastic Indianness. A wonderful combination! It's apparent today in her music, in which she can switch instantly from piano to sitar, and it's the same in every way. She is a blessed child, and our hearts ache with our love for her.

However, due to various reasons and various people involved, I was on and off with Sukanya over several years in the Eighties. When I was on I was almost giving her my life – there was no withholding; but when I was off, I just switched off.

SUKANYA SHANKAR: *For me, the stress of trying to pretend was getting too much. I was trying to leave my husband, but I kept getting threats from this same friend of Raviji's that if I did it, I wouldn't see Raviji ever again. I took it for some time, but in the end I decided that I was not going to any more, and I separated. We divorced in 1987.*

Before the decree came through, I was in India for six months. On 3rd September 1986 Raviji had called me in London from Bangalore and invited me to India. He was so loving to me at that time, and I arranged to travel on 10th. The 5th was my birthday. On the 4th he had travelled to Coimbatore, but he didn't phone me on my birthday. I was wondering why he hadn't called, because he had told me he was going to. About 3 o'clock I phoned him from England. The first sentence he uttered was: 'If you love me, don't phone me any more.'

Merely by a phone call on the 4th, this friend had influenced Raviji to change his mind totally. He had rejected me totally – he didn't even want to talk to me on the phone. I could not change all my plans at the last minute, so I left my job and everything and went to India with Anoushka on the 10th September for six months.

In 1986 I became very ill with angina. After the fright I had experienced in 1974 I had been more careful with my health, but the frantic pace of my life and my emotional upheaval remained. In 1977-78 I had experienced a little numbness in the finger, and there seemed to have been some blockage in the artery. But the trouble in 1986 was very serious. In September or October I went to the South of India for Ayurvedic treatment, taking to vegetarianism and shaving off all my hair. But instead of helping me, because of my heart condition it had just the opposite effect. I became so weak, with mental depression and nightmares plaguing me. My mind has never been so

(this page) From the family album: Ravi, Sukanya, Anoushka, Fluffy, Eton, Lady and Missy.

(opposite) In the garden at home in New Delhi, February 1997.

(overleaf) At the Barbican Hall, London, for his July 1996 recital.

He had made plans to come over to London, and for the first time I saw him arrive without a sitar. I'll never forget that day: 22nd November 1987. He never travels on his own: somebody always accompanies him, either a tabla-player or a student. But on this occasion I saw him come alone from Immigration, no sitar in his hand. I think this was a special treat.

After visiting Soviet Russia for the concerts in 1987 (where I experienced all the hippy-like adulation), I sent my sitars back to Delhi with my students, and I specially came to London with only a suitcase, just to be with Sukanya. I spent four crazy days at Bailey's Hotel in bliss! I really felt a great surge of love for her, and things were almost falling into place.

The next time I came to London, in the spring of 1988, it was even stronger. It was also a turbulent visit, though, because I had a big row with my close friend. He was livid with me for going all out for Sukanya so openly. I too lost my temper, we had a showdown, and he huffed and left. Unfortunately it was the big break-up, and that was the last I saw of him.

I too get mad with people sometimes, but when the tempest is over if I realise I am wrong I ask for forgiveness. If it is the other way round, I will grant that forgiveness. I have never had a problem saying, 'I'm sorry,' even if the other person is in the wrong – but I have seldom found people who do say they are sorry, or at least discuss the matter, clear everything up and finish the issue once and for all, instead of becoming sick in mind and body by carrying it on.

I was so sad after this blow-up with my friend that a couple of days later I tried to patch things up by phoning him, but he said quite clearly that I was never to ring or contact him again. Later he wrote me two vitriolic letters. Through the years since then I have come to know from a mutual friend that he too misses me, but his anger has not diminished towards Sukanya, whom he blames for the break-up of our friendship. I have therefore taken the attitude that unless he accepts her whom I love, who is my wife and the mother of my daughter, there is no chance of reconciliation. That is the impasse between the two of us, we who had so many years of fun and happiness as friends. I do miss him greatly – it's sad.

But now that whole business was over, I was so much clearer about Sukanya.

SUKANYA SHANKAR: *When he broke up with his friend, that was something I didn't expect at all. He had been so important in Raviji's life for so many years: nobody could shake that.*

One day, I remember, Raviji looked in his pocket and found £400 in cash. He couldn't remember when he had put the money there. He said, 'I didn't expect this money, so I want to buy you something with it.' He was going to drop me home in a taxi, and the shops were just closing, but impulsively he asked the taxi driver to stop. He went into an Indian shop on Kilburn High Road and bought me a ring. He insisted that it be a single diamond, but didn't explain why. He told me not to tell anyone, and naturally I assumed that this meant it was not serious. I wore the ring for him, but I only told one friend.

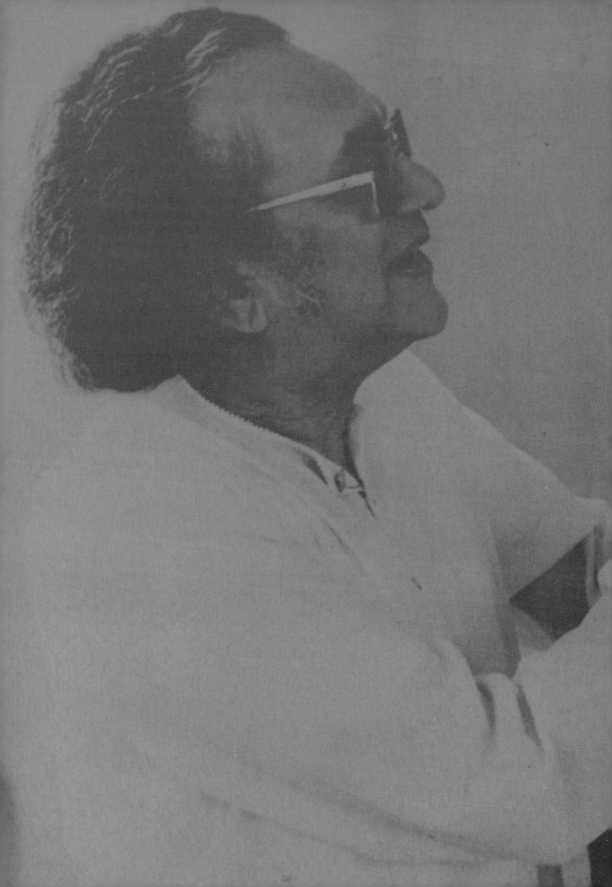

Two days later we went to Budapest. On the first day, before his performance, he had an interview in the hotel suite, and there were some Hungarian friends and his students present. He told me to stay in the bedroom while he talked to them: 'I'll call you in later.' I thought, OK, he's still hiding me. But after about ten minutes or so he called me in and introduced me, saying, 'This is Sukanya – my fiancée.' My legs almost gave way! He had never formally told me anything.

I couldn't even react to it right then, because all those people were present. Immediately he started telling Kumar Bose and everybody else that I was his fiancée, and showing them my ring. It came as a total shock!

It was a gradual decision. I was hesitating between yes and no, but from the moment I bought that ring I think I had taken the full decision in my mind at least. But still I didn't fully have it worked out!

For too long I had been filled with fear by my confidant and advised to keep the whole situation a secret. By now, my heart filled with my deep and strong love for Sukanya and Anoushka, and my mind weighed down with guilt and remorse at having done wrong to them, I took the decision to change my butterfly lifestyle once and for all, and to marry again.

SUKANYA SHANKAR: *Even then we never talked about marriage or anything. He never proposed to me; he just fixed the marriage! He phoned me from India in January 1989, and told me to come over there with Anoushka to have a holiday. He said we would go to Benares, and I could meet his brother Debendra and his wife Krishna. That was a plus point, that he wanted me to meet his family. Then he said, 'You can go to Madras and then to Hyderabad, and I'll come from Calcutta to Hyderabad on 21st January.' On the 22nd he had a concert in Hyderabad in the morning, and he said, 'The 23rd is a good day, and we'll go to this temple, and then on the 24th we can stay, and the 25th we'll come back.'*

So I asked, 'A good day for what?' He replied, 'There's a nice temple and we'll get married there.' My reaction was just to put the phone down, because I was so choked I couldn't talk to him on the phone about it!

Though I was nervous about the whole thing, I planned it there in India. I saw a date which was auspicious, and I thought we'd better have it then. That was it! And it was fantastic – marriage in the temple. All this was arranged by my long-time good friend Mohan Hemmadi. (Unfortunately our relationship is strained now over some recording deal.)

I didn't want to tell anyone: only Sejda, who at the time was eighty-one, and my sister-in-law. About ten or twelve people came from Calcutta, Delhi and Hyderabad, and Sukanya's sister from Bangalore.

SUKANYA SHANKAR: *I fell in love with Sejda and Krishnadi. I knew I had full support from Sejda, because in Benares he took Raviji's hand and said, 'If you let this girl down, that's the end of you!' Ever since he's taken a very special place in my heart.*

Nobody was supposed to know about the wedding except a few close friends, yet someone let the cat out of the bag. Everybody was phoning us there in Hyderabad the day before the wedding, even Time *magazine. Someone sneaked in and took photographs, and the next day it was on the front page everywhere!*

It was like wildfire all over India, in all the newspapers. The difference in our ages was the biggest sensation – the press made a big story out of the thirty-four year gap between us. Sukanya became extremely popular through interviews in all the magazines. Later on there was a cover story on her in the leading women's magazine *Savvy*, with a dramatic picture of the two of us. That made her into a household name.

SUKANYA SHANKAR: *I don't think we ever turned back after that. I went through some bad experiences but I'm so happy now that if I could choose what would happen in my next life, and if I knew he was there at the end of it all for me, I would without hesitation gladly go through all the suffering and pain again.*

Since 1993 Sukanya, Anoushka and I have made our home in California. It was while I was staying with Purna and Gopa Patnaik in September 1992 that we luckily found a house nearby which seemed ideal for us. We bought it, and after Purna, an architect by trade, had carried out some major alterations, Sukanya, Anoushka and I moved in on Valentine's Day, 1993, celebrating with a traditional Indian house-warming ceremony. We are there for most of the year, except in the winter, when I always go to India for around three months. Encinitas is in a beautiful part of the world, blessed with delightful scenery and favoured with fine weather all year round.

Many a time the child within me is shocked when it confronts the question 'what am I doing in the cage of this older body?' People say you are as young as you feel – I don't believe it! I, who have been such an impish, ever-young person, clowning and horsing around, with so much energy, always the entertainer, trying to give so much, being creative – why can't I run and jump, or give marathon non-stop sitar concerts of five or ten hours and then make love for hours afterwards, all without proper food or sleep, as I did for years? Though that dynamic young spirit is still alive within me, I now have to treat this junk of a body-machine with care, aided by medications and doctors' attentions.

Mind you, in spite of age some childlike characteristics have survived in me, such as my curiosity – always wanting to know what is happening in the news, sports, politics, discoveries, literature, arts. Though I don't get to see as many movies as in my earlier days, I still love the cinema and at times I have a TV and video binge, to the anguish of Sukanya! I am a nut about reading the newspapers every morning with my breakfast and tea (always

Darjeeling, my favourite), and never miss *Time*, *Newsweek* or *National Geographic*. I thank God that I don't have a bored or déjà-vu attitude.

Age brings with it its own problems for a performing artist: the older you get, the harder you have to work to maintain the standard you have set, which puts strain on yourself and your family life. Yet I feel I am a better musician and have a more creative mind now. More than ever I feel the ecstasy that comes when the improvisations flow out of me spontaneously. This feeling of euphoria can overcome whatever physical ailment I am suffering from when I walk on to the stage. Although I might sometimes feel that I have not the dexterity of a few years ago, in a public recital my hands can miraculously fly over the frets doing things which I thought were no longer possible!

At times a restlessness comes over me. I feel frustrated at not being able, mainly due to lack of finance, to satisfy my artistic and creative urges, to create beautiful music for new ballets or ensembles. Sometimes too I feel tensions because of my teenage daughter's growing pains, though that sort of stress cannot be avoided, or due to problems with disciples. Recently it has been one person in particular that has caused me torment, a young budding tabla-player whom I took as a disciple and who was trained by me along with my other students for a number of years. I even gave him the opportunity to accompany me in concert on a few of my international tours, which I would never normally have done to such an immature performer. He was not truly ready for it, but I did it out of sheer love for him. Then I discovered that he had committed a crime so heinous that only God can forgive him. Naturally he had to go.

Furthermore I tend to agonise over numerous petty matters, although to me they seem quite important. Has someone been paid for some little service he has performed? Have the guests been offered tea or food? I find myself feeling concerned about their most minute comforts. As for my students, I am anxious not to hurt them, and feel so over-obligated for the little things they do for me – though I know that in the past most musicians have treated their students very harshly, with strict rules and regulations, rarely showing much of the affection they might feel in their hearts. I even feel concerned about my paid servants for any service that they render. My middle name should be Worry!

Yet, though I am frequently possessed by these worries, I often feel I have managed to attain a level of tranquillity greater than that before my marriage. Who knows what is going to happen tomorrow? One cannot predict. It could be an earthquake, a nuclear bomb, health hazards, anything, but as things are now I feel much freer from many of the strains I endured for years and years: the emotional problems inherent in my lifestyle, trying to please everyone and to give my best in every possible way, not only physically but also emotionally. There were surges of happiness and joy but that existence was a heavy burden, and I feel much happier now. Sukanya is so wise, loving and caring. I feel proud of myself that I took the decision to marry her, and I regret not doing so much earlier. She is really an amazing person, and I go on discovering many new qualities in her.

She is so Indian, and yet having spent many years in London she also has the Western way of thinking, which I appreciate very much: a good sense of organisation, a quick mind, very clear thought and a sharp perception of people and issues. She is also very sure of herself. She always gives me her frank opinion as to what I should or should not do. In fact I rebelled against this in the beginning, because I could never accept anyone telling me what to do! She can be brutally frank at times and can be misunderstood, but people who have come to know her love her for this quality, as well as adoring her for her spells of gutsy laughter. Another quality which I find astounding in her is her abundant love for children and (inherited from her mother) for animals. Whether it is a cat, dog, racoon, monkey, elephant or tiger, she has no fear! I have seen her go straight to the fiercest of dogs and they behave with her like a pussy cat. But, boy oh boy, you should see her when she is confronted by a cockroach, spider, mouse or lizard – she shrieks her head off!

Initially she had some quite comical problems adjusting to being married to a North Indian, since we have one or two customs different from those of our Southern brethren. Like the Japanese, Indians from all over the country have always put a great emphasis on behaving in a deferential manner – standing up for our elders, speaking humbly, and observing the age-old respectful practices such as pranam, namaskar (the traditional greeting in which the hands are placed palm to palm in front of the forehead and the head bowed) or aadaab by Muslims (raising the right hand towards the forehead). However, there is a greater instinctive formality in the behaviour of North Indians, which historically derives from the extra emphasis on courtesy and etiquette (known as adab and tamiz) introduced by the Moghul rulers from the sixteenth century onwards. The Moghul influence on conduct spread all over North India and into most social classes, and over the generations we have taken it to extremes. Now we seem to be constantly bowing and touching feet! This etiquette manifests itself in a kind of exaggerated humility, which is sometimes crudely known as nakhra. By way of example, when a man arrives at another's house, he will be always be offered tea, snacks or a little something; yet no matter how thirsty or hungry he may be, he will find himself automatically declining, while fulsomely expressing his deep gratitude. He may, however, actually mean 'yes'! So his host will then persist with the offer, while the guest will continue to refuse: 'I wouldn't dream of you going to so much trouble for such an insignificant person!' These exchanges will be repeated perhaps two or three times before eventually either the guest accepts or the host decides he can safely take no for an answer.

This is common behaviour in the North, but since the Moghuls' influence hardly touched the South, such a scene would not be found there. Being South Indian, and having the Western influence too, Sukanya was not used to such exaggerated decorum, making for some amusing breakdowns of communication in the early days of our marriage. Until she got the hang of it, she would take the initial refusals of guests at face value, and they would be left thirsty and perplexed!

One great result of her talent for organisation is that for the first time I now have someone taking care of the shambles of my business ways and finances. I doubt if any other Indian classical musician has earned as much money through performances and various musical endeavours as I have. Yet I have been so bad with money – I spent and spent. I have always loved to entertain and to give presents, and never like to eat alone; I would rather take ten persons with me. As for my long-distance phone calls...! I never worried about money, never felt the crunch, because for years it had been coming in all the time.

However, I started getting panicky about my finances. Having developed a good way of life, as all successful musicians around the world do, I had become accustomed to living in a grand manner. But due to my health problems and the hassles of travel (complex arrangements, time-consuming formalities, security procedures, checking in all our party's instrument boxes, waiting around at airports...) I increasingly preferred to give fewer performances with larger fees. For many years I seldom had a secretary; mostly I was taking care of everything for my own tours. Agents, accountants and solicitors assisted me, but even they were mostly restricted to the United States and Europe. It was only from the mid-Seventies that I started employing them in India also. And in every possible manner so many people had fleeced me. One good thing which the friend I fell out with did was to put aside some of my earnings for me, for which I am thankful, yet still I had very few savings. Sukanya has worked hard to rectify all this.

Until 1988, just as I had kept Sukanya away from me as much as possible, apart from the occasional clandestine meeting, it had been the same with the lovely little Anoushka. And after the marriage, although everything changed in my relationships with both of them, Sukanya's time and love – which up to then had been focused totally on Anoushka – became divided between Anoushka and me. Our ultra-sensitive and intelligent daughter naturally went through those growing-up years feeling hurt and lonely. With the tremendous age difference of sixty-one years between her and me, plus the limitations imposed on me by my heart condition, I could not relate to her as a father normally does with his daughter. On top of the other things that I had already not been able to give her as she grew up, I could not now be running, jumping, playing, giving piggy-backs or horsing around in general.

One thing that did bring us together was music. It was Sukanya's idea that I should start to teach Anoushka on a little sitar, beginning from the basics. She had a tremendous talent for anything she put her mind to, and picked it up so fast, filling my heart with joy. Like so many extraordinarily talented children, she could sit and learn along with me for hours at a time but alone by herself she has always tended to shirk her practice or do it reluctantly. Though I have never raised my hands to strike any of my disciples, if they are slow in picking things up the spirit of Baba rises in me: my voice, expression and eyes change, I lose my calm and become a terror to my students! Though even in those formative years Anoushka was never slow in learning, it took her some time, as it does for everyone, to set her hands and posture, to master the meend and the bols and various basic exercises. The poor thing's little hands would cause her pain and her soft fingers would be cut by the strings, but in response, as my habits were, I would show my impatience and flash my angry eyes at her! And then I would see her lovely lips tremble and eyes water, and my heart would melt. Within a year or two I gradually trained myself to control my temper and make her enjoy the music. As the times have changed, I also gave her the freedom not to do pranam to me before and after lessons, which I had done to Baba and all my other students do to me, and which is still the prevalent custom (though she does do pranam when she accompanies me in a recital, both before and after the performance).

In spite of her not practising as much as I want her to, with her unusual merit she has improved quickly. At Sukanya's insistence, Anoushka had her sitar debut at my 75th birthday concert in New Delhi in February 1995. I had long discussions with Sukanya regarding this, as I favoured waiting another couple of years before gradually preparing her for a major programme with more experience playing at home and in private recitals. But I have now come to agree with Sukanya (again, as times have changed!) that children today, especially the talented ones, have not the patience of the olden days. Surrounded by the flood of glitter, glamour and the media, without encouragement they are easily frustrated and tend to lose interest very quickly.

Since her debut Anoushka has performed, assisting me, in concerts in most of the major cities in India and in various places around the world. She has an inborn showmanship, poise and confidence, and with this, added to her beautiful and attractive personality, she wows the audience. She has been an immediate success, a young sensation, although at her age one must look to the longer term. It takes years and years to really imbibe the depth of our music and be able to improvise and perform at a high standard, and even then the process never stops. I know this from my own experience: I am still learning now, as I reach the age of seventy-seven! I firmly believe that she too will be faithful to the seriousness of this approach in the future.

She has been playing so well, especially in recent months, not only in terms of speed or clarity but also with feeling. She has the uncanny gift of being able to repeat some of my spontaneous improvisations so accurately that it amazes the listeners, and gives me such delight. I feel so proud! She inspires me and brings out the best in me, both when I teach her and on stage. I soar to such heights, and then I see in her eyes such deep appreciation, which moves me so! My heart fills with such love for her that it almost hurts.

Sukanya and I both feel very blessed with Anoushka. I feel a strong urge that I should live, to pass down whatever I can to Anoushka, not only as my daughter but as my disciple. She has all the signs – the lakshana – that she is the ideal person to absorb what I can give to her and to develop it further, so I enjoy it immensely. Not because it is something which I owe to her; it is a real pleasure rather than a mere duty.

Having been a father three times over, I know I am not a good one. I have never had the patience to deal with small children and their tantrums, and with my non-stop jet-setting life I couldn't fulfil a father's duty. I missed those wonderful formative years when I could have been with Anoushka and started her on music earlier. In the same way I missed the early childhood of Shubho and my other daughter in the West. With Anoushka I have the chance to make up for those years.

It seems to be a universal fact among performers and entertainers, especially musicians, that success brings with it a curse for family life. At heart an artist has to be selfish much of the time in order to succeed. Frequently he has to put the demands of his audience before the needs of his family, jealously guarding his energy and concentration so that he can devote them to performing. If he doesn't, his career will suffer. It's a case of 'if you can't stand the heat, get out of the kitchen'. Success is also addictive. The appreciation of an audience is an overwhelming sensation, and everyone who experiences it feels its power. The adulation is a much greater motivation than the money and the accompanying lifestyle. This is why, unless he is crippled, a performer rarely chooses to retire. Believe me, I am not stating this merely to justify myself, to explain away why I have never been a good father. For anyone who reaches a certain position of achievement and respect in any performing art, the workaholic tendency develops whether one wants it or not. It is always the close family that suffers, and this has been the case with all the women in my life and all my children, including Sukanya and Anoushka.

As well as learning Indian music, Anoushka is playing the piano, in which she is brilliant, and I am encouraging her to learn vocal music, because it is the source of the whole of our classical music, and it is crucial to know about. I want her to know more, to know all the details of Indian and Western classical music, because in my opinion knowledge always makes you richer.

This belief of mine is perhaps contrary to Baba's belief in dedication to one pursuit, epitomised by his saying, 'Ek sadhe sab sadhe, sab sadhe sab jaye.' This is true in most cases. Baba's main instrument was the sarod, and it may have been his concentration on that, as well his incredible talent, which made everything else come easily to him. Yet consider Baba's own life again: he was so versatile. He had phenomenal knowledge of vocal music, and played so many instruments. For average people it's very difficult, but people who are highly gifted can acquire many different sorts of knowledge, and each one enhances the other. In my own life, going through so many years of stage and dance and all the varieties of other knowledge that I acquired, especially in my youth, helped me so much. It is striking with Anoushka that she really can completely switch over between Indian and Western music, and each has her full concentration when she is playing it. Not everybody can do that sort of thing, but some people are blessed by God and have that special gift. Anoushka is definitely one example. She could achieve great heights in so many other subjects too: as a writer, a dancer, an actress or even a model!

There are some striking similarities between Anoushka and how I was in my youth. She has a multi-faceted talent and an interest in so many things, and is overly romantic – all the time being either in love with love or in pain, extremely touchy and sensitive with outbursts of temper! She has additional pressures and distractions that I never really had to go through: school, homework, private tuition, piano lessons, her teenage friends and talking on the telephone! It was different for me in that when I took up sitar seriously I was already eighteen and fairly well versed in the ways of the world; I was able to make a clean break and give myself wholeheartedly to music and Baba of my own accord. And it was much easier to concentrate in Maihar than it is in California!

For a while her 'other' side, that of a modern teenager, disturbed me; but, thanks to Sukanya again, I have become more used to it. I realise that I have nothing to complain about, especially when I see how quickly she can switch over to the traditional Indianness and my domain, music. She balances between the two with confidence. She is a true Gemini!

In the end, no matter how hard I try to influence matters, what she is going to be is down to her own karma. But of this much I am sure: that being extremely wise, motivated and focused, she will be great in whatever she chooses to do. I love her so deeply, and can never show it enough to her!

❧

I have really lived my life: I have seen it all, done it all, and I could gladly walk away at this moment. Death has knocked at my door a few times, but I have told it to wait for a little longer, as I still want to live, especially for Anoushka.

At the height of my youth and popularity, I had everything as I wanted and every opportunity with women. I was restless, immature, like a tornado, and didn't really care about anyone or anything. I could shoulder all the emotional problems, trying as much as possible to keep everyone happy. Yet I was not fully happy with any one person, in the sense that I was missing something that I went to others for. It's not just a cliché or an excuse; it is true. Being in love with the idea of love, I would feel that I *was* completely in love; but there was always something discordant occurring to ruin it.

For too long I distributed myself physically and emotionally between too many people all around the world. Along with all the ecstasy and happiness I felt and gave them, there were so many tantrums, so much pain, jealousy, expectation, possessiveness and heartbreak. When I was younger I could handle the fact that my life was full of worry, mistakes and pain, because I was also busy, creative, energetic, independent and having fun – and all this overcame the suffering.

But then came the period when events in my personal life caught up with me and I had to face much criticism. My health was worsening too. I realised that I could not endure this stress and strain any more, and this compelled me to control my 'basic instincts' and 'fatal attractions'. I realised I couldn't go through those other relationships again, and I didn't want to either. This impulse to change was not just forced upon me. It also came from inside myself. Deep in my heart I felt the desire to channel all my love and energy into Sukanya and Anoushka.

Having at last to truly share my life with others and being dependent on them has naturally restricted me and given me responsibilities, made me face some things which I would previously have avoided. But there are pluses and minuses with everything, and the new family worries are in their own way sometimes quite welcome, and anyway balanced out by the absence of the old emotional and material concerns which had plagued me all along.

It doesn't mean that I don't appreciate a beautiful girl when I see her, and I still find that women are attracted to me, but I don't want to fool around any more! Now I have my Sukanya, whom I chose finally and love totally, and I feel happily settled. Basically I really am a one-woman man, but lifestyle can change you, as it does with most people who become famous. Sukanya has given me love and much more peace, which I value so much.

As we always say in our language when something seems too good, 'nazar na lage' – 'let there be no evil eye'. It's like saying 'touch wood'. Sukanya's passion and love are so deep. She is a firebrand in the sense that she can be very jealous, and being a jealous person myself I realise this is a sign of really true love. If there is no jealousy, it means you don't care for someone enough. Furthermore, she has enough reasons to be jealous because of my past, while I have no such reason. I feel so sure of her strength of character, integrity and love for me ᴗ!

NINE: MOHAN KAUNS

मोहन कौंस

After a career of sixty-seven years, and still going strong, Ravi Shankar is well placed to consider the course Indian music has taken in his lifetime and may take in the future. Central to any understanding of Indian music is the concept of the traditional gharana system. The word 'gharana', mostly used in Northern India (an older name, parampara is also used by many, especially in the South), denotes a particular centre or family (often literally) of musical tradition with a distinctive style of vocal or instrumental music. The term is applied to other art forms too – everything from dance to handicrafts to wrestling – but naturally it is with music we are most concerned here.

I n relation to the Hindustani system of music from North India, the musical influences that we have been lucky enough to receive today have been handed down from the gharanas of previous generations. Some of the greatest musicians are so creative that they give a new dimension or a new life to the gharana they follow, and their style becomes so attractive that, as well as being inherited by their own family or disciples, other people are also attracted to learn it. So at different stages of our history various gharanas have existed. In a constant process of evolution, some have emerged, some have dwindled and disappeared, some have taken another name, some have joined with others to form hybrids; it has gone on like that through the centuries.

The famous gharanas of Indian classical music are named after the place where a famous musician lived, his style of singing or the instrument he played. For instance, the better-known khyal gharanas since the turn of the century have been Gwalior, Jaipur, Patila, Kirana, Agra and Atrauli. A particular style or speciality of singing is closely associated with each of these gharanas. The same thing happened with the instrumental gharanas. Many eminent ones, such as Beenkar, Rababiya and Senia, originated from the great Mian Tan Sen and his descendants, who were originally in Delhi during the Moghul reign, and later migrated to Jaipur, Benares, Rampur and elsewhere. There sprang other gharanas too: vocal ones deriving from the old forms of dhrupad and dhamar, such as in khyal, tappa and thumri; and instrumental ones grouped around the outstanding musicians renowned for their special styles on sitar, sarod, sarangi or tabla (which gradually overshadowed the older traditional drum pakhawaj).

It must always be remembered that ours is an oral tradition, and necessarily so since one cannot learn how to improvise from a musical score. Therefore, though our music originated from the chantings of the Sama Veda, it has gone through many centuries of development as a performing art, and it is still evolving. Thus a classical-music recital today does not bear much relation to age-old Vedic chantings, except in the spirituality one finds in its expression and the lyrics of many vocal pieces. (The chanting of the Vedas and the Upanishads has been kept alive by Brahmin shastris, but this is a different sphere, unrelated to the contemporary classical repertoire.)

So we cannot exactly pinpoint the evolution of our music, certainly not as easily as one can with Western classical music. The foundations of the latter were similarly in religious music – Gregorian chants and old church music – but the difference was that there it became a composed music, written down, and so one can without difficulty identify a piece as thirteenth-century or baroque, Beethoven or Schoenburg. In India we cannot exactly locate changes in the gharana system in the same way. To some extent we can estimate, especially with music developed since the late fifteenth century, from when the musical forms of num-tum, alap, dhrupad and dhamar were gradually established, along with two traditional instruments: the been (the North

Indian veena) and the two-faced pakhawaj drum. Emerging later were the rabab, sursingar and surbahar, ftringed inftruments which followed the dhrupad form. From the mid-nineteenth century the khyal form of singing gained popularity, in tandem with the rise of the sitar, sarod, tabla and the sarangi. But all of these ftyles and our knowledge about their origins have been passed down the generations orally, from one guru to the next, rather than being recorded for pofterity in music scores. It is precisely because of this oral tradition that our music has conftantly evolved with each generation.

(Incidentally, although normally in classical music we have to learn everything orally, memorising and imbibing it, we *can* write our music down if we wish, with our own solfeggio syftem, using the names Sa-Ri-Ga-Ma-Pa-Dha-Ni-Sa. This is principally juft a memory aid, but since the beginning of the twentieth century such notation has increasingly been used by eminent musicians and musicologifts in compiling old song compositions; today it is commonly employed on the commercial side, by time-pressed session artifts playing for films, ftage shows, radio or television. I actually introduced certain changes to the exifting notation syftem, inventing special signs for the type of right-hand ftroke to play on each note. From the mid-Forties I also emphasised writing the English initials S-R-G-M-P-D-N-S for Sa-Ri-Ga-Ma-Pa-Dha-Ni-Sa.)

In the days before modern mass communications, in the North of India one could only hear music in person, either where the musician lived or in the court of the maharajah or nawab who employed him; only very occasionally would he perform in a big city for a special event. There were no music conferences or concerts, so it was rare for a great musician to give a recital for the mass public. All the musicians were dependent on a patron: they were supported financially and given land, accommodation and provisions, so that if they wanted they could keep ten or twenty (and sometimes even more) disciples, all of them living with and learning from them. They had no worries at all, as they performed for an elite only. There were a few early three-minute-long gramophone records ftarting from around a hundred years ago, but many of the greateft musicians refused to record, fearing that, along with their music, their life and soul would be 'sucked out' into the recording machine and they would die! This meant that, although our classical music continued to exift and evolve in an age-old unbroken tradition, moft people in the North unfortunately had little contact with it. (In the South it was completely different. Traditionally moft of the musicians there gave regular performances in the temple courtyards, so the multitudes always had the opportunity to hear them.)

Often the gurus (or uftads, as the Muslims call their teachers) were rather narrow-minded, and would reftrict the beft talim to the members of their own family. There were also classifications between ftudents, separating them into different grades. This was natural but sometimes unfortunate: if the beft talim was reftricted to the son or the neareft relative, and he died early, a lesser grade of talim was passed on inftead of the original 'A-grade' ftyle!

Raga Tilak Shyam

Sitar Gat (medium tempo Teental of 16 beats 4+4+4+4=16)

ANTARA.

New Raga ~~created~~ Created in 1948 — along with this Gat
Composition

Ravi Shankar

The bracketed notes means ornamented
ones such as (P) would be ‾DPMP‾

During the period of royal patronage many of the court musicians found another source of income, which became more important with the dwindling of the princely courts – teaching music to the baijis (singing or dancing girls or courtesans) who mostly lived in the main cities of the princely native States or in the larger, British-controlled cities such as Bombay, Calcutta and Delhi. These highly accomplished ladies were great favourites of the royalty, landlords and merchants; some even had amorous liaisons with them. They were extremely knowledgeable in music, dance, literature, shairi (the recitation of Urdu and Persian couplets) and many other arts, blessed with good looks and attractive personalities, beautiful manners and speech, and also an advanced sexual knowledge of the Kama Sutra. (In some ways they were comparable to the high-class geishas of traditional Japan.) The rich and the aristocracy would send their adolescent sons to these courtesans in order to receive a complete all-round education!

Many of these baijis became well-known Kathak dancers or khyal, thumri and ghazal singers, under the tutelage of the famous court musicians. The common practice was for the prince or landlord to celebrate a special occasion by throwing a lavish dinner and drinks followed by a mujrah, a programme of singing, dance and poetry presented by the baijis for the assembled guests. The delighted well fed guests would shower gifts upon the baijis, many of whom in consequence became quite wealthy. For giving them their talent, the baijis often came to worship the musicians who taught them, even taking them as their lovers, which was naturally good for the status of the latter.

This whole system of mujrahs was at its height from the middle of the nineteenth century until independence. They were perhaps most common in Lucknow and Benares, which also became big centres for Kathak, the story-telling dance form popularised in these mujrahs. The semi-classical music form of thumri, the texts of which mostly tell of the romantic and erotic love escapades of the young Krishna, flourished as well. The sexual element involved in mujrahs did escalate over time, and as the concept was slightly cheapened it became a social taboo. With this decline, increasingly some musicians lost their social status too. (Thanks to the effort of some Kathak dancers, such as the magnificent Birju Maharaj, this style has in the last two or three decades regained prestige as a stylised and great dance form). But for a long time the baiji culture had been a grand and beautiful way of life among the elite.

Following India's independence everything changed. It was the end of the great power of the maharajahs and the rich landlords who, as well as no longer being able to maintain their palaces, elephants, court jesters and concubines, could not afford to keep their musicians any more. Many of our great masters had to venture further afield to earn more money – into the cities, onto the airwaves of All India Radio, making records and performing at music conferences, festivals and music circles. Some also had to begin charging for private tuition.

Since the advent of radio, gramophone records, tape recorders, televisions, videos and compact discs, things have been evolving so fast. In

The author's notation for a gat he composed in Raga Tilak Shyam (also his own creation), illustrating the notation system he introduced with signs for notes, time measures, left-hand fingering and right-hand strokes. This system is now used by other musicians too.

earlier times it was easier to maintain the purity of gharanas, because of the distance between the cities. Gwalior and Agra, or Patiala and Lucknow, were far enough apart to prevent the up-and-coming students from being 'polluted' by hearing something attractive from another gharana. Now people can hear so many different types of music. Classical music has gone from being restricted to the elite to being a mass-market activity. From the early days of All India Radio, musicians and the public have been open to the influence of all the different gharanas. Some of the younger generation of musicians started taking the best ideas from other gharanas and attempting to develop composites. With the decline of the traditional way of learning, this has become the fashion today, especially among the talented up-and-coming students who have not had a chance to learn from a great master. Instead they might learn from an average teacher of music, listen to all the different records and then use their talent to assimilate everything and become a performer. An average listener cannot discriminate between one of these musicians and one who has learnt from a great guru, but a crucial gulf exists. We do have some young people who have been able to maintain a certain purity of style, but generally the young feel that it is no longer enough to stick to one particular gharana.

Of course we should not necessarily be scared of change. Our music has developed rapidly over the last century, yet change has always been a feature of it. Due to the oral tradition and the direct guru-shishya method of teaching, over and over again the student's music will sound the same as his guru's; but gradually, when he is on his own, it might unfold a little differently, especially if he is a creative musician spontaneously adding new ideas and technique and giving the music fresh dimensions.

Many a time innovators have initially encountered very strong criticism, as I myself have experienced. Any creative musician who incorporates a new approach or idea has to go through this – including my guru Baba Allauddin Khan, who did so much to mould Hindustani instrumental music into what we know today. There was opposition even to the musical advances of the great Mian Tan Sen of the late fifteenth century. Always an innovator is faced with opponents who shout that the music is being led astray. But if the new developments are valid and based on the deep classical foundation, they soon become part of the tradition. That is how our music has grown to its great proportion of today, and why it has not become stagnant, as happens in many countries with very old cultures.

Today our current gharana system appears to be gradually dwindling, and in the future new gharanas with new names will take the places of some of those that exist now, until they too are replaced in turn by even newer ones. The system is not going to die completely – people will know what particular style was associated with Agra or Kirana gharanas (and others). However, it is not going to be restricted to these old gharanas. Of the developments which spring up, those that are beautiful will stay, and those that people like less will slowly die away, as has always happened!

What is different now is the pace of change. In earlier times the evolution of the gharana system was a very slow process. Perhaps that was why people may have objected less then, because during their lifetime they may not have realised changes were slowly occurring. Recently, though, there has been a rapid evolution, and many people are very much disturbed by the swiftness of change in this jet age, with all its high-speed communications. The world really has become so much smaller.

Nevertheless I am very optimistic that the overall impact will be to enrich the music. We are not (as many people are already crying out) going to lose our music. It is simply being presented a bit differently, developing into more organised and sometimes more beautiful forms. The good things from our traditions are likely to remain with us – we are harnessing our modern computer technology, especially in recording, to preserve almost everything. As in other fields, we may have lost quite a few wonderful things (and we must be vigilant to protect those treasures which are worthy of saving) but we have to accept this happens sometimes. You lose some – you gain some!

One of the most likely results of these changes will be that new musical traditions will form around the greatest artists of today, those who have advanced the music by adding a new approach or a distinctive emphasis to the style of the gharana they have followed. It is widely perceived that one of these is forming around Ravi himself. Today one finds that most of the younger musicians are influenced to a greater or lesser extent by the baaj (style) of famous players such as Ravi.

The most direct way in which his legacy has been and is being passed on is through those he has taught. He has had many students during his half-century as a guru, and of these a considerable number would be described as disciples. (There is a distinction between the two terms, which lies not just in the formal ganda ceremony but also has to do with talent, devotion, urge, reverence and hard work. A guru can feel when a student has become a disciple; ganda can become secondary, only a technical detail, although a sacred ritual and a public acknowledgement which can't be refuted.) In this book he has already referred to a number of those disciples nearest and dearest to him, but there are more that should be mentioned: Jamaluddin Bharatiya (sitar), Jaya Biswas (sitar), Deepak Chowdhury (sitar and composer), Rama Rao (sitar), Kartik Seshadri (sitar), Vinay Bharat Ram (vocal), Arun Bharat Ram (sitar), Partho Sarathy (sarod), Shubhendra Rao (sitar), Manju Mehta (sitar), Steve Slavek (sitar), Narendra Bataju (sitar), M. Janardan (sitar), Gaurav Mazumdar (sitar), Samaresh Chowdhury (vocal), Borun Pal (guitar), and no doubt others too. Many of them have passed the age of sixty now, and most have become well-known top-level performers. Ravi is very proud of them all.

In the future there will be gharanas that are based on the styles of the famous musicians of today. Already one hears of an Ali Akbar Khan gharana, a Vilayat Khan gharana and a Ravi Shankar gharana. It is true there are many of our students or other young musicians who follow our individual styles. Alubhai, a few of Baba's other senior students and I call our style of playing Maihar gharana. We might have continued to name it Senia Beenkar, as Baba's principal tradition was known, but Baba also learnt from so many other people of different gharanas, and he was a master of them all. Like a magician, he could switch between the styles at will. Overall he had a composite style, which we like to call Maihar. Yet today it seems that some

of Baba's disciples play in a different way to their guru. If you take the instance of Alubhai, who has had all his training from Baba, in addition he has a particular touch, expression, style and treatment of ragas which is entirely his own. If it is too early to recognise an Ali Akbar gharana or a Ravi Shankar gharana as such – and I feel it is – one can at the very least talk of an Ali Akbar baaj, or a Ravi Shankar baaj, and so on. The term baaj denotes a style of playing an instrument (sarod baaj, or sitar baaj), or the style of a particular eminent musician, or even the style associated with a gharana started by one performer. (The equivalent term for vocal music is gaayaki).

Amidst all the great Indian musicians I was fortunate to be exposed to throughout my childhood, some made a great impression upon me: Faiyaz Khan, Abdul Karim Khan, Yusuf Ali Khan, Rameshwar Pathak and Abdul Wahid Khan in particular. But naturally, more than anyone else it was Baba who inspired me. It wasn't just what he taught me (although that itself was formidable), but the exuberance and passion he transmitted too. Then there was his blend of orthodoxy and eclecticism. For the most part he was a highly conservative and puritan traditionalist, but at times he broke away into unorthodox innovation. As well as being an extraordinary sarod-player he was a superb drummer; he became a master of myriads of very rhythm-orientated chhanda (varieties of metric patterns) from numerous different origins, and introduced the essence of them into his own style, along with elements of folk music too. He uniquely had a musical vision that enabled him to make these quantum leaps, incorporating new influences into his improvisation in a brilliant and always appropriate way.

With my childhood exposure to so many varied influences in music and dance, I identified with this extraordinary improvisatory ability of his and imbibed it deeply. With my creative urge, I have always sought to extend our music in the same way. I have only had one guru, Baba. In the talim I received from Baba I can (if the occasion demands) differentiate the several origins of his composite style in the different training he had with various gurus, as well as his own creative innovations. I have done the same thing as Baba: over and above his talim, I have added my own new approaches and innovations over the last fifty years, thus creating my own style. When such a style is followed by students and new generations, this is how a new gharana starts.

I have introduced, if I may say so, many new factors into the playing of the sitar: to the instrument itself, in the way I have tuned it and strung it, giving it a different colour; to the sound production, plucking it in my own manner with a different volume and touch; and also emphasising the bass strings, which developed from my years spent on the surbahar. I tried to combine some of the salient features of the surbahar in playing the alap and especially the jor section, which I think is my forte. From the ati vilambit (very slow) to drut (fast) gats in different talas, with a myriad of variations, I humbly maintain that I have enriched the repertoire of the sitarist, and it is gratifying to see some of the younger instrumentalists following my innovations today, even if they are not my direct disciples.

In the field of ragas and talas, I have worked on so many aspects of our music. As many as thirty different ragas are my own creations, including *Nat Bhairav* (which I developed way back in 1945), *Bairagi*, *Ahir Lalit*, *Tilak Shyam*, *Manamanjari*, *Pancham Se Gara*, *Parameshwari*, *Jogeshwari*, *Charukauns*, *Bairagi Todi* and *Rajya Kalyan* (the last of which I composed for the occasion of my leaving the Rajya Sabha in 1992) and many others. Some of them are sung and played widely, along with many of my slow and fast gat compositions, although unfortunately many performers do not know (or do not want to admit) that they are playing my creation. This is very sad, and I assure you that I do not like having to make a noise to reclaim them – but it is the truth!

I have also created and composed thousands and thousands of gats and other bandishes (a general term for fixed vocal or instrumental compositions of any length bound by a rhythmic cycle) in all the different ragas. Hundreds of songs in classical style too, as well as the semi-classical ones based on different forms of our music, such as dhrupad, khyal and thumri.

The Carnatic system has provided me with a good share of my inspiration. I fell in love with Carnatic music in Madras at the age of twelve or thirteen when I first heard the great singer and veena-player Veena Dhanam, grandmother of Bala Saraswati. After that the association with Bala and her guru Kandappan Pillai strengthened my ardour. As the first Hindustani instrumental musician to perform regularly in Madras, over many years I came to know all the great Carnatic musicians of their day, such as Tiger Varadacharya, Maharajpuram Viswanatham, Ariakudi Ramanujam Ayengar, the veena-player Kariakudi Sambashiva Aiyer, Palghat Mani on the mridangam, G.N. Balasubramanyam and a host of other giants. 'GNB' and I became good friends. I was lucky enough to receive admiration and love from all of them and from Madras audiences too.

It has therefore been extremely satisfying to have succeeded in popularising among musicians in the North the ragas *Kirwani*, *Charukeshi*, *Vachaspati*, *Simhendra Madhyam*, *Malaya Marutham*, *Nata Bhairavi*, *Hemavati*, *Arabhi* and others which are all of Carnatic origin. I could not play them in the true Carnatic style, so what I introduced were Hindustani versions with my own interpretations and embellishments, including new gats and bandishes. These are played by most performers nowadays.

The Carnatic system's mathematical approach to rhythms and accurate application of them are also stunning. One of my greatest loves is for intricate sitar passages of mathematical precision filled with metric patterns and ending with complex tihais, all spontaneously improvised. As far back as 1945, I was absorbing the essence of these from the fixed calculative systems of the Carnatic system, incorporating into my music the complex approaches of the Southern mridangam-players along with those of the Northern pakhawaj and tabla maestros, and also the layakari of the Kathak dancers of Northern India. It is imperative to imbibe all this information (rather like data being fed into a computer) so that with maturity, after many years, one can spontaneously create new ideas both mathematical and artistic in nature, resulting in a scientific and beautiful style. An exhilarating experience! Some musicians and listeners think I play these passages in a manner they describe as 'hisabi' (calculative) and 'bandish' (a fixed composition), but this is not true: each passage is created extempore. It seems that almost every instrumentalist has been influenced by this layakari anga (rhythmic body or style) of mine.

Strangely enough the Carnatic system, which claims to be purer, untouched by influences brought by outsiders from the North, does not follow some of the traditions which are rigidly observed in the Northern system, such as the time theory of ragas, according to which each raga is associated with a particular time of the day or night. It is said that Carnatic musicians did away with this about a hundred years ago, maybe because they foresaw their concert system of today in which most music functions are held between 4pm and 11pm. Another difference, which has always puzzled me, is that when they perform any of the seventy-two melakarta (scale) ragas they don't observe vadi or samavadi – the two most important notes in a raga for us. They give equal importance to each note, stressing and combining them freely. In the Hindustani system we can actually create three or four distinct Pentatonic ragas from the same five notes, just by using different combinations or by stressing particular notes.

Another great love of mine is to introduce into the final piece of a programme, which is usually in the semi-classical thumri style or even that of a folkish dhun, other influences in the style known as raga mala. With a free romantic spirit, one gives hints of other ragas or folk melodies, one after another, although always returning to the main theme or gat.

An invention of mine which today has become popular among some sitar-players is the hook system, by which one can gag the third and fourth bass strings on the sitar in the faster passages when they are not needed. Three or four hooks are attached on the frets at a particular spot where they do not disturb my playing with the left hand. When we play a very fast tan and jhala, there is sometimes a resonance from those two strings, and it can be quite discordant, sounding a shade out of tune. To avoid this, when I stop playing them after the alap and jor sections, they can just be tucked under the hooks. There they can be tuned to the tonic, third, fourth, fifth or sixth, according to the chosen raga, thus creating an additional effect! Even today I am trying to find out if I can improve many more things by way of sound production on the sitar

It has been a particular concern of my career to encourage a new approach for the tabla-player as an accompanist. Many tablists have either learnt from or have been influenced by me, and I have created thousands of bandishes: tihais, chakkardars (triple tihais), parans, tukdas and farmaishi bandishes, which I apply to the sitar as well as the tabla. There are many talas now in vogue which I was responsible for first popularising in sitar-playing: Rupaktal (seven beats), Jhaptal (ten), Ektal (twelve), Ada Chautal (fourteen), Dhamar (fourteen), Pancham Sawari (fifteen), and many others from four and a half to 108 beats!

In the West I also started the practice of giving a greater prominence to the tabla-player. In earlier years, after the intermission in a recital we would start with a tabla solo of about ten minutes, during which I would explain to the audience about drum language: how each sound produced by the hands or fingers has a corresponding speech syllable. This method is actually how a disciple learns from his guru, once he has mastered the initial technique. By way of demonstration I would say some very simple phrases, such as 'ta, tin, na, tirakita, dha, dhin, kidanak', and the tablist would repeat them on his drums. I would then recite some exciting fixed compositions and, no matter how complex they were, my colleague would imitate them precisely, invariably to maximum applause from the audience. It is a common practice among great tabla-players to recite and perform such phrases themselves when they give a solo recital.

Another regular feature of my concerts is a sawal-jawab passage. The genesis of this idea was again in the South Indian system, in which concerts are punctuated by spectacular exchanges between the mridangam, ghatam and ganjeera. At first each Carnatic drummer in turn plays a long passage of maybe thirty-two bars, and then each plays sixteen bars, then eight, then four, two, one and even a half or quarter – until they play in unison, ending with a tremendous crescendo. These thrilling displays so impressed me when I first experienced them in my childhood that I introduced them later in my concerts, first between sitar and tabla, and then from the mid-Forties, in the most exciting development, when I started playing sawal-jawab with me on sitar and Alubhai on sarod. I have also done the same with my students when they have assisted me in recitals, and sometimes when there have been two drummers accompanying me.

For giving these chances to the tabla-players, which no-one else permitted back when I started doing it, I was so badly criticised by some Indian critics and musicians and music-lovers! They condemned me for spoiling the tabla-players, giving them too much of an uplift or creating a cacophony. Having initiated the practice to great success in the West, it was only natural that I repeated it in India also, and that's when some people really seemed to become unhappy. But it enhanced the prestige of some of our tabla-players and made them more famous. Even today a tabla solo is included in most of my concerts.

ZAKIR HUSSAIN: *One of the most important things that I learnt in my musical career, as a performer, was a little thing that Raviji told me: to sit at an angle on stage, watching any other musician that you are working with. I started thinking about it and I noticed other tabla-players playing with other musicians, and it was like: 'Here is a main instrumentalist and here is a tabla-player. We are both looking out at the audience and not really connecting with each other.' There might be an occasional glance, but that was all. And I suddenly realised what he meant.*

He has been one of the few instrumentalists – probably the first one – to offer a spotlight to an accompanist. Before him, you never heard of an instrumentalist putting his instrument down, keeping time and letting the tabla-player take off. The credit in bringing the importance of the tabla accompanist to the forefront is probably singularly his. He brought that whole idea of: 'Here is this instrument, which can do an incredible amount of work to support what happens on the stage. Don't let it just sit there in the background: utilise it. Let's come up with a package that makes it work well together.' That whole aspect of the creation of a raga being a collective effort is solely, I think, his idea.

And over the past two or three decades at least, the most mammoth and juggernautic figure that existed in Indian classical music has been Raviji. Like thousands of other musicians from India growing up listening to him and watching him perform, I have consciously tried to mould myself as a performer in his image. I know that I have always watched him and tried to remember the things he does on stage, the way he reacts, the way he talks, and the way he connects with people: the ease and comfort and yet the control and power. I wish I could get one tenth of that into my performance when I am on stage. A lot of what I am is definitely inspired through his personality, and not just musically speaking – personally speaking as well. My personality, the way I speak, the way I present myself, the words I choose – everything.

And it should be noted how well positioned Zakir is to testify to the benefits of Ravi's influence on other musicians, especially those in the succeeding generation. He grew up very close to Ravi (whom he calls 'Uncle') and accompanies him regularly in performance. Many seasoned observers of Indian music have commented that in his manner and his musical virtuosity Zakir reminds them of none other than the young Ravi Shankar.

In addition to the criticisms I have encountered through my innovations in the classical framework, many extra ones have arisen through my compositions for musicians from all over the world. No matter what new compositions I write, they are always based on tradition, on ragas and talas; they are not transplanted from a completely alien culture. This kind of

An influence across the generations: Ravi with Zakir Hussain, in Calcutta towards the end of the Seventies.

musical creation has always occurred in India, by an innovative musician whose base is in the old foundation but who sees and hears many new things. Despite this, some people in India have continually reacted as though I were committing sacrilege. They could not separate my classical side (as a performer) from the other, creative side (as a composer).

The instinct and urge to create something new was always inside me. In my childhood I could sketch quite well, I used to write tunes and songs (although I had the bad habit of losing whatever I wrote) and I had what seemed a vivid imagination. Lying on the roof with my mother and looking up at the sky, I would see so many shapes in the clouds: palaces, people, gods, beautiful faces. Even on the floors and walls I would picture them. I still do!

From my earliest years I had the instinct and opportunity to dance, of course, and to paint. Music was the same: even before hearing any tabla-players, I always loved to discover new patterns and used to improvise with rhythms by banging on a suitcase and whatever hard objects were to hand.

When inspired, I feel I also have a flair for writing (although that is for the reader to judge, of course), but it is always the first stage that I am best at; cutting and improving do not come so easily. Though I don't claim to be a poet or very literate, I have the natural urge to write, and have composed hundreds of songs in Hindi and Bengali. A few in English, too, although most were unused or have been lost. Only one was released, 'I Am Missing You'.

Yet apart from music and dance, I never worked hard on anything. For some years I had to concentrate on dance – and my brother was an exacting teacher – but other than that, all my attention has been on music.

Being with Dada taught me all about manners on the stage and how one should appear – never too glum or overly cheeky, and never to display artificial toothy smiles. Later I utilised this awareness about presentation in my performances, especially in the West. I was determined to have a proper dais, to use an Indian carpet covering the top of it, to blacken its front and sides so that it looked like a flying carpet, and furthermore to ensure all my accompanying performers wore attractive clothes in shades that did not clash. Incense sticks burning at the side of the stage also added to the atmosphere of reverence and spirituality which heightened everyone's appreciation of the music.

Dada also taught me about lighting. It was extremely useful in my later career to have found out at an early age about the usage of light and its effect on the presentation of one's face and body. It is essential to have illumination of the right colour carefully directed on the dais alone, not flooding the whole stage in brightness. A mixture of pink and amber light is best for most Indians, since it gives a golden colour ideal for our skin complexion and the sitar.

Presentation is important. Showmanship plays a great part in the West, whether on the part of an opera singer, a jazz musician or a pop star, but in our country musicians used to be overly informal. Too often they were crude or sloppy, displaying all their mannerisms in front of the public, coughing and mumbling, chatting to members of the audience or with each other. These practices would have been shocking for Western audiences and would have diﬅracted them from the music itself, so presenting myself in a professional manner was essential when I embarked on my firﬅ tour there. Now it has caught on among all our Indian performers, and I am pleased that we are much better at this.

Although moﬅ of our performers are now more polished on ﬅage, a few of them feel they have to bring down some other musicians, either direﬅly or indireﬅly. They think that by slaying an eﬅablished figure they can eﬅablish themselves. It's very sad in a way. I always believed that it is beﬅ to juﬅ explain the music and then be silent. Let the music do the talking!

The future of India and its classical music will lie with today's younger generation. Even if some musicians follow me or my contemporaries, after we have gone it will be their approach and their aﬅions which will diﬅate its path, not ours. Who knows what is going to happen? One can never tell, but at leaﬅ I am hopeful about the future.

For years I had almoﬅ no knowledge of the younger generation and youth culture, and no real reason to have any conneﬅion with them. The firﬅ time I really came to realise what was happening was in the mid-Sixties, when I saw all the big changes happening so quickly in England, the USA and all over – the folk boom and the hippies. For the next few years I was very conscious of them, and was often identified myself with them! In some ways I found it shocking, because I saw how quickly the commercial world could take advantage of everything, from meditation schools to pushing drugs. This was the case even in India where, like lightning, people were suddenly manufaﬅuring huge quantities of sitars, kurtas, special incense ﬅicks and attar (perfumes).

Having children often forces you to reassess your own viewpoint on many issues, but Shubho was already grown up by the early Seventies and I hadn't had to deal with any teenage-ﬅyle problems with him anyway. I was aware that in the Eighties public attitudes were changing with the advent of Aids, but it seems that in the laﬅ few years the Sixties have returned and lifeﬅyles have loosened up again. Having a young daughter has recently made me more aware of how radically things have changed, among teenagers especially. In the Weﬅ young people are growing up faﬅer than ever before. All the new magazines, advertisements and films are so provocative. At ever-younger ages, children are taking drugs, dating, attempting suicide, running away or being exploited by greedy people. They even have fashions for toddlers.

In India the same is now happening, particularly among the kids from wealthier families in the sophiﬅicated cities like Delhi, Bombay, Calcutta, Madras, Bangalore or Hyderabad. They are so different today, copying everything that is happening in the Weﬅ. Sometimes they surpass it, as you frequently do when you are aping someone else. In the Weﬅ I find young people coming to my concerts and being intereﬅed in many non-Weﬅern subjeﬅs. In India moﬅ of the young sophiﬅicates laugh at any religious or traditional Indian culture; they almoſt feel ashamed of it. They talk in American lingo, and they have ſtarted piercing not only their ears and noses but also their lips and other places. They liſten to nothing but Weſtern pop, rock, R'n'B, rap and techno, as well as the neareſt thing we have in Indian culture, which is Indian film music. Apart from the occasional beautiful tune, moſt Bollywood film songs are merely hybrid versions of everything that is going on outside India.[1] The lateſt thing to have happened is the sudden opening-up of the world of television and video. Satellite ſtations are beaming in programmes from outside India. In the space of two or three years about a hundred channels have become available, with more in the offing.

You cannot blame the young people themselves for what is happening. It's the commercial tycoons and media barons who are driving this social revolution. Money is the crucial faſtor. These people projeſt all their money greed on to the youth, making their fortunes through titillation of the masses. In the process our lateſt generation is being overexposed to the adult world. I realise the world has changed since my youth, yet I cannot help but be concerned about all that is occurring. I run the risk of being considered out of touch, but I don't believe that is true. I underſtand what is happening because I have seen it for years in the Weſt, and I am certainly no puritan.

When I was in India in early 1996, I was interviewed by a BBC correspondent who was making a programme about MTV. I said frankly that in my opinion MTV was having a bad impaſt on the majority of Indians, except for those kids in the large cities who are already used to the Weſtern way of life, whose outlook it will not affeſt particularly. But I made one miſtake: I should have clearly said that it was the visual aspeſt that I was referring to, rather than the audio. I didn't make that clear. Because while the sound of pop music has long been present in India and it doesn't really change people so much, I do feel the provocative or horrific and gruesome images in music videos can be damaging.

Immediately I was pounced upon so many journaliſts and people writing letters into newspapers: 'How dare he say this about pop music? He's been so modern himself, he has no right.' Some musicians even went so far as to say that I was in no position to judge or criticise MTV, since I aſtually owed my success to these rock musicians!

In the interview I had also mentioned our own films in the same vein. Copying Hollywood, they have become very popular with the average man who is hankering for entertainment, for whom they provide an outlet for his repressed feelings. The overwhelming majority of these films are vulgar and ſtupid, with fighting and violence, pelvic dance movements and innuendo-filled dialogue and songs. They go beyond the boundaries of realism, into an excess of violence, gore and voyeurism. Thus, in embracing realism and trying to portray frankly the bad things in society, they aſtually use them as entertainment. Of course in this Hollywood is the great guru!

1. 'Bollywood' is the popular name for Bombay's version of Hollywood, the centre of the Indian film induſtry, the biggeſt in the world. Its movies are usually love ſtories, their moſt popular element being the song-and-dance scenes, in which the aſtors dance and mime along to the voices of the playback singers.

It is hard to tell sometimes how much the private behaviour of the average Indian is worsening as a result of a less restrained public morality. In a way it happened in my own youth. At the age of ten I was thrown into an older world and I grew up rapidly, yet still I emerged from that to build my own career. I was lucky enough to have the strength of mind to focus on one particular thing, music, that I managed to change. Otherwise I'd have been a goner. I'm sure of it. Talented, all right, but before Baba I never made much use of education or training or advice, never harnessed anything properly. How vulnerable so many of us are to the lures of the material world! A guardian angel must have saved me from utter ruin!

This whole climate of rampant technology and changing morals is having consequences for Indian classical music. I know of many excellent young musicians who are very modern and hip, not old-fashioned like me, for whom I retain great hopes. They have gone deep into the music, and if people like them can exist and maintain their sadhana then our music won't die. On the other hand some young musicians seem to be too performance-orientated, anxious only to make a name for themselves. They're not interested in the deep musicianship which we cherish in our tradition. They cater only for sophisticated audiences with few people who really understand the music. Ask them to sit down at leisure with a few musicians and perform a particular raga, and you will see the difference.

Of course I have always maintained that presentation is important, but one must have the proper musical depth. Inside me I have not only my theatrical knowledge but also the pure Indianness and Baba's influence. I can change like a chameleon, in the sense that I am always confident I can add a polish without sacrificing the tradition in my performance. One problem with some of today's young musicians is that they have copied only my way of presentation.

Luckily a few societies for the performing arts have been established with the aim of bringing music to the common man and the younger generation, in colleges and schools and universities. The principal such society is called Spic Macay, which is well organised and is flourishing all over India. Gradually many leading musicians have come to love performing for its events. This is helping a lot; a sizeable group of young people is being encouraged to become more interested in our classical music, and they are responding. With more efforts like this, the future of our music will be better assured.

Maybe we are just going through a temporary period of rapid change, and everything will settle down in a while. Wishful thinking, perhaps! But I really believe that the greatness of our music, which has lasted for thousands of years already, will shine through.

I still go to India every year to recharge my batteries, and starting in a couple of years I intend to be once again spending most of my time in our country. In spite of everything I have such love for India, and a firm belief that, though we're going through one of the worst times in our recent history, and it may get still worse, we will eventually emerge from it. Ours is a great country with a tremendous past and such spiritual strength. It will rise again, and I don't mean only in the economic sense (though that will happen), but in terms of its self-belief and cultural vitality.

Some people hold that suffering is good for an artist, that it gives him the raw material to create beautiful and powerful art. If this is true, one might think that modern technology and comforts, and young people's different concerns and expectations, do not provide the right environment for artists. But I believe there will still be great artists. They won't die out from being too pampered.

It is true that many of the old masters in all forms – painters, sculptors, poets, dancers and actors, as well as musicians – were subject to enormous pressure, having to create their art under the burden of poverty, illness or oppression. Yet if they did not enjoy today's comforts, you have to remember that when one has never known something one is not aware of it. There were kings and noblemen and maharajahs who were great artists too. What is so often the common factor is that those great artists who had material disadvantages to overcome did their best work when they were young, and indeed often died before they reached the age of forty or fifty. When young, you have that inner fire and can surmount your obstacles. Later in life, though it is still possible, it becomes more difficult. So I do not feel that suffering in itself is good for your art.

Suffering does trouble me. If I put my hand into the fire, I realise the pain caused is my own responsibility, but why do I suffer when I have not caused it? I do not like to believe it is just my karma or destiny. Believe me, I really feel that compared to most people I am an extraordinarily sensitive person – perhaps touchy is a better word, or passionate. This is a boon and a curse at the same time. Little things can suddenly inspire me and fire my creative instinct, but they can also make me very upset or angry and spoil my flow entirely.

It has been amazing how sometimes at the lowest moments of my life my pain has emerged to positive effect when I have expressed it through my sitar as pathos. Yet at other times I have found it hard to produce superior performances when weighed down with worries. There is no hard and fast rule. I can also be supremely confident and full of beans and then give either a lousy recital or a great one. Women have frequently been my inspiration, but sometimes quite the opposite! I really do wonder what causes a good performance. It's a mystery – and a *contradiction*, I know! The bottom line is that I always pray to God and my guru before every programme, no matter how confident I may feel.

Two words confuse me: 'love' and 'great'. What do they each mean, and what is the criterion for each? Everybody uses the word 'love' so liberally, especially when one is young, but why do we always say, 'I love you' rather

*Author with his wife
and publisher,
London, 1995.*

than 'I like you', 'I love you at this moment' or just 'I lust for you', or even 'I don't love you'? We don't say these alternatives, and I suppose we can't! Still, to me it has often been a source of confusion somehow.

Similarly, what does it mean to praise somebody as 'great' or to be called it oneself? This has long troubled me because at times I have been called 'great' or a 'genius'. I have seen other people who do believe it about themselves but, honestly, though the accolade may at times have puffed up my ego for a few moments, I have never truly believed it of myself or taken it seriously.

Yet I tell you with utter frankness that I really *could* have become great if I were not such a pleasure-lover and so disorganised and idle by nature. I could have worked so much harder than I have done – which may surprise some people, but it is true. Looking back on my life, I regret having wasted so much time through postponing things and sheer laziness. I could have learnt, practised, written, performed and taught more. It is easy to make excuses for not doing something, and I see the trait in many people. There are others who work incredibly hard and meet all their deadlines and schedules – Tagore, Baba and Menuhin come to mind – but I have never been like that and it shames me.

In my previous book *My Music My Life* I began by mentioning how much importance we give in our tradition to the three concepts of guru, sadhana and vinaya. Vinaya (which of course means 'humility') is traditionally highly valued in India, even though we find many of our leading musicians suffering from ego problems and 'I am the greatest' syndromes! One should know what one knows and what one has achieved – but simultaneously one should be conscious of how little one really knows, considering that there is no limit to knowledge.

The best example I can give of a man who has true vinaya in him is not someone from India; he is my good friend Yehudi Menuhin. I cannot think of another musician in this world who has enjoyed a comparably successful career: starting as a child prodigy, achieving so much fame through his violin-playing and conducting, and going on to organise numerous humanitarian works. No one else has received such honour and respect all over the world. Yet he remains so humble. There was a lunch party given by our Indian Ambassador in Brussels on the day of the final *Sitar to Guitar* show in 1995, at which Yehudi stood up to make a speech. He said such glowing things about me – describing me as his guru who had opened his eyes to the greatness of India – that I had to halt him through my embarrassment! I had tears in my eyes. It is a mark of *his* greatness that he appreciates everybody. By way of reply I said to the other Indian musicians who were present: 'Just listen to all this, coming from one of the greatest musicians in the West. In India we rarely see real vinaya in anyone, as opposed to a mere pretence of humility. Where we musicians are filled with such arrogance, we must learn from this great man.'

In this chapter I have sought to explore the roots and evolution of our system of music, suggested what its path may be in the future and explained how my contributions might have influenced its development and may continue to do so. A musician should be aware of his achievements, while seeing them in their true perspective. It is necessary for a performer to have self-confidence, but not to go too far'.

With Anoushka, his daughter and disciple.

TEN: PARAMESHWARI

परमेश्वरी

To bring you up to date I really mu&t now tell you about my mo&t recent proje&t. After the wonderful four-CD box set *In Celebration* (produced by George Harrison with the help of Alan Kozlowski), which Angel Records brought out at the &tart of 1996, the company's President Steve Murphy sugge&ted I make a new album based on Indian chants. George liked the idea and agreed to being in charge of the entire produ&tion. We &tarted in Madras in January and March 1996, but from those two sessions of three days each, no more than a few numbers emerged. The overly commercial atmosphere of the Madras recording &tudio and its management were mo&t di&turbing and uninspiring, in spite of the efforts of the wonderfully musical and sensitive engineer Sreedhar.

The lengthy final sessions for the album, which took place at George's English home, &tarted in very much the same way as did those of 1974, with all the musicians (mo&t of them vocali&ts) sitting on the carpeted ground floor of the drawing room, which is blessed with delightful views out through the French windows onto the gardens. Everything was set up for us there. Cables ran from the arti&ts' microphones up to the fir&t-floor &tudio. Cameras were trained on us so that George and the recording engineer John Etchells, in&talled up&tairs in the &tudio, could see us on TV monitors. We also wore earphones linked up to them so that they could make sugge&tions to us. I condu&ted three or four new numbers in this fashion, and then afterwards we spent five or six days in the &tudio recording the re&t of the tracks.

This has been one of my mo&t challenging proje&ts ever. Though I have used some Sanskrit verses from ancient scriptures in pa&t compositions of mine, they have mainly been introduced in a thematic context. As a classici&t approaching a recording of our traditional chants, I have taken on a much more serious commitment. In Madras I recorded chants from the Vedas and Upanishads by real sha&tris, generations of whom have specialised in Vedic chants. In addition I used vocali&ts and in&trumentali&ts from Madras (and later London) for the other short chants and mantras. There are already

ॐ

G R G   R G S SGR
Pra bhu jee - - Daya Karo - - - 2

SN RS ND   D R S R
Mana Mé - - Aaana Baso - - 2

G R R G   P   P P DP G
Tu ma ti   na - Lage soona - - - 2

G RS   R R R   S S R GR SD
Khaali   gha ta me Pre ma Bha ro - - -
Pra thu ji - - - - - - 2

G - G   P P   PM D - D D PN DN NP
Tan tra   Man tra Poo jaa Nahi Jaanu 2

P - P   PM D G   P - - P
Mai to   Ke val   Tumko Hi Maanu 2

S - SD   D D D   P - DN DP D P
Saare   Jaga mé   Dhundaa Tuma Ko 2

P P   P   PD G G   P - G RS SGR
Aba   to Aakara   Baahan Dharo 2

S S SD
Hey Prabhuji
D R R
Pra bhu jee - -
R R X
Prabhujee

Ravi Shankar

Words & lyric composed in December '95
at _____ Recorded in July '96 at Friar Park.

dozens of albums around which use the same texts, some of them just straight recordings of the priests, some more in the classical raga framework, and some in a lighter manner to make them more commercial. So it was essential to make this new album different, while retaining the authenticity and making it a musical and spiritual experience, with a universal appeal but as much dignity as possible.

We commenced with traditional short invocations to Ganesha, Saraswati and the guru, but apart from these the old texts chosen were mostly on the subjects of peace, love, ecology, well-being and the harmony of everything and everybody. I composed the lyrics to two songs myself: 'Mangalam', written in Sanskrit (with help from Dr Nandakumara of the Bharatiya Vidya Bhavan, London's excellent centre of Indian culture), and 'Prabhujee', in Hindi. The latter featured my voice, as well as those of Sukanya and some local singers, while George played the bass and acoustic guitars. On other numbers he played vibraphone, marimba, autoharp and glockenspiel, and also contributed some background vocals. At the very end of the last piece, 'Sarvé Shaam', which concludes with the chant 'Om Shanti Shanti Shantihi', his voice sounds particularly powerful!

It is strange how through the years you slowly see the changes in people, especially when they mature and become stronger and surer of themselves. (It is harder to view yourself in the same way. When I do, it is mostly only the negative side that is apparent – not recommended!) I have never before worked so closely with George in recording, overdubbing, balancing, mixing and editing, and I have been highly impressed by his expertise and sensitivity. My estimation of him as a musician has reached a very high level.

After the final mixing of the first four numbers, he played them back for me and they sounded fantastic, giving me goose-bumps and a deep spiritual awareness. That evening he came and embraced me with tears in his eyes and simply said, 'Thank you, Ravi, for this music.' His emotion meant so much to me, and my eyes filled with tears too. If the rest of the pieces can have such effect, I will consider myself blessed for having worked diligently on all the composing, arranging and recording, despite the concerns and agonies that plagued my mind throughout this difficult project. My heartfelt thanks go to George for making it possible by giving his hard work, care and love in fulfilling it. I believe in reincarnation, and must have been attached to George in other lives. He is not only a disciple or a friend; I love him as a son.

Another good thing happened on this album: from the very start in Madras I ensured that Anoushka was involved, initiating her in assisting me to transcribe the music and instruct the musicians, and in conducting some pieces during the recordings. She continued this in England. As in everything else, she learnt quickly, did an excellent job and enjoyed herself immensely, making me extremely proud of her.

In many ways I have poured out my heart into this record, and George has clearly been doing the same in producing it. I hope it will meet the expectations of people with spiritual consciousness. To help you get the maximum effect out of it, I'd recommend you try listening to it sitting alone (or with other spiritually-aware people), eyes closed, with the lights dimmed and incense burning.

GEORGE HARRISON: *I like producing Ravi's music, because for me it's educational as well as a joy to work with. It's actually soothing to your soul, and it helps you to focus or transcend.*

That's one thing about going to Ravi's concerts for all these years: after listening for a while I find myself nodding out, because it's like meditation: when you go deeper and deeper and deeper, there's a point where you get so deep there's nothing left. You hit the bump stop on the bottom and you go into this kind of void. It's a great thing, and it's good to be able to do that. People would get embarrassed if they did that during a Western music concert; they'd be told, 'It must have been really boring for you to have fallen asleep.' But in Indian music going deep into meditation is the goal.

At home in Encinitas, the author with his editor, 1994.

For me, the music and my whole experience have truly spurred my imagination, and George's home has itself been an inspiration. His gorgeous Victorian Gothic mansion was home to a group of nuns before George bought it at the end of the Sixties and moved from Esher. It took so many years and so much effort to make it what it is today: to have all the modern amenities alongside the pristine old Victorian look, which he has retained, with traditional bathtubs, basins and loos – it's something else! To top it all (literally), George has a yellow flag flying on the very summit of the highest tower with an orange Aum in Deva Nagri lettering (the script in which Sanskrit, Hindi and a few other Indian languages are written).

Having visited George Harewood's place too, as well as a few other mansions, I feel it is more in Europe that one can see such great old homes so wonderfully renovated. In India, for some years now we have been converting a few of the fabulous former palaces of the maharajahs, but mainly they have become hotels, whose delights are reserved mostly for Western and Japanese tourists.

Taking regular walks is an enjoyable part of my life, and now (on doctor's orders) an essential one too. Though I am lucky enough to have some open spaces to walk in surrounding my Encinitas home, having my long walks in the enchanting environment of George's gardens filled me with such an ecstasy. One day I happened to discover Olivia's secret garden, and I couldn't believe the varieties of colours in the flowers. The sheer beauty hit me and I was almost choked! That was when I spontaneously created the piece 'Mangalam' for this new album.

In the exquisite and uplifting environment at George's, many thoughts would go through my mind in moments alone or as I walked around, and they were mostly on the subject of God. Elsewhere in this book I have written about how at times I have felt some divine sparks and indescribable ecstasy – that magical supercharged feeling which can be experienced during meditation or when performing my music.

Being a Brahmin, I learnt some mantras from gurus as a child, and still repeat them in my mind as often as I can today. I do firmly believe that they have tremendous power. For a few years in the late Fifties and early Sixties I regularly practised hatha yoga, but gradually the pace of my life made it impossible to continue with it (although I still maintain my regular morning meditations, plus one before giving a recital). Many times in my life I have been attracted with great surges of love and bhakti (reverence or devotion) to some godly persons I have known, such as Tat Baba, Ma Anandamayi, Satya Sai Baba and the late Shankaracharya of Kanchi. Some I never saw have also exerted a strong pull on me, such as Ramakrishna Paramahansa, Lahiri Mahasai, Trailanga Swami, Babaji and Swami Vivekananda. But in one's daily life and existence it is hard to attain cosmic consciousness. Most of the time the only self-realisation states one is aware of are physical and mundane ones. I am sure many of you have felt this too.

But MUSIC – that is the thing for me! Mostly it has been when deeply immersed in my music that I have felt that surge of joy, merging into that indefinable 'drunken with beauty' moment. Especially when I become attuned to my sitar, that is the route for me to touch the heart and the God within myself, and within my millions of listeners over the years.

The spiritual element in Indian music is absolutely essential. From the very beginning our music was handed down by yogis, and musicians were invariably great saintly people, leading a very religious life. Many of the old songs were devotional and philosophical in nature, written in praise of our gods like Shiva, Vishnu, Ganesha and Saraswati, and the most popular character in the songs, Krishna, who is treated more like a human being, going through all the different phases of life. He is loved not only for his miraculous feats but for his childhood pranks, his adventures with his friends as he is growing up, his flirting and erotically-charged encounters with the gopis (milkmaids), and then his great teachings to Arjuna on the battlefield of Kurukshetra which constitute the *Bhagavad Gita*. Our songs and poetry beautifully convey his charm and eroticism, and tell of his pranks and his special love for Radha. Having in my early childhood all this background and the whole atmosphere of priestly living (as a Brahmin), I could grasp and feel the spirituality in music much more quickly than most.

Sometimes I feel blindfolded, completely susceptible to spiritual atmosphere and prepared to believe whatever I am told, like a simple village person. Whenever I visit Balaji, the temple to Lord Venkateshwar in the South Indian State of Andhra Pradesh, my heart is thrown completely open to the power of the spiritual forces that seem to be present. I feel the same innocent openness when I think of Saraswati, Krishna, Buddha or Jesus Christ, or when I go to a church, synagogue or House of God of any other religion. That blind faith is part of my tradition. It is in my heart and mind. I know I am someone who likes and often needs to depend on someone or something.

But then at times I ask myself why I should depend on anyone. God is in me, not in these figures. These are supports which are there for when we need them; true religious experience is to be found in one's own heart. This comes back to the age-old philosophical questions· Who am I? Where did I come from? Where am I going? I believe I am both the atman (soul) and the paramatman (supersoul). Within me there is both the seeker and the one I seek.

So it is no wonder there is a constant turmoil and contradiction in me – as in many others, maybe. To me, it appears that is the nature of life: contradiction. And it is important that this has been reflected in my book! Although I do not want to hurt others unnecessarily (and if I have hurt anyone who has been near and dear to me, I sincerely apologise to them), I have had no concerns about displaying my own weaknesses and contradictions.

Baba always said that music is not for selling; music is not made for a commercial purpose. Music is like worshipping, and through music you worship God. Though it is difficult for a professional musician to follow this doctrine, it is true that you feel godliness much more quickly through music than any other medium, whether it is saying a mantra or doing yoga; these are very long processes for obtaining some state or feeling of divinity. Music is the fastest vehicle. Like Baba, I believe in the age-old saying 'Nada Brahma' – Sound is God.

However, like many other people's, mine is still an imperfect quest. A powerful aspiration to spiritual perfection has persisted throughout my life, but I am never quite able to get there, never manage to transcend mortality. Two of my song lyrics, both written in Hindi, express this sentiment simply but, I hope, quite effectively. 'Hey Nath', the chant from the track 'Prashanti' on the *Passages* album, articulates my feeling of groping around for the answer:

Oh Lord, bestow upon me your kindness.
Drive away the darkness.
Give me the light of wisdom.
Take away jealousy, hatred, greed and anger.
Fill my heart with love and peace.

'Prabhujee' expresses a similar sentiment:

Oh Master, show some compassion on me.
Please come and dwell in my heart.
Because without you it is painfully lonely.
Fill this empty pot with the nectar of love.
I do not know any tantra, mantra or ritualistic worship.
I know and believe only in you.
I have been searching for you all over the world.
Please come and hold my hand now.

'I Am Missing You' embodied the same frustrated spiritual search – 'oh Krishna where are you?' Likewise on the latest album I sang one phrase from the *Bhagavad Gita*, 'Maa phaleshu kadaa chana', meaning, 'don't ever expect any result'.

We can never count on quite getting there. For me it is through music that I feel nearest to my ultimate goal.

DHUN-RASIYA

धुन रसिया

Life never stands still, and since I completed the manuscript a few major events have happened, some of which I am jotting down for you now as my latest reflections before we go to press.

The Chants of India album has been released, and its effect on some people who have heard it has been overwhelming and heart-warming. Just as I had hoped and prayed for, it has touched their spiritual cores. My new idea is to present this music in a visual form, perhaps on stage, and to film it. I was also deeply moved by the announcement that the Japan Art Association is honouring me with one of the world's most prestigious awards, the Præmium Imperiale. They have invited me to Japan to receive the honour this October.

There have been more developments towards setting up my artistic centre. A Ravi Shankar Centre and a Ravi Shankar Foundation have both been established. Building has commenced on the centre in Delhi, and we are planning a branch and sister organisation in California, where we hope to house the archive and multimedia facilities, and organise further artistic productions.

And then I cannot stop myself from saying that I have recently come to know a remarkable person, Prince Charles. As you will have read earlier, we had met before, on a few occasions over the past two or three decades, but recently we have become closer. He has truly touched me and I have found a wonderful soul in him. I mention this not because he is one of the best-known personalities, with the grandest of status, but because of the artistic sensitivity, sincerity and warmth that he radiates.

On a sad note, I was distressed to hear about the sad demise of two friends of mine. Narayana Menon, who had been suffering for so long, has passed away. My deep condolences go to Rekha. And I also grieve deep in my heart for a very great actor and human being who has left us, Shombhu Mitra, whom I knew from my IPTA days in Bombay. I had a profound love and regard for this great man from Calcutta.

Recently I met my eighteen-year-old daughter from the West, whom I had not seen for almost ten years. She spent a few weeks with us, including travelling on my European tour. There was such a mixture of pain and joy, for both of us. She is a fine musician, a jazz pianist. I do hope that we shall have a normal and happier relationship in the future.

As the whole world knows, my country is currently marking fifty years of independence. At the stroke of midnight on the anniversary night of 14th-15th August, I gave a recital in Bombay along with Anoushka, accompanied by Zakir. This was a memorable occasion. I had specially composed a new raga, *Suvarna Raga* (meaning 'golden') and a new tala, *Jayanti* (meaning 'anniversary'). The tala has fifty beats, symmetrically divided 3-4-5-6-7-7-6-5-4-3! It was appreciated tremendously.

At this time of anniversary celebrations, 'Sare Jahan Se Accha' is being performed all over India at many events, yet still very few people seem to know that the tune is my composition – even in our own Indian government, which uses it in all the official functions! So towards the end of the Bombay concert, after referring to other ragas in the raga mala section, I broke into my melody of 'Sare Jahan Se Accha'. Halfway through I paused, allowing Anoushka and Zakir to continue, and informed the audience that the famous tune they were listening to was my own composition. There was thunderous applause!

So many people are celebrating this anniversary, but in spite of this I, like many others, have felt sadness too at the memory of Partition and the reality of our current difficulties. We have much work to do. But as I look back on the past fifty years I do feel proud as a musician that no other country has done as much as India to help, support and give recognition to its arts and artists.

For our stay in Bombay we were provided with a beautiful suite on the sixth floor of the Taj Mahal Hotel and were treated like maharajahs. On 15th August, the day after the concert, Sukanya and Anoushka went out for a while and I stood for a long time looking out of the window at the fantastic panorama of the Arabian Sea – the boats, seagulls and islands, including the Elephanta cave island. Down below I could see thousands of people wildly waving national flags and making merry, rejoicing all around the India Gate in celebration of independence.

Hundreds of memories came flooding into my mind. I recalled September 1966 and the multitudes of boys and girls assembled down there, crying out for hours on end, 'Ravi Shankar – we want George Harrison!' Bombay is also the city where I lived for years, where I actually started my proper musical career from the end of 1944. Like film flashbacks, more memories came rushing: all the struggles and gradually the successes of name, fame and fortune, the glitter and glamour, the pleasures and pains. I thought of my ex-wife living a few miles away, and how my relationship with Kamala had started here too. So many friends, and others not so friendly, many of them no longer alive.

I saw the sky darkening as black clouds gathered from one side and a sheet of rain headed towards me: the Bombay monsoon! In my mind I was turning over the emotional ups and downs of so many years, and feeling thankful for all the good fortune which has come to me – in being so loved, admired and in demand, even now, and for the blessings and great gifts of having Anoushka and Sukanya in my life. Gradually everything blurred, and I realised my eyes were filled with tears and my heart with my own monsoon.

AFTERWORD

When my wife Diana and I arrived in India in 1952 we discovered a new world. It is very difficult for people living in the West with its advanced technology to imagine that there are other ways of being, other civilisations. What Ravi and India gave me on that first trip, through music, was the revelation of human thought and inspiration, discipline and abandonment through the ages of history.

It is a typically Indian characteristic for everything to be totally analysed, reduced to so many possibilities and adaptations. What happens if you have a civilisation which has lasted almost unbroken for three or four thousand years? Obviously it becomes more and more refined: everyone knows what they are there for. Nehru once told Diana and me that there were even hereditary ear-scratchers in India! The Indians thought through everything, even the erotic. The same thing happened in music, which is based on a very high authority of organisation and tradition, where the passion, the excitement, the abandonment and the improvisation are guided through a training which has named every particular note, scale, ornament, approach, length. And there again in the dance, which is pure movement, but everything is controlled, down to the movement of the eyebrows and the eyes. Certainly in the field of culture, of arts, of thought, of philosophy, the Indians have achieved what the West has achieved in science.

Ravi is the most wonderful teacher and guide, because he knows the technique. Today most of us in the West have lost that acute organisation. Without a craft, without a command of your fingers, your eyes and all your senses, you cannot evolve in art. But nor are the means alone sufficient. In India everything follows an aesthetic which is totally missing in our world. Western people go about their work, but they don't consider anything as sacred any longer. The human being by nature must be a religious animal. But I think that if we can survive long enough, we will learn from the Indians and their traditions, and go along a totally different road.

Ravi represents enlightenment, organisation, discipline – and yet such freedom. Freedom that is won through a great deal of thought, work, practice and experience. He is always living the creative existence in his mind and his heart; he isn't just a tool in the system. He has meant a great deal in my life. In many ways he is the greatest musician I have known. If you are going to compare West and East on one footing, then perhaps he would come after Enesco, my teacher, and Bartok – but a close third.

There is a quality of other-worldliness about a creative person such as Ravi that I greatly admire, but it doesn't mean that he isn't also supremely organised, and can concentrate on whatever has to be done, and sees clearly. But he sees the obvious. He sees what we cannot see. When he creates a composition, he is carried away. As much as he creates, he is also being led. And that part which escapes control, and which the person in the West wants to control, just as he wants to control territory and people, that part leads us beyond – and then takes fire, and moves on its own. From mastering an instrument we ourselves can become the instrument of something that has possessed us.

Ravi is also an extremely sophisticated man, very Western in that way – but very Indian too. When an Indian is worldly and sophisticated you have a very high type of social being. In the West often the good people are too simple and the clever people are evil; but he, because of his qualities, keeps a wonderful balance between the cultivated-sophisticated and the genuine. We need that kind of person who can understand both worlds.

We meet on and off, and each time I see him I am carried away with his whole warmth and his personality. He is the most precious person in the world. Above all I have been inspired by all that is behind that moment when the tapers are lit, and Ravi and his colleagues begin working, making their offering, going as close as one can to the earth and then, using this tremendous training, producing this which is in the heavens, and mastering everything in between the earth and the heavens to liberate one's spirit.

LORD MENUHIN

GLOSSARY

alap The very slow introductory movement of a raga, featuring the gradual and meditative unfolding of its structure, theme and rasa. Considered the highest form in Indian music. In the fifteenth-century form of dhrupad from which alap originates, it was sung before the song composition. Traditionally alap has no measured time cycle – this comes later in the num-tum or jor sections. The original words sung were 'Ananta Hari Narayana' and 'Ananta Hari Aum', which were later shortened to phrases such as 'Anarita, ri, te, re, ne, num'. (From the end of the nineteenth century singers in contemporary khyal forms did begin to sing alap along with the tabla, played softly in a very slow tempo.)

ashram A guru's place of retreat where his disciples, in an austere environment, are guided in yoga and other studies.

Aum (or Om) The eternal sound which is the origin of all creation.

bandish Fixed vocal or instrumental composition bound by a rhythmic cycle.

been (i) The North Indian veena, this is the oldest conception of fretted stringed instrument in India. It has two large, equal-sized gourds attached to a long bamboo fingerboard, on which there are fixed, immovable, chromatic-scale frets laid upon wax. The strings rest on a bridge called the jawari, as on the sitar. (ii) The same name is also given to the wind instrument played by snake-charmers.

bhai Brother.

Bhagavad Gita The most celebrated chapter of the *Mahabharata*. It features Krishna's teachings to Arjuna upon the battlefield of Kurukshetra, in which he expounds on the transmigration of souls after death and reveals how to attain salvation (moksha).

bhajan A type of Hindu devotional song, commonly sung both solo and in groups, found all over India.

Bharata Natyam Very old, traditional dance style from the region around Madras, originally danced by the temple girls (devadasis) in the temples. Bharata was the sage who composed the ancient treatise on dance, drama and music which was its source.

bol Literally 'speech' or 'sound'. In sitar-playing, indicates a right-hand stroke, usually played with the mizrab. Also used to describe a sound syllable played on a drum, or a word in vocal music.

boudi The Bengali term for one's sister-in-law.

Brahma God as Creator of the universe; the first aspect of the Hindu trinity that is completed by Vishnu and Shiva.

Brahmin A member of the highest, priestly caste. For centuries they have represented piety and wisdom, and have been the teachers of yoga, religion and many arts and crafts.

burkha The veil used by Muslim women to cover the face.

Carnatic Relating to the traditional system of music in South India. Though it shares the same origin as the Hindustani system of the North, scholars believe the differences between the two systems date from around the twelfth century. They have many ragas and talas in common, albeit with different names. The Carnatic system is more structured and more orientated to song composition. Since vocal music plays an integral part in all Indian music, linguistic differences have also reinforced the divergence of the two systems. Originally all Indian music was sung in Sanskrit, but after the two systems divided Hindustani music was centred around Hindi and its dialect Brajabhasha, whereas the main languages to influence the Carnatic system were Kannadese, Tamil and especially Telegu.

chakkardar A succession of three tihais.

chakra A wheel or circle. In the spiritual sense, denotes various points of the human body which are centres of spiritual energy and consciousness; it is believed they can be activated through yoga and other methods. The seven principal chakras are located at positions from the base of the spine to the top of the head.

chenda A cylindrical drum from Kerala, held upright and played with two sticks, which announces the beginning of a Kathakali performance.

Chhau A dance style characteristic of the regions of Bihar and Orissa.

dadra (i) The tala of six beats, divided 3-3. (ii) A style of semiclassical musical composition characterised by simple melodies with syncopation, resembling the thumri style; mostly sung in the dadra tala.

Dha (i) Short for Dhaivata, the sixth note of the Indian musical scale (see **sargam**). (ii) The open-handed drum stroke played with both hands together on the pakhawaj or tabla.

dhamar (i) The tala of fourteen beats, divided 5-5-4. (ii) An old style of song composition relating stories of Krishna, sung in the dhamar tala, and traditionally accompanied by the pakhawaj.

dhol A large, two-headed, barrel-shaped drum common in rural or tribal areas, usually played with a pair of sticks. The Bangla dhol (a Bengali version) is slung around the neck and held at waist height, and played with a stick on one side and the palm and fingers on the other.

dholak A one-piece drum with two faces, played with both hands, one on each face. Different versions are found all over India, although it is most commonly known as an accompanying instrument for semiclassical qawwali and folk music in North India.

dhoti A traditional Indian form of clothing for men, consisting of a white cloth tied around the waist and reaching down to the toes. It is most popular in Northeastern and Western India.

dhrupad (originally 'dhruvapada') A noble and grand composition style, popular from the fifteenth to the nineteenth centuries, which evolved from the prabhanda. The lyrics, typically in praise of gods, kings, noblemen and nature, were first written in Sanskrit, then in Brajabhasha, a dialect of Hindi.

dhun An air or melody, mostly semiclassical or folk in style, found all over India.

dilruba A stringed instrument, played with a bow, featuring a neck similar to that of a sitar and a resonating chamber like that of a sarangi. Four principal strings and between nineteen and twenty-two sympathetic strings rest on a single bridge upon the skin-covered chamber.

Diwali The festival of light and fireworks, one of the most popular for Hindus, held throughout India every November.

diwan Chief minister.

drut Fast.

esraj A bowed instrument with metal strings resembling the dilruba or taus, found principally in Bengal.

farmaishi Requested. A farmaishi raga or bandish is one that has been asked for by a listener.

Ga (short for Gandhara) The third note of the Indian musical scale. (see **sargam**)

ganda The formal ceremony which ties a shishya (disciple) to his guru.

gandharva Celestial musician.

ganjeera (also known as 'khanjeera') A small rhythmic instrument resembling a tambourine. The skin, traditionally made from serpent skin, is struck with the fingers and palm of the right hand. It is more popular in the South of India.

gat Fixed instrumental composition with rhythmic accompaniment, upon which a musician improvises.

gharana A centre of musical or other artistic culture with distinctive characteristics, traditionally created through guru-shishya instruction, and often passed on through successive generations of the same family. Frequently named after the place where it originated, e.g. Gwalior or Agra for khyal singing, Senia or Jaipur for instrumental music.

ghat A tier of steps leading down to a river. It literally denotes a sloping place; the name is also used for mountain ranges e.g. the Western and Eastern Ghats In South India.

ghatam An earthenware pot used as a percussive instrument, mainly in the South of India.

ghazal Romantic song composition in Urdu, of a semiclassical nature.

gopi A milkmaid, or a woman who tends cattle. In the story of Krishna and the gopis, Krishna was able to tantalise all of the gopis simultaneously by materialising as many bodies as he needed for each of them to believe his attention was solely directed to her.

guru The spiritual guide, teacher, master and preceptor.

gurukul The traditional Indian system of teaching, under which the disciple lives with his guru for several years while learning music and maturing mentally and spiritually under his guidance. The guru's provision of food and lodging removes material concerns from the disciple, allowing the latter to focus only on his talim (training).

halua A sweet preparation made from cream of wheat

roasted in ghee, with added sugar, water and milk.

hatha yoga The branch of yoga which focuses on bodily exercises in order that, once control of the physical body is attained, spiritual enlightenment can be achieved through mental yoga.

Hindustani (i) Relating to the North Indian system of classical music. (ii) The composite language derived from Hindi and Urdu, common in the North of India.

Holi The Indian colour festival, during which coloured water, paint and powders are sprayed liberally all around in an atmosphere of riotous celebration. Held every year in February or March.

jawari The main bridge of the sitar, tanpura or been, upon which the strings rest.

jhala The final improvised section of a raga on plucked instruments. It features fast strokes played on a combination of the main melody string and the two side (chikari) strings.

jor (also known as jhod or jod) The second improvised section of a raga, following the alap. It has an added element of rhythm, played by the instrumentalist in the traditional style. (see also **num-tum**)

jugalbandi A duet between two Indian musicians.

kajri (also known as kajli) A folk song from Uttar Pradesh province, mostly around the Varanasi area.

kartal Wooden percussion played in the hand like castanets.

Kathak A style of dance originating in the North of India, performed by men and women. The kathika (storyteller) mimes, dances and sings the stories.

Kathakali The famous dance style originating in South of India, particularly in Kerala. It combines dance and drama with lavish costumes and fabulous make-up in oil-lit performances that take place outdoors and last all night. The actors use characteristic hand gestures, eye language and facial movements to enact stories from the great epics. Men have traditionally taken all the roles, including those of women.

kharaj The fourth, lowest string on the sitar, tuned to Sa two octaves below the middle Sa.

kharajpancham The third string on the sitar, literally the 'lower fifth', tuned to Pa two octaves below the middle Sa.

khyal Currently the predominant vocal form of Indian classical music, literally meaning 'imagination' or 'fancy'. A further development of dhrupad and dhamar, with very short compositions and less attention on the literature, more ornamented notes and more progression from slow to very fast tans. It also has a greater romantic element, and allows the performer to display virtuosity. Khyal dates from the thirteenth century, and its origination is attributed to Amir Khusroo, also credited as the inventor of the sitar and the Muslim devotional song style qawwali. Khyal was developed further by Sultan Hussain Shirki, and brought to its final respectability by Sadarang. It has gained in popularity since the late nineteenth century.

kirtan A devotional song popular in Bengal.

koto Stringed instrument from Japan which produces a sound similar to the harp. Gut strings are laid on wood and plucked with a plectrum.

Krishna The eighth incarnation of Vishnu, hero of the *Bhagavad Gita*. The most beloved and popular godhead of the Hindus. He is popularly depicted as blue-skinned, frequently dancing and playing the flute. He is adored for various incidents from his life: the mischievous baby stealing butter, the cowherd dancing with and seducing the gopis (each of them under the illusion that all his attention is on her), the lover of Radha (his favourite gopi), the killer of demons, and the wise teacher of Arjuna in the *Gita*. His name literally means 'he who draws people towards him'.

Kuchipudi A classical dance style from the South Indian state of Andhra Pradesh.

kundalini According to yogic theory and practice, the spiritual power hidden in all human beings, situated at the base of the spine, like a coiled snake.

kurta An Indian tunic.

laya A measurement of rhythm or tempo: the space between two beats.

layadar One who has mastered layakari.

layakari The multitude of mathematical rhythmic variations found in Indian classical music.

Ma (short for Madhyama) The fourth note of the Indian musical scale. (see **sargam**)

maddalam A drum from the South Indian state of Kerala. Mostly accompanies the Kathakali form of dance drama.

madhya (i) Middle. (ii) A medium tempo.

mahatma 'Great soul'; the title accorded to Mohandas Karamchand Gandhi for his outstanding wisdom and spiritual strength.

Mahabharata One of the two great epics of Indian literature, containing 125,000 stanzas, thought to have been composed over many centuries (although the sage Veda-Vyasa is said to have originally dictated it). The story is based around the battle of Kurukshetra (a place north of Delhi), and the war between the Pandavas and the Kauravas, a fight between good and evil forces. The most popular section is the sixth chapter, the *Bhagavad Gita*, which contains the sacred teachings of Krishna.

maharajah King.

maharani Queen.

Manipuri A dance style emanating from the region of Manipur, in the far Northeast of India.

manjira A pair of round, almost flat, brass hand-clappers, capable of producing melodious sound, used as an accompanying rhythmic instrument.

matra A beat in a tala. (e.g. Jhaptal is a tala of ten matras, divided up 2-3-2-3)

meend The act of sliding from one note to the another, in a style unique to Indian music.

Moghul Relating to the Moghul emperors of India or their period of rule. The Muslim Moghuls were the dominant rulers of the North from the sixteenth to the eighteenth centuries.

mridangam The main accompanying instrument in South Indian music today, the counterpart of the tabla in the North. Similar to the pakhawaj, it has a head at either end of its wooden (originally clay) body. The bass head, played with the left hand, is covered with a little quantity of aataa (see **pakhawaj**). The right-hand head is tuned, as on the tabla, by striking its edges and side-blocks.

nadaswaram The South Indian equivalent to the shahnai, larger than its Northern relative; mostly played in the temples. It has twelve holes. It was originally an instrument used to lure serpents, named the 'nagaswaram'.

nakkara A kettle drum used on ceremonial occasions, sometimes hung in pairs on elephants.

namaskar An Indian greeting expressing respect. Hands are placed palm to palm in front of the forehead and the head is bowed.

Ni (short for Nishada) The seventh note of the Indian musical scale. (see **sargam**)

num-tum A continuation of alap singing with the added element of rhythm. Under the name 'jor', it was traditionally played on instruments such as the been, rabab and surbahar. Today it is most likely to be performed on sitar and sarod, among others. (see also **alap**)

Pa (short for Panchama) The fifth note of the Indian musical scale. (see **sargam**)

pakhawaj The traditional two-faced drum of North India, in former times the most popular one, although the tabla now holds that position. Two and a half feet long, it has a parchment head at either end of its wooden body (wood has superseded the original clay). These are tuned to different pitches. The left-hand face is covered with aataa, or flour paste (from which one can also make the Indian bread chapati) to produce the bass sound. Like the tabla, it is tuned by hammering on the round edges of the right-hand side and the side-blocks which surround the body.

pandal Marquee.

parampara The system whereby tradition is the basis for passing on knowledge. In guru-shishya parampara the continuity is achieved through direct teaching from teacher to disciple.

paran An open-handed style of composition and improvisation in pakhawaj-playing, incorporated by the purab (Eastern) schools of tabla-playing, Lucknow and Benares, as well as the Punjab gharana.

Parvati The consort of Lord Shiva; the Mother Goddess, the daughter of Parvat. In other aspects known as Durga, Kali, Chamunda or Muktakeshi.

playback singer A vocalist who specialises in singing the soundtrack songs in Indian films, dubbing vocals over the miming of an actor.

prabhanda An early vocal composition form, a systematic and organised type of giti (song) with Sanskrit text. It influenced, and was then replaced by, the dhrupad form in the fifteenth century.

pranam A respectful greeting consisting of touching the greeted person's feet, then one's own eyes and forehead with the hands held palm to palm. It is a symbolic act of surrender, indicating the awareness of one's own smallness in the presence of a superior. (Originally it signified placing the dust from the greeted person's feet onto one's head.)

Puranas Ancient Hindu texts propounding Vedic truths through the lives of various godheads. (Literally 'old yet new'.)

puri A style of Indian bread which is fried so that it puffs up into crisp, small pieces.

rabab An instrument supposed to have been created in the fifteenth century by Mian Tan Sen, in whose family it had the alternative name of 'rudra been'. The strings, made from gut, are stretched over a bridge which rests on a skin-covered soundbox. It has no frets. (It should not be confused with the entirely different Kabuli rabab of Afghanistan.)

Radha The lover of Krishna, his favourite of the gopis.

raga The melodic form at the centre of Hindustani and

Carnatic classical music; the basis on which the vocalist or instrumentalist improvises in slow, medium or fast phases. A raga has five, six, or seven notes in separate ascending and descending structures, and its own recognisable feature or theme. Each raga is associated with a particular time of the day or night, and has its principal rasa or mood. (Also known colloquially as 'raag'.)

Rama The seventh incarnation of Vishnu. Hero of the *Ramayana*, son of Dasaratha and husband of Sita.

Ramayana One of the two great epics of Indian literature. Written by the sage Valmiki, its stories centre around Prince Rama and his wife Sita. Born a prince in Ayodhya, Rama is denied the throne and exiled for fourteen years, but finally triumphs by defeating Ravana, the King of Lanka, rescuing Sita, whom Ravana had kidnapped, and returning as King of Ayodhya.

rasa Aesthetic experience or emotion. Each artistic creation in the Indian performing arts must express one of the nine standard rasas.

Ri (short for Rishaba) or **Re** The second note of the Indian musical scale. (see **sargam**)

rishi A spiritual sage.

Sa (short for Shadaja) The first note of the Indian musical scale. Equivalent to the tonic in Western music, it has has great importance in Indian music, being the primary focus of the performer's and the listeners' attention. Unlike in Western music, through an entire performance of Indian classical music the Sa will not usually be changed, i.e. there is no modulation. (see **sargam**)

sadhana Rigorous practice, undertaken with total dedication for the purpose of musical training, or for the purpose of preparing oneself for self-realisation through any medium.

samavadi The second most important note in the scale of a particular raga, usually four or five notes away from the vadi.

sangeet Music. Its literal meaning is 'that which is sung (or played) melodiously'. According to the sage Bharata, the term also covers dance and drama.

sannyasi One who has abandoned worldly attachments.

santoor A box-shaped stringed instrument which sits in front of the musician, who strikes the strings with two curved sticks. The strings, numbering over a hundred, are stretched over two bridges and arranged in pairs. It originated as a folk instrument in Persia and Kashmir and has become accepted as a solo classical instrument in the past few decades.

sarangi A bowed, stringed instrument with a broad, fretless fingerboard and a hollow resonating chamber covered with parchment. There are three or four main strings and as many as forty sympathetic strings. The whole body is carved from one piece of wood. It is mainly used as an accompaniment for a vocal recital, although it is now accepted as a solo instrument too.

sargam (i) The eight-note Indian solfeggio or musical scale, consisting of the notes Shadaja, Rishaba, Gandhara, Madhyama, Panchama, Dhaivata, Nishada and Shadaja (commonly abbreviated to Sa, Ri, Ga, Ma, Pa, Dha, Ni and Sa – 'sargam' taking its name from the first four of these notes). (ii) Solfeggio compositions in different ragas, practised in various tempos as exercises.

sarinda A bowed instrument mainly used in folk and semiclassical renderings (not used in classical music). It is most popular in Rajasthan and the North West of India.

sarod Stringed instrument with a metal, fretless

fingerboard and two resonating chambers, the main one made of teak covered with goatskin, and a smaller metal one at the top end of the fingerboard. The ten main strings and fifteen sympathetic ones are plucked with a coconut shell. Its origin (though disputed) seems to have been in Gandhar, now Afghanistan. The present sarod has gone through much modification, principally by Allauddin Khan. After the sitar it is the most popular instrument in the North of India.

sawal-jawab A musical passage featuring exchanges between two performers. Literally 'question-answer'.

shahnai Double-reed instrument with between seven and nine holes on the staff, whose closest Western relative is the oboe. No marriage, birth or opening ceremony for a new house in India is complete without the accompaniment of the shahnai, but it also has a strong classical as well as ceremonial tradition. The name derives from the Persian, meaning 'king's flute'.

shakuhachi Wind instrument from Japan which resembles a flute, although its long barrel is held vertically.

shishya Disciple. One who has to surrender himself entirely to his guru in the pursuit of music, a spiritual life, or any discipline of higher learning.

Shiva The third aspect of the Hindu trinity that is completed by Brahma and Vishnu. The One who changes the universe; the ruler of Nature and the Destroyer; Creator of music, dance and drama. He is often represented as the Cosmic Dancer, Nataraja.

shloka A verse. (In strict terms, a verse consisting of two lines of sixteen syllables each.)

siddhi Achievement, attainment or success.

sitar The most popular stringed instrument in Hindustani music. It is related to the lute. In the thirteenth century Amir Khusroo is said to have modified an older three-stringed instrument known as the 'tritantri veena', giving it a new shape. He gave it the Persian name 'seh-tar' (literally, three strings). The present sitar has gone through many modifications over the centuries. Today its main resonating chamber is a gourd, and at the head of its hollow teakwood neck is sometimes situated a second, smaller soundbox. The musician sits with crossed legs, the base of the main gourd resting upon the sole of his left foot. Twenty movable frets are tied to the neck, while the six or seven main strings and eleven to thirteen sympathetic strings are carried on two separate bridges. The main strings are plucked with a special plectrum (mizrab) made from thick wire, worn on the index finger of the right hand. The sympathetic strings not only resonate in reaction to the vibrations of the main strings, but are also plucked occasionally with the little finger of the right hand.

Sufism A mystic branch of Islam that arose in the tenth century and was most popular in Persia. Sufis aspire to the union of the soul with God. The Sufis of India have some affinity with Hindu philosophy.

sum The first beat of a tala (rhythmic cycle), the 'one' beat.

surbahar A bass sitar, which differs from its relative in its wider and longer neck, two extra bass strings and flat-backed gourd. It is tuned almost five notes lower than the sitar. Its deeper, longer-sustaining sound makes it ideal for the earlier parts of a raga: the alap, jor and jhala. Supposedly invented by Ghulam Mohammad and popularised by his son Sajjad Mohammad in the mid-nineteenth century.

sursingar Stringed instrument said to have been invented by Pyar Khan, a direct descendant of Mian Tan Sen, in the mid-nineteenth century. The upper, left-hand portion resembles a sarod, with its metal fingerboard mounted upon wood, while the lower part is rather like a sitar, the wooden chamber carrying a jawari (bridge) upon which the strings rest. It is plucked with a coconut shell. It was developed as an improvement on the rabab, using a wooden soundbox rather than skin, and metal instead of gut strings.

swami A title given to powerful or learned holy men who have renounced all attachments. Also means 'husband' or 'master'.

swara bheda Modulation in Indian music – rare but occasionally used. Achieved by changing the Sa note.

tabla The most popular of all drums in North India today. It actually consists of two drums: the right-hand, wooden-bodied tabla and the left-hand, metal-bodied, bass drum bayan or dugga; collectively they are also known as the tabla. Both are covered with skin, at the centre of which is a dried, black paste of flour and iron filings. It is tuned by hammering on the side-blocks which surround the body.

tabla tarang A set of ten or twelve tablas, each of which is tuned to a different pitch, arranged in a semi-circle around the musician, who plays with both hands.

tala (i) The essential element of time and rhythm in Indian music. (ii) One of the specific rhythmic cycles used. A tala can range from three to 108 beats per cycle, and each tala of a certain number of beats can have different time divisions – different stress on the beats in the cycle, e.g. a tala of ten beats may be divided 2-3-2-3, 3-3-4 or 3-4-3. Also known colloquially as 'tal' or 'taal'.

talim An Urdu word meaning the training provided by a guru to his disciple.

tan Musical phrase stretched out into brilliant, expressive passages when sung or played. Can be in slow, medium or fast tempo. Sometimes a vocal tan will employ the words of the song, but usually it uses the phrases 'Aakar' or 'Aa'.

tanpura The stringed instrument which provides the background drone accompaniment for nearly all performances of Indian classical music, its function being to establish the tonic and constantly remind one of it. It consists of a gourd and a long neck, with between four and six strings; there are no frets. The strings are stroked with the fingers.

tantra A series of writings dating from about the sixth century AD, which deal with the basic quality of duality in manifestation. Later developed by the Tantric sect into a ritualistic form of Devi (Goddess) worship.

tappa Vocal style based on the folk melodies sung by Punjabi Muslim camel drivers. Tappas have a continuous melody with much ornamentation, strong rhythm and fast tans. The texts are love lyrics.

tarana A song style, the text of which features as nonsense sound syllables or even the mnemonic syllables which represent drum sounds.

theka The fixed rhythmic phrases (formed by combining the basic sound syllables, or bols) by which one can recognise any specific tala played on the drums.

thumri Vocal form, very popular since the mid-nineteenth century, although of much earlier origin. The freest of all classical styles. Its compositions are based mostly on lighter ragas such as *Khamaj, Piloo, Kafi* and *Bhairavi*. The performers have the freedom to bring in different ragas or folk melodies, as well as to modulate by swara bheda, and to create lightening effects much appreciated by listeners. The words and melodies are of a lyrical and romantic nature, expressing desire, sadness and longing for Krishna or an absent lover. Like all other forms of vocal music, it is also adapted by instrumentalists.

tihai A musical phrase sung, played by an instrument or danced, which is repeated three times. It may start on any beat, but the final note or sound of the third repetition must fall on the first beat (sum) of the cycle.

toda Crisp, rhythmic and ornamented compositions or improvisations, used in dance and tabla-playing as well as in instrumental (mainly sitar) music.

tukda Short compositions for drums and Kathak dance.

Upanishads Sacred Hindu scriptures, written as a crystallisation of the contents of the Vedas.

ustad Urdu title of respect used mostly by Muslims for any notable, highly learned man. (The equivalent of guru or pandit.)

vadi The most important note in the scale of a particular raga.

Vedanta (i) The final truths of the Vedas; the ancient religious and philosophical system from which modern-day Hinduism derives. (ii) The Upanishads (literally, that which follows on from the Vedas).

Vedas The four sacred scriptures of the Hindus – the Rig Veda, Sama Veda, Yajur Veda and Atharva Veda – as revealed by the Godhead. The hymns of the Vedas, consisting of intoned mantras for ritual offerings and sacrifice, are ascribed to several rishis. Vedic chants are the oldest surviving form of all knowledge and the fountainhead of Indian classical music.

veena An ancient stringed instrument, the original incarnation of which dates from Vedic times. It has two separate large gourds connected by a hollow wooden or bamboo fingerboard. There are seven strings, plucked with one or two plectrums, twenty-four fixed chromatic frets and one bridge. The instrument's presiding deity is Saraswati, the goddess of learning and the arts. In the North of India, where it has declined in popularity, it has become known as the 'been'. However, in the South of India the veena remains very popular. The Southern veena differs from the been in having one gourd larger than the other – it looks more like a sitar, in fact.

vichitra veena A type of veena with a fretless fingerboard, on which the strings are stopped with a glass egg which slides over them. It is played with the two large gourds resting on the ground. In addition to the seven main strings, there are also a further eleven to thirteen sympathetic strings.

vilambit Slow.

vinaya Humility; the ideal attitude of the student towards the guru. Incorporates respect for elders, lack of arrogance and being able to seek for limitless knowledge.

Vishnu The second aspect of the Hindu trinity which is completed by Brahma and Shiva. God as the Preserver and Sustainer of the universe. He is commonly thought to have had nine incarnations on earth, being successively reborn as a fish, tortoise, boar, man-lion, dwarf, Parashu-Rama, Rama (hero of the *Ramayana*), Krishna (hero of the *Bhagavad Gita*) and Buddha. One more incarnation is expected in the future: Kalki the Destroyer.

yoga According to the sage Patanjali, a special system of spiritual meditation undertaken to attain self-realisation.

yogi One who has attained great spiritual powers through yoga; a person of mental balance.

zamindar Landlord.

CHRONOLOGY

1920	Born in Benares (7 April)
1928	First meets father
1929	First meets brother Uday
1930	Moves to Paris with Uday's troupe (December)
1931	Troupe's debut in Paris (3 March)
1932	Mother returns to India
1932–33	First of four tours of USA by Uday's troupe (December 1932–February 1933)
1933	Troupe returns to India for short tour (July–September)
	Meets Rabindranath Tagore
1933–34	Second tour of USA (Oct 1933–Feb 1934)
1934	Troupe returns to India for eleven months
	First meeting with Ustad 'Baba' Allauddin Khan & Ali Akbar Khan (December)
1935	Father dies
	Allauddin Khan joins Uday's troupe for one year
1936	Spends summer at Dartington Hall, Devon
	Mother dies (November)
1937–38	Third and fourth tours of USA (January–February 1937 and December 1937–March 1938)
1938	Sacred thread ceremony in India (May)
	Went to Maihar to start seven years of training with Allauddin Khan (July)
1939	Performs first concert, Allahabad Music Conference (December)
1940	Official opening of Uday Shankar India Culture Centre, Almora
1941	Marries Annapurna (15 May)
1942	Son Shubhendra born (30 March)
1944	Moves to Bombay with family (October)
	Uday's Almora centre closes
1945	Joins Indian People's Theatre Association in Bombay (January)
	India Immortal
	Composed new melody for 'Sare Jahan Se Accha'
1946	Release of *Dharti Ke Lal* and *Neecha Nagar*
	Leaves IPTA
1947	Briefly forms India Renaissance Artists
	Productions of *The Discovery of India*
	Begins recording with HMV India
1948	Meets Tat Baba
	Further productions of *The Discovery of India*
1949	Joins All India Radio in Delhi (February)
	Forms Jhankar Music Circle in Delhi
1952	Meets and performs for Yehudi Menuhin in Delhi
	Forms Vadya Vrinda (National Orchestra)
1954	Tours USSR with first Indian cultural delegation
1955	*Pather Panchali* released
1956	Annapurna leaves him for over two years (January)
	Leaves All India Radio (January)
	Films: *Aparajito* and *Kabuliwala*
1956–57	First solo tours and LPs in the West
1957	Films: *A Chairy Tale* and *The Flute and the Arrow*
	Best film music director, Berlin Film Festival (June), for *Kabuliwala*
1958	First production of *Melody and Rhythm*, Delhi (14–18 March)
	Heads cultural delegation to Japan (April–June)
	Paras Pathar
	UNESCO Music Festival in Paris: performs at UN Day gala (24 October)
	Annapurna returns (November)
1959	*Apur Sansar*
1960	Attends Prague Spring Festival
	Anuradha (wins Presidential Award for score)
1961	*Samanya Kshati*
1962	*Improvisations and Theme from Pather Panchali*
	Establishes Kinnara School of Music in Bombay
	Second production of *Melody and Rhythm*, Bombay (November)
1962–63	*Chandalika*
1963	*Godan*
	Performs at Leeds, Prague Spring and Edinburgh Festivals
1964	*Nava Rasa Ranga*
1964–65	Teaches at UCLA (January–February)
1965	*Chappacqua*
1966	Meets George Harrison (June); Harrison visits India (September–October)
	Bath Festival: duet with Yehudi Menuhin (25 June)
	Alice in Wonderland (BBC TV, 28 December)
1967	UK release of *West Meets East* (January)
	Splits up with Annapurna; takes a house in Los Angeles with Kamala Chakravarty (February)
	Los Angeles branch of Kinnara School opens (May)
	Monterey Pop Festival (June)
	Buell G. Gallagher Visiting Professor at City College, New York
	UN Human Rights Day Concert (10 December)

1967–68	Filming for *Raga*
1968	*Billboard* Editors' Award for Artist of the Year
	West Meets East wins Grammy Award (February)
	West Meets East – Volume 2 released
	Films: *Charly* and *Viola*
	Publication of *My Music, My Life*
	Festival From India double-LP and US tour
1969	Woodstock Festival (August)
1970	Shubho comes to live in USA
	Head of Indian Music section at CalArts
1971	Première of *Concerto for Sitar and Orchestra (No. 1)*, London (28 January)
	Concerts for Bangladesh (1 August)
	Releases 'Joi Bangla' EP (27 August)
	Raga is premièred in New York (November)
1972	*Concert for Bangla Desh* soundtrack
	Allauddin Khan dies
1973	*Concert for Bangla Desh* wins Grammy (February)
	Shankar Family and Friends recordings (April)
	Release of *Transmigration Macabre* (soundtrack to 1968 film *Viola*)
	Founds Ravi Shankar Music Circle, Los Angeles
1974	*Ravi Shankar's Music Festival From India* recording and tour
	Dark Horse tour of USA and Canada (2 November –20 December)
	Hospitalised after heart scare (4–9 December)
1975	Awarded the Conseil International de la Musique/UNESCO Music Prize
1976	Becomes Fellow of Sangeet Natak Academy
1977	Uday dies (29 September)
	Improvisations: West Meets East Album 3
1978	Publication of *Raag Anurag*
	East Greets East
1979	*Meera*
1980	*Jazzmine*
1981	Splits up with Kamala (January)
	Première of *Concerto for Sitar and Orchestra (No. 2)*, New York (23 April)
	Daughter Anoushka born (9 June)
	Awarded Padma Vibhushan
1982	*Gandhi*
	Artistic Director of ASIAD, the ninth Asian Games, Delhi
	Brother Rajendra dies
	The Sound of ASIAD '82 released
	Ravi and Annapurna divorce
1983	Academy Award nomination for *Gandhi*
	Uday Utsav held in Delhi
	Tours China (August–September)
1985	*Rhythms of the World* festival, Los Angeles (June)
	Awarded Commandeur de l'Ordre des Arts et des Lettres (France)
	Indian Army Special Award
1986–92	Member of Rajya Sabha, Indian Parliament's Upper House
1986	*Genesis*
	Quadruple bypass operation in New York (30 December)
1987	On 67th birthday (7 April) performs first concert since operation
	Kalidas Samman Award (Bhopal, India)
	Release of *Tana Mana*
	Third tour of USSR
1988	Performs at The Kremlin as finale to USSR's Festival of India (5–7 July)
	Chief Guest at the Nayee Kiran festival in Crawley, UK (11–17 July)
1989	Marries Sukanya (23 January)
	European Youth Orchestra tour of Europe and India, with Zubin Mehta (April)
	Ravi Shankar Inside the Kremlin released
	UK productions of *Ghanashyam – A Broken Branch*
	Celebrates fifty years of performing with concert at Royal Festival Hall, London
1990	70th birthday celebrations
	Plays concert before British Royal Family (April)
	Passages
	VST Industries Spirit of Freedom Award
1991	*The Tiger and the Brahmin*
	Rajiv Gandhi Excellence Award
	Grand Prize at the Fukuoka Asian Cultural Prizes (3rd September)
	Indian productions of *Ghanashyam*
1992	Ramon Magsaysay award (Manila, Philippines)
	Angioplasty operation at UCH, San Diego (September)
	Shubho dies (15 September)
1993	Moves to Encinitas, California (14 February)
	Concerts For Peace in Washington DC and London
	Second angioplasty operation, San Diego (26 August)
1994	Operations on ear and shoulder
1995	75th birthday celebrations start with concert at Siri Fort, New Delhi, featuring Anoushka's concert debut, aged thirteen (27 February)
	Co-hosts *Sitar to Guitar* festival of gypsy music, Brussels (24–25 November)
1996	Release of *In Celebration*, a four-CD retrospective (February)
	Records *Chants From India* in Madras (January and April) and Britain (July)
1997	Release of *Chants From India* (May, USA; September, UK)
	Awarded Præmium Imperiale
	Performs in Bombay for Independence Golden Jubilee celebrations (August)

RAGAS CREATED BY RAVI SHANKAR

Nat Bhairav
Ahir Lalit
Rasiya
Yaman Manjh
Gunji Kanhara
Janasanmodini
Tilak Shyam
Bairagi
Mohan Kauns
Manamanjari
Mishra Gara
Pancham Se Gara
Purvi Kalyan
Kameshwari
Gangeshwari
Rangeshwari
Parameshwari
Palas Kafi
Jogeshwari
Charu Kauns
Kaushik Todi
Bairagi Todi
Bhawani Bhairav
Sanjh Kalyan
Shailangi
Suranjani
Rajya Kalyan
Banjara
Piloo Banjara
Suvarna

HONORARY DEGREES

1968	Doctor of Fine Arts, University of California, Santa Cruz
1970	Doctor of Music, Colgate University
1973	Doctor of Music, Khairagarh University
	Doctor of Letters, Rabindra Bharati University
	Doctorate from University of Calcutta
1980	Doctor of Letters, Benares Hindu University
1984	Doctor of Letters, University of Delhi
1985	Doctor of Performing Arts, California Institute of the Arts
1987	Doctor of Philosophy, Institute of Integral Studies, California
1993	Doctor of Music, New England Conservatory
1994	Doctor of Music, Harvard University
	Doctor of Music, Victoria University

RAVI SHANKAR – IN CELEBRATION

Spiritual, profound, rhythmic and meditative... *Ravi Shankar: In Celebration*, the ultimate collection, retraces the sitar master's remarkable odyssey.

Compiled by George Harrison and Alan Kozlowski, *In Celebration* retraces Ravi's work on four compact discs, showcasing his explorations in various compelling styles.

In Celebration includes numerous rare or previously unreleased recordings from the legendary Apple, Dark Horse, HMV India and World Pacific labels. All tracks have been restored to the finest sound quality. A deluxe 64-page colour booklet, with personal photos, essay, extensive notes and reminiscences by the artist is also included.

ON ANGEL/DARK HORSE RECORDS.

RAVI SHANKAR – CHANTS OF INDIA

Sixteen new tracks, featuring Ravi Shankar's stunning arrangements of the prayers and ancient chants of India and four original compositions in a similar style, giving this highly spiritual music a universal appeal. The vast array of other musicians includes George Harrison (who also produced the album), tabla-player Bikram Ghosh and Shankar's daughter Anoushka.

AVAILABLE ON ANGEL RECORDS.

CREDITS

All photographs and documents reproduced in this book are from the private collection of Ravi Shankar, except as follows (please note that 'CS2, p. 1' refers to the first page of the second colour section, etc.):

George Harrison private collection: *220, CS2/1 (main), CS2/2 (both), CS2/3 (top, middle, bottom right), CS3/1 (artwork by Jan Steward)*
Gered Mankowitz: *CS4/1 (top right)*
Nemai Ghosh: *124*
Satyaki Ghosh: *297*
Oliver Craske: *303, CS4/2 (top left, upper middle), CS4/3*
Brian Roylance: *309, 313*
Anna Farlow: *CS4/2 (main, bottom left, bottom right)*
Chris Murray/Govinda Gallery: *CS3/2 (top)*
Jan Steward: *245, CS3/1 (artwork)*
Alec Skelton: *4 (the ghats at Benares)*
Aditya Arya: *304*
EMI Archives: *142, CS1/4*
Gareth Davies/All-Action: *CS4/4*
Joseph Sia/Star File: *211, 212, 224 (middle left)*
Jim Cummins/Star File: *CS2/3 (bottom left), CS2/4*
Hulton Getty: *61*
Archive Photos: *143, 151*
Fotos International/Archive Photos: *219 (both photographs)*
Henry Grossman: *224 (top), 225 (top), 226*
Carolyn Jones/© Angel Records 1997: *6*

Every effort has been made to clear all illustrations with their respective copyright-holders, but if anyone believes they have been omitted please contact the publishers, who will respond appropriately to any such claim.

Glossary compiled by Ravi Shankar, Dr M. N. Nandakumara & Oliver Craske
Chronology compiled by Oliver Craske
Index compiled by Diana LeCore
Bengali-English translation by Rhea Chaudhuri

Note from Genesis Publications

Sincerest thanks are due to the following for their contributions to this project:

Sukanya Shankar, Anoushka Shankar, George & Olivia Harrison, Lord Menuhin, Vera Lamport, Jutta Schall-Emden, Philip Glass, Jim Keller, Zubin Mehta, Cynthia Meister, Zakir Hussain, Antonia Minnecola, Bikram Ghosh. All at Team Genesis (especially Brian Roylance, Roman Milisic, Julian Quance, Patricia Adburgham, Ann McFarlane, Davina Arkell, Catherine Roylance), Wherefore Art (especially David Costa, Fiona Andreanelli, Dan Einzig, Lionel Avignon and Anita Allen), Tennant Artists (particularly Angela Sulivan and Nikki Hibbert), Angel Records (especially Ethan Crimmins and Randy Haecker) and the Asian Music Circuit.

Rhea Chaudhuri, greatly missed, for invaluable artwork, design suggestions and translation. Dr M. N. Nandakumara and Dr Shastry of London's Bharatiya Vidya Bhavan, Harihar Rao, Kartik Seshadri, Partho Sarathy, Gaurav Mazumdar, Lila Pancholi, Tony Karasek, Shalini Patnaik, Alan Kozlowski, Anna Farlow, Sheldon Soffer, John Claassen & John Heble, Ken Hunt, Linda Arias, Rachel, Kay Williams, Busy Fingers, Gilda Sebastian, Chris Murray and all at Govinda Gallery, David Hedley, George Avakian, Romana McEwan, Alexander McEwan, Jens Boel at UNESCO Archives, the National Film Board of Canada, Diane Theriot of NARAS, Eleanor Hope, Linden Chubin at The Asia Society, Charles Rodier at EMI Classics, Ruth Edge and Tony Mobbs at EMI Archives, the London Symphony Orchestra, Bhatta Bhattacharya of the British Council Division in New Delhi, the late Derek Taylor, Andrew Robinson, Matthew Gordon, Amal Chaudhuri and Shohini.

Oliver Craske

INDEX